The *Unusually* Useful Web Book

June Cohen

New Riders

1249 Eighth Street, Berkeley, California 94710
An Imprint of Pearson Education

The Unusually Useful Web Book

International Standard Book Number: 0-7357-1206-9

Library of Congress Catalog Card Number: 2001095011

Printed in the United States of America

First printing: June 2003

9 8 7 6 5 4 3

Trademarks

Warning and Disclaimer

Associate Publisher
Stephanie Wall

Production Manager
Gina Kanouse

Senior Product Marketing Manager
Tammy Detrich

Publicity Manager
Susan Nixon

Senior Development Editor
Jennifer Eberhardt

Senior Project Editor
Lori Lyons

Copy Editor
Jake McFarland

Senior Indexer
Cheryl Lenser

Composition
Gloria Schurick

Manufacturing Coordinator
Dan Uhrig

Interior Designer
June Cohen

Cover Designer
Aren Howell

For my mother, Shirlene, who taught me to read and encouraged me to write.

And for my father, Richard, who taught me to do crosswords in pen.

The
Unusually Useful Web Book

contents at a glance

contents

about the author

June Cohen has been a leading developer of web sites and multimedia for more than a decade. In 1991, she led the Stanford University team that developed the world's first networked multimedia publication. Then, in 1994, she helped launch HotWired.com, the first commercial content site (and spin-off of *Wired Magazine*). While at HotWired, she founded Webmonkey.com, the much-loved web-developer's site used by millions. Later, as HotWired's VP of Content, she played a key role on a range of innovative sites, from Animation Express to the HotBot search engine. June holds a BA from Stanford, where she was editor of *The Stanford Daily*. After years in San Francisco, she now lives in New York City, where she occasionally talks about things other than the web.

about the cartoonist

Alex Gregory has been contributing cartoons to *The New Yorker* since 1999. Thirty-three of his unpublished cartoons appear for the first time in this book. By day, he's a TV writer who has written for *The Late Show with David Letterman*, *The Larry Sanders Show*, *Frasier*, and *King of the Hill*. He lives in Los Angeles and isn't ashamed to admit that he likes it.

about the technical reviewer

Steve Sanchez is the founder and CEO of iNexus.com, a Los Angeles–based firm that consults, builds, and promotes Internet solutions for business. Over the past 10 years, he has worked with leading companies in industries such as travel, medicine, and publishing, creating sites that work for both owners and users. A long-time evangelist for strengthening the online user's experience, Steve is a "raving fan" of database-driven web sites, web communities for business, and technologies such as dynamic Flash, VR tours, Active Server Pages, and Microsoft's .NET. He enjoys photography, travel, sailing, and scuba diving. He lives in Los Angeles with his wife and four children.

acknowledgments

This book has been a long time coming. And a lot of people helped get it there. The idea started percolating four years ago, during lunch break brainstorming with Kristin Windbigler, then the Executive Producer of Webmonkey (and always my close friend and collaborator). Jeffrey Veen—friend, colleague, superstar--took the idea to his publisher, and *The Unusually Useful Web Book* got its start.

experts

The content of this book has been shaped and reshaped over the years, as my ideas about the web— and the web itself—evolved. The most important influences were the interviews with dozens of industry veterans--some friends, some strangers— who generously shared their insights with me.

They include Andrew Anker, Adam Berliant, Carrie Bickner, Hillary Billings, Doug Bowman, Rick Boyce, Martha Brockenbrough, Sheryl Cababa, Kris Carpenter, Jason Cook, Cate Corcoran, Greg Dotson, Esther Drill, Janice Fraser, Jim Frew, Jesse James Garrett, Margaret Gould-Stewart, Lara Hoyem, Mark Hurst, Luke Knowland, Mike Kuniavsky, Hunter Madsen, Matt Margolin, Lance McDaniel, Noah Mercer, Peter Merholz, Jim Morris, Steve Mulder, Peter Naylor, Wendy Owen, Derek Powazek, Josh Quittner, Nadav Savio, Randi Shade, Emily Simas, Srinija Srinivasan, Pamela Statz, Taylor, Evany Thomas, thau!, Michael Twidale, Beth Vanderslice, Jeffrey Veen, Omar Wasow, Kristin Windbigler, Jason Wishnow, Indi Young, Jeffrey Zeldman, and Tim Ziegler.

The interviews helped me solidify ideas and confirm (or reject) theories. They also expanded the scope of the book. For example, many people independently mentioned—without prompting— that pull-down menus are an absolute disaster as a navigation device. I didn't know that, actually. But now I do. And you do, too. On a broader scale, I also heard—over and over again—that the real challenge of web development isn't technology or design or bandwidth or funding. It's people. People and their organizational politics. So I expanded the book to shed some light on workplace issues.

These experts are quoted throughout the book to highlight points, offer real-world examples, and bring the pages to life. However, I must emphasize that I interpreted and consolidated their ideas in accordance with my own editorial judgment and outlook on the industry. So responsibility for the content is ultimately mine.

editors and others

Many people have helped bring the book to life, but chief among them is my editor at New Riders, Jennifer Eberhardt, who pushed the book in all the right directions—inventing the idea of the "Take Action" worksheets and encouraging me to bring more to the book: More bullet points, more fill-in sections, more examples, more fun. More. She also had a terrible habit of innocently pointing out every place I'd gotten a bit lazy. I still haven't forgiven her for it. But her humor and insight and whip-smarts—and her understanding of the role venti coffees play in a person's life—were essential to making this book what it is.

Stephanie Wall, the associate publisher, forged the path for this book from my head to your hands. She has that rare ability to cut straight to the heart of the matter and focus on exactly those things that matter most. She made sure the message the book sent to the world was consistent with what lay in its pages. And she was also great fun to work with.

Technical Reviewer Steve Sanchez is the only person besides me who read every draft of this book, and his insightful suggestions helped push this book to become more visual, more engaging, and more complete. His influence is evident on every page, and I'm hoping to some day meet him in person.

I'm grateful to everyone at New Riders for their energy and enthusiasm. This book was truly a collaboration, and I couldn't ask for better, nicer people to work with. Lori Lyons edited and managed this book from layout to delivery, and did so with patience, humor, and an expertise I so appreciate. Aren Howell expertly designed exactly the right cover (and helped also to finalize the interior design). Gloria Schurick composed the pages (no small feat!), while fine-tuning and improving the design. Jake McFarland copy-edited the text, and made it sing. David Dwyer lent his support and made me laugh, Chris Nelson gave great editorial advice and told great stories. And Karen Whitehouse gave this book its start.

Several trusted friends with sharp pencils and sharper minds read the book as it made its journey from draft to draft. Jeffrey Veen reviewed an earlier draft with an eye toward the latest trends. Kristin Windbigler cheerfully pointed out (among other things), the topics I'd been avoiding that I really should have covered. Martha Brockenbrough alternately cheered and challenged the content of the book and filled the margins with comments, jokes, and several tracings of her daughter's feet. Guy Cohen read and edited large chunks of the manuscript, making the writing tighter and helping me to weed jargon out of the book. For example, when I casually used the word "iterative," he wrote, "I don't know what that means, and I went to college." In the final stages, other friends reviewed individual sections. These generous souls included Jay Greenspan, Matt Margolin, Noah Mercer, Nadav Savio, and Tim Ziegler.

But for all the effort that went into the writing, it may be the cartoons that emerge most memorable. Alex Gregory's pictures are each worth at least 1,000 of my words. Going through his file cabinet of cartoons was like finding buried treasure.

Outside of the book's content, many people helped me through the process of writing a book. My lawyer, Mary Luria of Davis & Gilbert, LLP (www.dglaw.com), who knows her way around a contract, let me tell you. Liz Ferris (www.lizferris.com) expertly transcribed all the interviews for this book and managed to accurately record many nonsensical industry buzzwords like "monetizing eyeballs."

Additional support came from all the neighborhood joints I rely on in New York: Visual Art Photo, Your Neighborhood Office, Basiques, Three Lives & Co., Grey Dog Coffee, and the Chocolate Bar.

And goodness, I feel like Julia Roberts at the Oscars, twirling my vintage Valentino and beaming at the camera so they won't yank me offstage…. Because I'm not done thanking yet.

colleagues

This book really began long before I sat down to write it. It's a product of many years and many web sites. But mostly, it's a product of conversations.

My first conversation about the web took place—as so many do—in a Palo Alto bar at 1 a.m. It was 1991, and we weren't talking about the web *per se*, but about a multimedia publication we wanted to build.

Our napkin scribbles became a working product, and that never would have happened were it not for the initial spark and determined follow through of Scott Kirk, and the ingenuity, innovation, and infinite patience of Noah Mercer. I'm forever grateful to them and also to Martha Brockenbrough, Adam Block, and N'Gai Croal for breathing life into that project.

But almost everything I know about the web, I learned at HotWired. Mostly the hard way.

For six years, I had the very great fortune to work at HotWired, a think tank, media lab, and Internet start-up in San Francisco. Everyone at HotWired influenced my thinking, and many of them will see a bit of themselves in these pages. I'm grateful to everyone who worked there for shaping my ideas and helping to shape the web, really. But there are a few people, in particular, whose influence has been deep and long-lasting.

First off, the people who made Wired happen: Louis Rossetto, Jane Metcalfe, John Plunkett, and *especially* Barbara Kuhr, who's been a mentor, inspiration, and friend, for many years.

Also Beth Vanderslice, who created opportunities for me and was always generous with her wisdom; Andrew Anker, who founded HotWired and never forgot to have fun; Cate Corcoran, with whom I learned just about everything I know about the web; George Shirk, who was full of surprises; Hunter Madsen, who taught me the phrase 'Dare to be obvious.' And also to each of these remarkable people: Doug Bowman, Chip Bayers, Rick Boyce, Liz Chapin, Kevin Cooke, Susan Copeland, Eric Eaton, Todd Elliott, Jim Frew, James Glave, jillo, Luke Knowland, Matt Margolin, Anna McMillan, Sabine Messner, Laura Moorhead, Mary Murphy, Peter Naylor, Wendy Owen, Steven Petrow, David Pritchard, Ian Raikow, Nadav Savio, Pam Statz, Taylor, rhau!, Evany Thomas, Joel Truher, Jeffrey Veen, Kristin Windbigler, Michael Winnick, and Gary Wolf.

inspirations

I don't actually know all the people who influenced this book. But I feel I should thank them, all the same. Like many people, I got a lot out of the web books written by Lynda Weinman (<designing web graphics>) and Steve Krug (*Don't Make Me Think*). Thanks also to Max DePree (*The Art of Leadership*), Donald Norman (*The Design of Everyday Things*), and Scott McCloud (*Understanding Comics*).

I should also thank Johann Sebastian Bach, who wrote the music I write to, though I don't suppose he'd be offended if I didn't.

friends and family

Although they don't necessarily know much about the web, the rest of these folks know a lot about friendship.

I don't think I could have written this book if I didn't have the very good fortune of living next door to such good friends. Thank you to Kate Gallimore (and Piers Davies, of course) for all the coffee breaks and cups of tea and font-buying sprees, and for literally being there for me throughout the writing of this book.

I also couldn't have written it without my sister and my brothers—Robin, Guy, and Glenn—who are the best possible people to go through life with. They made me laugh, kept me company, and brought me Chinese take-out when I was too busy

writing to leave my apartment. They've been great friends to me, and Guy would argue that they made me who I am by teaching me at an early age to persevere in the face of exhaustion and doubt. They taught me this in the form of "Training Camp," a fun game we'd play that involved training me to do handstands and catch balls, and then having me run around the house each time I missed while they chanted "Training Camp. Training Camp." Without that—and without them—I would surely be a different person, and I might never have finished this beast of a book.

My father, Richard, also did his share of character-building by encouraging me always to drink my coffee black, do my crosswords in pen, and face up to things that seem difficult. Thanks, Pop-Tart.

Thank you also to The Ladies for their endless support and late-night phone calls. Mady Wallen, Cathy Green, and Emily Simas listened patiently through a lot of very boring answers to the question, "How's the book?" Jen Sey, Rae Meadows, Sarah Blanch, Martha Brockenbrough, and Kristin Windbigler were always willing to talk about the maddening creative process. Lance McDaniel made everything fun. And Tam Edwards was always ready with advice or an ear, even if she made me go to Mary's Fish Camp to get them.

The final acknowledgement is saved for the first person in my life. My mother Shirlene: ballerina, actress, and Revlon girl turned nature photographer, mother, and muse. She played a big role in convincing me to write this book, and she encouraged me along the way with inspirational quotes in adorable emails like this one:

Dear Junie,

The heights by great men reached and kept
Were not attained by sudden flight,
But they, while their companions slept
Were toiling upward in the night.
(Henry Wadsworth Longfellow)

Love,
Mom
xxxxxx

Tell Us What You Think

As the reader of this book, you are the most important critic and commentator. We value your opinion and want to know what we're doing right, what we could do better, what areas you'd like to see us publish in, and any other words of wisdom you're willing to pass our way.

Email: errata@peachpit.com

introduction

"What better way to say 'we're a start-up that's going to make it' than a big, beautiful chandelier."

An introduction should begin at the beginning. And this book's journey began in the 90s, when I worked at HotWired. I had a problem that I was sure a book could solve.

It was San Francisco during the boom, and the web was growing so quickly and dramatically that it was hard to keep track of all the changes. Everything was new—from the technology to the business models—and we struggled to train our growing staff on everything we'd learned so far.

I would always wish I had a manual that I could just hand to new employees and say, "Here. This is everything we've learned about the web. Read it, and then we'll get started."

This, I hope, is that manual.

what this book is...and isn't

Whether you're building a site for a local restaurant, a multinational corporation, or your gardening club, this book can help. It's based on the idea that all web sites succeed for the same reasons. The principles that help the big dogs stay ahead of the pack can also help the little guy.

Now most web books are specialized, covering design, technology, or specific topics, such as community-building. But this book is for people who have to think about everything. It was written for web producers—or anyone who bears the primary responsibility for a site's success. And it covers a lot of territory, because they have to.

In this emerging industry, everyone wears multiple hats. You have to know a little bit about a lot to create a successful site. So this book covers the entire development process, from planning your site to designing, building, and maintaining it after it launches. The focus is on practical solutions to real-world problems—from increasing traffic to improving site speed to setting up an email list—in organizations that may or may not have money to invest in a solution.

What this book is:

- **A reference guide** for web professionals that fills in the gaps in your knowledge, reminds you of things you already know, and offers persuasive arguments for following— or avoiding—particular development paths.

- **A do-it-yourself workbook** that breaks down tasks—like improving site speed or increasing traffic—and gives you a step-by-step approach to effecting positive change on your site.

- **A glimpse behind the scenes** of web sites that face challenges similar to yours.

- **An introduction** to web development for professionals who are new to the field or for business owners who are bringing their organizations online.

What this book isn't:

- **It isn't a technical manual.** There are many, many books and web sites that will guide you step-by-step through the technical procedure of creating a site. I don't try to replace their work here. Instead, I offer an overview and point you toward more complete reference guides.

- **It isn't a design portfolio.** There are many books that offer lush examples of beautiful and innovative sites. They're great for inspiration and ideas! But in the interest of saving space, I've limited my use of images.

- **It isn't a get-rich-quick scheme.** I can't promise you there's a pot of gold at the end of your Internet rainbow. But this book can help you create a site that meets the needs of your customers and your organization. Maybe this will make you rich! But it probably won't overnight.

what we've learned about the web

Over the course of the last year, I had the great fun and good fortune to talk to nearly 50 web veterans about what they've learned. These industry experts (who are listed starting on page 344) came from a range of disciplines—design, engineering, marketing, finance—and spent the last 5–10 years working on a wide range of sites: from small start-ups like gURL.com and BlackPlanet (now leaders in their category) to corporate ventures like Levis.com. From small business sites like, say, The Yoga House of Bellevue, to large portals like MSN and Yahoo!.

These interviews helped me solidify ideas and confirm (or reject) theories I was hatching. They also expanded the scope of the book, bringing in lessons I hadn't yet learned (and from which I'll now be spared!). For example, many people independently mentioned—without prompting—that pull-down menus are an absolute disaster as a navigation device. I didn't know that, actually. But now I do. And you do, too. (See <u>why pull-downs are not for navigation</u> on page 113.)

The interviews also brought out a larger theme that greatly changed the content of the book. I heard—over and over again—that the real challenge of web development isn't technology or design or bandwidth or funding. It's people. People and their organizational politics. So I expanded the book to shed some light on workplace issues.

More than anything, these interviews confirmed my suspicions that there's a growing body of knowledge about web development that's broadly applicable across all kinds of sites and for all kinds of industries. It was striking to me how many web developers had independently reached very similar conclusions about what was working

and why. Also striking was how universal these lessons seemed, across sites large and small, independent and corporate, commercial and not-for-profit.

So, what exactly did we learn? Well, above all, we learned to focus on the user—to build sites that meet their needs, speak their language, and make sense to them, visually. We learned to start small and stay focused. We learned to evolve our sites over time to better meet our customers' (and business') needs. We learned to use clear (not clever) names for site sections. We learned to promote our sites online, to improve our rankings in search engines, and to encourage our customers to spread the word. We learned that site speed matters. We learned to use email to keep visitors coming back. And we learned how to collaborate, compromise, and communicate across disciplines—essential for the balanced teams that develop successful sites.

These lessons are incorporated throughout the book, of course. But you'll find highlights on the front and back covers that tell you —honestly— almost everything you need to know.

However, it's important to remember that the web is still in its infancy. The industry is in its very early stages, and a lot of things—including industry leaders, winning strategies, audience expectations, and interface conventions—will change over time.

But I have a hunch that many of these early lessons—focusing on the user, defining goals, evolving the site, labeling things clearly, testing thoroughly, and, of course, resolving office conflicts—will remain relevant for years to come.

June Cohen
New York City
May 2003

section 1

planning

your site

chapter **1**
deciding what to do

"After exhaustive research, innumerable high-level meetings, and a lot of hand-wringing and soul-searching, we've decided to stampede."

don't miss ...

The first step in creating a web site is the most important and perhaps the most difficult. You have to decide what to do. It's not enough, you see, to know you need a web site. You have to think about *why*.

Too often, companies simply hire someone to build something similar to what other companies have. And while they may end up with a workable web site, they miss an opportunity to really move their business and waste some money in the process.

It's a phenomenon Martha Brockenbrough sees all the time in her Seattle consultancy, where educating clients is a full-time job: "Often, a client's first question is 'How much is this going to cost?' But the real question is, 'What do you want this web site to do?' What do you want it to do for your business?"

"I primarily work with very small businesses," Brockenbrough explains. "And they usually have no idea what a web site can do. They just feel like they should have one. But that's the biggest mistake you can make! You should have very clear goals for what the web site can help you achieve."

And small businesses aren't the only ones blundering: Corporate giants are just as likely to stumble through their Internet strategy. Ask Jeffrey Veen, whose consulting firm Adaptive Path works with clients large and small.

"The first question I ask any client is 'Why do you have a web site?' Veen says. "I ask that question and sometimes there's just dead silence. They can't answer it beyond 'We *have* to have a web site. Our competition has a web site.'"

It's not enough to know you need a web site. You have to think about why.

So whether you're launching a new site or rethinking an old one, you should start with some provocative questions about why you have a web site in the first place.

Ask yourself:

- Why does my organization need this site?
- Why do my visitors need this site?

The answers will form the basis of your Internet strategy. Together, business needs and user needs will guide all your decisions. And if you answer these questions well, everything else—honestly, everything else—will fall into place.

what works on the web

In the late '90s, every business was suddenly expected to have a web site, whether or not they knew why. But this sudden rise to prominence preceded any real understanding of what the web was good for. Companies created web sites because they needed a web site, and that was that.

But 10 years later, a great deal has been learned about what works—and what doesn't—on the web. Whether you're launching a web company, building a site for your book club, or bringing your business online, there are some general principles you can follow to help you avoid the most common rookie mistakes.

4 great pieces of advice:

1. Match user & business goals.
2. Use the web for what it does well.
3. Emphasize functionality over fun.
4. Start simple & stay focused.

match user goals & business goals   The first thing you should figure out, as mentioned previously, is why you need a web site (<u>10 things the web can do for your business</u>, p. 11). But it's essential to think through not only what *you* need, but what your users need. For the web is a voluntary medium. People will only visit your site when they want to, and will only take out of it what they need.

So before you start planning, put yourself in the shoes of your typical users. Think about what they're coming for—and not just what you want them to take away.

"You have to answer the fundamental question, 'What is your objective?' before you go online," said Beth Vanderslice, former president of Wired Digital. "Know how your web site is going to get you closer to your customer—and why your customer will want to go there."

Balancing user & owner goals:

- **The corporate site.** A corporation may want to reposition itself through exciting design and beautiful prose explaining its strategy. But the customer just wants to find information on a specific product.

- **The portfolio site.** A designer may want to strut his stuff with an immersive multimedia presentation. But the potential employer just wants to learn who he is, where he studied, and what kind of work he does.

- **The grassroots political site.** A local cause may want to plump up its membership roster, raise money, and get people to events. But the visitor just wants to gain a deeper understanding of the issues.

Now, none of these goals are mutually exclusive. In fact, each of these sites can quite readily accomplish its primary goal while helping its visitors as well. But if the site owners don't consider both set of goals—their own and their users—everyone will lose.

use the web for what it does well Too often, web sites merely mimic another medium, with TV-like commercials, for instance, or documents that were designed for print. Both will appear slow, clunky, and misplaced on the web—because they are.

So before you recycle an old idea on to your web site, think through how it might be given a new life that's more appropriate to the medium.

"The Internet is at its best when it's letting you do something you couldn't do before, or do something faster and easier and cheaper," says Martha Brockenbrough. "What eBay did was take something that exists in the offline world—classified advertising—and use the power of the Internet to make it better. So you have to think, 'What's offline that could be improved with the power of the Internet?'"

emphasize functionality over fun This is a lesson many sites learned the hard way: The web is best used for utility, not entertainment. Many early web companies, including HotWired and the Microsoft Network, focused on entertainment, using TV and magazine models to describe their sites. And many corporate sites in those days were flashy and fun, focused on entertaining customers with animation and games.

"Back then, we would talk clients into doing the 'coolest thing ever' because that's what the medium had to offer," says Lance McDaniel, now VP of Creative at consulting firm SBI and Company, who worked on several of the earliest corporate sites, including those for Levi's, Dockers, and Harley-Davidson.

But times have changed. Most web users are now focused on getting things done, and most web sites now focus on useful, practical applications for their customers.

"For the most part, people don't use the web for pure entertainment," McDaniel says. "So if they're coming to, say, the Clorox web site, they're not there to be dazzled by your fun Flash animations. They're coming for information: 'My shirt's not white enough, how do I get it whiter?' or 'I just drank some bleach, what do I do?'"

And while McDaniel likes to reminisce about the early web, he doesn't miss it: "The web is much better now than it was when we started out. The fun sites are fun and the informational sites are informational."

Think about what users are coming for—and not just what you want them to take away.

Indeed, there's still room for fun online. There are successful entertainment sites—featuring games, animation, and music—But it's hard to finance them and hard to build a substantial audience. So for now, fun is the exception and not the rule.

start simple & stay focused   When you're working in a medium where anything seems possible, it's easy to get carried away. But the best results often happen when you keep the web site as simple as possible.

"I have really learned that less is more," says Janice Fraser, a partner at consulting firm Adaptive Path who has developed many multi-million dollar sites. "Doing a few things really well is far more important than having so-called full-featured web sites."

Simplicity, as a strategy, makes sense for more reasons than one. From a business perspective, it keeps the site manageable, maintainable, and priced within reason. But it also makes sense for users, who find streamlined products easier and more appealing than their complicated counterparts.

And once you decide on your key features, do everything you can to stay focused. "Figure out what needs to be on the web site, and leave it at that," says online marketing expert Hunter Madsen. It's common sense advice, but it requires a certain amount of restraint.

"It's easy to think of all sorts of fun things to add to a site that a customer might enjoy because he's a human being. But you need to stay focused on what he would find relevant because he's here for your product."

10 things the web can do for you

1. Reach new customers & markets. The web can help you find (and keep) new customers, regardless of location or lifestyle.

2. Convert people with a passing interest into customers. After seeing your ad, hearing your name or passing your store, new customers or prospects can visit your site and learn more.

3. Encourage repeat business. Using email and your web site, you can keep existing customers (or readers or members) informed about new products, articles, issues, or events.

4. Reduce bad leads by clarifying who you are, what you do and (importantly) what you don't do.

5. Follow up on ads & press coverage. When your organization places an ad or gets covered in a magazine, the web lets readers learn more.

6. Save money on printing & postage. Organizations large and small save money by replacing printed collateral and mailings with a web site and email.

7. Provide better, faster customer support. Although some customer service must be done live, many kinds of questions are better served by a web site, including company background; location and hours; and product specifications.

8. Save money on phone support. No matter what the size of your organization, fewer phone calls means more money and time.

9. Gauge customer interest in products or events. By looking at what visitors look at, you can get a rough sense of their appeal. This can be helpful when planning events, ordering new inventory, or predicting sales.

10. Stimulate creativity! Don't get carried away, but ... it's OK to have fun with your site!

writing a mission statement

I have only one hard and fast rule about developing web sites: I never, ever begin work without a written mission statement and project goals.

It's tempting, especially when working under time pressure or on a small-scale project, to skip this step. You figure: I know what I'm doing, and my team knows what they're doing. I don't need a formal mission statement. But you do. Even the smallest project—one that's measured in days instead of months—is measurably improved when you have the site's purpose in writing. And on more significant projects—a new site or a major redesign—it's perilous to proceed without it.

The mission statement, you'll learn, is a web team's best friend.

The written mission statement

- **Clarifies what you're creating** so everyone shares the same vision

- **Clarifies your objectives** so everyone agrees to the same goals

- **Prevents the project from slipping** off course—a major risk with web projects

- **Insulates you from the whims of others** by accomplishing the above

Of course, these advantages don't come free. Mission statements are notoriously hard to write, because they need to be both pithy and meaningful, capturing the essence of a site's purpose in just a few words. They should explain what you're doing and who you're doing it for.

Every mission statement should include

- Who the site is for

- What the site does

- How the site differs from its competition

Keep in mind, however, that the mission statement is for your staff, not your customers. It needn't (and I'd argue shouldn't) appear on your web site itself.

---

a model mission statement

Mission statements are notoriously difficult to write. So when crafting one for your site, it helps to have a model.

Try this Mad Lib-like template:

_____ is a _____
(site name)   (noun describing site)
offering _____to
              (type of service)

_____
(adjective describing audience)
_____who
(noun describing audience)
_____ to
("need" or "want")

_____.
(need filled by site)

Unlike competing sites, which

_____,
(description of competition, highlighting faults)
_____ will
(site name)

_____.
(verb-based purpose, distinguishing site from its competition)

The resulting mission statement should look something like this:

MySistersGarden.com is an online gardening center offering information, advice, and products to discriminating gardening enthusiasts who want the best possible products for their outdoor garden. Unlike other gardening sites, which provide either information or products, but not both, MySistersGarden.com will offer a comprehensive suite of garden-planning tools to assist in all phases of garden planning, from plant selection to landscape design to product purchase to year-round maintenance.

"If you cry 'Forward!' you must without fail make plain in which direction to go."

—Anton Chekhov

stating your goals

Once you've determined the general direction of your site—or its redesign—it's important to articulate what you expect from it. What, exactly, are you hoping your site will accomplish? What concrete goals should the site help you achieve?

The goals themselves will vary, depending on the type of site. But whoever you are and whatever your site's mission, you'll find it's critical—both for the project's health and your own—to define success ahead of time.

By stating your goals, you

- **Create attainable measures** of success shared by everyone in the organization.

- **Provide an objective framework** for making decisions.

- **Give company stakeholders a forum** to voice their expectations.

- **Force company stakeholders to sign off** on goals, freeing the development team to meet them as they see fit.

- **Help prevent meddling** by accomplishing the above.

By defining (and writing down) your goals from the outset, you accomplish both practical and diplomatic purposes.

On the practical end, goals create quantifiable, and hopefully attainable, goals for the project. Over the course of development, the project team can consistently refer back to them, ensuring that the project's on track and that decisions made along the way support the overarching goals.

On the diplomatic front, these goals create a forum in which all an organization's stakeholders can voice their expectations and demands of the site (or site redesign). By gathering opinions on the site goals, consolidating them into a short list, and then getting approval on these stated goals, the producer sets herself, her team, and her site up for success. They now know what is expected of them, and they have the freedom to effectively do their jobs.

---

typical goals...

for a new site

- Reduce phone calls about hours and location

- Reduce bad leads by clarifying what your organization does (and doesn't do)

- Increase sales in store, or attendance at events, by using online promotions

- Convert existing offline customers or members into online customers or members

for a redesigned site

- Increase pageviews after a redesign

- Increase return visitors

- Increase number of registrations, purchases, or other completed transactions

---

what kind of goals?

The goals for your site will vary, of course, depending on its focus, but they may include things like increasing revenue, cutting costs, attracting and retaining more users, developing leads for new customers, reducing phone calls, building a mailing list, or raising the company's profile.

Whatever the specifics, your goals should meet two basic criteria.

The web site's goals should be

- **Relevant** to the organization's goals

- **Measurable**, so you can objectively gauge their success and track their progress

- **Realistic**, so the site can actually succeed.

This last point can't be stressed enough. Web sites may be powerful, but they're not magic. You can't expect them to right all your company's wrongs.

Dig Deeper
how to encourage collaboration, p. 330.
how to speak the language(s), p.329.

setting goals for a company site

Many web sites are developed within the context of a company—with employees, projects, and products that have a history both with customers and with each other. Goal-setting is a challenge in this environment, because you're weighing what's best not only for the web site and the company, but also for the individuals involved in the project. It's a political process as much as a strategic one.

For have no doubt: Web sites are political. The site acts as a company's public face, and everyone wants their work to appear prominently on it.

But goal-setting can help. By encouraging co-workers to agree on objective goals—rather than specific, subjective solutions (about where buttons should be placed or what the sections should be called)—you help them see a common purpose and force them to ignore irrelevant conflicts.

The goals you set collectively will help steer your site in the right direction. But the purpose behind goal-setting is not only to chart a clear course, but also to get others on board. This buy-in at the beginning of the process gives you the information you need to be successful.

7 steps to setting goals:

1. **Identify stakeholders**, the people in the company with a vested interest in the site.

2. **Interview stakeholders** about what they need the site to achieve.

3. **Interview the CEO** or someone as high as possible in the organization about what they need the site to achieve.

4. **Interview the web team** that will build or work on the site.

5. **Write a consolidated list of goals.**

6. **Discuss, revise, and approve goals** at a meeting attended by all stakeholders.

7. **Begin work** on the site with goals in hand!

A good way to get started on goals is to touch base with each of the key stakeholders. Sit down with them one-on-one, and discuss what they (or their departments) need the site to deliver. It's best to focus this conversation on what the site should accomplish, rather than how it should look or what it should do.

> **The web site acts as a company's public face. Everyone wants their work to appear prominently on it.**

In these interviews, you're playing amateur psychologist, journalist, and diplomat. Your goal is not only to take in what stakeholders are saying, but to understand their motivations. Are they fearful for their jobs? Resentful over past wrongs? Competitive with another individual or department? Once you understand their real concerns, you can begin to address them.

In addition to the stakeholders, it's important to talk to the CEO or someone of high status. Nearly every web developer has a horror story about a CEO who pulled the plug on a web site just before launch, because it didn't line up with corporate goals, or because he didn't like surprises. The best way to avoid this is to solicit executive opinions early on.

After collecting all these opinions, the producer should write a consolidated list of goals that best represent the company's interests. These goals should be approved by the stakeholders at a meeting attended by all: This ensures that everyone important to the process gets on board behind the objectives and shares an understanding of success.

It's important to emphasize that this meeting is the moment for discussion and dissent: Speak now, cranky ones, or forever hold your peace! After the development process begins in force, you can't modify the goals without jeopardizing the launch date.

Persuasive powers failing you?
Rethink your approach:
how to get everyone on board, p. 341.

what will you do with your web site?

Although web sites can grow very complex, they begin with a few simple questions: What do you need from the site? What do your users need? Everything else flows from there.

determining direction

Why does your organization need a web site?

_____

_____

_____

_____

_____

_____

Why will your visitors need this web site?

_____

_____

_____

_____

_____

_____

Describe what your web site will do or be:

_____

_____

_____

_____

_____

_____

_____

setting goals

Do different people in your organization have different goals?

Marketing says: _____

_____

IT says: _____

_____

Human resources says: _____

_____

The CEO says: _____

_____

_____ says: _____

_____ says: _____

Write a mission statement for your site:

_____ is a _____
(site name)   (noun describing site)
offering _____ to
                    (type of service)

_____
(adjective describing audience)
_____ who
(noun describing audience)
_____ to
("need" or "want")
_____.
(need filled by site)

Unlike competing sites, which
_____,
(description of competition, highlighting faults)
_____ will
(site name)
_____.
(verb-based purpose, distinguishing site from its competition)

What are your goals for this site?

1. _____

2. _____

3. _____

4. _____

5. _____

deciding what goes on the site

It may be the single most challenging step of web development: deciding what goes on the site. Everything that's been researched and decided must be channeled into your site's features. Note: This step shouldn't be taken until the product plan is otherwise complete. You should know a lot about your users, your financial goals, and your competition (not to mention your schedule and budget) before you finalize what goes on the site.

4 steps to defining your site's features:

1. **Set your priorities** about what will be included. These should be based on both your business goals and your users' needs.

2. **Make a blue-sky list** that outlines everything your site could possibly do or offer.

3. **Identify core features** without which your site couldn't launch.

4. **Prioritize other features** you'd like to include.

Defining the feature set is a strategic challenge, a creative opportunity, and a managerial nightmare. You must first encourage innovation—in order to produce a long list of all the possible features your site could include. Then you have to enforce discipline to narrow the list down to its core elements.

There's one word for this process: *political.*

Within a company, the question of what stays and goes on a feature list can easily become a power struggle between individuals or departments. Your goal, then, is to skillfully navigate these political waters with organized, collaborative methods for prioritizing features.

setting your priorities

Before you begin imagining and prioritizing features, it's important to agree on the site's overall mission and goals (starting your goals, p. 13). This will give you an objective framework for evaluating the features you dream up.

making a blue-sky list

The first step toward defining your site's features is the most fun. You and your team need to generate ideas about everything the site could offer or do.

The goal is to brainstorm a long list of all the possible features your site could include. You'll rapidly develop and refine ideas about how the site should be organized, how it might help or entertain users, how it will generate revenue, and how it will be different from competing sites.

The leader's role in this process is not only to generate ideas herself, but also to create an open atmosphere that enables creativity in others. This isn't exactly easy, as anyone who's attended—or led—a bad brainstorming session can tell you. "There are probably three people in the world who know how to run a brainstorming session," joked Jim Morris, former Director of Software Engineering at Global Sports, Inc. "It's so hard to be an unbiased collector of good ideas" (how to run a brainstorming session, p. 326).

> **There's one word for this process: political.**

The result of these brainstorming sessions is what's often called a blue-sky list. And while this might seem like a futile exercise (because we both know the sky isn't all that blue, and you're just going to turn around and narrow the list down), it's important, because you never know where the winning ideas are going to come from, or when.

Your most important idea could emerge a few hours, a few dozen doughnuts, and a few pots of coffee into a brainstorming session. Or it could be suggested by a junior production assistant next to the copy machine at the end of the next day. Or it could come to you in the middle of the night a week later. The creative process is tricky that way. Ideas build on ideas in ways that are hard to explain.

But this we know: The most interesting ideas are generated when you get people of different backgrounds in the same room at the same time. So a cross-disciplinary meeting—though challenging to run—is often the best place to start.

identifying core features

Before you delve too deeply into prioritizing your lists, it may help to pull out the "must-have" features, without which the site couldn't launch.

Sometimes these core features will be obvious. If you're launching a commerce site, for example, users must be able to select a product and purchase it. No point in launching the site if they can't do that. But the core features for a media site would be less clear-cut.

So there's no one way to identify these features. But there are a few techniques you can try, particularly if the choice is contentious.

3 ways to identify core features:

1. **Follow the user's path** from entering your site to accomplishing her primary goal. The streamlined steps that make this happen may be your core features.

2. **Compare user goals and business goals** (see the chart, right). The overlapping area may contain your core features.

3. **Chart all the features** according to how easy and important they are. (See the prioritization chart on p. 19.) The core features will likely be in the top half of the chart.

prioritizing features

It would be nice if we lived in a perfect world, where all our ideas for important features made it on to our web sites. But the real world, as you know, is highly flawed. Most web sites are deeply constrained—by time, money, and expertise —in what they can produce.

So the path from your blue-sky list to your final site will be marked with difficult choices. After scoping down the project to its core functionality— the features without which the site could not function or could not meet the basic needs of your users—you may still need to do several rounds of prioritization.

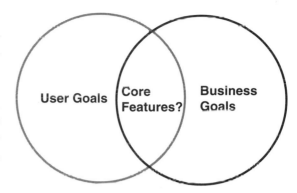

One way to identify core features: If the "must-have" features aren't otherwise obvious, you can match business goals with user goals and see where there's overlap.

For each feature, ask yourself:

- How important is this feature?

- How easy is this feature to implement?

importance

When rating the importance of a feature, there are three key elements to consider:

3 ways to rate importance:

- User needs

- Business needs

- Organizational needs

user needs   Plain and simple: If users don't need your site, they aren't going to use it. So the first factor to consider when prioritizing your feature list is what your users need or want (understanding user needs, p. 60). Examine each proposed feature and ask yourself: Is this necessary, or just nice? If your site omits major steps that the user must accomplish, you run the risk of being irrelevant. Conversely, if your site includes too many unnecessary features, it may appear bloated or confusing.

"He who attempts too much rarely succeeds."

—Dutch proverb

business needs Your other major concern—as you decide what to include—is financial. How much revenue must the site generate, and which features will figure most prominently in this effort? If revenue isn't the goal, then which features best support your other organizational goals?

organizational needs Another factor you shouldn't overlook is the role of the web site in your organization. Different constituencies within a company will place demands on the site: The marketing department may need to post press releases, for example, or human resources may need to post job openings. And while these goals may not rank highly in the overall priorities of the web site, their diplomatic importance (coupled with their relative ease of implementation) will often merit inclusion.

easiness

When gauging how easy a feature will be to produce, there are also three key elements to consider:

3 ways to gauge easiness

- Time constraints
- Budget constraints
- Staff constraints

time constraints It's always best when you can set a schedule based on how long the work will take, rather than vice versa. But the reality is that most web sites must be created within a tight schedule, and it's important to be realistic about how long tasks take before you begin (how to set a schedule that sticks, p. 324). Features that take longer to develop can always be phased in later, but it's best to plan this from the get-go, rather than to scramble when they don't get done.

budget constraints Money, like time, is always at a premium. And you definitely need to consider cost when planning your features. But remember to think beyond development: Some features are more expensive to maintain than they are to build. Some applications, for example, require more and better servers as the site becomes more popular. Most community features require moderators to monitor and guide discussions, and many editorial features require updated content that's expensive to produce.

staff constraints A site can only be as good as the people who create it. And sometimes it just isn't possible to find the right people to create the site or features you want. In this case, you might partner with another site or company to produce specific features. Or you might table the features in question until you can find the right team.

a prioritization process

In order to prioritize features, you need to consider both how important they are and how easy they are to produce. Sometimes, the site producer can do this in his head, weighing the different options and arriving at conclusions that will go more or less unchallenged. Lucky guy. Most producers face a tougher battle.

If you—like most site producers—need to justify your decisions about what stays and what goes, it helps to have an organized process. The prioritization chart (facing page) is an excellent tool (though not the only one) for making these decisions in a public and defensible way.

Planning what goes on your site?
predicting what users will want, p. 58
5 online revenue models, p. 70
structuring your site, p. 99
developing software for your site, p. 231
how to run a brainstorming session, p. 326

prioritization chart

This prioritization chart is a handy way of visualizing how different features should be prioritized on your web site. It makes explicit the process most of us would do in our heads, and it delivers similar results. But the chart is group-friendly and helps others in the company understand what decisions were made and why.

1. **Get all the important staff in one room.** Brainstorm the "Blue sky" list of all the possible features you could or would like to include.

2. **Identify the core features.** These are the "must-haves"—the features that the site absolutely, positively couldn't launch without. Set these aside. It isn't necessary to rank features that you must include (although it may be helpful to put them on the chart as a reminder that they exist and will be tying up resources). If you can't reach agreement on which features these are, carry them all over to the next step.

3. **Rank each feature for importance and easiness.** Importance here means either importance to the user, importance to the business, or both. Easiness here means how quickly and cheaply the project can be completed.

4. **Rank each of the features from 1-10** for each characteristic.

5. **Plot the features out on the graph at right.** Each bar represents one feature. The light block of each bar represents its easiness, and the dark block represents its importance.

6. **Note the location of each feature on the chart**, and note what that tells you about whether it should be included.

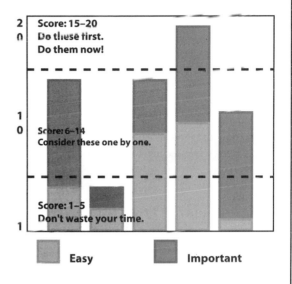

Score: 15–20
Do these first.
Do them now!

Score: 6–14
Consider these one by one.

Score: 1–5
Don't waste your time.

Easy   Important

Rank each feature 1–10 for importance and easiness.

For easiness:
1 = Very, very hard, expensive, and/or time-consuming
10 = Very, very easy, cheap, and/or quick
For importance:
1 = Completely unnecessary
10 = Absolutely essential

what features will your web site include?

defining the site's features

Use the space below for your blue-sky list of everything your site could possibly contain:

_____
_____
_____
_____
_____
_____
_____
_____
_____
_____
_____
_____
_____
_____
_____
_____
_____
_____
_____
_____
_____
_____
_____
_____

Which features must you include?

1. _____

2. _____

3. _____

4. _____

5. _____

Prioritize the remaining features on the following chart. Rank each feature 1–10 for importance and easiness.

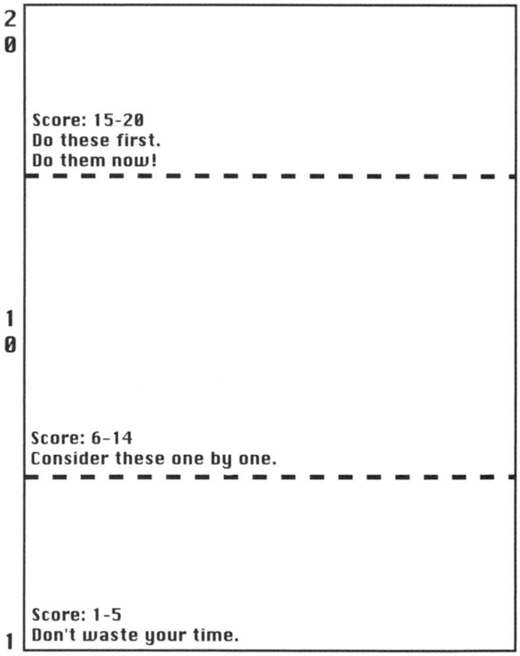

```
20
        Score: 15-20
        Do these first.
        Do them now!
- - - - - - - - - - - - - - - - - -
10

        Score: 6-14
        Consider these one by one.
- - - - - - - - - - - - - - - - - -

        Score: 1-5
 1      Don't waste your time.
```

"Look, we just raised $18 million in venture capital, so take the damn shovel."

take action**!**

writing
a plan

"Well-begun is half-done."
- Aristotle

why bother writing a plan?

It's astonishing to me just how many web sites get started without a clear idea of goals or priorities, not to mention business models. You hear it all the time: Companies announce web initiatives without specifying what's being built, hire designers without telling them what to design, plan launch parties without knowing what will launch. Honestly, it's a wonder anything gets built at all.

> **No matter how pressed you were for money or time, you'd never break ground on a building without a blueprint.**
> **Same goes for web sites.**

You wouldn't stand for this foolishness in other arenas. Consider architecture: No matter how pressed you were for money or time, no matter how much you prized innovation, you would never break ground on a building without a blueprint. It would be sheer folly to begin such a complicated and expensive project without a diagram of what you were building and assurance that it would—at the end of the day—remain standing.

Same goes for web sites. The product plan acts as a blueprint, describing the goals and purpose of your site before you begin building—in some cases, before you're entirely sure what you're going to build. It forces you to make decisions and confronts you with any inconsistencies or impossibilities before you waste too much time, money, and credibility.

By establishing goals from the outset, you'll help your development team focus its energies only on those initiatives that support the site's main goals while deflecting the distractions that inevitably arise along the way.

Why write a product plan?

- **It facilitates communication** by getting the whole development team on the same page and keeping them there.

- **It describes what you're building** *before* you start building it.

- **It clarifies your goals** so you'll know when you've achieved them.

- **It keeps you focused** as you move further into the development process.

- **It confronts you with unsolvable problems** before you waste too much time, money, and credibility.

- **It forces your boss** (and her boss, and other co-workers) **to sign off** on the vision behind the site—or express concerns at an early stage, when they can still be efficiently addressed.

So now we agree: You need a plan.

the basic plan

The product plan is your site's backbone. Written before you start development—and updated along the way—it outlines your site's overarching purpose, as well as its specific features and strategic goals.

The product plan

- Identifies who's in charge, whether it's a producer, project manager, or company owner.

- Identifies the team of people who will work on the site.

- Explains the site's purpose.

- Declares the site's goals.

- Identifies the target audience.

- Describes the site's features and how they'll work.

- Projects traffic and revenue.

- Outlines a promotion plan.

- Identifies potential competitors.

- Estimates the schedule and costs.

- Outlines assumptions upon which the plan is based or dependencies within it (If X doesn't happen, then we can't do Y).

The product plan outlined on the following pages is a close cousin to the standard business plan. If your background is in business, marketing, or product management, the structure will be old hat. The challenge for you will be integrating ideas about the online environment, which may run counter to the conventional wisdom in your field.

But if your background is, well, anything else, all the analysis and segmentation may be new to you. I assure you, as I'll assure you many times over the course of this book: It's simpler than it sounds.

And if you're short on time, remember: Anything is better than nothing. Even if your so-called plan contains only a few key sentences, it can make a big difference on the finished site.

don't get paralyzed!

Many producers skip the formalized planning process for fear it will expose too many unknowns. Not knowing exactly how things will turn out, they avoid writing anything at all. They become paralyzed by the uncertainty.

But the point of the product plan isn't to set things in stone, but to **get your best guesses in writing**. No web producer is 100% certain of what they're doing or where they're going at the outset of a project. The important thing is to capture your goals and your assumptions, so you can recognize when and if they change.

So relax. You're not expected to know everything. This is an emerging industry. You don't know enough. You'll never know enough. Just write down what's in your head and move on.

"Congratulations—phase one of naming this project's first phase is complete."

the basic product plan

The product plan is essential to a web site's success. Written before you start development work—and updated along the way—it outlines your site's overarching purpose, specific features, and strategic goals. So at the end of the day, you'll know whether you've accomplished what you set out to do.

Different projects demand different levels of detail. So whether your plan takes you five minutes or five months is up to you. But don't start work without it.

1. name

Your site will need a name and a domain name (ideally, these will be the same). Don't put this off until the last minute. Start considering names early in the development process, and make sure the needed domains are available.

Choosing a name isn't as easy as it may seem. It's a creative challenge to name any product or organization. But the web introduces its own complicating factors:

When choosing a name, consider

■ **Clarity.** On the web—more so than any other media or industry—it's helpful for the name to provide some clear idea of what the site is about.

■ **Legality.** Businesses from all different industries and locations compete on the web, which means domain names are scarce and lawsuits are rife. Be sure to investigate any possible trademark infringements before deciding on a name.

■ **Availability.** Sadly, you may come up with the perfect name for your site, only to discover the domain name's been taken—by an organization in a different country, perhaps, with a vastly different focus. The fact is that simple, straightforward domain names are hard to come by, and you may have to settle for your fourth or fifth choice.

See 3 ways to name your site, p. 33.

2. mission & goals

mission statement What's the big idea? Articulate clearly and succinctly the purpose of your site (or added feature). What is it for? Who is it for? How is it distinguished from other, similar sites? See writing a mission statement, p. 12.

stated goals Along with the mission statement, it's important to articulate specific, measurable, and (hopefully) attainable goals for your project before you begin work. Over the course of development, the project team can refer back to this list, to make sure all decisions support the overarching goals. See stating your goals, p. 13.

Goals may include

■ Increasing revenue

■ Cutting costs

■ Attracting and retaining more users

■ Changing user behavior

■ Raising company's profile

Stated goals are essential for every project, even those—like redesigns or new features—that don't require a formal mission statement.

See deciding what goes on the site, p. 16.

3. target audience

profile Describe your target audience, and be specific. Your site can't be for everyone. It's essential to know who you're targeting and build the site with them in mind. See profiling your users, p. 50.

You might describe your users by

- **Demographics.** Nationality, age, gender, profession, education, income, etc.

- **Psychographics.** Attitudes, interests, and motivation in seeking your product.

- **Webographics.** Length of time on the web, frequency of web use, point of access, connection speed, type of computer and browser.

- **Behavior & activities.** Sometimes the best way to describe a site's users is by what they do, not who they are. If you're building a game site, for example, then the most important description of your audience is that they're game players. Age, gender, and operating system are all secondary.

- **Site-specific experience.** Some sites will require greater detail about their users, specific to their site or company. A bicycle company, for instance, would have to think about what kinds of cyclists they're targeting: Hard-core single track mountain bikers, or parents who need tips on training wheels?

Size. Estimate the total size of your target audience and the percent of that market you expect to capture. Base your projections on the best and most accurate numbers available. If there's just no way to build an estimate with available statistics, then guess. Your best guess is always better than nothing at all. See estimating audience size, p. 52.

See learning about your users, p. 46.

4. traffic patterns

How will people use your site? How often will they come, and how long will they stay? How will they find you, and how will they remember to come back? This kind of qualitative analysis will help you make quantitative traffic projections.

The best way to predict usage patterns is to divide your audience into several segments you expect to behave differently. You could segment them by need (Why are they coming to your site?), experience level (New to the web? New to your product/site?), or origin (How did they find you?). See segmenting your users, p. 56.

Describe each audience segment by

- **Motivation.** What are they looking for?

- **Entrance point.** How did they find you? Will they enter your site through the home page or a link to an interior page?

- **Site use.** What part of the site will they use?

- **Frequency of visits.** Will they return daily, monthly, never?

- **Page views per visit.** How long will they stick around?

Given the usage patterns of your different audience segments (and the relative size of each segment) guesstimate your traffic levels.

Remember, this isn't an exact science, so don't worry if you have a few gaps in your research. The purpose here is to get your best guesses in writing so you can plan accordingly.

See evolving your site, p. 254.

the basic product plan (continued)

5. revenue model

How will your site make money? Always begin with the most obvious plan (providing leads for your existing business, for example), but also consider the full range of options that are working on the web right now. Some of the strongest business models are based on multiple revenue streams, developed over time.

5 revenue models that work online:

- Generating leads for an existing business
- Advertising
- Product sales
- Subscriptions and user fees
- "Match making"

As in other sections, be specific. If you plan to make money through advertising, for example, be sure to include projections for the number, size, and placement of ad banners on your site. Be sure to also include your assumptions on important variables, such as price of advertising, sales-per-customer, or sign-up rates. When any individual variable changes, it will affect your overall projections.

See <u>making money</u>, p. 68.

6. feature set

Describe your site (succinctly), in terms of content, services, and utilities. What are the elements that make up the overall experience, and how will they fit together? Which features are essential to the site's success? Which can be phased in over time?

List your site's features, including

- **Central service, content, or utility.** Product database, search engine, news articles, etc.
- **Content areas.** Will they be updated? How often?
- **Content feeds.** Stock quotes, news headlines, weather, etc.
- **Personalized features.** Recommendations, customized pages, etc.
- **Related links.** Within your site or to other sites. Will these be automated or chosen individually?

- **Ads.** Number, type, and placement.
- **Site search.** If needed.
- **Help section.** If needed.
- **Archive.** If needed.
- **Multiple versions of site.** For printing, emailing, or delivering content to handheld computers.
- **International versions.** If needed.
- **Potential partners.** Your product plan should include a brief list of any possible partners, including technology or content providers.
- **Details, details.** If you're serious about documentation—and you should be!—you can develop this section over time to include a more detailed technical specification, design brief, editorial brief, and site map. These can all be added at a later date.

See <u>deciding what goes on the site</u>, p. 16

7. competition

Write a brief overview summarizing your competitive outlook, including the following:

▓ **A short list of competitors** with names, URLs, and parent company.

▓ **Your points of differentiation** vis-á-vis the competition.

▓ **Your aspirations** vis-á-vis the competition. (How big do you want to be? How much of their audience can you steal? Which segments of your audience can they poach?)

In a separate document, list and describe your competitors on the web in greater detail, including the following elements:

▓ **Site name**, URL, and parent company

▓ **Feature list**

▓ **Revenue model** (advertising, subscriptions, etc.)

▓ **Approximate size** in terms of visitors and/or page views

▓ **Subjective rating** telling if they're good at what they do

Be sure to notice the things your competition is doing well—and copy them.

See sizing up the competition, p. 38.

8. marketing plan

How will you get the word out about your site? What kind of budget have you assigned to site promotions, and how will it be best spent?

Your marketing plan should probably include

▓ **Linking programs** for promoting your site on search engines, directories, and sites related to yours

▓ **Email programs** for both deepening your relationship with site visitors, and—in some cases—recruiting new customers

▓ **Word-of-mouth programs** that will encourage your existing customers to spread the word for you

▓ **An online advertising budget** so you can strategically purchase placement on key sites

▓ **Cross-media strategies** so you can promote your site in the real world

See promoting your site, p. 278.

9. team

Every web site needs a clear producer or product manager—that is, if you want it to succeed. It's important to have a single person responsible for driving a project forward and making final decisions, but it's also important to have all the key disciplines represented from the beginning.

At minimum, you should identify

▓ Producer or project manager

▓ Technical lead

▓ Design lead

▓ Production lead

This should go without saying, but it's also important to identify key decision makers before you start making decisions—and certainly before you begin building the site. If a senior manager has the power to overturn decisions, she should be consulted in the earliest stages to avoid wasted work.

See assembling a web team, p. 332.

the basic product plan (continued)

10. schedule & budget

Project success is at least partially judged by completing the site on time and on budget. Be sure you know your constraints before you begin work.

budget   Never underestimate the importance of a budget. Everyone loves to hate them, but they're an essential tool for managing your project.

"Having a budget is a really good thing," said web veteran Dave Thau, author of *The Book of JavaScript*. "It sounds funny, but a lot of people just don't have one. Then costs will run away from you, and if you don't have a budget, you don't realize that they're running away."

You may have a budget imposed on you. But you won't be able to estimate your expenses until you've finalized your feature set. (If you don't know what you're building, you won't know what it's going to cost.) To build an estimate, start with your staff costs, both while under development and after launch. Estimate salaried staff, as well as non-salary costs, including consultant payments, licensing fees, special marketing or promotions (media buys, trade shows, and press tours), and required travel. And don't forget the backend—the more complex your site, and the more popular it proves, the more expensive your servers and bandwidth will be.

schedule   The budget for your project often determines the people and resources you have available, and this in turn helps determine how long it will take. Before you begin work, outline project milestones with projected dates for completion. Be sure to include any dependencies built into the schedule. (Often, one phase must conclude before another can begin.) Leave time for testing and QA, and always, always, always pad the schedule to accommodate the delays that inevitably occur. See how to set a schedule that sticks, p. 324.

See managing a web project & team, p. 320.

11. assumptions

What are the assumptions upon which you're basing your plan? Are you assuming the existence of a particular audience? Are you assuming that a particular technology will work, or scale to a larger audience? Are you assuming there's an unmet need your site will fill? Do you have any basis for these assumptions? What will make or break this product? Does it depend on being first to market? Does it depend on being cheaper, faster, or just plain better than its competitors? Does it depend on a particular technology being available, functional, or scalable? Does it depend on a particular individual? Does it depend on world events or pop culture trends? Does it depend on being seen as "cool"?

writing your product plan

A written product plan is the foundation of a successful site. Start yours now by filling in the blanks. You can expand on your answers in the chapters to come.

What will you name your site?

_____

_____

What is your mission statement?

_____

_____

What are your specific goals?

1._____

2._____

3._____

4._____

Who are your users and what do they need?

Segment 1:

_____

_____

Segment 2:

_____

_____

Segment 3:

_____

_____

Who are your main competitors?

1._____

2._____

3._____

How will you make money?

❑ Generate leads for business.

❑ Advertising.

❑ Product sales.

❑ Subscriptions or user fees.

❑ Match-making.

❑ We won't, but we'll save money.

How will you promote your site?

_____

_____

How will your site be used?

_____ pageviews per month   _____ visitors per month

Length of average visit:

_____ minutes or _____ pageviews

What is your overall budget?

_____

When is your launch date?

_____

When is your launch date?

this is a: ❑ hard launch date   ❑ soft launch date

Who is your team?

❑ Producer/project lead

_____

❑ Design lead

_____

❑ Technical lead

_____

❑ Production lead

_____

assumptions

This plan is based on what assumptions?

_____

_____

Under what conditions will you need to rethink your strategy?

_____

_____

chapter 2
naming your site

"We can't call him Kevin—that domain name has been registered."

don't miss ...

The name game is a challenge in any industry, but it's complicated on the web by several factors, including the dearth of domain names. Unlike business names—which can be repeated in different towns or different countries or different industries—domain names are one to a customer.

So, while a Joe's Hardware in Teaneck, New Jersey would normally coexist peacefully with a Joe's Hardware in Phoenix, Arizona, the two will likely butt heads online. For there can only be one joeshardware.com.

This became a problem in the late '90s, when the web's popularity took off. There was a rush on domain names, and many companies were left empty-handed. Soon, the possession of a straightforward, easily understood domain name was both a status symbol and a point of professional pride.

When choosing a site name, consider

- **Clarity.** On the web, it's important to be clear about who you are and what you do. Your name is a good place to start.

- **Legality.** Businesses from all different industries and locations compete on the web, which means domain names are scarce and lawsuits are rife. Be sure to investigate any possible trademark infringements before deciding on a name

- **Availability.** Sadly, you may come up with the perfect name for your site, only to discover that the domain name's been taken. Simple, straightforward domain names are hard to come by, and you may have to settle for your fourth or fifth choice.

choosing a name

No matter what kind of site or business you're naming, your basic goal is always the same: You want a name that sticks in users' minds and helps you stand out from the pack. But there are three distinct philosophies on how to accomplish that goal online.

3 kinds of site names:

- Dot-com names

- Unusual names

- Combination names

the dot-com name   One popular approach to naming web sites is to choose the most generic name possible, and add a "dot-com" on the end – as in computers.com or news.com—or an "e" on the beginning, as in eToys or eGreetings.

This naming trend hit its peak in the late '90s, when nearly every word in the Oxford English Dictionary was registered as a dot-com domain name. Long-standing companies repositioned themselves as internet start-ups by renaming themselves or spinning off new businesses with "e" and "i" in the name. The motivation was largely financial: an effort to reassure stockholders about a company's internet strategy and convince investors that it deserved a dot-com valuation.

It should come as no surprise, then, that companies began shedding their dot-coms as soon as the financial climate turned. In 2000, many recently minted dot-coms changed their names back.

the unusual name   An alternate naming philosophy leans toward unusual, and not necessarily descriptive, names. This is sometimes referred to as the "empty vessel" approach to branding: You choose a word with little or no intrinsic meaning—an "empty semantic vessel," if you will—so you can define your brand and the word at the same time.

This approach is well-suited to established businesses as they come online, such as Gap.com, Walmart.com, and Marthastewart.com. But for new businesses it's risky, because it doesn't make your life any easier: It won't help your search engine listings, and it won't help users understand what you do.

Despite the risks, this approach has worked wonders for some of the web's most successful sites, including Amazon.com (the leading retail store), Google (the leading search engine), and Yahoo! (a leading portal). Whether they succeeded because of their names or despite them is anyone's guess.

the combination name   It's hard to decide between these two approaches, because—if you're like me—you want it all. On one hand, you want a name that's distinctive so it will stick in users minds. On the other hand, you want a name that's clear, so users will immediately have a sense of what you do.

There is a middle path. It's possible to choose a name that reaps the benefits of both approaches.

A combination name is

- **Meaningful.** It communicates something about what the site does or who it's for.

- **Memorable.** It goes beyond generic words to uniquely brand the site.

This is no small task, but it can be done. A few successful examples include Babycenter, Ask Dr. Weil, BlackPlanet, and Animation Express.

registering your name

Once you come up with a name for your site, there are a few hoops to jump through before it's officially yours: Acquiring the domain name and registering the trademark—or at least making sure that you're not infringing on someone else's.

To make the name yours:

- Register the domain name.

- Register the trademark.

register the domain name   Just about everyone who's built a web site knows the frustration of domain-name registration. The process itself is simple enough: Just choose a name, choose an internet host, and pay the annual licensing fee. Easy enough—if you can find an available name. More and more businesses come online each year and find fewer and fewer "dot-com" names available. Fortunately, there are now alternatives, like .biz and .info (See choosing a suffix, p. 34).

Provided that you find a domain name you want, you can register it through a web-hosting service (See acquiring a domain name, p.35) for around $100/year.

register the trademark   If you're serious about your web site, you should think about registering the name as a trademark. And even if you're not so serious, you should make sure the name doesn't infringe on another company's mark.

A trademark is a word, name, symbol, or device that uniquely represents a specific company or product, and cannot be used by others. For instance, the Nike name, the "swoosh" logo, and the phrase "Just do it" are all trademarked by Nike, Inc.

Trademark law applies in the online world as well as the terrestrial. If your domain name uses a word or phrase that is trademarked by someone else, they can sue you for it. And the last thing you need is an intellectual-property suit six months down the road.

So make sure you're in the clear. First, do a trademark search through the U.S. Patent & Trademark Office (http://www.uspto.gov). Then do a web search on the word or phrase. You should know of any similar names before you make your choice.

The cost to register a trademark is around $350, and it can only be done for words or symbols that are—or will be—used for commercial purposes.

3 ways to name your site

1. dot-com names

Dot-com names are based on a generic word that describes the site's focus:

- artdealers.org
- drugstore.com
- efax.com
- weather.com

benefits

- Customers understand what you do because your business focus is communicated with your name.
- Customers remember your URL because it's straightforward and related to your line of business.
- Search engine rank improves because name contains important keywords.

drawbacks

- They're very 1999 and may not age well.
- They aren't distinctive. Customers can easily confuse you with similarly named competitors.
- They can be limiting if you plan to expand off the web.
- Dot-com names don't exactly inspire consumer confidence.

2. unusual names

Unusual names have little or no intrinsic meaning, so the name can be defined by the brand:

- Amazon
- Google
- Napster
- Yahoo!

benefits

- They're distinctive. Customers are less likely to confuse you with competitors.
- They lack intrinsic meaning, so you can "own" the word. You define its meaning as you define your brand.
- They're memorable.

drawbacks

- They're vague. Customers may have a hard time understanding what you do. You'll have to work harder to explain it to them.
- They don't help you rank well on search engines, because the name doesn't contain relevant keywords.
- Customers may pass you by—not realizing you provide a relevant service.

3. combination names

Combination names take the middle path with names that are distinctive but clear:

- Ask Dr. Weil
- BabyCenter
- BlackPlanet
- Guru

benefits

- Customers quickly grasp what you do even if it wasn't immediately clear when they heard the name.
- They're distinctive. Customers can differentiate you from competitors.
- They're often memorable.

drawbacks

- They're easily mimicked. Though they're not entirely generic, combination names can often be closely copied by the competition
- They don't usually help you rank well on search engines, because the name doesn't necessarily contain relevant keywords.

Required Reading

No student of the web should miss Josh Quittner's classic article on registering McDonalds.com. "Billion Registered," *Wired Magazine* (August 1994) p. 124

choosing a suffix

When you register a domain name today, you can choose your suffix (or "top-level domain" as they're called). Although .com is by far the most popular, there are currently 260 other options: 247 country-specific domains and 13 global top-level domains.

There haven't always been so many choices. When the domain name system was first introduced, only six top-level domains were created.

6 original top-level domains:

- **.com** for companies
- **.edu** for universities
- **.gov** for government agencies
- **.mil** for military organizations
- **.net** for network service providers
- **.org** for all other organizations

Country-specific domains were soon added, giving each nation control over its own top-level domain.

Country-specific domains include

- **.cn** for China
- **.uk** for Great Britain
- **248 others**

But by the late 90s, this was no longer enough. The crush of applications for domain names created a need for more top-level domains. Many were proposed, and as of this writing, seven were approved. (One more—.pro—is under consideration.)

7 new top-level domains:

- **.biz** for businesses
- **.info** for all uses
- **.int** for international organizations
- **.aero** for the air-transport industry
- **.coop** for cooperatives
- **.museum** for museums
- **.name** for individuals

---

understanding web addresses

The URL (Uniform Resource Locator) is the standard format for a web address:

http://www.foggymorning.com

This is read as "H T T P colon slash slash dubya dubya dubya dot foggymorning dot com."

http
stands for hypertext transfer protocol. This is the "language" computers speak to each other when transferring web pages and their elements.

www
refers to the specific server (or computer) that stores the web site. Web sites may have limitless numbers of servers and may name them whatever they want. But the standard name for a web server is www.

foggymorning
is the domain name. When combined with the top-level domain (in this case, .com), it creates a unique identity, which may not be duplicated by any other site, worldwide.

.com
is the top-level domain. It identifies what type of organization owns the site. The ".com" in this URL identifies the site as a commercial organization.

what about ip addresses?

Web addresses can be expressed either in numbers or words. People find it easier to remember names than numbers, so we use domain names like foggymorning.com. But computers prefer to communicate with numbers. So every domain name is correlated with a unique number, or IP address. So foggymorning.com could also be found with an address like this:

http://234.56.78.525

IP addresses consist of 4 numbers, each less than 256, connected by periods.

(See how web pages are served, p. 200.)

acquiring a domain name

How can I check if a domain name is available?

Easy. You can do a simple, no-commitment web search through any web-hosting service (or other accredited registrar). The list of registrars is at http://www.internic.net.

How do I register a domain name?

You can register a domain name through almost any web-hosting service (or other accredited registrar). Note: You must have a hosting service for your site before you can register a name. This is why most people register through a web host: You can register for the name and host at the same time.

How much does it cost?

It costs roughly $100/year to license a domain name. The hosting service usually charges an additional one-time registration fee and a monthly fee for hosting the site—even if you don't build it. However, some hosts offer discounted "parking" fees to reserve a site before you actually build it. Note: You can't buy domain names outright; you license them annually.

Does the price vary?

The licensing fee is the same for all domain names within the same registry. Meaning: All .com names will cost the same per year, but .biz names may have a different fee. The biggest variation in price will be for the hosting service. Monthly charges range widely (and so does the level of service).

What if the name I want is taken?

Count on it: The name you want will be taken. It's very hard to find a simple domain name, and the obscure ones are taken, too. Your best bet is to think of a different name altogether, but you could also register it under a different top-level domain (.biz instead of .com). You could add a differentiating word on to the domain, such as seedmagazine.com instead of seed.com, or you could see if the owners want to sell. To find out who owns it, do a "whois" search on internic.net. Often, this only reveals the hosting service, but you can sometimes obtain contact information from them.

What if someone else registers my company name ?

If a domain name violates your trademark, you can file suit against the owner. Find the dispute-resolution policy at http://www.icann.org/udrp/.

Should I register more than one version of my name?

Possibly. Many site owners register more than one name to avoid customer confusion. Many sites register common misspellings of their names (genealogy.com also owns geneology.com). Many register the same name under different top-level domains (The San Francisco Museum of Modern Art owns sfmoma.com and sfmoma.org). And some register different variations of the name (The store Williams-Sonoma owns williams-sonoma.com and williamssonoma.com).

Do I have to choose a hosting service before I register my domain name?

Yes. From the moment they're registered, domain names must be linked with a specific server, so the site can be found (<u>how web pages are served</u>, p. 200). However, you can always change hosts later on.

what will you name your site?

Never underestimate the importance of a name. As the first thing users learn about your site, it sets the tone for their experience and helps them understand—and remember—who you are.

What do you want the name to convey about your site?

1. _____

   _____

2. _____

   _____

3. _____

   _____

4. _____

   _____

5. _____

   _____

What are your competitors named?

1. _____
2. _____
3. _____
4. _____
5. _____

What are some possible names?

1. _____

This is
❏ generic/dot-com   ❏ unusual
❏ combination

2. _____

This is
❏ generic/dot-com   ❏ unusual
❏ combination

3. _____

This is
❏ generic/dot-com   ❏ unusual
❏ combination

4. _____

This is
❏ generic/dot-com   ❏ unusual
❏ combination

5. _____

This is
❏ generic/dot-com   ❏ unusual
❏ combination

Which names are available?

Name

1. _____

Trademark OK?   Domain Available?
❏   ❏

2. _____

Trademark OK?   Domain Available?
❏   ❏

3. _____

Trademark OK?   Domain Available?
❏   ❏

Which name do you want?

Name   Domain Reserved?

1. _____   ❏
2. _____   ❏
3. _____   ❏

chapter 3

sizing up the competition

"On the plus side, we are the <u>only</u> coffee chain with that God-awful burnt bitter aftertaste."

don't miss ...

Underestimating one's competition is a classic mistake made in all walks of business. But it's epidemic on the web, where competitors may not be immediately visible or obvious.

Excuses abound: In a fast-paced development environment, it may seem easier to ignore the competition than to analyze it. And teams that are innovation-focused often resist the idea of examining other sites—as if it would undermine their creativity to acknowledge the work of others. Non-profit sites often skip this step altogether, assuming that competitive analysis applies only to commercial sites.

But they're all mistaken. Competitive analysis is essential for all sites—commercial and noncommercial, heavily contested or alone in its field—because it gives the product team key information.

3 reasons to do competitive analysis:

1. You always have competition.

2. The web introduces new competitors.

3. Competitors give you ideas.

you always have competition   Many sites assume they have no competitors because they haven't seen anyone else do the same thing online. It's a common mistake, because it's a common situation. In a rapidly growing medium, millions of companies have been, for a time, the first or only entrant in their particular fields. (Though many define their fields rather narrowly. For example, "We're the first one-hour online photo developers with personalized photo albums in Miami, Florida.")

But most sites *do* have competitors, even if they're not immediately apparent. There may be sites doing what you do in a different geographic location. Or there may be sites doing something similar—in the eyes of your customers. There may also be off-line competitors—stores, books, software, TV shows—that already fill the need you're addressing or that are poised to follow you online.

And even entrants who remain alone in their fields, such as unique entertainment sites and specialized services, need to look outside themselves. For there's always competition, even if it's only for users' time.

the web introduces new competitors
Everything powerful is also dangerous, and the web's greatest power is one businesses fear the most. The web allows businesses to achieve geographic distribution in a way that's never before been possible. So even if you run a local business, your competitors may no longer be those you pass on your way to work. They may appear, seemingly from nowhere, online. (Can you say "Amazon?") (identifying competitors, p. 40)

The good news is that the web also gives you *access* to your competitors—if you view them as a source of ideas and potential partnerships.

There's always competition, even if it's only for users' time.

competitors give you ideas   It's useful to evaluate your competitors, because it opens your eyes to potential threats. But it also opens your mind to possibilities: in product direction, in partnerships, and in strategy. By anticipating your competitor's next move, you just might think up your own.

Before you launch a site, you should take a long, hard look at similar sites, and see how they solve the problems you face. They're usually full of ideas on what to include, what to highlight, and how to organize it all (evaluating competitors, p. 42).

And if your business (and your competition) is firmly rooted in the terrestrial world, the web is a great tool for analyzing off-line competitors as well. Take restaurants, for example. It can take months to visit and assess a wide range of your competitors. But the web lets you glimpse into their kitchens and dining rooms without placing a single order.

identifying competitors

The first step in analyzing your competitors is identifying who or what they are. Begin, as always, with the obvious: A simple list of known competitors operating in your sector.

Broaden this list by looking online. Who will you be competing with on the web? All your known off-line competitors may come online, but there may be new competitors as well. If you're a local business, you may face competition from national outfitters.

Now broaden your mind. Think about the user need you're addressing. What other sources will people turn to when confronting this need? Books? Magazines? Informational web sites? Trusted friends? (<u>understanding user needs</u>, p. 60)

You can, of course, put the web itself to use in identifying competitors. Begin by browsing the online directories, like Yahoo. Their hierarchical categories will let you see, at a glance, the other sites in your category. Pay special attention to any competitors who advertise in these areas or whose functionality is highlighted within the portal. These are probably your most significant competitors, or at least the ones hustling the hardest.

Search engines offer another convenient tool: Simply search on those keywords relevant to your site. Both the ads and the listings will point you toward potential partners and competitors.

Also, make sure you pay attention to what the big guys (Amazon, Microsoft, etc.) are doing. A competition with these 900-pound gorillas could be deadly, but a partnership could be a tremendous boost.

where competitors come from

Online competition often emerges from unexpected sources, because the web allows sites to expand *vertically* or *horizontally* with relative ease.

2 ways for competition to emerge:

- **Vertical competition** comes from sites that offer multiple services related to one topic.

---

where to look for competitors

Not sure who your competitors are? Here's where to look:

- **On Yahoo!** Look at the sites listed in your category on Yahoo! or other directories.

- **On a search engine.** Do a search for keywords related to your site. Look at both the ads and the listed sites.

- **On the newsstand.** Look for magazines, books, and TV shows related to your site.

- **Look at ads on your competitors' sites** (or your own!) and in relevant publications.

- Find the latest industry ratings from **Nielsen NetRatings** or **Media Metrix** (<u>how the rating systems work</u>, p. 246).

- If you can afford it, **research services** like Nielsen offer hoards of helpful information, such as which sites your customers visit after leaving yours or which sites have a user base that overlaps with yours.

- **Horizontal competition** comes from sites that offer a single service related to multiple topics or product categories.

Many sites start small, then expand either horizontally or vertically over time. Amazon, for example, started out as a bookstore and expanded horizontally, adding other product categories (CDs, software, toys, etc.). Babycenter, on the other hand, is a classic vertical site; it started out as an information resource for new and expecting parents, and added both community features and a store over time.

Required reading

Are you a large company threatened by upstarts? "Identify your competitors before they destroy you." *Harvard Business Review* (November 2000).

action section

who is your competition?

On the web, your competition may not be immediately obvious. It may come from companies in other industries or even other countries. But remember: There's always competition, even if it's only for your customer's time.

identifying competitors

Who are your known competitors?

1. _____
2. _____
3. _____
4. _____
5. _____

What sites might become competitors?

1. _____

The competition will be: ❏ vertical ❏ horizontal

2. _____

The competition will be: ❏ vertical ❏ horizontal

3. _____

The competition will be: ❏ vertical ❏ horizontal

4. _____

The competition will be: ❏ vertical ❏ horizontal

5. _____

The competition will be: ❏ vertical ❏ horizontal

Do any related sites have partnerships with portals?

1. _____
2. _____
3. _____
4. _____
5. _____

According to Nielsen NetRatings, what are the top-ranked sites in your category?

1. _____
2. _____
3. _____
4. _____
5. _____

When you search for the keywords that are most important to your site, which sites appear on the first page of the listings?

On Alltheweb:

_____

_____

On AOL search:

_____

_____

On Google:

_____

_____

On HotBot:

_____

_____

On Lycos:

_____

_____

On MSN search:

_____

_____

On Overture:

_____

_____

On Yahoo!:

_____

_____

evaluating competitors

There are two ways to size up your competition: financial and functional.

2 ways to evaluate the competition:

- **Financial analysis** looks at the health of an overall business—company size, investors, sources of revenue, and traffic to site.

- **Functional analysis** looks at what a business is doing on the web—how its sites are organized, what features it offers, and how fast it is.

financial analysis

The first way to analyze a competitor is to look at the health of their business: Is it profitable? How stable is the business? Does it have multiple revenue streams? Is its market growing or shrinking? How many people does it employ? Who has the business partnered with?

This is the traditional approach to competitive analysis, which is important in any business. There are multiple sources for the information. If your competitors are public companies, much of this information will be public. Some large private companies may be profiled along with public corporations, on Hoovers.com. But if they're privately owned, you'll have to look harder: Research agencies like Nielsen can offer insight into the size of their audiences and businesses; newspaper or magazine articles may also offer insight, and the site itself may tip a competitor's hand: Corporate pages often include staff directories, lists of partners and investors, and press releases on product releases and corporate earnings.

functional analysis

The second way to evaluate a competitor is to look at its web site and assess how well it's working. This allows you to both understand what you're up against and generate ideas for your own site.

If you're launching a site for your restaurant, for example, look at other restaurant sites. Notice how they're organized and what features they include.

---

understanding your competitors

Not sure how well your competitors are doing? Here's what to ask:

- **How well are they doing?** For online competitors, look at traffic levels (How high? Growing or shrinking?) as well as revenue and company size.

- **In what direction are they heading?** What have they done lately? What partnerships have they announced? What do they emphasize on their front door? What do they downplay? What audience do they address?

- **What works well on their site?** What do you like about their web site? What seems to be popular? What makes sense to you?

- **What are they doing wrong?** What's not working on their site? Is it confusing? Slow? Do the features work as expected?

Are there standard buttons or headings? Where do they put their contact information? Do they include a menu? Photos of the dining room?

Noticing these details will help you solve the problems on your own site, and it will also help you understand your users' expectations. Often, you'll find conventions have developed within your particular industry (designing for web conventions, p. 84).

It's important, though, that you actually *use* each feature on these sites, because functionality can be deceiving: Features may work differently from what you assume, or they may not work at all. Features that sound great often fail to deliver on their promises.

It's also important not to get caught up in the bells and whistles. Although they may be fun to look at, the coolest, prettiest sites are rarely the most effective.

"Whoever is winning at the moment will always seem to be invincible."

—*George Orwell*

how good is your competition?

	Competitor 1	Competitor 2	Competitor 3
Name			
Traffic (if known)			
Revenue (if known)			
Search ranking			
Key features			
Navigation system			
Site search			
Email service			
Performance **–Front door K size** **–Front door load time** **–Speed of features**			
Technical choices			

chapter 4

getting to know your users

"Do we actually have to go to your parents? Can't we just visit their web site?"

don't miss ...

Of all the mistakes a site owner could make, the most common—and the most perilous—is to underestimate the power of the user.

Ask Mike Kuniavsky. A long-time web developer and author of *Observing the User Experience*, Kuniavsky has seen more than his share of wayward web sites. From 1999–2000, he consulted for more than a dozen companies—mostly start-ups in San Francisco.

"Every company I worked with failed," he said. "And they all failed for the same fundamental reason: They hadn't thought about the value they were giving people—and whether people wanted that value."

"So the main thing I've learned is that before you make a product, you need to know that it satisfies someone's need and that someone will want to pay for it," he said. "This is true for just about any business, but it's especially true for web sites."

Web sites have to pay special attention to their users, because the web demands so much of them. Customers must actively remember to visit your site, and they must actively navigate it once they arrive.

Other industries have it easy:

- **Stores** get foot traffic from busy streets and shopping malls, and customers can just wander around and browse.

- **Magazines** get noticed on the newsstand, and readers can just flip through the pages.

- **TV shows** lure people who flip past with the remote control, and viewers can just sit back and watch.

Web sites, however, get few accidental visitors. There's no natural way to browse the web (except perhaps through portals, and that's very directed), so users only find your site when they seek it out. And once they arrive, their work's only just begun. They have to figure out what your site does, how it works, and where to find what they need.

For there's no passive option on the web. Although many users would prefer it, you can't

just watch a web site. You can't even *read* a web site without making decisions about where to go and how to get there.

If users can't find, understand or navigate your site, you've lost them. And you've lost.

So whether you like it or not—whether they like it or not—users are in control of their own web experience. If they can't find, understand, or navigate your site, you've lost them. And you've lost.

Your web site, then, isn't for you. It's for your users. It should be organized the way they think and written in a language they understand.

The user's opinion, you see, is the only one that matters. And this is hard for site owners to accept. They like to trust their own instincts, and this backfires on them. Because it's the user's opinion—not theirs—that matters.

This is a particularly thorny issue for web agencies, whose clients are used to rejecting ideas simply because they don't like them. Lance McDaniel, VP of Creative at SBI and Company, says it comes up all the time: "Inevitably, a client will tell us he doesn't like something about the interface—or his *wife* doesn't like something about the interface. And I have to remind him, 'Look, you're paying us millions of dollars to build a site your *users* will like. Not you. And not your wife.'"

The user-centered approach can be hard for clients to understand. But it's in their best interest, McDaniel said. "If we just did things our clients *liked*, we'd be wasting their money."

Indeed, most successful sites (if not most successful businesses) have learned to put their users first. "You have to be really truthful about who your customer is," said Hilary Billings, chairman and chief marketing officer of RedEnvelope. "Know who your customer is, and what they need from you. And let that guide you. Don't try to outsmart your customer. Build a business for them."

learning about your users

Because your site's success is dependent on what your users need and want and do, it's important to learn as much about them as you can. By following your users—identifying who they are, anticipating their needs, analyzing their behavior, responding to their requests—you can build a successful site, almost every time.

But you're not just learning about users for the sake of it. All user research should be directed toward the goal of improving your site.

5 key questions in user research:

1. **Who are my users?** Having a profile of your typical user helps you build the site with them in mind. See profiling your users, p. 50 and visualizing your users, p. 54.

2. **How many are there?** You can't plan an event without knowing how many people will show. Same goes for web sites: The number of users impacts costs and revenues. See estimating audience size, p. 52.

3. **How do they access the web?** People experience the web differently, depending on their location and equipment. The more you know about their set-up, the better you can tailor your site to their needs. See profiling your users, p. 50.

4. **What do they need?** The most important thing to learn about your users is what they need from you. By filling a real need, you give people a reason to keep coming back. See predicting what users want, p. 58 and understanding user needs, p. 60.

5. **What do they do?** When it comes right down to it, this is all that really matters: What do users *do* once they're on your site? See understanding user behavior, p. 62.

It's easier to answer these questions on the web than in many other industries. Online surveys make data collection more convenient, and traffic logs let site owners see exactly how people use their sites—where they come from, where they click, how long they stay, and what they do.

For example, instead of *asking* people what they like about your site—or what they use and how often—you can just run a traffic report and see for sure. This reduces your reliance on opinion-based research, such as focus groups.

quantitative vs. qualitative research

There are a lot of ways to learn about your users (See tools for user research, p. 48). You can field surveys, conduct interviews, analyze traffic patterns, and run usability tests. There are methods for every budget and temperament, and each one helps you gain specific insights into the user.

Because there are so many techniques, it's important to know when and how to use each. First, though, some basics: There are two kinds of user research: qualitative and quantitative.

2 kinds of research:

- **Quantitative research** gives you objective, measurable facts—the kind of data you'd put in a chart.

- **Qualitative research** gives you subjective opinions—the kind of data you'd put in a sentence, not a chart.

Quantitative data is usually the first thing you reach for when making a user-related decision. You want to know if there's anything definite on which to hang your hat, such as a traffic report showing that a feature is popular or industry data showing that other related sites are popular. See predicting what users want, p. 58.

In the absence of quantitative proof—or to supplement it—you look at qualitative data, such as customer feedback or focus group results showing that consumers express *interest* in a feature. Generally speaking, though, you want to follow what users do and not what they say.

Quantitative data can help you decide what to do. Qualitative data can tell you how to do it.

Once you've decided to launch a site, qualitative data becomes very important—as a way to get inside the user's mind. Let's say, for example, that you run a banking site, and you've decided to add a bill-paying feature. You should go out and talk to your customers about how they currently pay their bills. After a few interviews, you'll have a good sense of what your bill-paying application needs to do. (See <u>understanding user needs</u>, p. 60.)

So quantitative data can help you decide what to do, and qualitative data can tell you how to do it.

When to use quantitative research:

- To understand who your users are

- To understand how people use your site

- To assess which features are most popular

- To predict how new sites will perform

When to use qualitative research:

- To understand how users accomplish and think about a task

- To identify what confuses users

- To understand what people think of your site, brand, or organization

Again, what's unique about the web is the amount of quantitative data that's readily available and the way it can shape a site's evolution. See <u>monitoring and evolving your site</u>, p. 240.

key steps in user research

Each stage of site development should be accompanied by a round of user "discovery" to learn what you need to know about what your users need.

before site launch

- **Do traffic analysis or market analysis** to confirm that there is consumer interest in the site you're planning to launch.

- **Create a user profile** to identify and describe the target audience.

- **Estimate size of target audience** so you can plan accordingly.

- **Interview users** about what they need from your site, and how they get by without it.

as you design

- **Run usability tests** to (1) make sure your assumptions are correct, and (2) catch any mistakes in the interface that you may have missed.

after you launch

- **Study your traffic logs** to learn how people are actually using the site: Where do they come from? How long do they stay? What features do they use? Where do they exit?

- **Run usability tests** to help you answer specific questions about how the site is used. Why are users choosing one path over another? Why do they leave?

- **Study customer feedback** to understand how people feel about your site and to identify what's frustrating or angering them.

- **Field a user survey** to learn more details about your audience and confirm they are who you think they are.

tools for user research

	market analysis	traffic analysis	user surveys	personas & scenarios
what it is	Research gathered from the media and research firms offering insight into industry trends.	Research gathered about how your site is used by customers.	Questionnaires distributed to a statistically significant portion of your users.	Personas are fictional characters, representing typical users. Scenarios tell the story of how they use your site.
kind of data	Quantitative and qualitative.	Quantitative.	Quantitative and qualitative.	Qualitative.
how it works	Many firms issue reports on specific topics and market segments. Firms like Nielsen and Media Metrix also offer tools for customized reports about specific users or market segments.	Using traffic-analysis software, your web site can be monitored, revealing how many people visit, how long they stay, what they do, and other details.	The survey is usually fielded on your site and served to a portion of incoming users. Data is collected through user input forms and analyzed.	Personas and scenarios are invented by your product team (or a consultant) to bring your typical user to life.
what it's good for	Crafting strategy, estimating the size of your potential market, predicting long-term trends, identifying competitors and potential partners.	Understanding how your site is actually used. Prioritizing site features and determining site direction. Tracking long-term growth. Identifying problem areas in interface.	Getting an accurate demographic and "webographic" snapshot of your users.	They help web teams visualize users in a more personal way. It's easier and intuitive to picture "Eric" using your site than a nameless, faceless "user."
why it's imperfect	Some feel that analyst reports are treated as gospel, when in fact they're largely conjecture.	The enormous amounts of data can be hard to slog through, especially if you don't have good traffic-analysis software.	Online surveys interrupt traffic to your site. Can be labor-intensive and disruptive to run.	Some feel that people take personas a little too seriously, considering they're fictional.
when to use it	Early in the planning stages, while crafting product plan and determining site strategy.	Should be used consistently—if not fanatically—on an ongoing basis.	Six months after launch, annually, and before any major redesign.	As you plan and design your site.
how long it takes	Varies. You can read a report or find a statistic in an hour. In-depth study could be full-time.	Varies, depending on what you're trying to learn.	Around a month. A few days to write the survey, four weeks to field and analyze.	A few hours to invent them.
where to learn more	learning about your users, p. 46.	understanding user behavior, p. 62. monitoring and evolving your site, p. 240.	profiling your users, p. 50.	visualizing your users, p. 54.

task analysis	focus groups	feedback analysis	usability testing	preference rating
Research gathered from users on how they approach the problem (or tasks) addressed by your site.	Studies conducted with small groups of customers to understand their attitudes toward a particular product or problem.	Studies of communication from your customers, including email, and phone calls.	Studies conducted with users (in a lab) to see how they navigate and interpret (or misinterpret) your site.	Studies conducted with users to determine which features they think are most important.
Qualitative.	Qualitative.	Qualitative.	Qualitative.	Qualitative.
Users are interviewed about how they currently accomplish the tasks related to your site. The facilitator later breaks down the comments into tasks and sub-tasks.	A moderator leads the group in a discussion of your site or related topics. The product team often observes the session live from behind a two-way mirror.	Customer feedback can be collected and analyzed in a systematic way to reveal what topics move users to contact you.	Users are observed trying to accomplish a task on your site. They may be asked to explain their thought processes or choices. Sessions are observed live or taped.	Users are interviewed and led through a series of preference-rating exercises, such as sorting cards.
Helps you understand how users get things done and how they think about the problem. This helps you decide which features to include and how to organize them.	They help you predict consumer response to a new site or feature and understand consumer feelings about your brand or site.	Providing clues to who users are, what they want from you, and how you're letting them down. Identifying areas of the interface that may be broken.	Making sure visitors can actually use your site. Identifying and correcting problems with the interface, navigation scheme, section names, etc.	Helpful for clarifying what's important to customers. Can settle internal debates over priorities and help you narrow down the feature list.
Users don't always tell the truth, and don't always remember all the relevant steps.	The results are very subjective—both the comments and the interpretation. A strong personality can dominate the group.	Only reliable as an indication of what makes people mad. Feedback is usually negative and can be unpleasant to read	Results can easily be misinterpreted. Also, they only test if something *can* be used—not whether it *will* be used.	Users don't always do what they say they'll do.
After outlining a site plan, but before finalizing the features or beginning design.	Before launching an expensive new initiative or redesign.	Ongoing, throughout life of site.	During development of a new or redesigned site. Ongoing tests are also useful.	While planning the site or a redesign and before finalizing the site's feature.
Anywhere from a few hours to a few months, depending on how complicated the task is.	A few weeks. The focus group lasts only an hour or two, but recruiting and analysis take longer.	Varies.	Varies, depending on the number of users and how accessible they are.	A few hours—if you have access to typical users. Recruiting is what takes the longest.
understanding user needs, p. 60. defining the feature set, p. 26.	understanding user needs, p. 60.	understanding user behavior, p. 62.	understanding user behavior, p. 62. designing for the user, p. 82.	understanding user needs, p. 60.

profiling your users

The user profile paints a portrait of your audience in broad statistical brushstrokes. Though necessarily crude, it's an important tool for understanding your audience.

Before you launch a site, your user profile will describe the visitors you hope to attract. After launch, you can field a survey to confirm these assumptions. (See surveying your users, opposite page.)

5 ways to profile your users:

1. Demographics

2. Webographics

3. Psychographics

4. Behavior & activities

5. Site-specific experience

What you want to know is who your users are and what they need from you. But the characteristics you highlight will vary according to your site's focus. Some sites may define their users by demographics, looking primarily at age, race, or gender to describe (and size) their audience. Other sites care less about who people are and more about what they do. A financial site, for instance, may care little about the age, gender, or even income of their visitors, so long as they're active stock traders.

But all sites have to pay attention to so-called "webographics." It always helps to know how people access your site so you can best build it for them.

demographics This census-type information is usually the first component of any user profile. It's the easiest to collect in a survey of your users. And if you're building a site for a particular population—residents of a city, members of a club, people within a certain profession—you can also find data elsewhere: census reports, almanacs, and professional organizations are all good resources.

The basic demographic profile:

- Age
- Gender
- Race
- Nationality
- Geographic location
- Education level
- Income level
- Marital status
- Occupation

webographics I'm sorry about the term, "webographics." I really am. But I haven't come across another way to describe people's experience with, attitudes toward, and behavior on the web. And this is significant when developing a site.

The basic webographic profile:

- **Years online.** How long have users been online, and how well do they know their way around?

- **Frequency of use.** How often are users online? How long is each session?

- **Access point.** Are users connecting from their home, office, school, or somewhere else (library, cafe, etc)

- **Time of use.** Are users online during the week or on weekends? Morning, afternoon, or evening?

- **Connection speed.** Are users connecting through high-speed, always-on access (like a cable modem at home or a T-1 at work) or a dial-up connection?

- **Computer type.** Are users on a Mac, PC, or something else? Are they on a new high-end system with a fast processor or an older system that's struggling?

- **Browser.** Which browser do users employ, and which version? Which plug-ins do they have installed?

- **Monitor.** What size and resolution are users' monitors? Desktop or laptop?

- **General online behavior.** What do users do online? What tasks do they accomplish? What sites do they visit? Do they make purchases, contact friends, check the weather, download software?

psychographics Psychographics are less straightforward. They cover attitudes, interests, personality types, and other fuzzy factors that make people people. Depending on the nature of your site, there are a lot of different factors that might fall under psychographics.

At Wired, for example, we always targeted the so-called "early adopters": people (mostly men) who are the first to try new technologies before they're adopted by the masses.

Other psychographic icons include the Yuppie (young upwardly mobile professionals), the DINK (double income, no kids), and the soccer mom. Feel free to invent your own.

behavior and activities Most web sites are action-oriented: They're about accomplishing specific tasks and getting things done. Which is why, in many cases, you'll be less interested in who your users *are* than what they *do*, both online and off.

Are they getting married soon? Do they trade stocks? Play online games? Cook? Ski? Throw a lot of parties? Make sure your user profile covers whatever activity is most important to your site.

site-specific experience In many instances, you'll want to focus on factors specific to your business, product, or web site. For example, if your site promotes a particular product, you'll want to clarify whether you're targeting prospective customers or those who already own the product. If you're creating a site for a city—say, Barcelona, Spain— are you targeting the local or the turista?

---

surveying your users

The best way to learn for certain who your users are is to ask them. And the best way to ask them is to field a survey on your site.

A questionnaire can be served—in a pop-up window or the main browser window—to all your site visitors or just a certain percent. Usually, the questionnaire will be optional and offer some incentive to those who finish (it's tiring to complete surveys). Answers are collected through user input forms and analyzed later.

3 ways to field a survey:

1. **Do it yourself** by writing a questionnaire, serving it on your site, and programming the code to collect user input.

2. **Buy surveying software**, such as the package from Inquisite (http://www.inquisite.com), and use it to run the survey.

3. **Work with a research firm** and let them deal with it.

Similarly, if your site is focused on a particular topic, you might want to clarify whether you're targeting experts or novices. Which isn't to say you can't target both; most sites serve multiple constituencies. But you need to be aware of the natural breaks within your audience, clear on which group is the most important to you, and explicit about how you're targeting each of them. (See segmenting your users, p. 56.)

🛒 **Buy this book!**

The Handbook of Online Marketing Research: Knowing Your Customer Using the Net
Joshua Grossnickle & Oliver Raskin $39.95
Step-by-step instructions on sampling, surveys, segmentation, and everything else you need to know to research your web site visitors.

estimating audience size

One of the first things you want to determine, as you begin work on a new site, is the size of your potential audience. This is crucial for three good reasons: backend, revenue, and costs.

3 reasons that size matters:

1. **Building the backend.** A site's technical needs change as its user base grows. As visitors increase, a site needs more bandwidth and more powerful servers. If you have an application-backed site, you may also have to overhaul the backend code to run more efficiently at higher capacity.

2. **Predicting costs.** The more popular a site is, the more expensive it is to maintain. You need more (and more powerful) servers, more bandwidth, and possibly more staff (more customer service reps, more community moderators, more fulfillment operators, etc.).

3. **Predicting revenue.** If your site needs to make money, as most do, your success will largely rest on your ability to find (and keep) customers. So before you begin, you should know they exist in sufficient numbers to support your site.

It's easy to overestimate your potential audience, especially when you're passionate about the site's subject matter. And it's also easy to overestimate your draw. In most cases, you'll be lucky to attract 10% of your target audience.

To determine the size of your potential user base, you'll first need to describe them. See profiling your users, p. 50, for help with creating a useful profile.

If you have the money to invest in a research service, you can get excellent numbers from agencies like Nielsen NetRatings and Media Metrix. Even if you don't, you can learn a lot by combing through their web sites for press releases and public studies.

But if you can't find the exact statistics you need, you can calculate a pretty good estimate by combining census data and industry estimates.

1. Begin with the entire Internet universe (the number of people online)—whether in the world, your country, or your city.

2. Choose the distinguishing factors of your audience, and estimate their percentage of the whole. This is your target audience.

3. Estimate what percentage of the target audience you can reasonably expect to capture. 10% is a nice, hopeful number to start with.

Let's take an example. Say we're creating a new web site that targets women in Singapore. How big an audience can we hope for in our first year?

1. According to Nielsen, Singapore's total online population is 2.3 million.

2. Although precise data isn't available, we'll estimate that 40% of Singapore's online population is female (women usually lag behind men).

   2.3 million × 40% = 920,000 women online in Singapore.

3. Since we have a substantial marketing budget, we'll aim to capture 10% of this market in our first year:

   920,000 × 10% = 92,000 users

So our goal for year one is to attract 92,000 unique visitors to our site.

Finding statistics on the web
Nielsen NetRatings
http://www.netratings.com
MediaMetrix
http://www.mediametrix.com
TheCounter
http://www.thecounter.com

action section

who are your users?

The first step toward serving your users is identifying—specifically—who they are. Though the details you include will vary depending on the focus of your site.

demographics

Age: __% Under 18   __% 18–24   __% 25–34

    __% 35–49   __% 50–64   __% Over 65

Sex: __% Male   __% Female

Race: __% African American   __% Caucasian

    __% Asian/Pacific Islander   __% Hispanic

    __% American Indian, Eskimo, or Aleut

    __% Other

Education: __% Some high school   __% High school

    __% Some college   __% College

    __% Some post-grad   __% Post-graduate

Marital status: __% Single   __% Married

    __% Widowed __% Divorced/separated

Income: __ % Under $20,000   __ % $20–49,000

    __ % $50–74,000   __ % $75–100,000

    __ % $100–150,000   __ % Over $150,000

Nationality:

_____

Location:

_____

Occupation:

_____

psychographics

What are the unique distinguishing factors of your audience?

_____

webographics

Access point: __% Home   __% Work

    __% School   __% Other

Access speed: __% Modem __% Cable modem

    __% DSL   __% T1/high-speed work

Frequency __% <1 hour/week   __% 1–3 hours/week
of use: __% 4–10 hours/week __% 10+ hours/week

Time of use: __% Morning   __% Afternoon

    __% Evening   __% Late night

Years online: __% First year online   __% 1–2 years

    __% 3–4 years   __% Over 5 years

Platform: __% Windows   __% Mac

    __% Unix   __% Other

Browser: __% Netscape   __% Internet Explorer

    __% Other

activities

What (relevant) online activities do your users participate in?

_____

site-specific profile

Who is your site geared toward?

❑ First-time visitors, new to your organization and site.

❑ Offline customers, familiar with your company but NOT the site.

❑ Returning visitors, familiar with both your organization AND your site.

❑ All of the above.

visualizing your users

When you're trying to build a site with your users in mind, it's helpful to have an image of who they are. But user profiles, while valuable, can be hard to warm up to. They paint a picture of the user in broad theoretical brushstrokes and are often more useful to advertisers than the development team.

To really picture the user, it helps to build a story around them—using personas and scenarios.

You can visualize your audience using

- **Personas.** Fictional characters who represent your site's users.

- **Scenarios.** Fictional, but true-to-life circumstances under which a typical user might visit the site.

creating personas

Personas are fictionalized characters, based on the user profiles you've developed for each segment of your audience. These characters help bring your users to life by taking the stereotype and giving it a name, a face, a job, and perhaps a dog—all the trappings of fictional characters that allow them to become real to us.

This way, as the team is developing and designing the site, they can ask themselves what "Madeline" or "Eric" would do, rather than just thinking generically about "users."

> **Personas help tell the story of your site. And humans need stories.**

Though slightly, well, *cheesy*, personas can be quite helpful for creating awareness and understanding throughout an organization. They help tell the story of your site, and humans need stories.

Creating a persona is relatively easy and fun. Start by giving him or her a name. Then fill in the details of her life, using your site's user profile. Run through all the major demographic information: How old is she? Where does she live? Where does she work? Add in details: What are her

---

a sample persona

Name: Madeline
Age: 32
Profession: High school history teacher
Home: Palo Alto, CA
Married? Yes
Kids? Not yet
Car: Honda Civic
Internet access: Home and work

A high school teacher, Madeline occasionally checks email during her lunch break. But most of the time, she uses the web from home, where she and her husband have high-speed access. She uses the web a few times a week, to find source material for her lesson plans or research purchase decisions.

---

hobbies? What kind of car does she drive? What's the last book she read? Does she own a pet?

Be specific—and feel free to be funny! But remember to stay within the stereotypical confines of your user profile. Don't give your persona too many unusual characteristics. They'll just distract you from the bigger picture.

Once you have your persona's basic stats down, you should think about issues specific to your site's focus: Why would she come to your site? What needs does she have that aren't being met? What problems does she need solved? Think also about her Internet use: How does the Internet fit into her daily or weekly routine? What sorts of things does she do on the web? Is she comfortable online?

Also: Does she have a spouse? Does she happen to have a spouse who happens to embody one of your other user segments? I thought so. It's helpful, actually, to have your personas interact with each other. So, if one fictional couple happens to embody two of your user segments, all the better.

Finally, don't forget to picture the personas: Find clip art or magazine ads with models who look the way you imagine your personas. Make posters with their pictures and descriptions, and hang them in your development area or throughout the organization—in the conference rooms or the bathroom stalls or above the coffee maker. They're great conversation starters (and it's OK if people laugh at them a little. No need to take yourself *too* seriously!)

you are not your user

When you're building a web site—especially a site on a topic you know well and care about—you may find yourself assuming that everyone in your audience is just like you. If you're drawn to the subject matter, and fit into the target demographic, it's easy to convince yourself that you're the average user.

But you're not. You know more about the topic, more about your site, and more about the web. This means you know less than you think about what your real users want.

This is one of the hardest lessons for web developers to learn. As author of *Observing the User Experience*, Mike Kuniavsky, likes to point out: "You are not your audience. You don't see things like they do, know what they know, want what they want, or work how they work."

Even if you do fit squarely within your site's user profile, you still aren't you're audience. It's impossible for you to figure out what a person "just like you" would think of your site or need from it. And if you make assumptions about your audience based on yourself, you run the risk of building a site that suits no one but you."

"This is something I'm always called to task for," laughs Lara Hoyem, senior marketing manager of BabyCenter. A parent of two, Hoyem says she tends to assume that other parents are just like her. She has to fight that impulse when she's considering promotion techniques or content strategies.

"For example, I'm a minimalist in terms of what I buy for my kids," she says. "I just can't imagine why anyone would buy a bassinet. Why would you buy another piece of furniture? Just put them in bed with you!"

"So I have to remind myself," she said with a smile, "Not everyone's like you. Some people like bassinets."

And all web developers need this reminder. Otherwise, they'll unconsciously design the site for themselves.

"The most important thing to think about when you think about users is that they don't think the way you do. They never do," says information architect Jesse James Garrett, author of *The Elements of User Experience*.

> **"You are not your audience. You don't see things like they do, know what they know, want what they want, or work how they work. "**
>
> **—Mike Kuniavsky**

"You're never designing for yourself," he explains. "You're always designing for someone else. What that means is that you have to be able to identify your own prejudices and your own preferences and be able to cast those aside when you're making design decisions. It's a difficult thing to do."

Indeed, it's hard to set aside your preferences. Often, our biases are so deeply ingrained, we don't even realize they're there. Unchecked, though, they'll shape everything about the site—from the features you include to the way the site is organized to the names you choose for sections.

Jargon, in fact, is a common problem on web sites, because the words used within an industry are never the same as the lay-terms that customers would recognize.

"One of the hardest transitions for people in a given business to make is from the mind of the seller to the mind of the buyer, and from the language of the seller to the language of the buyer," says online marketing expert Hunter Madsen.

"So what you often see in web sites is jargon—sometimes hilariously piled upon itself—so that some higher concept for the product is articulated in the abstract, which is completely impenetrable to the visitor."

However you do it, it's important to spread the idea. The more awareness you build around the idea of these personas, the more receptive your organization will become to making user-centered decisions. And that, as you know, is a very good thing.

creating scenarios

To really put your personas to work, you're going to want to create some scenarios, describing true-to-life circumstances under which they might be using your site. Scenarios should describe the situation that led the personas to your site, and the ways in which they use it.

It's important, though, to get the whole picture. Scenarios should include all the distracting details that might happen in a person's life as they use your site.

"Scenarios should be messy," says usability expert Jeffrey Veen, a partner with the consulting firm Adaptive Path. "Just like real life—where the kids are screaming and the modem is slow." It's important to capture these distracting details, in order to stay as true to the actual user experience as possible.

"Don't make everything work like magic," Veen says. "Be real."

Keep thinking about the user!

designing for the user, p. 82
how people navigate the web, p. 111
usability testing, p. 129
typical traffic patterns, p. 248

segmenting your users

It's a rare site that attracts a monolithic user base. Most audiences can be split into groups of customers with different needs and goals.

Creating a site that serves all of them is a real challenge. But by segmenting your users early on, you can identify the different ways people will use your site.

Not all users are equal. It's important to decide which are the most important to you.

For example, let's say you're building a site for a crafts store in Santa Fe, New Mexico. Your first group of users may be Santa Fe residents who already come to your store and who want to check in on your new arrivals. Your second target group may be Santa Fe residents who haven't found your store yet. The third may be tourists planning a trip to Santa Fe, and the fourth may be craft lovers looking to buy online.

Of course, not all users are equal, and it's important to decide which are the most important to you.

Our Santa Fe store would probably prioritize the first group—existing customers. (After all, the people most likely to buy in the future are those who've bought in the past.) The store's other priorities would depend on its goals and its assessment of the market. Is there a large untapped crafts market in Santa Fe, or should the store look outside the city to grow the business?

These are the types of questions that a site owner must answer as she decides who her site is for. By acknowledging—and then prioritizing—these different groups, you can consciously build a site that serves at least one—and probably all—of them better.

action section

create personas for your users

It's easier to build a site for "Lucy" or "Virgil" than it is to design for an anonymous "user." Create 2 personas to represent your users, then spin the scenarios in which they'd use your site.

Persona 1

(Draw or paste picture here)

Name:
_____

Age: _____

Location:_____

Occupation:

_____

Income: _____

Marital status: _____

Kids?

_____

More about him/her:

_____

_____

Why does she/he need your site?

_____

_____

Describe a typical scenario of him/her using your site:

_____

_____

Persona 2

(Draw or paste picture here)

Name:
_____

Age: _____

Location:_____

Occupation:

_____

Income: _____

Marital status: _____

Kids?

_____

More about him/her:

_____

_____

Why does she/he need your site?

_____

_____

Describe a typical scenario of him/her using your site:

_____

_____

predicting what users will want

Whether you're launching a new site or evolving an old one, your goal is to predict what users will want.

2 ways to learn what your users want:

- **Watch what they do.** Your traffic logs can tell you how people use your site: Which features are used and which are ignored?

- **Ask what they think.** Using surveys, focus groups, or customer interviews, you can ask users how they'd respond to a new feature or what they'd want in your site

watching what users do The most reliable way to learn what your users want is to watch how they currently behave on your site: What features do they use? What products do they look at? What articles do they read? How long do they stay?

This is the great advantage of web sites: You can see—with great precision—how your site is used. (See monitoring & evolving your site, p. 240.) Few industries enjoy this luxury (which is why they rely more heavily on *asking* users what they want).

You can also look outside your own site for insight. Using market research tools—like those from Media Metrix or Nielsen NetRatings—you can study traffic patterns for other, similar sites.

asking users what they think If you're launching a new site—or adding a feature unrelated to your current site—your traffic logs won't tell you if it's a good idea. So in these cases, you'll want to ask users what they want. Using focus groups, user interviews, or surveys, you can ask users (or people who fit their description) what they think of your proposed idea. Do they need it? Will they use it?

Now, if you've already decided to build a particular site (a grocery-delivery service, say), it's *essential* to talk to users about what they need from it. (See understanding user needs, p. 60.) But if

---

tools for learning what users want

- **Traffic analysis** tells you which parts of your site are the most popular.

- **Market analysis** tells you which other sites on the web are popular.

- **Task analysis** helps you understand how users currently accomplish specific tasks.

- **Focus groups** tell you how customers might respond to a particular feature or site.

- **Preference rating** tells you how customers would prioritize features on your site.

- **Surveys** let you collect user opinions.

See tools for user research, p.48

---

you're still deciding *what* to do, consumers are a little less helpful.

Focus groups and surveys *can* help you predict consumer response. But bear in mind: Users don't always do what they say they'll do. They may express interest in sites they'll never use or feign disinterest in those they use often.

A real-world example: When you ask city-dwellers why they like urban life, most will mention cultural outlets, like opera or ballet. But let's face it: Most of them have never stepped foot inside an opera house.

> **Users don't always do what they say they'll do. They may profess a deep interest in features they'll never use.**

Same goes for web users, who may profess a deep interest in features they'll never use. Maybe they like to *think* they would use the feature. Maybe they think it's a neat idea for someone to use. Or maybe they're just being polite. Whatever the reason, users are reliably unreliable in predicting their own behavior.

your site is not the center of the user's universe

Your web site may mean the world to you, but it's only one small part of your users' lives. And the sooner you recognize this humbling fact, the more effective your site will be.

"It's natural to overestimate the importance of your product," says online marketing expert Hunter Madsen. "But it's not helpful. You have to remember that unless your product is a heart-lung machine—which they need and for which there is no substitute—your product's not as important to them as you'd like it to be. And it never will be."

In order to effectively build or promote a site, you have to "understand the role of your brand in the universe of the consumer," Madsen says. And for most sites, it's a cameo appearance.

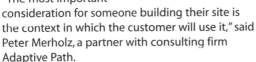

It's helpful, then, to get the bigger picture. "The most important consideration for someone building their site is the context in which the customer will use it," said Peter Merholz, a partner with consulting firm Adaptive Path.

And the big picture is often a humbling one. You can't assume that the user understands your site—or even that you have their full attention. "It's very unlikely that someone is using your system so much that they develop the understanding of it that you have," Merholz explained.

And if you're trying to teach them about your site—or encourage them to 'hang out' there—you probably need to adjust your thinking.

"You have to look at the web site as a part of someone's life," says Mike Kuniavsky, author of *Observing the User Experience*." And you have to look at the other parts of their life in order to understand how they're going to use this one

little, tiny, itsy-bitsy part, which—if you're doing a really good job—they'll use for an incredibly short period of time."

This is difficult to remember, because it goes against our own experience. We spend so much time thinking about our own web sites that it's inconceivable to us that users wouldn't do the same.

But they won't. And you have to accept this if you're going to effectively serve them. "Their goal is not to hang out at the web site," Kuniavsky explains. "Their goal is somewhere else. Their goal is to have a couch or buy insurance or know what's happening in Pakistan."

> ## "Do not punish people for leading their lives while they're using your site."
>
> —*Peter Merholz*

So you need to account for their lack of time, knowledge, and, well, interest when you design your site. "You need to make sure that interactions are obvious, that you're not using jargon, that you respect the user's time, that you allow them to do things that they need to do in five or ten minutes," Merholz said.

Similarly, you have to remember that people get distracted while they work, and it may take them longer than expected to complete tasks.

"The number of sites that have session time-outs after 20 minutes—causing all the work that person has done to disappear—that, I've never understood," Merholz said. "That person on the other end of the screen might have had to walk their dog, deal with the baby, answer the phone, whatever it is."

"Do not punish people for leading their lives while they're using your site."

understanding user needs

Once you've decided what kind of site (or feature) you're launching, your users can help you design it. It makes sense, after all, to know how your users work before you decide how your site will work.

"Design is now inseparable from user research," said Jeffrey Veen, author of *The Art & Science of Web Design*. "We literally do nothing until we talk to people. We try to go into a project with no assumptions, and just hear how people approach the task."

> **You should know how your users work before deciding how your site will work.**

So instead of designing a site and then seeing if people can use it, Veen starts off with what people can do. The question he tries to answer: How do they do things without this site?

"So if you're building a banking site, you could just copy an interactive application, like the ATM, that exists already. But it's better to just go talk to people about how they balance their checkbooks. And listen. And notice the steps. If you talk to 10 people about that, you'll see how to make your application."

planning a new site

Let's say you're planning a gardening site, which will offer advice and supplies. Since you're the site owner, chances are you know a thing or two about plants. You're probably one of those perfect people who grows an herb garden on his Manhattan rooftop, or plants an organic orchard within a month of buying her first home at 22.

Being such a person, you probably have your own ideas about site features. However, as we've discussed, you're not building this site for yourself. (See you are not your user, p. 55.)

So you need to learn how *other* people in your target audience accomplish relevant tasks—in this case, planning and planting a garden. By understanding how they currently operate, you can identify their needs, and ways to meet them. Also, if you understand how users *think* about the tasks, you can create a navigation system they'll intuitively understand.

task analysis

Task analysis is a fancy way of saying "talk to people about how they get something done." It involves interviewing typical users about how they approach and accomplish a specific task related to your web site. Note, however, that you're not asking them about the site itself. You want to know what they do, not what they'd like in a site.

6 steps in task analysis:

1. **Clarify the user goal** that you're studying.

2. **Recruit users** to interview. They can be current customers or people who fit the description of your typical user.

3. **Interview users** about how they accomplish the goal—not just on your web site, but in general.

4. **Record the interview** by taping it and/or typing up the answers.

5. **Identify the key tasks and sub-tasks** that your user mentioned.

6. **Convert tasks into features** on your site.

Usually, the interview covers the whole range of tasks that the user must complete en route to the final goal. (If the goal is planting a garden, then tasks may include deciding what to plant, buying the seeds, designing the garden, and so forth.)

The interviewer asks a series of open-ended questions, allowing the user to describe her approach in her own words. An effective interviewer will follow up to get more complete responses, but refrain from putting words in her mouth, or re-framing her answers to fit his own ideas. The goal, after all, is not only to understand the task, but also how the user *thinks* about it.

> **The goal is not only to understand the task, but also how the user thinks about the task.**

Afterwards, read through the transcript with an eye toward identifying tasks. Usually, you'll be able to identify discrete tasks within the user's responses.

The next step is to group similar tasks together. You may find, for instance, that one user read magazines, visited a botanical garden, and drove around his neighborhood—all to get ideas about what his garden could look like. All these tasks might be categorized under "getting ideas."

One easy way to group tasks is to write each sub-task on a Post-it note, then cluster them into groups of related tasks (See chart, opposite). You can create a separate Post-it chart for each user interviewed. By comparing them, you get a sense for different users and how their needs may overlap or diverge.

converting tasks into site features

You should be able to map the tasks mentioned in your interviews to a list of potential site features. Any prominent task without a corresponding feature—or worse, a prominent feature without a corresponding user-generated task—is a red flag.

For example, if your CEO has his heart set on a personalized weather chart but no users mentioned "checking the weather" as a task pertinent to the site's mission, you've got a good argument for standing up to the boss. Similarly, if many users mention a task that you don't address—you should think about incorporating it.

getting good results from task analysis

Task analysis is a method for analyzing how users accomplish a task related to your site:

■ **Recruit representative users.**
Ideally, each user should fit squarely within one of your predefined audience segments. If using a friend or acquaintance (to reduce costs), ask them to "represent a group." To ensure quality (and sufficient quantity), users should be rewarded for their time, with cash or goodies.

■ **Ask good, open-ended questions.**
It's essential to be open-minded and to ask open-ended questions. Don't let your own business goals taint what you ask or how you interpret the answers. Also learn the vocabulary of the subject before beginning interviews. Know what you're talking about, and how to talk about it.

■ **Find a good interview spot.**
It's best to do face-to-face interviews, which allow for visual cues. Ideally, a private, quiet, interview space outside of the company office. Phone interviews are an acceptable way of achieving geographic spread, but the results won't be as good as in face-to-face interviews, which generate more detail and a greater sense of connection.

■ **Generate an accurate transcript.**
Always record the interview, even if you have someone typing simultaneously. The typist should record both the questions and the user's responses. The transcript should include the user's own words and expressions.

■ **Analyze the results.**
Include all the steps users mentioned— even if you think they're unnecessary or irrelevant to your site. Pay attention to when and where they get things done. Pay attention to what frustrates them or takes too much time. Notice the words they use to describe tasks. Don't allow your personal opinions or knowledge of the business goals taint the analysis.

understanding user behavior

So far, our user research has been pretty theoretical. We've painted a statistical portrait of our users and created fictional characters to personify them. We've talked to users about their wants and needs. That's all well and good, but what you really need to know is how (and whether) they're going to use your site.

traffic analysis

The best way to understand user behavior (and perhaps the best way to understand users, period) is watching how they actually use your site. How long do they stay? Where do they click? Do they make a purchase? Find important features? Only your traffic logs know.

You can learn a great deal from your traffic logs about who your users are and how they interact with your site. Traffic analysis can tell you how they arrived at your site (from a search engine, through a link on another site, etc.), how long they stayed, where they clicked, and the features or pages they chose. (See monitoring and evolving your site, p. 240.)

> **Traffic analysis and usability testing work hand in hand to show you how your site is used.**

Log files can also reveal "user clues"—hints about their identities or backgrounds—such as their host domains (i.e. intel.com, stanford.edu), the times they visit, and their computer systems and browsers.

Traffic analysis and usability testing work hand in hand to illuminate your site's potential pitfalls (and its stunning successes). Traffic analysis presents facts, but can raise more questions than it answers. For example, your log files may reveal that 90% of your users leave your site after the first page. But logs don't tell you why. Is the site too

---

tools for understanding user behavior

- **Traffic analysis** helps you see how visitors actually use your site: Where do they come from? How long do they stay? What features do they use?

- **Usability testing** helps you identify the problems people have when they try to use your site or one of its features.

- **Customer feedback** sheds light on specific grievances your users may have.

---

slow? Is it malfunctioning? Is the design confusing? Did users end up there by mistake? What?! Usability tests attempt to answer these questions by shedding light on the user's thought process during a typical session.

usability testing

Usability testing gives you a chance to see real people use your site in a way that simulates the actual user experience while allowing for questions. Do they understand what the labels mean, where the links lead, what the buttons do? Does the interface work the way they think it will work? Can they complete a given task?

Nothing is as powerful—or as instructive—as watching real users struggle with your interface. And struggle they will. No matter how good your initial design or how talented your design team, some aspect of your interface—the navigation system, the labels, the sequencing of events—will likely confuse your users. (See designing for the user, p. 82.)

"Your most unhappy customers are your greatest source of learning."

–Bill Gates

By putting your site in front of users early in the design process, you can catch significant problems early enough to correct them. For usability testing sometimes turns up problems that are more than skin deep. You may discover problems with your site's functionality or conceptual structure that force you to rethink your approach.

> **Listen to what they tell you. Customer feedback is the most direct path you have to users' brains.**

So the greatest favor you can do for your users—and your product team—is to integrate usability testing into every step of the design process. You should begin testing as soon as you have a prototype on paper—just sketches of the interface, really—and continue testing until you complete the site. Test early and often (at least twice before launch); this is the best way to catch mistakes and avert a user disaster.

This might sound complicated and expensive, but it need not be. The beauty of usability testing is that it can fit any budget. Of course, it's nice to have a state-of-the art usability lab and a full-time testing and recruiting staff. But usability testing can be done competently with a camcorder, a part-time tester (you, perhaps?), and a small budget to compensate volunteers.

In a pinch, you can even test the site with friends and family. As usability expert Steve Krug writes in *Don't Make Me Think*, "Testing one user is 100% better than testing none. Testing one user early in the process is better than testing 50 near the end."

customer feedback

The final clue to understanding user behavior is also the most obvious: Listen to what they tell you. Customer feedback—email, phone calls, or actual letters—is the most direct path you have to user's brains. It's honest, candid, and—importantly, it's proactive: Brought to you by the users themselves, rather than offered in response to your questions.

Now bear in mind that customer feedback always skews negative (people are more likely to let you know when they're outraged than when they're delighted), so it isn't an accurate gauge of overall consumer feeling. It is, however, an accurate portrayal of user frustration. You can safely assume that every angry email you receive represents the experience of at least 10 users—nine of whom simply left in a huff without bothering to tell you that you'd lost their business.

So it's important to pay attention to what the cranky users are telling you. People don't usually write in about run-of-the-mill frustrations—slightly confusing design, slightly annoying features, somewhat slow pages—they write when something has them fuming.

So it's important to give credence to these letters, even when they're written in a rather irrational tone. A wise manager views customer feedback as a valuable research tool. And also an opportunity.

Customer feedback gives you a chance to turn angry customers into loyal customers. These cranky letter-writers are very vocal, active people who tell people what's on their mind. If you win them back, you've gained a very powerful advocate.

One more note on customer feedback: If you have a large enough organization, and you're high enough up the ladder, it's easy to be shielded from the experience and reactions of actual users. But it's important to expose yourself now and then. You need to understand: What confuses your users? What do they like? What do they hate? What frustrates them? And why?

50 ways to lose your users

1 Email your customers about a one-day sale, then unplug the server so no one can get through.

2 Require users to register before entering your site. Don't offer any previews—in fact, don't even tell them what you do!

3 Serve lots of "rich-media" ads without testing them first. Watch your users' computers crash!

4 Carefully construct a considerate privacy policy—and then ignore it.

5 Buy slower servers.

6 Fill customers' screens with pop-up windows.

7 Fill customers' screens with pop-up windows that open more pop-ups each time you try to close one.

8 If that doesn't work, try pop-unders.

9 Regularly change the location of features on your site, ensuring that regular customers can never find anything! Ever!

10 Add a new whizzy JavaScript thingy every week. Watch your customers' computers crash!

11 Put an audio soundtrack on your home page. Don't let users turn it off. This is great for the cubicle crowd.

12 Specifically create links to pages that don't exist, so all your users can see the incomprehensible server errors.

13 Reorganize your site, but don't offer redirects to the new pages. None of the links to your site will work!

14 Eliminate all custom-made help pages. Replace them with incomprehensible server error messages.

15 Serve every page of your site in a new pop-up window. Make sure the new windows include neither the "Back" button or the "Print" button. That'll keep them from getting attached to you!

16 Create really compelling content and hide it behind obscurely named links.

17 Remove the underline from all your links, and make them the same color as the text. Let users guess where to click.

18 Change the navigation system on every single page. Users are lazy—they'll give up soon enough.

19 Change your site name and URL every month. That'll throw them off your scent!

20 Replace your home page with a really big image map, displaying an extended visual metaphor for your site sections.

21 Embed a really cool Flash movie on every page of your site.

22 Better yet, embed the same Flash movie on every page of your site.

23 Let customers place their entire order—and give you their credit card—before telling them that everything on your site is out-of-stock.

24 Hire exceptionally surly customer service representatives.

25 Ask users to fill out a survey. Make it really, really long, and then—this is important!—make sure the "Submit" button doesn't work.

26 Redesign your front door with lots of big rainbow-striped letters.

27 Fire your copy editor. Let the engineers and designers do the writing.

28 Fire your designer. Design the site yourself, as you've always wanted to.

29 Disable site search so every query turns up "No matching results."

30 Better yet, randomize site search, so a search for sneakers displays last season's prom dresses.

31 Serve Exit ads in pop-up windows as users leave your site. It's the online way of saying, "And STAY out!"

32 Serve exit ads when they exit your exit ads. See how many windows you can open at once!

33 Make your text really small—and italic.

34 Include lots of links. I mean LOTS!

35 Charge a lot for shipping!

36 Share customers' email addresses—without asking.

37 Sloooow down your customer service.

38 Customer service? What customer service?

39 Use non-secure servers for commerce transactions, and tell users it's "at your own risk!"

40 Don't keep an accurate inventory: Charge for products you don't have!

41 Choose curious color combinations.

42 Serve banner ads that say "If this is flashing, you've won!"

43 Email all your customers weekly—or better yet, daily, just to tell them what's on your mind.

44 Tell users they can unsubscribe from your email list, but make sure they can't!

45 Add background images—in dark colors—to every page.

46 Make sure error messages pop up during check-out. Force the customer to re-enter information every time.

47 Create a gift registry, but forget to take addresses for the people receiving gifts.

48 Change the nav bar options on every page.

49 Bury your contact information.

50 Two words: More pop-ups!

"These days, most of my sales are online."

making money

"Money is better than poverty,
if only for financial reasons."
- Woody Allen

Throughout the late 90s, there was a lot of hype and hullabaloo about the magical, rule-breaking, paradigm-bending, economics-defying properties of the Internet. Everyone, it seems, was getting rich quick.

But the bubble burst and the money dried up. And now many people believe the Internet was merely a flash in the pan, and that no one really makes money online. But the truth, as usual, is somewhere in between.

> **There *is* money in them there hills. You just have to know where to look.**

People *are* making money online. And they're not making it magically. The sites profiting on the web are using a simple set of time-tested revenue models, which have been adapted to suit the online environment. And they're making more than $80 billion per year.

So you see, there *is* money in them there hills. You just have to know where to look.

the revenue models

At first, the idea of outlining Internet revenue models may seem impossible. After all, there are billions of web sites, and they cover the breadth of human experience. Sites take the form of stores, games, magazines, meeting places. "Content" sites alone can be splintered into a million subcategories: art exhibits, travelogues, recipe collections, and so on.

So while it's impossible to anticipate the goals of every web developer, we can outline their financial options. In observing the range of successful strategies used over the last 10 years, it's possible to categorize them into five basic revenue models, each of which have been used by a startlingly wide range of companies and individuals.

5 online revenue models:

1. Generating leads for an off-line business

2. Product sales

---

4 steps to making money online

1. **Define your goals.** Whether you're bringing your company online or building a web business from the ground up, you should outline your expectations, so you know how to reach them. (See <u>stating your goals</u>, p. 13.)

2. **Do the obvious first.** Before you try to spin straw into gold.com, dare to be obvious. Use the web to support your existing business—by distributing information and generating leads. Once you've exhausted the obvious routes, then it might be time to branch out.

3. **Consider all five online revenue models.** Although the web is used as an extension to nearly every business under the sun, there are only five basic revenue models that work on the web. Make one—or several!—of them work for you. (See <u>5 online revenue models</u>, p. 70.)

4. **Get creative.** The web opens up new opportunities for companies ready to seize them. Once you have your bases covered, don't be afraid to try less-than-obvious paths.

---

3. Advertising

4. Subscriptions and user fees

5. "Match-making"

See <u>5 online revenue models</u>, p. 70.

Whatever your business, you'll do well to follow one of these approaches. And you'll find you have a lot in common with other, seemingly unrelated businesses—in different industries—that make money the same way online.

"Money is like a sixth sense without which you cannot make complete use of the other five."

—*W. Somerset Maugham*

considering your options

Figuring out how to make money is like deciding what to do with your life. It's an overwhelmingly broad question until you find a system for making choices.

If you run an existing business or organization, the smartest way to approach the money question is to begin with your current customers (or members, or readers—however you define them) and what they need from you.

Ask yourself:

- **What do your customers need from you?** Will they be willing to pay you for any of these services? If so, think about subscriptions & fees, p. 71.

- **What would your customers buy from you?** Is there anything you could sell that they would want to buy? If so, consider product sales, p. 70.

- **What do your customers need from each other?** Are there ways you can help them connect with each other? Would they be willing to pay for this service? If so, think about a match-making service (not just for dating, but also for jobs or products), p. 71.

- **What do other people need from your customers?** Are there other people or companies who want to reach your audience? If so, think about advertising, p. 71.

Now, if you don't have an existing business—if you're just dreaming up your next venture—you should also, of course, begin with *someone's* needs. Ask yourself: How can you harness the power of the Internet to make something easier, faster, or better?

eBay, for example, took classified advertising and made it work on a vast grassroots scale. You, however, should start smaller. Think of a specific problem for a smaller group of people, and solve it.

"I still beat my tail against a log, but now it's digital."

"The bigger your site is, the harder it is to get attention," said Josh Quittner, editor of the magazine *Business 2.0.* "But if you have a really wonderful, small, beautifully designed, simple-to-navigate, obvious site that provides real value to whoever you identify as your market, people will find it, and sooner or later it will take off. "

why pick just one?

Although it's always best to start small and simple, it's also smart to grow over time, gradually adding all the revenue models that make sense for your customers and your business.

For example, BlackPlanet (now the Number 1 site for African Americans) makes money from three of the five available revenue models. They run advertising throughout their site and collect user fees for their dating service. They also recruit volunteers for market-research studies and earn some additional revenue that way. See how BlackPlanet got users to register (and pay) p. 262.

BabyCenter followed a similar approach. They started by defining their audience: pregnant mothers and parents of small children. Initially, they made money entirely from advertising, but they later added a store to sell the products that new parents need.

5 online revenue models

Although the web is used as an extension to every business under the sun, there are only five basic revenue models that work online. By placing your business within one (or more) of these models, you can learn a lot from other companies with whom you didn't think you had much in common.

1. generating leads

How it works: Web sites can be used to **bring in new business**. By explaining exactly who you are and what you do, you can build interest in your organization that leads directly to the leads you want— whether that means new members, customers, or clients.

Who it works for: Almost everyone can successfully use the web this way. Companies can find new buyers for their products. Non-profits can find new members. Hotels and restaurants can find new customers. Charities can find new volunteers. Service professionals, from accountants to wedding photographers, can find new clients.

How much it's worth: N/A

Why it fails: You can only generate leads if people come to your site, and they'll only come if they can find it. Sites should be listed in search engines and directories, as well as with any sites pertinent to your field or location. You should also let existing customers know you have a web site: Put your URL in your ads, in your store window, and on your business card. Anything you can do to get the word out.

2. product sales

How it works: Commerce sites make money in a fairly traditional manner: **They sell things.** And people buy them. Products may range from airline tickets to pedigree poodles, and from couches for consumers to computers for corporate accounts.

Who it works for: Any company that sells products directly to its customers through catalogs or retail stores. Amazon, of course, is the celebrated leader in this category. But there are many other success stories, from travel site Expedia to specialty store RedEnvelope to tiny crafts shops around the world.

However, this model hasn't worked as well for companies that sell through a middleman. Levis, for example, launched one of the earliest online stores, but they no longer sell on their site. They now focus on generating leads for the stores that sell their products.

How much it's worth: Online consumer spending totalled $73.2 billion in 2002. This estimate includes travel sales. Retail spending alone totalled an est. $43 billion. (Source: Research firm comScore.)

Why it fails: As with any commerce-based business, web sites sink or swim based on the number of customers they attract and how much money they spend —balanced by the cost of running the business.

Web retailers often face ultra-competitive pricing. Online businesses also fail when customers can't figure out how to use their site.

3. advertising

How it works: Advertising-based sites earn money by **exposing their visitors to ads**. The ads may take the form of animated banners, interactive presentations, or simple links. The amount a site earns is dependent on both the number of ads it runs and how much advertisers are willing to pay per ad.

Who it works for: Sites with a large audience that can be subdivided into specialized groups. For example, news sites or portals that can target ads against particular types of content and search engines that can target ads against particular searches. (So a search for "Honda hybrid car" yields banners or links for car dealers online.)

As in other media, smaller, more specialized sites can also do well if they have an audience that advertisers value.

How much it's worth: Advertisers on American sites spent an estimated $6.38 billion in 2002. (Source: Research firm eMarketer.)

Why it fails: If a site can't attract a large enough audience, can't attract an audience that interests advertisers, can't target ads meaningfully, or can't get users to click on ads, they'll have trouble attracting advertisers. On the other hand, if they run too many ads on each page or try too many annoying experimental ads at once, users may turn away.

4. subscriptions & fees

How it works: Subscription or fee-based sites charge users money to gain **access to specialized content or services**. The type of service dictates the method of payment (either a flat subscription or fee-per-use). The perceived value of the service dictates how much the site can charge.

Who it works for: This category just began to take off in 2002 with successful sites ranging from content sites like Salon to video-rental service NetFlix to ESPN's Fantasy Football game. Also, many software companies are moving in this direction: Rather than selling packaged software to be installed individually on users' machines, they're increasingly offering subscription-based online access to applications, ranging from site search (Atomz) to corporate fulfillment software (Ariba).

How much it's worth: American consumers spent $1.3 billion on online content in 2002. (Estimate doesn't include games, software, gambling, or pornography). (Source: Online Publishers Association.)

Why it fails: If users don't see enough value in the service, they simply won't pay. But there's also a psychology to the sale: Most fee-based sites offer users a taste of their content or service before requiring payment. Sites that ask for too much too quickly often find themselves rebuffed.

5. matchmaking

How it works: Matchmaking sites are all about **making connections**. They bring together buyers and sellers of all kinds—in jobs, real estate, relationships—and profit from each successful match.

Who it works for: The runaway success in this category is the auction site eBay. There are many others, however, in other sectors: personals sites, which match people looking for relationships; jobs sites, which match companies with potential employees; and real estate sites have all proven successful for a number of sites.

How much it's worth: N/A

Why it fails: The number one reason matchmaking ventures fail is lack of critical mass. You have to attract enough buyers and sellers to create a viable marketplace. If your site doesn't grow big enough quickly enough, it won't gain the momentum it needs to take off.

making money from product sales

It's perhaps the first rule of retail: A store should seem alive, inviting, and, of course, legitimate—that is, if you expect people to shop there. But so many merchants abandon the basics when they go online. "A lot of people, when building e-commerce stores, just totally forget to treat it like a store," says Lance McDaniel, VP of Creative at SBI and Company.

Hilary Billings is one of the few who stuck with what she knew. Previously a vice president at Pottery Barn, Billings joined RedEnvelope in 1998 as chairman and chief marketing officer. "One of the reasons I came to the web is that I found the web shopping experience to really be lacking as a consumer," she said.

"There was an enormous amount of energy and money and time going into the development of features that I felt were ahead of the customer," Billings explained. "Whereas some of the basics—just having an easy-to-navigate website and images that were beautiful and easy-to-see—were missing."

Over the last five years, Billings built RedEnvelope into one of the web's most compelling stores; its secret lies in a simple interface and striking images.

"I've always been a deep believer in the fact that people want a functional shopping experience," Billings said. "But that alone is not enough. It also has to be an enjoyable shopping experience. So everything we've done is to try—within the constraints of a website, of which there are many—to make it as pleasurable and enjoyable as possible."

What are you selling?

- A few unique products
- Gifts or luxury items
- Considered purchases
- Big-ticket items

what customers want

- **An easy way** to find products they want.
- **Competitive prices**.
- **Help making decisions**—especially if it's a considered purchase. Photos, descriptions, and product reviews help.
- **Security** for users when submitting their email address and credit card number.
- **Responsive customer service** to give customers the sense that someone's minding the store.

unique products   Whether you're selling the perfect mousetrap or hand-woven carpets, the trick is finding the people who want them—or rather, helping them find you.

gifts or luxury items   When you're selling things that aren't a necessity, it helps to make shopping fun. For inspiration, look at RedEnvelope, which focuses on stylish gift-giving. The site's creative categories let you choose gifts by the recipient, occasion, or lifestyle (the spa seeker, the gadget guru). And their signature packaging leaves an impression.

considered purchases   Considered purchases are those higher-ticket items—like computers and consumer electronics—that people research before they buy. The key here is offering context: The more you can help customers research their decisions, the more likely they are to buy from you (so long as your prices are competitive).

big-ticket items   Big-ticket purchases include cars and homes; they can be researched online, but are purchased in person. The key here is to move customers toward closing the deal: Encourage them to phone or email you, provide a dealer locator, suggest appointment times—anything you can do to both build trust and move the relationship forward.

making money from advertising

Since almost any site can accommodate ad banners, almost every type of site has. A revenue model that was once restricted to media companies is now open to all comers: chat rooms, software products, personal home pages—you name it.

But the simplicity of the model is deceiving. Advertising—as any site owner who's tried it can tell you—is a far cry from easy money.

Advertising revenue depends on:

- **Traffic** to your site, which correlates with the number of ads you can serve.

- **Price** advertisers are willing to pay for ads.

- **Performance** of ads, which is usually measured in click-through.

traffic A common misunderstanding among site producers is that traffic = money. The more traffic you have, the more ads you can run. But that doesn't mean anyone will pay you for them. You need to have a user base that advertisers value—or a way of targeting ads toward a specific subset—to lure advertisers.

price Ad revenue is based not only on the number of ads you serve, but the price each ad commands. Prices can fluctuate widely, depending on the type of ad, the type of site, and even the time of year. But price generally correlates with the perceived value of the users and the context: The more valuable the audience, the more interactive the ad unit, and the more targeted the placement, the higher the cost.

performance All advertisers in all media are looking for results: They want to increase sales, raise awareness, create desire. Whatever their goal, they want to reach it.

But the impact of most advertising is fuzzy at best: How do you know the effect of a given TV ad? How many people actually saw it? How many people will buy your product as a result?

what advertisers want

- **A targeted audience.** They want to reach the right people at the right time.

- **Impact.** It's not enough to reach the right audience. Advertisers want to know their message was heard.

- **Proof.** Advertisers expect to receive reliable, audited accounts of how their ads did on your site.

All this changes on the web, where *everything* is quantifiable. You can tell exactly how many times an ad appeared and exactly how many times users clicked through. But this accountability hasn't worked in favor of web sites. The more sites deliver, the more advertisers demand of them, and the less tolerant they are of campaigns that don't yield high results—as measured in click-through.

"The expectations of what the medium can deliver have never tapered off," said Internet advertising pioneer Rick Boyce. "The pressure has been on the Internet to do more, and deliver more, than any other medium has been expected to. I used to really resent that."

"In fact, I still do," he added with a good-natured grin. "Unfortunately, what marketers want, are expecting, and now increasingly demanding, is to understand what's happening along each step of the 'purchase funnel.' And that's extraordinarily difficult. And they want all that from the Internet media marketplace, which continues to face tremendous downward pricing pressure."

"It's really a hard business."

making money from user fees & subscriptions

For many years, conventional wisdom held that people wouldn't pay for anything online. There was an abundance of free information and services, and people were uneasy about using credit cards online. It seemed impossible to charge for anything.

But people are always willing to pay for things they need or want. And many online players—from newspapers to software to games—are now making a living through user fees and subscriptions.

3 ways to collect user fees:

- Subscription-only services

- Tiered services with free and premium offerings

- Pay-as-you-go services

subscription-only services   Subscription services charge users an up-front fee for unlimited access to content or services over a set period of time; nothing is given away for free. Great work if you can get it!

But not many businesses can get away with a subscription-only model, because web users rarely invest money up front in an unknown quantity. Only deeply compelling services or established brands can pull it off. A success story: Both *Consumer Reports* and *The Wall Street Journal* bucked the industry trend in 1996 by establishing subscription-only content sites that continue to this day.

tiered services   Tiered services put the psychology of salesmanship to work on the web. They offer users free access to a site—or, rather, part of a site—and then sell them premium services or content. This approach has worked for a wide range of businesses, including magazines, research services, software, and games.

what subscribers want

- **Value.** They'll pay for a service they need that they can't get elsewhere.

- **A free sample.** They want to try the product before committing to a subscription.

For instance, the financial information service Hoover's Online offers free access to its basic descriptions of companies and industries. But its premium services—in-depth reports, competitive profiles, targeted searching—require an annual subscription.

The tiered approach has also worked well for ESPN. Its sports news is available free, but users a-plenty pay to join fantasy sport leagues (baseball, basketball, and football) timed with each major league season. Sports fans pay around $30 per season to assemble and coach a team (based on pro athletes) and get a shot at the (fantasy) championship.

This model works for software, as well. Atomz provides a free, basic version of its site search engine, which brings search capabilities to sites with under 500 pages. Although customers can use this free service indefinitely, Atomz uses it as a lure for their full-featured services, for which customers pay a monthly fee.

pay-as-you-go services   Pay-as-you go services allow consumers to sample a site little by little, paying only for the content or services they use. The fee may be applied based on the service rendered or time elapsed. Content sites, for example, may charge by the article, whereas game sites may charge by the hour.

The problem with this model is that the payment system really isn't there yet. Once consumers can make true micropayments—a few pennies per article, for instance—this model will become far more viable. (See <u>online payment options</u>, p. 76.)

making money from match-making

Matchmaking is all about connections: connecting people to people, connecting people to jobs, connecting people who want a particular product to people with the products they need.

So match-making sites play the role of middleman. They make money by bringing together buyers and sellers, and facilitating successful transactions. The job's not that different from the traditional romantic match-maker, like the one in the famous song from *Fiddler on the Roof* ("Matchmaker, match maker, make me a match. Find me a find, catch me a catch...").

Good match-makers—whether they're of the old-fashioned or the new-fangled online variety—all have a lot in common. They have access to a lot of people, they understand the criteria of a good match, and they can help people articulate what they're looking for. They also know how to arrange a safe environment to explore the idea of a potential match.

3 ways to charge for match-making:

- Subscription services
- Pay-as-you-go services
- Commission-based services

subscription services Subscription services grant unlimited access to the system for a specific period of time. This fee is the same, regardless of how often you use the system or whether you find a successful match.

For example, the dating site Match.com charges users a monthly subscription fee (roughly $25) for full access to the site. However, Match.com lets you sample the service for free: You can browse the system and post your profile before you join. But you have to pay if you want to contact someone or reply to someone who's contacted you.

---

what match-seekers want

- **A large selection** of potential matches to choose from—whether that means people, products, jobs, or something else.

- **Effective ways of searching** for the right match. They want the site to help them describe what they're looking for, find potential matches, and evaluate how good each match is.

- **A safe, confidential way of exploring** a match before committing to it.

---

pay-as-you-go services Pay-as-you-go services charge a set amount each time you use the system, but this access can take different forms, depending on the site. For example, the employment site Monster.com charges a set rate for employers to post a single job listing for a set period of time (usually 60 days).

Same dating sites use the same pay-as-you-go approach, but they go about it differently. The personals service on Nerve.com lets you post a profile and browse the system for free. You pay a small amount (roughly $1 per message) each time you want to contact someone—or reply to someone who has contacted you.

commission-based services Commission-based services charge a set amount—or percentage—for each *successful* transaction. This obviously wouldn't work on dating sites (how would you define "successful"?), but it is commonly used on sites where a clear dollar value is attached to the transaction, or sale.

Commissions are often charged—to one or both clients—on used car sites, real estate sites, and auction sites, such as eBay.

online payment options

If you plan to sell things over the Internet, you'll also need to plan out how people will pay for them.

Collecting money online:

- **Credit card.** The most basic payment method requires a merchant account and a secure server to process the transaction.

- **Online cash.** Online cash services, such as PayPal and Yahoo! PayDirect, let you exchange money between two online accounts set up for this purpose.

- **Micropayments.** Micropayment services will someday allow you to pay for services in tiny increments—a few pennies or less.

- **Cash, check, or money order.** These are sent by mail.

credit card Credit cards may be the most familiar method of collecting online, but they aren't the cheapest or the easiest. If you have an existing business, you already know about merchant accounts. If you don't, you're about to learn. In order to receive credit-card payments online, you have to first establish a merchant account with an FDIC-insured merchant bank.

Be warned: This is a bureaucratic process, and a costly one. Between account set-up fees, processing fees, and transaction fees, you'll pay quite a bit for the privilege of accepting credit cards. So smaller merchants sometimes use cash-payment services like PayPal.

online cash Online cash isn't exactly cash. These services—like PayPal and Yahoo! PayDirect—play the middleman, letting you transfer money directly from one person to another, while ensuring that it actually gets where it's going (and taking a cut for themselves, of course).

"You'll be happy to know I just invested in a company which is developing technology which will allow me to wirelessly beam e-dollars to you, but to answer your question: Sorry dude, no change."

PayPal is the best known e-cash service, commonly used on auction sites like eBay, where individuals are selling to each other. It's a simple system. Users set up a PayPal account by transferring money from a bank account, charging it to their credit card, or sending a personal check. They can then buy online using this account. When someone buys from you, the amount is transferred from their account to yours (with roughly a 3% commission).

micropayments Micropayments allow users to pay tiny amounts of money—a few pennies, say, or less—for a service they use online. This approach would be perfect for content sites of all sizes: The tiny payments would mean little to any individual consumer—Why not pay a penny for an article, so long as it's easy to do so?—but it could add up to significant revenues for the site.

The trick, then, is making it easy. And that's the missing piece in this puzzle. Although several early players attempted to put such a system in place, none gained critical mass and they all died trying. File this idea—lovely as it is—under "someday."

"There was a time when a fool and his money were soon parted, but now it happens to everybody."
—Adlai Stevenson

how will you make money?

It's a million dollar question if ever there were one: How will you make money online?

How will you make money?
(Check all that apply)

❑ Generating leads for an existing business

❑ Product sales

❑ Advertising

❑ User fees and subscriptions

❑ Match-making

If you're selling products, what kind?

❑ A few unique products

❑ Gifts or specialty items

❑ Commodities

❑ Considered purchases

❑ Big-ticket items

Specifically, what will you sell?

How many items will you have?

If you're selling advertising, what kind?

❑ Banners

❑ Buttons

❑ Text-based links

❑ Pop-up ads

❑ Sponsorship

Who will advertise on your site?

If you're selling subscriptions or user fees,
how will you charge?

❑ Subscription-only service

❑ Tiered service

❑ Pay-as-you-go service

What service will you be selling?

If you're match-making, how will you charge?

❑ Subscription-only service

❑ Tiered service

❑ Pay-as-you-go service

Who or what will you be matching?

How will you collect money?

❑ Credit Card

❑ E-cash service like PayPal

❑ Micro-payments

❑ Check or money order, in the mail

❑ I won't collect money online

designing

your site

designing for the web

A MODERN ADAPTATION OF THE CLASSIC LOVE STORY

GREGORY

don't miss ...

Everyone loves design. Perhaps because we're visual creatures, perhaps because design is seen as "fun," or perhaps because design is easier to understand, than, say, engineering—everyone has opinions on how a site should look and feel.

But people often underestimate what goes into site design. Like beauty, design is more than skin deep. A site's design begins with its structure and functionality—and only ends with the choice of colors and fonts.

Focus first on how well the site works, and only then on how good the site looks.

Web sites, you see, must be used—not just viewed—so they don't have the luxury of simply looking good. You have to focus first on how well the site works, and only then on how good it looks.

"Design is never just about visual aesthetics anymore," said Doug Bowman, principal of Stopdesign "You have to consider usability. You have to consider the technology. You have to consider how things render on the page, and the flow from one page to another."

In many ways, web design is a study in constraints: Technological, conceptual, and aesthetic. On the technology front, pages must be built in HTML, delivered over often-slow network connections, and displayed on different kinds of systems.

But the conceptual challenge is even greater: People have to understand—almost immediately—what your site is, what they can do there, and how they can find what they're looking for.

Finally, there's the aesthetic challenge. Despite all the other constraints, your site should still, if at all possible, have some style.

These are indeed great challenges. But they aren't unsurmountable. "The web is inherently constraining," said Jeffrey Veen, author of *The Art & Science of Web Design*. "But constraint breeds creativity."

the well-designed web site

Beauty might be in the eye of the beholder, but good design is not. Unlike art, design is meant to be used, and can be judged more objectively.

The well-designed web site:

1. **Lets the users accomplish their goals.** Your design must be —above all else—intuitive and functional for users. It should allow them to smoothly—almost effortlessly—accomplish their goals. (designing for the user, p. 82.)

2. **Makes its purpose clear.** The web is an ambiguous medium. Designers must work overtime to make the site's purpose and functionality clear to the user, even if a site's purpose is to delight, surprise, and amuse—that, too, must be clear. (front door design, p. 140.)

3. **Follows conventions.** Over the years, conventions have emerged for how sites should look and work. When you follow these conventions, you make your users' lives easier (and yours, for that matter). Your web site doesn't have to look like everyone else's, but it should work the way people expect it to. (designing for conventions, p. 84.)

4. **Speeds along.** Your web pages have to load quickly. That is, if you want people to use them. You'll need to weigh the trade-offs between the effects you want and the speed they'll cost you. (designing for speed, p. 92.)

5. **Displays well in different environments.** Unlike other media, web sites appear differently to different users, depending on their computer, browser, and monitor. Good web design rises to the challenge—appearing differently, perhaps, but functionally across a range of user environments. (designing for different systems, p. 90.)

6. **Has some style.** Despite all these constraints, it's possible to design a site that's stylish and appropriate to your brand. (visual design, p. 138.)

designing for the user

The success of your site rests quite literally in the hands of your users. So when you're designing a site, you need to focus on what your users want to do, not what you want to say. After all, your web site is for your users, not you. And the more you think about them—their goals, their expectations, their abilities—the more effective your design will be.

4 steps to user-centered design:

- **Focus on the user and the user's goals.** You can't design a usable site unless you know how it will be used. Understanding the audience should be your top priority. See getting to know your users, p. 44.

- **Provide intuitive pathways through the site.** After you know what users want, help them find it through the organization of content, the order of events, the labeling of links. Well-designed sites lead users down clear paths to what they want. See site organization, p. 98.

- **Follow interface conventions.** Over the past 10 years, conventions have evolved for how sites look and behave. If you follow them, users will understand your site more quickly. See designing for web conventions, p. 84.

- **Test! Test! Test!** No matter how much you know about how people use the web, you'll always be surprised by what you find. See usability testing, p. 129.

User-centered design begins at the beginning: with the user's needs and goals. "Everything that happens on the site—whether it's structure, or labeling, or visual design—should be appropriate to the specific users you're designing for," says Steve Mulder, Manager of User Experience for Terra-Lycos.

The biggest mistakes, he said, happen when companies fail to recognize "the importance of designing a product based on user needs."

And you don't learn what users need through usability testing alone. Usability tests come at the end of the design process, but user research should begin before you start designing.

> **User-centered design begins at the beginning: with the user's needs and goals.**

"Design is now inseparable from user research," said Veen. "We literally do nothing until we talk to people. We try to go into a project with no assumptions, and just hear how people approach the task."

"Unless you are, for some reason, designing a web site for yourself to use, you've got to talk to the people who are going to use it. You've got to!" Veen said. "That's the difference between art and design, right? If you want to make art, that's great. But if you're going to design things for people to use, then it's a totally different process."

And this process can be harder than it sounds. "The idea of a user-centered approach to design is very simple," says Nadav Savio, principal with Giant Ant Design. "I think people generally understand it, but people mistake the simplicity of the idea with the idea that it's simple to do. It can actually be incredibly hard."

"A lot of time you'll ask, 'What's best for the user?' and it's a difficult question to answer because there isn't one monolithic user. Even if you know exactly who's going to use your site—and even if you're only designing for two people—it can be hard to figure out what works best for those two people. Even if you ask them. People are not always good at knowing what's going to work best for them."

So user-centered design requires not only research, but also good instincts and common sense. "You need to balance user research with the fact that you're a smart person, and you can make your own decisions," Veen said.

Putting the user first?
understanding user needs, p.60
understanding user behavior, p. 62
how people navigate the web, p. 111
usability testing, p. 129

10 ways to make your site more usable

1. **Think about the user.** This is perhaps the most obvious statement you could make about web site usability, but it's also the most important. Web designers should not only understand their user's goals and needs, but also put themselves in the user's shoes and imagine what it's like, for instance, to be on a 15-inch monitor, on a dial-up connection, with the kids screaming in the background. See <u>getting to know your users</u>, p. 44.

2. **Follow conventions.** Over the last 10 years, conventions have evolved for where things should appear and how they should look on a web page. (Think of the shopping cart icon in the upper-right corner.) These conventions are your friend. They save you the trouble of reinventing the wheel with every site you build; they allow you to assume some basic user knowledge. They allow you to focus on your unique design challenges, rather than having to twiddle around with the placement of each icon. See <u>designing for web conventions</u>, p. 84.

3. **Label things clearly.** The specific words you use to label site sections can determine whether or not they're used. People rarely click on things they don't understand, so site sections should be named clearly and intuitively. Resist the urge to make up clever little names that need an explanation. See <u>naming site sections</u>, p. 122.

4. **Avoid jargon.** Every industry and every company has its own jargon for describing its business and the world. Unless you're building an intranet, you'll need to translate everything into a language the rest of us can understand. See <u>what does jargon mean?</u>, p. 123.

5. **Don't use your org chart as site navigation.** Too often companies divvy up their web sites to mirror their organizational structure, assigning a link on the home page to each department. This might satisfy internal politics, but it rarely serves the user. See <u>structuring your site</u>, p. 99.

6. **Avoid lengthy instructions**. Unless you're building an interface to a complicated, specialized application that's essential to its users, your site shouldn't require lengthy instructions—largely because people won't bother to read them. "Resorting to instructions is an admission of failure," says professor Michael Twidale of the University of Illinois, Urbana-Champaign.

7. **Pay attention to detail.** When it comes to a user interface, details count. Seemingly small matters like alignment and labels can make a big difference in user comprehension.

8. **Make links look clickable.** This is a simple rule, but it sure makes sense: If you'd like people to click something on your site, make sure they know it's clickable. Links should look like links. (They should be underlined.) Buttons should look like buttons. See <u>designing for web conventions</u>, p. 84.

9. **Focus on organization more than navigation.** Your site's navigation—the visual elements that guide the user—is important, but the site structure is more important. If your underlying organization doesn't make sense to users, no amount of visual ingenuity will make it work. See <u>site organization</u>, p. 98.

10. **Test, test, test!** The best way to improve the usability of your site is to test it with real users and modify the site to reflect what you learn. See <u>usability testing</u>, p. 129.

designing for web conventions

In the mid-'90s, when the web was still young and the stock market sensible, people looked at web sites with fresh eyes. They didn't have many pre-conceived notions about what a web site should do. There were plenty of opinions, sure; but hard and fast notions about how a web site should behave hadn't yet developed.

Five years later it's a different world. The web has been integrated into tens of millions of lives, and users have come to expect certain things.

4 kinds of web conventions:

■ **Navigation systems.** People habitually look to the top or left of a web page to find navigation, and several specific systems—like tabs and "breadcrumbs"—have also become conventions in their own right. See <u>navigation systems</u>, p. 114.

■ **Icons and other visual elements.** Like stop signs on the street or playback controls on a stereo, certain symbols—like the shopping cart—are now recognized by most web users. See <u>visual conventions on (and off) the web</u>, p. 87.

■ **Placement on the page.** People have developed expectations about where certain elements should appear on the page. The logo should be in the upper-left corner, for example, and the shopping cart icon in the upper-right corner. See <u>how people see web sites</u>, p. 86.

■ **Color.** There aren't many color conventions, but a few have emerged: Blue, for example, often means a link. But people bring their own cultural expectations to the web—green might mean "go" or "money" or "Erin go Bragh," depending on who's looking. See <u>color on the web</u>, p. 146.

These expectations have changed the way designers design. In the early days, we made everything up as we went along. But we no longer have a blank slate. Depending on your outlook, you can bemoan your loss of freedom or rejoice that someone else has done the hard work for you.

"We were completely flying blind when we started," said Jeffrey Veen, who joined the staff of HotWired in 1994. "Because no one had ever done web design before. We copied some conventions from magazines and books, and some conventions from computer operating systems. But now there are conventions for the web."

"If you're an e-commerce site, you can put your different products in tabs across the top, and it'll work," he explained. "People know what that means. Especially if you put the shopping cart in the upper right-hand corner and the logo in the upper left-hand corner. You can call that boring, but it will work! You have a foundation to start from, and you can innovate on top of that."

Granted, this is a mixed blessing. The emerging conventions are by no means perfect, and it can be hard to break the mold, even if you design a genuinely superior system. "Going against conventions is an uphill battle," said designer Doug Bowman. "For better or worse, users have gotten used to certain conventions and placements on the page."

These conventions have been largely set by the sites used most often—portals like MSN, stores like Amazon, news sites like CNN.com. And it's hard for smaller sites to deviate too widely from the norm.

"As the large web businesses gain dominance, they define the expectation for web sites in a much deeper way," said Hilary Billings, chairman and CEO of specialty gift store RedEnvelope.

Customers expect, for example, an Amazon-like check-out process. "Even though our check-out is much better for our business, customers get confused because it doesn't follow Amazon's," Billings said. "So we have to model some portions of our web site—the very functional portions of our web site against the big sites out there, because they've set the customers' expectations."

why you should follow design conventions

Over time, conventions emerge In all industries to make our lives easier, our products better, and our communications faster. There are conventions for everything from traffic signs on highways to playback controls on a stereo.

And conventions are now emerging on the web, dictating where certain elements should appear, what they should look like, and how they should work. (Think of the shopping cart icon in the upper-right corner, which leads users to the check-out process.) Some designers resist these basic conventions out of a desire to be original. And while innovation is always needed, this push-back is a bit misguided.

> **"Don't break the rules just to show off how different you are."**
>
> *- Michael Twidale*

What would happen, for example, if every city had a different traffic system: If street signs used different shapes and colors; if red and green no longer meant stop and go?

Drivers would have to learn these systems on-the-fly and far more accidents would happen.

On the web, of course, the stakes are lower. No one dies from poor web design. But companies and products suffer when visitors can't use their sites.

Conventions, you see, are a way of helping users make their way on the web. What they've learned on other sites should help them navigate yours.

"As more and more customers are buying more on the web, they want it to be a faster and faster experience," says Hilary Billings, chairman and CMO of the specialty gift store RedEnvelope.

"Customers want to go autopilot," she explained." They don't want to have to stop and think; they just want to click through really quickly. And it's a lot easier for them if the functional parts of all the major sites are virtually identical. It makes the shopping experience much easier."

And this applies, of course, to all web sites—not just online stores.

"If I'm on a site, I hope there's going to be some sort of corporate logo somewhere near the top, near the left-hand corner, and when I click on it, it will take me back to the top-level page of the site," said Michael Twidale, a professor of library and information science at the University of Illinois, Urbana-Champaign. "So if I get lost, I'll always be able to find my way back."

"That's an emerging convention," he said. "And it's really irritating when it's not there."

"Now, I'm not saying we all have to follow all the world's conventions," he explained. "But you shouldn't change a convention just to be different. That would be like General Motors saying, 'Well, Ford has the brake and accelerator this way round, so we'll have it the other way round just to be different.'"

"If you want to break the conventions because you've thought of this fabulous new usability innovation, that's OK," he said. "But it better be 10 times better than what we've got. Only break the rules when you're going to do something useful with it. Don't break the rules just to show off how different you are."

Jeffrey Veen, author of *The Art & Science of Web Design*, also takes a measured approach to following and breaking interface conventions. He embraces conventions, but also encourages designers to keep pushing the limits. "I completely 100% believe in following conventions," Veen said. "And you have to completely internalize, understand, and know why conventions work before you can start to break them. And then you should! Because we're not done yet!"

"But you can't bury your head in the sand, and say, 'I'm gonna do it different! I'm gonna be innovative!' without first understanding all the rules. You can't be James Joyce without first knowing grammar."

how people see web sites

When users arrive at your site, you have only a few seconds to orient them. You must explain where they are, what they can do, and how to do it. You must do all this in just a few moments. "If it ain't 100% usable in 15 seconds, you've failed," John Shiple wrote on Webmonkey. And his estimate is probably a little high; web users are an impatient bunch.

To design an effective interface, you must first understand how users will see your site when they arrive.

1. how users take in a web page

It's seen over and over again in usability labs: People habitually scan web pages the way designers have traditionally arranged them: with site identity top-left, the main content center-right, and additional navigation down the left side. Users typically glance at the top of the page to orient themselves, then look toward the center. If they don't find what they're looking for, they shift their eyes (and mouse) to the left, where they expect to see navigation.

2. where users expect things to be

Whether or not they realize it, web users have developed expectations about where certain elements will be placed on the web page. This is also seen in usability labs: Testers habitually look toward the place on the page where they expect something to appear (often hovering the cursor over it). They expect to find the shopping cart icon near the upper-right corner, for example, and information about the organization—"About us,""Contact us"—at the bottom of the page.

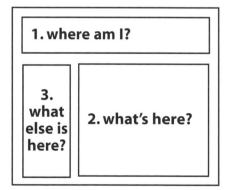

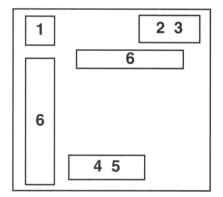

How the user takes in a web page. People tend to scan web pages the way they've "traditionally" been designed, with the logo on the top, featured content in the center, and navigation on the left. Source: Inspired by a diagram in Jeffrey Veen's *The Art & Science of Web Design*.

Where users look for common elements. Usability studies show that people have expectations for where particular page elements should appear.

1. Logo, leading back to front door
2. Shopping cart, leading to check-out
3. Help
4. About us
5. Contact us
6. Site navigation bars

Source: Optimal Web Design (www.optimalweb.org) and other sources.

visual conventions on (and off) the web

Visual conventions arise out of need. In so many aspects of our lives, we need quick, easy ways to communicate important concepts—like "poison," for example, or "bathroom" or "Stop!"— in ways that can be almost universally understood, even by those who don't read or speak the language being used.

Of course, not all conventions are a matter of life and death. Visual symbols and other conventions arise in many industries simply to make our lives easier—or, in the case of comics, funnier. Here are a few examples from some familiar worlds—including, of course, the web.

on the road

in public places

on consumer electronics

on the web

This is a link.

Check-in: April ⬦ 24 ⬦ 🗓
Check-out: April ⬦ 26 ⬦ 🗓

◀ Gooooooooooooogle ▶
Previous 1 2 3 4 5 6 7 8 9 10 11 12 **Next**

in comics

The value of conventions is that they don't need to be explained. Most people know that a right-facing arrow means **Play** on a stereo or VCR. And the lines behind a **cartoon car** mean it's moving. These conventions are relatively new (25 and 75 years old respectively), but widely understood. Web conventions, too, are taking hold. Most users now understand that a **shopping cart** icon leads to the check-out process. Also: A **question mark** leads to Help, a **printer** icon will print the page, and an **envelope** will send email. Users also recognize that underlined words are **links**. They know how to use **pull-down menus** and how to navigate through pages of **search results**.

designing for HTML

The first fundamental challenge of web design is to create pages that look and behave the way they're supposed to using HTML, the page-layout language that controls the appearance of everything on the web. (See underline building your first web page, p. 196.)

From a design perspective, the problem with HTML is that it isn't a design tool. It was developed to define the structure of documents (distinguishing headlines from paragraphs from lists), not their appearance. Many visual effects used in print design simply aren't possible with HTML.

To achieve even simple effects—like creating two columns of continuous text—you have to get creative with the technology. The designer must learn to work with—and around—the limitations of HTML in order to produce interesting designs.

"You've got to exploit the medium," says Jeffrey Veen. "You have to understand it inside and out. I just don't think you can do good web design without knowing HTML—without getting deep into it."

Of course, not everyone goes quite as deep. Most successful designers understand the medium's possibilities. But not all of them learn to program. Sheryl Cababa, a product designer with Microsoft, argues that designers can learn the limitations of HTML without learning the actual code.

While she herself can hand-code pages, she doesn't think it's essential. "I know designers who've had an incredible impact on every product they've worked on, who aren't at all technical," Cababa says. "They just understand how things should function. And they don't need to know the magic behind it in order to design something that really works and is really usable."

"Building web pages with HTML is like painting a portrait with a paint roller."

— Steve Mulder

5 keys to HTML design

1. **Learn the limitations.** As with any medium, you have to know your constraints. You should understand how pages are structured, how text is treated, and how images are included before you begin. See how web pages are built, p. 191.

2. **Surrender some control.** Designers get themselves in trouble when they try to control every last pixel on the page. It's just not possible. You can't control the exact placement of everything on your site. Your site will appear differently for different users. Accept this. You are not in control. Try very hard to accept this.

3. **Don't try to re-create print designs.** HTML works differently from page-layout software such as QuarkXPress and Photoshop. There are many things you just can't do, and you might kill your design—or your production manager—trying. It's best to start from scratch, structuring the page to take advantage of the web.

4. **Learn to live without your favorite fonts.** On the web, you can use only those fonts that your users have installed on their computers, so you'll have to learn to love Arial, Times, and Verdana. And while you can include images of text in any font you want, you should only do this sparingly. See typography on the web, p. 150.

5. **Test! Test! Test!** Your design will appear differently on different computers, browsers, and monitors. Some variation is inevitable, but you should know what the variations are before you decide to accept them. Sometimes small changes in the code can make a difference between displaying perfectly and not at all. See designing for different systems, p. 90.

choosing software for web design

Although you could create a web site using nothing but a text editor, most professionals rely on a range of software tools to help them accomplish specific tasks

HTML-editing software

How it's used: For designing and building pages. Most HTML-editing software allows you to design pages in a visual environment, while the program creates the HTML. You can also do it in reverse: creating the code yourself and using the editing software to observe how it will look.

Choices include:

- Macromedia Dreamweaver
  http://www.macromedia.com
- Macromedia HomeSite
  http://www.macromedia.com
- Adobe GoLive
  http://www.adobe.com/golive
- Microsoft FrontPage
  http://www.microsoft.com/frontpage

other page layout software

How it's used: Some designers use a non-web layout program such as Photoshop to mock up pages, before they build them in HTML. This allows them to work more quickly and comfortably. However, it's important they understand the limitations of HTML before taking this approach. Otherwise, they'll design pages that just can't be built.

Choices include:

- Adobe Photoshop
  http://www.adobe.com/photoshop
- QuarkXPress
  http://www.quark.com/

site-mapping software

How it's used: To create the chart that visually represents the site structure. (Note: You don't necessarily need software for this; it can often be done on paper.)

Choices include:

- Microsoft Visio
  http://www.microsoft.com/office/visio
- SmartDraw
  http://www.smartdraw.com

graphics software

How it's used: For producing, editing, and compressing images. Some software focuses on one type of image (photographs versus illustrations), and some focus on a particular process, such as compression.

Choices include:

- Adobe Photoshop
  http://www.adobe.com/photoshop
- Macromedia Fireworks
  http://www.macromedia.com
- Equilibrium DeBabelizer
  http://www.equilibrium.com

animation software

How it's used: For designing and producing animation.

Choices include:

- Adobe AfterEffects
  http://www.adobe.com/aftereffects
- Macromedia Flash MX
  http://www.macromedia.com

designing for different systems

Unlike print-based designs, which are distributed to everyone in exactly the same way, web sites are seen differently by different users. Your site will be viewed by users with different computers, browsers, monitors, color capabilities, and connection speeds.

All of these factors affect the appearance of the site, altering its dimensions, colors, and typefaces, as well as the overall size of the browser window and the size and placement of elements within it.

Design differences arise from:

- **Platform**
- **Browser**
- **Plug-ins**
- **Monitor**
- **Color capability**

platform   People use the web on just about every computer (and every operating system) ever made, including Windows, Mac, and Unix. Colors may appear differently on different platforms, and different fonts may be available. Also, platform sometimes affects font size; text often appears larger on Windows than it does on the Mac.

browser   Users view the web through many different versions of many different web browsers, and different browsers support different design features. Inconsistent support for stylesheets is the biggest problem today; it varies even between different builds of the same browser.

plug-ins   Not everyone has plug-in technologies, like Flash, installed properly. So if your site uses plug-ins, not everyone will be able to see it. Because of installation problems, it's hard to estimate how many people you're excluding. See understanding Flash, p. 166.

monitor   People use monitors of different sizes and resolutions, and this dictates how much space you get on their screens. See where's the fold? p. 91.

color capability   There are slight differences in color on different platforms. And older computer systems don't display the full range of colors. See color on the web, p. 146.

Your challenge is to design a site that functions across the board. It doesn't have to look the same in every browser—it doesn't even have to look good in every browser—but it should work.

6 steps to cross-platform design:

1. **Identify your target audience.** Research the browser/platform they're most likely to use.

2. **Choose a single browser.** Design your site with it in mind.

3. **Research the differences.** What separates your target browser from the rest. Small changes can make the difference between a site that works on many browsers, and a site that works on only one.

4. **Accept the differences.** Your site will not look exactly the same in all browsers and platforms, no matter what you do.

5. **Degrade gracefully.** Your design should function and display reasonably in other browsers. To accomplish this, you can serve alternate pages for different browsers, but try to limit yourself to two: one design for the target browser and one for the other browsers.

6. **Test! Test! Test!** No matter how well you've researched the differences, you might still find problems when you test.

where's the fold?

Designers often talk about getting links or images "above the fold." It's a strange term, really, for a flat medium, but it was borrowed from one that made sense. "Above the fold" Is actually a publishing term for the top half of a newspaper's front page—above the crease that folds the newspaper in half. Everything above the fold, it's believed, is more likely to be read.

On the web, the conceptual "fold" divides everything the user sees when they first access your site—and before they have to scroll—from everything below.

The "fold" presents 2 challenges:

1. **Figuring out where it is.** The fold hits at different places for different users, depending on their browser, platform, monitor, and the number of toolbars they have showing. The biggest issue is monitor resolution, which measures how many pixels appear on the screen (a pixel is a tiny square dot of color—the smallest visual unit on the screen).

At the time of this book's writing, the most common monitor resolution is 800x600 pixels, which leaves a slightly smaller space for the actual web site (after you account for the "chrome").

2. **Fitting things above it.** No matter where you decide the fold is, there isn't much room above it, and everyone will want their pet feature, link, or ad to appear "above the fold."

The "chrome" is the toolbars and scrollbars that frame your site. Users control how many toolbars they have showing.

The "fold" is the imaginary line between what a user initially sees and what she must scroll for. It varies from user to user, producing sometimes dramatic differences in site appearance.

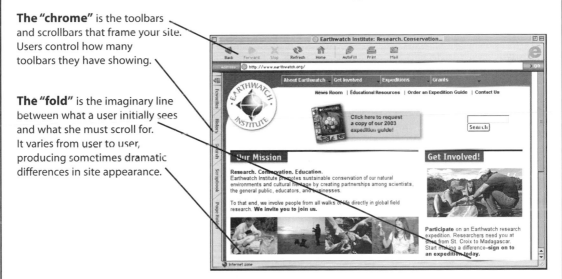

designing for speed

If speed weren't an issue, web site design would be a whole different ball game. Sites could incorporate many more images with richer, fuller color; structural design could be more complicated; functionality could be enhanced (or obscured, as the case may be); video and animation could be incorporated more freely.

But that's not the world we live in. Our world is filled with impatient users, tempting distractions, slow connections, and fast-moving competitors. Speed matters in our world.

The best web designers have adapted their style to the constraints of the medium, using speed-friendly techniques (color, words, placement, pacing) and creative tweaks to convey meaning and emotion within a site that's also usable and fast.

"For me, as a user, the simpler the better," says designer Jeffrey Zeldman. "So I carry that through in my design. It's all about simplicity."

"For me, web design is about removing everything extraneous, and then sizing and positioning only the elements that are absolutely needed—and being willing to accept a simpler version of those elements if it speeds up the site."

> **You should know where—and why—you're sacrificing speed. Be conscious of the trade-offs.**

Web designers also know there isn't a single universal solution. The need for speed varies from site to site, depending on its focus and audience.

"Speed is important, and it needs to be thought through from the beginning," says designer Wendy Owen. But it doesn't hold equal weight on every project. "It depends on the product and it also depends on which part of the product. In web applications, speed is really important—especially if the site's replacing, say, an ATM. But if you're designing a web page for an event, you may be willing to sacrifice speed for a little more glitz."

The most important thing is to know where—and why—you're sacrificing speed. If you understand what slows sites down, you can design efficiently and be conscious of the trade-offs.

What slows sites down? There are a lot of factors that contribute to drag—some visual, some technical—and you'll want to address them all. (See improving site speed, p. 218.) But the key issues in design concern the construction of the page and the number and size of images.

What slows you down:

- **Images and multimedia.** The number and size of images on your site (not to mention the animation, audio, and video) will affect how quickly your pages are transferred to the user's computer.

- **Page construction.** Complicated or sloppy HTML will affect how long it takes the browser to draw your pages. Also, designs based on stylesheets download faster than those based on tables and font tags.

- **Poor organization or non-standard design.** If users can't find what they're looking for, your site will seem slow to them—even if it loads quickly.

The classic problem graphic designers have is when they translate print designs directly to the web without considering how the pages could be better constructed for the medium. Print-style designs create all kinds of problems: they're laid out in a way that's hard for the browser to re-create, they're heavy on graphics, and they use specific fonts that can only be matched using an image of the text. In other words, they're slow.

So whether you're adapting a design from print or designing anew for the web, here are six tricks that will speed up your pages.

Speed errors. The Lincoln Center web site makes a lot of classic speed errors. The main problem: The design is based on images, and the images haven't been compressed enough. The "Welcome" paragraph, for example, takes up 32K and is barely legible. Plain HTML text would have been a better choice. And each tiny link to each site section takes up 28K. These could have been done in HTML text, or at least could have been much smaller.

8 tricks to designing for speed:

1. Surrender some control.

2. Eliminate the extras.

3. Compress all images and multimedia.

4. Replace images of words with words.

5. Repeat images throughout the site.

6. Mind the details of your HTML.

7. Switch to stylesheets.

8. Follow design conventions.

1. Surrender some control Let me just come out and say it: Most designers are control freaks. We like to make sure everything is exactly the way we want it. Perfect little fonts and perfect little logos and perfect little lives. Well, I hate to be the one to break it to you, but you have to learn to let go. At least when it comes to your web site.

One of the biggest speed eaters on the web is overly controlled design. If you try to control your site's appearance down to the pixel, you've probably wasted a lot of space doing it. You've included images of words when you could have just used text. You've designed buttons when you could have used forms. You've used complex tables embedded within tables when you could have simplified the design.

A better approach is to accept the web for what it is: A flexible medium where speed is key and pages appear differently in different environments. Experienced web designers embrace this challenge and create innovative sites within these constraints.

2. Eliminate the extras Take a long, hard look at everything on your site, especially on the home page. Consider the images, the animation, the scripts, and ask yourself, "Is this essential to the user experience?" If the answer is no, it's got to go.

3. Compress all images and multimedia Image "optimization," as it's called, might well be the most important way to speed up your site. Optimization is the blanket term covering everything you can do to reduce the size of your images—cropping them, redesigning them, compressing them—so they can be easily transferred.

The goal is to produce an image with the best possible appearance and the smallest possible file size. Compression techniques will vary based on the type of image (photos are different from line illustrations), but every image on your site—without exception—should be compressed to improve overall speed. See preparing images & multimedia for the web, p. 202.

4. Replace images of words with words Generally speaking, you want to convey as much of your site's content as possible through plain HTML, using images only where they'll have the most impact.

One of the most obvious signals that a designer hasn't quite transitioned to the web world is an insistence on turning words into images (designed exactly as he wants them to appear), rather than typing them into HTML. Although it might make you feel better to include your particular favorite font, let's face it, it doesn't always make much of an impact on the user. Even if the user does happen to notice that your headlines are in a nice font, and they say to themselves, "Nice font!" it might not justify the trade-off in speed.

There are other reasons to leave text as text and save images for pictures. For one thing, images of text aren't searchable. This affects both the accuracy of your internal site search and your ranking on search sites such as Google. (See <u>improving your search rank</u>, p. 309.)

The other problem is that images of text are unreadable to blind people, whose screen readers can translate HTML text, but have no way of "reading" a picture. (See <u>building for accessibility</u>, p. 182.)

What's wrong with images of text?

1. They're slower than HTML text.

2. They aren't searchable and can't be indexed.

3. They aren't accessible to blind people.

That said, there are times when you might choose to present limited amounts of text within an image; if it helps—really helps—you create the right look and feel for your brand.

But you have to know how to strike the balance between function and form. My personal guideline is that taglines and headlines can sometimes be displayed as images, but anything longer than a sentence should be in HTML.

5. Repeat images throughout the site One easy way to speed up your site, with minimal strife, is to take advantage of the browser cache. All browsers have the built-in ability to cache—or temporarily store—images after they're downloaded.

If a user arrives at your home page, which displays your logo, and then clicks to a second page—which also has your logo—their browser will re-display the same logo, rather than downloading it all over again. This greatly decreases the download time—and hence increases the speed—of the second page.

Note, however, that this technique only works if you use the exact same image, with the exact same name, stored in exactly the same place. You'll need to centrally store your images (a good idea anyway) to take advantage of this technique.

If you use slightly different versions of the same image throughout the site (for example, varying the category name under the logo), you might consider breaking it into two images, keeping one piece consistent (and reusable), while varying the other.

6. Mind the details of your HTML The perceived speed of your site depends not only on how quickly the elements are transferred across the web, but also on how quickly the browser can draw the page. Complicated—or just plain sloppy—HTML can significantly slow down your site.

Here's how: When a browser first accesses a web page, it begins drawing as fast as it can. Using the HTML file as a guide, it creates a layout for the page—flowing in the text and leaving room for the images, which appear after they've downloaded.

But your HTML might not provide enough information for the browser to accurately draw the page. The browser might know, for example, that an image should be included, but has no idea how much room it will take up. So nothing can be drawn until the big, fat image loads.

In some cases, the browser will begin drawing the page and then "realize" it's made a mistake (the image is too large for the space it allotted, for example). The browser will then clear the window and redraw the page, to the dismay and annoyance of the user.

3 most common HTML speed traps:

- Image height and width aren't specified

- Table height and width aren't specified

- Too many tables are nested inside each other

7. Switch to stylesheets   There are a lot of reasons to convert your site to a stylesheet-based design: It can save you a lot of production time; it can make your site compatible with all browsers; it can bring you into compliance with web standards; it can make your site accessible to the blind. And it can also make your site faster. (See understanding stylesheets, p. 162, and why you should follow web standards, p. 186.)

Thanks to a clean structure—no messy tables, no need to repeat and re-repeat style for text—sites designed with stylesheets load much faster than those designed with tables and font tags. The savings in speed and bandwidth can be staggering. Wired News, for example, reduced the size of its pages by half when it converted to stylesheets (even though the design itself became richer). And

ESPN cut 50K off each page when it converted. With 40 million pageviews per day, that amounts to an astounding bandwidth savings of 2 terabytes per day (one terabyte is a million megabytes).

Read more about these redesigns in DevEdge: http://devedge.netscape.com/viewsource/.

8. Follow design conventions   There's more to site speed than fast-loading pages. Your visitors have things to accomplish on your site, and if they can't quickly and intuitively navigate it, their experience will be slow and frustrating.

One way to ensure a quick and easy experience is following the design conventions that have evolved on the web. If you place elements where users expect them to be and structure transactions the way they expect, they'll move through your site more easily and enjoy it more.

"As more and more customers are buying more on the web, they want it to be a faster and faster experience," says Hilary Billings, chairman and chief marketing officer of RedEnvelope, a specialty gift store.

"Customers want to go autopilot," she explained. "They don't want to have to stop and think; they just want to click through really quickly. And it's a lot easier for them if the functional parts of all the major sites are virtually identical. It makes the shopping experience much easier."

See designing for web conventions, p. 84, and improving site speed, p. 218 for more details.

chapter 6

organization & navigation

"Information…Information…"

don't miss …

1 Structuring your site p. 99

2 6 ways to organize your site p. 102

3 Creating site maps & schematics p. 108

4 12 navigation systems p. 114

5 Action section: How will your site be organized? p. 120

6 Why section names should be clear, not clever p. 126

In many ways, web design *is* organization and navigation. Although visual flourishes—such as color, imagery, and style—might get more attention, it's the structure of the site that determines its success.

A well-organized site will lead users effortlessly toward their goals, because its sections correspond with their needs. Its language makes sense to them, and its navigation is consistent and clear. But a poorly organized site (one that was built hastily, or with only the owner's needs in mind) will confuse users, and inadvertently keep them from the information or services they need.

The organization, after all, is the backbone of your site. Like the supporting beams of a house, it provides the structure on which the visual design rests.

> ## It's the structure of a site that determines its success. A well-organized site will lead users effortlessly toward their goals.

Still, many people have trouble separating the two areas of web design. And sites suffer when the two are confused. "You have to separate the functional or structural design from the communication design," says Peter Merholz, a partner with consulting firm Adaptive Path. "People tend to get hung up on the final expression without considering the underlying functional framework."

But the framework is the most important piece. If you haven't organized your site in a way that makes sense to the user, no visual wizardry can make it work for them. "If nothing else, a web site must work before it ought to look good," Merholz said. "It better do what it sets out to do."

Despite its strategic importance, site structure has often taken a backseat to the flashier aspects of design. But its importance is finally being acknowledged.

"I moved from doing content work to doing information architecture because it became more

---

the well-organized site

Site structure might not be the sexiest aspect of web design, but it's the most important. A well organized site makes the user's job easy— as it should be! Three separate elements contribute to a well-organized site.

The well-organized site has

- **A logical structure.** Your site should be organized in a way that makes immediate sense to the user. Site sections should correspond with the user's needs, and similar things (or tasks) should be grouped together. See site organization, p. 98.

- **Consistent navigation.** Users rely heavily on site navigation for orientation (Where am I?), context (What else is here?), and direction (How do I get there?). Your navigation should provide clear pathways that lead users quickly and intuitively to the things they need. See site navigation, p. 110.

- **Clear labels.** The names you choose for site sections go a long way toward helping users find what they need. Don't be clever. Don't be smart. Just be clear. See naming site sections, p. 122.

---

and more clear to me that structure—more than anything else—was the defining element in a web site," says Jesse James Garrett, author of *The Elements of User Experience.* "The key to a successful site is having it be well-structured."

And corporations, as well as consultants, are reaching this conclusion.

"Information architecture has overtaken visual design as the most critical component in web design," said Lance McDaniel, VP of Creative for consulting firm SBI and Company. "The design of the information now outshines the visual design of the site, and gets more credit for its success. Whereas before, it was kind of a red-headed stepchild."

site organization

Although it isn't as exciting as the visual design or as prestigious as the engineering or editorial content, the organization—or information architecture—is often the crucial factor in a site's success.

While information architecture falls under design, it's intimately linked with strategy. You need a clear idea of who the site is for, and what it's supposed to accomplish, if you're going to organize and design it effectively.

You'll need to set goals for the site before you begin the organization process. (See setting goals for a company site, p. 14.) If these decisions aren't made—or aren't communicated to the design team—the vague directives will cascade through the design process to the finished site. A muddled mission will reveal itself to the user through confusing categories or an inconsistent interface.

"Successful site architecture requires the organization to agree on common goals," says Jesse James Garrett. "And if you can't get the organization to agree on those common goals, you're not going to have a successful architecture or site."

Site organization is based on

- **User goals.** The most important thing about a site's organization is that it makes sense to your users and corresponds with their goals when they arrive at your site.

- **Business goals.** Site organization must also address your organizational goals, emphasizing those features or products most important to your success.

- **Classification systems for the content.** The content or services on your site will likely fall into natural categories (or groups of overlapping categories).

Your site organization should be the best possible marriage between these three sometimes-conflicting criteria. Now if your site has only one subject, one business goal, and one kind of user (with only one need), the organizational task will be completely straightforward. But the reality is usually far more complicated.

> **You need a clear idea of who the site is for—and what it's supposed to accomplish—if you're going to organize it effectively.**

Sites usually have several user groups, each of which has different needs at different times, several different types of content—which don't necessarily mesh together neatly—and different goals for the site, depending on who you ask in the company.

"It's challenging to create a nice, neat structure without any gaps in it," Garrett says. "And the challenges tend to come about either when you're serving audiences with really divergent needs or when you have internal corporate strategies that somehow end up working at cross purposes."

"It's nice to paint this idealized picture of the project where the company has one strategy and that one strategy is clearly articulated," he says. "But in fact that's not the case. Companies have lots of different strategies—different ones at different phases in their life cycle."

And there isn't always a lot of agreement on which strategy—or whose—is most important. "More than any other aspect of web development, the information architecture is likely to be the ship that runs aground on the rocky shores of corporate politics," Garrett says. "All the internal battles for resources in an organization—the battles for support for different corporate initiatives, the battles for visibility to the higher-up executives—all of these things end up getting played out in the decisions about site architecture."

structuring your site

Although different sites face different structural challenges, their designers go through similar steps to create an information architecture.

The particular process might vary from person to person and project to project. You might use different tools, try different tactics, and produce different documents, but the essential steps are the same.

4 steps to structuring your site:

1. **Take stock of what you have.** The first step toward organizing a site is figuring out what exactly it will include.

2. **Decide what's most important.** You can't organize (much less design) your site until you know which elements are the most important. What are most users looking for? What do you want them to use?

3. **Choose an organizing principle.** Most sites are structured around one or more organization systems. Some are organized by date, for example. Others by category or the type of user.

4. **Categorize the content.** The final essential step is to actually organize all your content in a way that will make sense to your users.

1. take stock of what you have

The first step toward organizing your site (after you've defined your site goals) is getting your arms around what you're dealing with. What exactly will your site include?

For many sites a simple list summarizing site content will suffice. But some require a full inventory to account for all their existing content.

---

lesson from the trenches

your site shouldn't mirror your company

One of the most common mistakes designers make is to model their web site after their company structure, giving each department a section and front-door link.

It's a "classic error," says Michael Twidale, library and information science professor at the University of Illinois, Urbana-Champaign. "It's fine if you're producing a corporate intranet, because you can assume everyone knows what the organization hierarchy is. But if it's a public web page, you've got a problem."

"If your site becomes a territorial map to your company, that's not going to give you the results you want."

–Wendy Owen

The problem is that your internal structure is irrelevant to your users. Their goals rarely map on to your org chart, and your department names will likely confuse them. It can be hard to explain this to co-workers who want a prominent place on the site.

"We have to acknowledge that there's a lot of internal politics in web design," Twidale says. "Everyone naturally believes the job they do is crucial to the organization. That means you think your department should be on the front page. You want to be on the top of the front page!"

You'll have to educate your co-workers if you're going to produce a successful site. "You shouldn't structure your site like your org chart," says designer Wendy Owen. "If your site becomes a territorial map of your company, that's not going to get the results you want."

2 ways to take stock:

1. **Make an outline.** A basic outline covering the types of content or services that will appear on your site is often all you need when you're launching a new site, especially if it's relatively small in scale.

2. **Take a content inventory.** If you're redesigning an existing site, or launching one that's large in scale, you'll want to list, in painstaking detail, every single piece of content (articles, product listings, images) available for the site. These are the lists you'll work from as you begin categorizing and organizing the content.

2. decide what's most important

As you organize your site—and before you arrive at a final structure—it's important to decide which elements in your site are the most important. What will most users be looking for? What does your financial success depend on?

"One of the biggest mistakes I see on sites is a lack of clear hierarchy," says Wendy Owen, a principal with Giant Ant Design. "Making clear decisions about what's most important really helps the user understand the experience."

But many organizations find it easier to duck these decisions. They prioritize what the boss wants to prioritize, or—perhaps worse—give everything on the site equal weight.

"Too many sites shirk their obligation to organize materials based on user needs," says designer Jeffrey Zeldman (www.zeldman.com). "When committees (instead of user needs) drive the architecture, we get sites that give us one-click access to everything instead of guiding us through a carefully planned experience."

"One-click access to everything sounds good, but is bad because it overwhelms the visitor," he explains. "If you visit a New York diner with a 25-page menu, you'll end up ordering coffee and eggs because you just can't cope with the endless array of choices."

This is one thing on a menu, but quite another on the web. "People have to eat, but they don't have to linger at your web site," Zeldman says. "If you overwhelm them with too many choices, they'll go elsewhere."

You should remember, too, that not all visitors are equal. "There are usually different people in the audience, but every user group doesn't deserve the same importance," Owen says. "For instance, if you're selling shampoo on your site, and that's 90% of your business, then you're going to focus on your shampoo users. You're not going to give equal play to your razor blades, which account for only 5% of your business."

3. choose an organizing principle

As you organize your site, you'll need to choose an organizing principle around which the site will be structured. Stores, for example, are usually organized by product category, and online diaries are usually organized by the date of the entry.

Although each site presents a unique structural challenge, most can be organized one of six ways: by category, by task, by user, by language or location, by date, or by corporate department (which isn't recommended). (See 6 ways to organize your site, p. 102.)

4. categorize the content

The final organizational step is the most important. You have to break up the site's content into meaningful categories or sections.

In some ways it's a simple process. All you do is arrange things into logical groups—similar things go together, dissimilar things don't. But the actual process isn't so easy. You have to consider user needs, business needs, and classification systems inherent in the content itself. There are many ways to approach the problem, and there's often more than one viable solution.

It's a task both satisfying and frustrating, because an elegant solution will often seem obvious once crafted. But there are many paths to the elegant solution, and each designer has to find the right one for herself. (See how to create the information architecture, p. 101.)

lesson from the trenches

how to create the information architecture

It's not hard to understand what an information architect does: They organize a site's content in a way that makes sense, giving the site a meaningful structure. But it's a little harder to picture how they do it.

"When you hear people talk about information architecture methodology, they'll talk about every part of it except for the part where they actually construct the architecture," laughs Jesse James Garrett, a prominent information architect and author of *The Elements of User Experience*.

"They'll talk about all the research, and all the thinking, and all the planning that happens up until the point that they create the architecture. Then they might talk about all of the things they do to validate the architecture after it's been built. But the actual creation of the architecture is kind of a mystery to us."

The mystery lies in the brain's ability to sift through information until it falls into a neat structure. There are a lot of different ways to facilitate this process, and different techniques seem to work for different people.

But most of the time you'll start with an outline that lists all the content on your site. Then you'll rearrange the outline, trying different organization schemes and different groupings, until a workable solution reveals itself.

"My process typically will involve making lists," Garrett says. "I'll make lists. Sometimes I'll make outlines on the computer, sometimes I'll doodle on my white board."

His preferred method makes use of unused business cards. "I'll take a stack of my business cards, flip them over, and write the names of elements on the back. Then I sort of slide them around on a table and get a feel for how they're fitting together."

This exercise helps him picture the natural groupings, or recognize when certain things need to be clustered more closely together. The physicality of it appeals to him: "That exercise—pushing business cards around on the table—has been really good," he said. "There's something about working in a tactile fashion that engages the brain, in a kindergarten activity hour kind of way."

It's also not a bad way to get rid of excess business cards. "If they came in boxes smaller than 500, I'd have to come up with some other way to do it," he laughs.

> **"At some point, you almost feel a gravitational pull toward a certain solution."**
>
> *- Jesse James Garrett*

Like most information architects, Garrett says he works through a number of possible directions, before the best solution reveals itself.

"I'll usually toy around with a few different ideas before settling on a particular architectural approach," he says. And the determining factors always come back to site strategy: What does the business need the site to accomplish? What do the users want to get out of the site?

"There's a sort of co-evolution kind of process," he says. "I'm usually working on both levels at once. As I'm working through the content, and pushing those business cards around, part of my brain is thinking about the content and part of my brain is working out the strategic issues at the same time."

"At some point, you almost feel a gravitational pull toward a certain solution. Then you know that the conceptual model is starting to come together, and the content elements just start falling into place."

6 ways to organize your site

1. by category

Use this when all your visitors have the same basic task in mind—whether that task is to research a topic, buy a product, or discuss an issue.

Category-divided sites are probably the most common on the web today. These systems divide a site by the topics or categories of information they offer. Content sites, for instance, might be divided by the types of articles they offer, commerce sites by the type of product, and community sites by the discussion topic.

2. by task

Use this when your site allows users to accomplish several distinct tasks which may or may not be related to each other.

Task-organized sites attempt to identify the various goals a user might have in mind, and point the user speedily in the direction of accomplishing them. One reason this works well is that it correlates with the mentality of web users, who are usually focused on what they can do next.

Nerve.com organizes its personals site according to the different things users can do to find their perfect match.

BlackPlanet
Forums give users a place to discuss issues and interests. Because everyone is there for the same basic purpose, the forums are organized by topic.

3. by user

Use this when your site serves two or more distinct groups of users with different (though often related) goals and interests.

User-organized sites group together tasks and topics that are of interest to a specific type of person, and they funnel users into the appropriate area. This organization system works well for matchmaking sites, which bring together "buyers" and "sellers" (or employers and job-seekers, as the case might be).

User-based systems are also effective on content, commerce, and corporate sites that focus on different types of customers. Babycenter, for example, divides its site by pregnancy stage and baby age; National Geographic has special areas for kids, parents, and teachers; the clothing company Levi's sorts users by country; and the furniture company Herman Miller has distinct site areas for customers, designers, and investors.

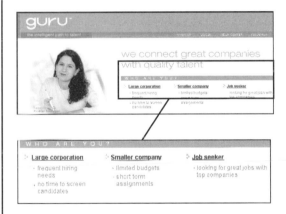

Guru matches companies with consultants, and vice versa. So the site is organized by user—funneling employers and job seekers in different directions to get specialized services intended for them.

4. by language or location

Use this when your visitors speak different languages or live in different geographic regions requiring different content or services.

Many sites are organized by language or location, to meet the needs of a far-flung, or linguistically diverse user base. However, this is less an organization system and more a way of funneling users into different sites, each of which will then be organized by different criteria that are appropriate to the content.

Levi's funnels different users to different sites, based on their geographic region. Each site offers content based on the language, culture, and available products in the region.

The Guggenheim Museum in Berlin welcomes users in English or German ("Welcome" vs. "Wilkommen").

continues

6 ways to organize your site (continued)

5. by date or order

Use this if either the date or order of elements is essential to user understanding—as in timelines, journals, event calendars, or step-by-step instructions.

Generally speaking, web sites are less dependent on dates than other media. Print publications rely on dates, because they publish discrete, complete issues that correspond with a publication date. Most web sites are more fluid, updated without ceremony multiple times per day or a few time each year.

There are exceptions, however. Web logs (called "blogs" for short) are online journals that are organized by date, beginning with the most recent entry and going back through time. And other types of sites—timelines, event calendars, etc.—are obviously well-served by a date-dependent structure.

Zeldman.com is the personal site of designer Jeffrey Zeldman. Like all blogs, it's organized by date, with the most recent entry appearing first.

6. by corporate department

Use this only when you're designing an intranet, when your departmental structure is relevant to your audience (as in a university site), or when the company's political climate leaves you *absolutely no other choice*.

One of the most common—and understandable—mistakes designers make is to model their web sites after company structure, giving each department a section and front-door link. This solution serves a political purpose within the company, but it doesn't serve the user.

The problem with this approach is that your internal structure is irrelevant to your users. Their needs rarely map on to your internal hierarchy. Let's say, for example, that you visit the site for your local art museum, because you read about an upcoming lecture on Picasso, and you want to find out when it is. Would that lecture be listed under "Education," "Events," or "Programs?" Hard to say. Unless, of course, you work in the museum, and then you'd know that the modern art lecture series is organized by Marilyn in the Programs department.

See your site shouldn't mirror your company, p. 99.

Like most schools, **Brown University** organizes its site by department, with different site sections for the admissions office, the athletic department, the Alumni Association, and so on.

creating fun categories

A site's organization should be intuitive, but it needn't be boring. Sites—stores especially—that sort their wares into creative categories serve a real user need: They help people find things they didn't know they wanted. And let them have fun in the process.

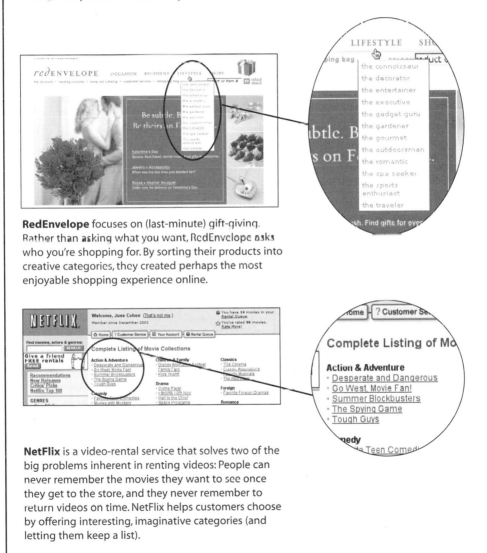

RedEnvelope focuses on (last-minute) gift-giving. Rather than asking what you want, RedEnvelope asks who you're shopping for. By sorting their products into creative categories, they created perhaps the most enjoyable shopping experience online.

NetFlix is a video-rental service that solves two of the big problems inherent in renting videos: People can never remember the movies they want to see once they get to the store, and they never remember to return videos on time. NetFlix helps customers choose by offering interesting, imaginative categories (and letting them keep a list).

combined organization systems

Only rarely can an entire site be structured using a single organization system. Usually, sites need several systems—presented simultaneously or in sequence—to categorize all its content and guide its users toward what they need.

The Guggenheim Museum has several branches in different cities, each of which has different exhibits and serves different local and international audiences.

1. Front door organized by location.

The front door of guggenheim.org sorts users by which museum location they're interested in. (Mousing over each image reveals the city in which the distinctive building is located).

2. Local site organized by language.

The front door of each individual Guggenheim site (including the collection in Venice, pictured) initially sorts users based on language—in this case, English or Italiano.

3. Local site organized by department.

The front door of the New York Guggenheim offers six sections (organized roughly by department) which are repeated throughout the site on a page-top nav bar. Departmental organization is rarely ideal, but it works, in this case, because the departments correspond with user tasks.

4. Site section organized by category.

When users enter "The Collection," they're presented with six different ways to view the artwork.

The Guggenheim Museum uses different organization systems **sequentially** to move users toward the information they need.

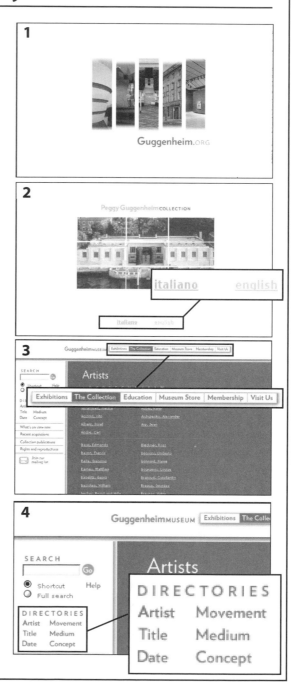

Herman Miller is a furniture company, known for both its sleek office systems (including the Aeron chair, pictured) and classic home furnishings by well-known designers, like Eames.

1. By product category.

Most of Herman Miller's front door is dedicated to their products. They organize their furniture into two main categories (Work Environments and Modern Classics) and offer entry points for both.

2. By task.

The front door also offers quick links for other tasks (aside from looking at the furniture): reading about Herman Miller, looking for jobs, and so on.

3. By user.

The front door is designed primarily for customers, so it offers other clear entry points for users in other categories (designers, investors).

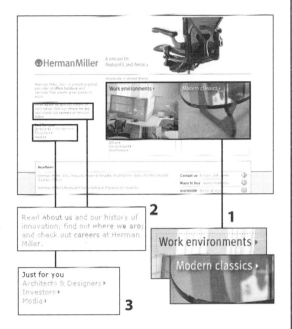

Hewlett Packard is a technology company, known for its printers, computers, and other high-tech products.

1. By user.

Visitors can identify themselves by the kind of company or office they're buying products for (home & home office, small & medium business, enterprise, etc.).

2. By product category.

Users can also choose the particular product they're looking for (printers, PCs, handheld devices, etc.).

3. By task.

The front door also offers quick links to other tasks, such as reading about HP or looking for jobs there.

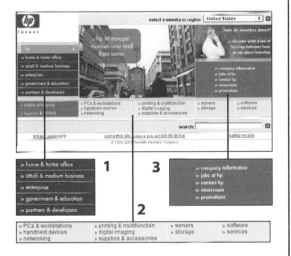

documenting site structure

Once you've made decisions about the structure of your site, you'll need to document your ideas and decisions in a way that others can understand.

Several forms of documentation have evolved to help web teams visualize site structure, communicate organizational decisions, and track changes as a site evolves. These visual tools include the site map, the page schematic, and the user path. They're often used together, to represent different aspects of the site structure and user experience.

3 ways to visualize site structure:

1. The **site map** provides a bird's eye view of the site, showing how site sections are organized and how they fit together.

2. The **user path** shows the screen-by-screen experience of users as they move through your site or accomplish a given task.

3. The **schematic** shows all the elements that will appear on a given page and how they relate to each other.

1. the site map

Also called a flow chart, the site map shows the organization of site sections and how they fit together.

Each box represents a page on the site, beginning with the front door. A stack of boxes usually represents a set of pages with the same design and similar content (like those in a searchable database). It may also represent a site section that's described on another map.

Each line represents a connection between pages—or a path that users may follow. As such, each line or group of lines presents a navigation challenge.

The site map is usually created by the information architect—or whoever's organizing the site—after they've arrived at an organizational structure, but before a navigation system's been designed.

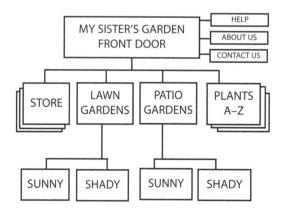

2. the user path

Also called a user flow or a flow chart, the user path outlines the screen-by-screen experience of the user as they make their way through your site or accomplish a specific task.

Each box represents a screen that users see as they move through an experience.

Each line represents a path users could follow. The purpose of the user path is to make sure all possible paths are anticipated, including those taken in error.

Each diamond represents a decision point. The lines that extend from the diamond represent each possible user path

The user path is most important in application- or transaction-based sites, when a user is registering for a service, buying a product, or using a tool on your site. But it can also be helpful to picture—and improve—the user experience on any site.

3. the page schematic

Also called a wireframe or storyboard, the schematic shows all the elements that will appear on the page, and roughly where they'll appear.

Each box represents an element on the page (an image, a nav bar, a headline) without specifying about how it will look.

A schematic is usually produced for each type of page—or each template—on the site before visual design gets underway. However, the level of detail may vary. Some are produced in great detail, showing precise page placement. Others take a rougher cut, showing only the basic elements and suggestions on relative placement.

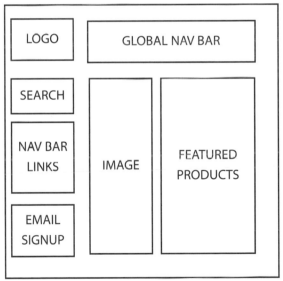

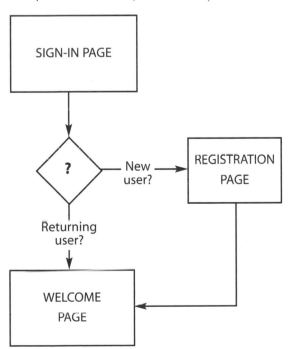

site navigation

In many ways, good web design is good navigation. When we say that a site is well-designed, or that it works well, what we usually mean is that it has excellent, intuitive navigation.

Navigation is the visual expression of a site's structure, and it's the basic problem that must be solved, in the course of designing a site. It's no small problem. Unlike magazines, or stores, or products in the physical world, web sites are abstract: The user has no way of *intuitively* sensing the scope of your site or where they are within it. (See how people navigate the web, p. 111.)

Your navigation must provide all these clues. It has to tell users what you offer, orient them to where they are, and point them toward their next destination—all simultaneously.

What users learn from your navigation:

- **What your site offers.** By scanning your navigation bar (or whatever system you use), visitors get a sense for what your site contains.

- **How your site is organized.** Many users look to navigation to get a handle on how the site is structured. This way, they can create a context for where they are on your site, and navigate more confidently.

- **Where they are within your site.** On the web—as in the physical world—a good navigation system will always point out where the user is. (Think of a map with a big red X saying "You are here.")

- **How to find what they're looking for.** This is the essential task of site navigation: To get users where they're trying to go—as quickly and efficiently as possible.

When designing navigation, it's tempting to assume you have a loyal audience who'll learn about your site over time. But an honest look at

---

8 bad ideas for site navigation

There are a lot of different ways to let users navigate your site. Some are better than others, but none are worse than these. I know, because I've tried them. All of them. Even the flying, floating things.

1. **Pull-down menus**, which conceal your site's sections instead of revealing them.

2. **Home-made icons**, which users will not come to recognize, no matter how hard you try to make them.

3. **Color coding**, which no one will even notice, much less attach meaning to.

4. **Visual metaphors** like a picture of an office or sales desk that users can click around. They'll find it quaint, at best.

5. **Cute, clever names** for sections that your users won't visit (because they don't understand them).

6. **Navigation elements that move around** and appear in different places on different pages. Repeat after me: "I will not disorient my user. I will not disorient my user."

7. **Navigation elements in unexpected places.** Surprises have a time and place. Your site's navigation is not it.

8. **Flying, floating things** that the user has to grab as they zoom around the screen. Your navigation should not be a game, unless your entire site is a game. And even then, your navigation should not be a game.

---

your log files will likely show otherwise. "You should design your interface for the first time someone uses it," says Cate Corcoran, former Director of Online Communications for PeoplePC. "Also, design all of the pages so they can be useful standing alone. Not everyone will come in through the front door of your site."

how people navigate the web

In order to design effectively for the web, you have to first understand how people behave when they're online. For the web is fundamentally different from print, TV, or other media to which it's often compared.

People use different media differently:

▦ **People read magazines.**

▦ **People watch television.**

▦ **But people navigate the web as if it were a physical space.**

Although the computer screen is physically flat—more one-dimensional than a book, even—people move through the web as if it were a physical space. They scan each page for navigational cues, then move forward mentally, closing in on their destination. "Where should I go?" they think, instead of "What should I read?"

This is no small difference. The transition from reading a magazine, for example, to using the web requires a cognitive shift: When a person stares into a monitor, the cursor on the screen (controlled by the mouse in her hand) becomes an extension of her physical body. So the task of navigating the web feels very much the same, mentally, as navigating a physical space.

This is exactly what Marshall McLuhan might have predicted. In the early years of television, McLuhan published influential theories on how people interact with—and are shaped by—media. "All media are extensions of some human faculty—psychic or physical," he wrote in The *Medium is the Message*. "The wheel is an extension of the foot. The book is an extension of the eye…clothing an extension of the skin…electric circuitry, an extension of the central nervous system."

If users do project themselves into the screen (the cursor becoming an abstract representation of the body), this goes a long way toward explaining not only how people feel online, but also how they act. Most people navigate web sites as if they were running through an airport, looking for their gate: Quickly, purposefully, and sometimes desperately.

designing for users on the run

Theory aside, the spatial nature of the web is what makes navigation so important. In many ways, designing a web site is more like designing a public space than a printed page.

Users arrive at your site with a purpose in mind, and your goal in designing the site is to get them to their destination as quickly as possible, providing the most direct pathways marked by the most universally recognized symbols.

Most people navigate web sites as if they were running through an airport, looking for their gate.

So web design is an architectural problem, as much as a visual one. And as architectural problems go, it's a challenging one, because people can't rely on any of the visual clues—or other senses—they use to navigate real-world spaces.

In the real world, people can size things up more easily: They can see how big a building is, and they can see who else is there. They can tell how noisy it is, and what it smells like. They can see where the doors are. And if they get lost, they can always retrace their steps or ask someone for help.

But the web is abstract, and it offers no such clues. Your senses are limited to what you can see in the browser. And there's no one around to help you if you get lost. So it falls to the site's design—and particularly the navigation—to fill all these roles. It must communicate what kind of site it is, tell users what's there, orient them to where they are, point them to where they're going, and show them how to get back.

No one said it was going to be easy.

global and local navigation

Most sites face complex navigation issues that have to be solved in layers. The overall organization of the site poses different problems than the functionality of an individual site area. So all but the smallest and simplest of sites will grapple with issues of global and local navigation.

3 types of navigation:

- **Global navigation** shows users where they are within the site and how to get somewhere else. It should remain consistent throughout the site.

- **Local navigation** picks up where global navigation leaves off, giving users tools to move around—or accomplish tasks within—a specific site section.

- **Network navigation** displays links to other sites within a larger network.

global navigation   Also called sitewide or persistent navigation, global navigation helps users navigate the site to find the areas of interest to them. So global navigation tends to concern itself with hierarchies of information or broad categories. Global navigation usually appears in the same way and at the same place on every page, listing the same items. Though it should offer some visual clue about which section the user's in.

local navigation   Once the user arrives at their "destination" within the site, local navigation takes over. It usually tackles the functionality issues in a specific application, the classification issues within a particular topic, or the page-turning functions within an article.

Global, local, and network navigation are all used within his page on **Webmonkey**. (1) T**he network navigation bar** (sometimes called a "branding bar") leads to Webmonkey's corporate parent, Terra-Lycos. (2) **The global navigation bar** leads back to the Webmonkey front door and offers a pull-down menu of site features (not pictured). **Global navigation** is also offered through (3) **breadcrumbs**, which show you where you are on the site. (4) **Local navigation**—to other pages in the article—is accomplished through links down the left hand side.

network navigation   More political than practical, network navigation brings in a layer of navigation that's often irrelevant to the user but important to the business. Sites that are part of a network—or are owned by a corporate parent that controls other sites—are often required to link to the other sites.

balancing layers of navigation

It can be hard to decide how much navigation should go on any individual page: Too much and you run the risk of obscuring your subject matter by literally squeezing it off the page. Too little and users may lose track of where they are.

The balance between global and local navigation is struck differently on different sites. On directories, for example, there's very little local navigation. The rigid global navigation often extends into local areas. Games and art exhibits are at the other end of the spectrum, with almost no global navigation—except a button to return to the front door.

why pull-down menus are not for navigation

Because they neatly conceal a lot of information in a small space, and because they're widely understood, pull-down menus are a popular choice for navigation systems. Unfortunately, they don't work very well.

"I've learned that you should never use pull-down menus for anything other than filling in forms," says Peter Merholz, a partner with Adaptive Path. "They should not be used as navigation elements."

"Pull-down menus are a highly effective way of burying information that you want your users to see."

—*Peter Merholz*

The problem is that pull-down menus conceal information. And unless the user can reliably predict what's being concealed—as in a list of countries or months of the year—they won't know what's in the menu, and they won't bother to look.

"People won't have a clue about it," Merholz says. "They'll just ignore it. Pull-downs are a highly effective way of burying information that you want your user to see."

Martha Brockenbrough, former managing editor of MSN.com, couldn't agree more. MSN tried using pull-down menus, but found them ineffective. At the time, the site attracted around six million users per day to its front door. "But only 200 discovered the goodies that were lying, neglected at the bottom of the pull-down menus," Brockenbrough said.

"No one will find your content in a drop-down menu," Brockenbrough says emphatically. "No one can see what's in them. Don't use them. I guarantee you they will not work. They're not your friend."

creating a navigation system

There are many different ways to design a navigation system—tabs, bars, menus, icons, image maps, simple lists—and the solution for your site depends, of course, on the problems you need to solve.

In most cases, you can draw from existing navigation conventions and customize or combine them to meet your needs. A handful of navigation systems are serviceable to the vast majority of sites. (See 12 navigation systems, p. 114.)

There may, however, be times when you're tempted to design your own system. But remember: Innovation always has a price. Non-standard systems are harder to design and harder for visitors to use. In most cases—and especially if you're not a trained designer—you'll be well served by the established navigational systems.

Remember: Innovation always has a price. Non-standard systems are harder to design, and harder for visitors to use.

"There's a reason left-hand navigation is a convention," says designer Jim Frew. "A lot of people use it. A lot of people understand it. It works. A lot of other, non-conventional interfaces can work equally well. But it takes a lot more diligence to make them work. More work, more skill, and more babysitting on the back-end."

If you decide to design a custom navigation system, it's still helpful to reference conventional systems—so your users will have a head start toward understanding yours. (See why you should follow web standards, p. 186.)

Whatever you do, don't design a system that people have to "learn"; if a navigation system isn't intuitive, it simply won't be used. "Your job as an interface designer is not to teach people anything," said Cate Corcoran. "They're not there to learn how to use your site."

12 navigation systems

1. tabs

Use this when your site is organized into categories—especially product categories.

Used most famously by Amazon.com, tabs create a visual reference to folders, allowing users to understand conceptually that they're within one of several parallel areas on the site. When a user clicks on a tab—say, the one that says "Music"—the corresponding folder moves to the front and the contents of that conceptual "folder" are revealed.

This visual metaphor was first used by Apple Computer on the Mac interface (which made liberal use of the file-and-folder metaphor), and it's widely used in software today. It's also widely used—and misused—on the web. Tabs work best when you have a series of distinct, but parallel, categories on a web site. This is why it's so effective on commerce sites: It's an excellent way to organize different product categories, while revealing the breadth of your offerings. However, tabs are awkward when they become a catch-all for unrelated site sections.

Amazon's tab-based navigation system has been widely imitated across the web, on stores as well as other types of sites.

2. left-hand panel

Use this as global or local navigation for almost any kind of site.

Used first—or at least most famously—by CNet, the left-hand navigation panel quickly became a staple, if not an uncontested convention, on the web. The reason it took off is because it neatly solves a wide range of navigation issues, and because it scales: As your site expands or its navigation needs change, you can easily add more links or buttons to a left-hand panel (extending the navigation further down the page).

The left-hand panel provides a simple, flexible, persistent source of navigation throughout a web site. It can explain the site structure, reveal sections that may have been overlooked, provide a permanent placement for sitewide functionality (such as a search box), and also set aside real estate for small ads.

CNN.com uses the left-hand panel to list other content areas, while the travel site **Expedia** uses it for search tools.

3. page-top nav bar

Use this as global navigation for almost any kind of site.

Nearly every web site makes some use of the page top for navigation. For some it's the primary navigational tool; for others it serves as either global or local navigation, leaving the other to be handled elsewhere on the page. Still others use this space for branding: a chance to simply identify the site while providing a nominal link back to the front door.

The gardening store **Burpees** uses prominent page-top navigation to make its purpose—and its product categories—clear.

4. breadcrumbs

Use this when your site contains a lot of hierarchical information, which users access by following a conceptual path deeper and deeper into the site.

Breadcrumbs give visitors a visual representation of where they are in the site and allow them not only to return to the front door (which you could do with a Home button), but also to partially retrace their steps and follow a different branch of the path.

The breadcrumbs offer users a list of links—separated by colons or slashes—that indicate the hierarchical levels they passed on their journey to the current page. A click will bring them back to any level.

Breadcrumbs are a staple on directory sites, such as Yahoo!, that offer access to deep, overlapping hierarchies of information. But other sites use this method as well: deep content sites like CNet, matchmaking sites like eBay, and commerce sites like Amazon all make use of this homing mechanism to provide the users with context.

Oh, and in case you haven't guessed, the term "breadcrumbs" is a clever little reference to the fairy tale *Hansel and Gretel*—two children who wander into the woods, leaving a trail of breadcrumbs to follow home. Of course, in the story, the breadcrumbs are eaten by birds, leaving H & G to fend for themselves in the witch-filled woods. Come to think of it, that's how a lot of web users feel.

> **Yahoo! Directory**
>
> Home > Recreation > Travel > By Region > Countries > **Thailand**

Yahoo! uses breadcrumbs to navigate its extensive collection of site listings.

continues

12 navigation systems (continued)

5. folders & files

Use this when your site includes several categories of information and each has subcategories that are relevant to the user (but don't all fit on the screen simultaneously).

The folder and file metaphor so widely used on computers today was invented at Xerox Parc in the '70s and first used on the Apple operating system. It's occasionally used on web sites, but technical difficulties have prevented it from becoming more widespread.

This approach works best when folders can be quickly "opened" and "closed" with the click of a mouse. But on the web this requires the use of add-on technologies, such as JavaScript or Flash. The growing prevalence and increasing reliability of these technologies makes files and folders an options for more and more sites.

Webmonkey uses folders to conceal—and then reveal—the contents of each section within its library.

6. hub & spokes

Use this when you have several sections that need to link back to the home page, but not to each other.

This is perhaps the simplest of web navigation methods, but it isn't very robust. It generally relies on a link that says "Home" or a logo/icon that represents the front door. On it's own, it only works for small, simple sites. And in most cases, these sites would be better served by a global nav bar that lets users click around. Why force them to go back through the home page?

Where this system is most useful is for sites that have rich, immersive experiences—like games or art exhibits—where you want to fill the screen and create an environment. In this case, you may want to minimize distractions or superfluous elements, such as a navigation bar. So the scaled-back system fits the bill.

The story-telling site **Fray** uses minimal navigation once a user begins reading a story. At the end of the story, you're offered a single link back to the front door of a section (in this case, "Criminal").

7. linear path

Use this when you have a narrative story to tell—or a transaction to complete—which relies on a sequenced order of events.

This system is typically used for local, not global, navigation. When a user is reading a story, or taking a quiz, or making a purchase, it's important for him to see things in a particular order. Questions must be answered in sequence, or a story must unfold in a logical order. In these cases, you'll want to offer very simple navigational controls, offering arrows forward and back, and perhaps that's it.

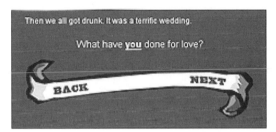

The story-telling site **Fray** lets users focus when they're within a story by offering stripped down, linear navigation from start to finish. Whimsical images often replace the usual arrows.

8. multi-page path

Use this when you have long articles—or a lot of search results—broken up into multiple pages, and you want to let users click around among them.

The multi-page approach was popularized first on search engines and is now widely used on both commerce and content sites to represent pages of options to the user. This system typically works two ways: Users can either click the Forward/Back buttons (or Next/Previous links) to move one page in either direction, or they can click on the number of a particular page and go straight there. It's effective for both showing the scope of the material (how many pages) and showing where the user is within it.

Gooooooooogle ▶
Result Page: 1 2 3 4 5 6 7 8 9 10   Next

Google (like all search engines) divides search results into multiple pages and lets users click through them—either by clicking "Next" or clicking on the individual number (or, in the case of Google, clicking on one of the "O"s in the Google logo). Content sites take a similar approach to long articles. They're often broken up into pages that users can click through.

continues

12 navigation systems (continued)

9. pull-down menus

Use this only when the content of the pull-down menu is completely obvious, as in a list of countries, months, or years.

Usually used as a component of a navigation system, rather than a system itself, the pull-down menu offer users a quick, space-efficient way of choosing between parallel—and mutually exclusive—items.

Because pull-down menus conceal information, they're best used to present a list that would be obvious to users, such as states, countries, months, or years. They're less effective—indeed, ineffective—when they contain non-obvious choices, such as site sections. (See <u>why pull-down menus are not for navigation</u>, p. 113.)

The **BBC** is very skilled at using risky navigation elements well. These pull-down menus work because users can easily predict what's inside them. The top menu is clearly labeled "Country profiles" and the item that appears— "Algeria"—is clearly a country. The lower menu is also clearly labeled, "Middle East Weather." But the first alphabetical city, Abu Dhabir, is a bit obscure. So they start the menu with an instruction, "Choose a city," which makes it clear what will be inside (Beirut, Cairo, and so on).

10 . the search box

Use this when you have a site of any size with content some users may want to search.

There are two kinds of web users: browsers and searchers. Browsers like to move around a site's organization system, getting a feel for how things are organized and navigating to the thing they're looking for through a series of links. They like context. Searchers, on the other hand, go straight for the search box. They like a direct route.

Just about every site will have both browsers and searchers in the audience, so you should, of course, make sure your site search works. And simply adding search isn't enough. You should have a search feature that lets you customize specific results—so you can learn the top 50 things your users search for and make sure you're providing good meaningful search results for them. (While you're at it, you can make sure it's easy to browse to the same items.)

L.L. Bean lets you jump directly to the product you want using the search box. They also do an excellent job customizing search results.

11. image maps

Use this when your site's organization corresponds with an obvious and literal image—a geographic map, for example.

Image maps are often terribly misused, but they work well when the site's subject matter maps easily and intuitively on to a visual image. Geographical references are an obvious fit, and others—product diagrams, medical diagrams, etc.—can also work.

Lonely Planet offers travel guides covering the entire globe. Users can choose their destination by clicking on a region (or by using the pull-down menus or search box).

12. lists of links

Use this when you have a short list of loosely related items or a long list of closely related items on your site.

Listen, there's nothing wrong with keeping it simple. And a list of links is about as simple as you can get. They reveal the exact contents of a site and its sections by…um…listing them. Lists may run across the top of the page, in a column down the page, in chunks across the front door, or anywhere they fit.

Most sites use lists of links somewhere within their navigation systems, to show—in the simplest way possible—what's available and where the users can go. And don't be surprised if your users love them. On Fogdog Sports (shown below), they've always been the most popular way to navigate the site.

A simple list of links has proven the most popular and easy method for customers to find what they need on **Fogdog Sports**.

how will your site be organized?

Your site's organization is in many ways its backbone. The rest of the site will be built on top of it. So the way you organize your site will dictate a great deal about how—and whether—it will be used.

site organization

How is your site organized?

❏ By category:
_____
_____

❏ By task:
_____
_____

❏ By user:
_____
_____

❏ By language or location:
_____
_____

❏ By date or order:
_____
_____

❏ By corporate department:
_____
_____

What is the secondary organization?

What are the most important things on your site?

1. _____

2. _____

3. _____

site organization

Draw your site map below:

Draw a schematic of your front door, showing how the elements will fit together:

action section

how will your site be navigated?

Your navigation is the visual expression of your site structure. It will explain your site to visitors and help guide them as they make their way through your site organization.

navigation systems

What kind of global navigation system will you have?

❑ Left-hand panel   ❑ Page-top nav bar

❑ Tabs   ❑ Breadcrumbs

❑ Folders & files   ❑ Hub & spokes

❑ Linear path   ❑ Multi-page path

❑ Pull-down menus   ❑ Search box

❑ Image map   ❑ List of links

❑ Other: _____

What kind of local navigation will you use?

❑ Left-hand panel   ❑ Page-top nav bar

❑ Tabs   ❑ Breadcrumbs

❑ Folders & files   ❑ Hub & spokes

❑ Linear path   ❑ Multi-page path

❑ Pull-down menus   ❑ Search box

❑ Image map   ❑ List of links

❑ Other: _____

Where on the page will your navigation appear?

1. Front door

2. Inside page

naming site sections

The question of names may strike you as trivial at first: A simple, superfluous detail to be tacked on at the end. Would that it were so! In fact, names are crucial to user understanding of what the site does and how it works.

Well-chosen names are invisible; they quietly point users in the right direction without calling attention to themselves. Whereas poorly chosen names slow users down, confusing them and undermining their confidence.

"Labeling is an important part of information architecture," says Steve Mulder, manager of User Experience for Terra-Lycos. "We've seen this in the usability lab. We've seen very simple naming issues completely prevent users from completing a task."

Section names should be

- **Short.** You don't have a lot of room to get your point across. So names should be short and to the point.

- **Consistent.** Section names should all use similar phrasing to show their relationship to each other.

- **Clear.** The more descriptive and literal your section names are, the more likely users are to click on them.

- **Jargon-free.** Customers don' t understand the specialized lingo of your industry. So you'll have to translate labels into a language they understand.

choose short names   Space is always at a premium online. You have a lot to convey, and not a lot of room in which to convey it. The width of the screen will always limit the width of your words. So pick the shortest, most accurate words(s) you can.

> "You must call each thing by its proper name, or that which must get done will not."
> —*A. Harvey Block, President, Bokenon Systems*

choose consistent names   When you're labeling several sections that will appear together on a nav bar, the names should be as consistent as possible. Ideally, the names or phrases should agree on the number of words, part of speech, verb tense, capitalization, language, and so on.

The issue here isn't grammar, but comprehension. Users will understand categories (and your site as a whole) more quickly if the names agree with each other. Humans are natural-born categorizers; if they perceive a parallel between sections, they'll immediately bundle them together, allowing their understanding of each new category to build on the knowledge of the previous category. But seemingly small inconsistencies will trip them up, making them re-sort the words in their mind.

> **The issue isn't grammar, but comprehension. Users understand categories more quickly when the names are consistent.**

Often, subtle changes in language can make significant improvements in user comprehension. (And this is an area where even split-second differences can impact a user's impression.) For instance, if you have areas on your site for both buying homes and buying cars, you should avoid mismatched names, like "Buy a Home" and "Cars." Instead, choose a single scheme: either "Buy a Home" and "Buy a Car" or "Homes" and "Cars." (See choosing consistent names, p. 124.)

choose clear names   The most important thing about the labels on your site is that they accurately represent the section's function or contents. In other words, you should call things what they are. Sounds pretty basic, but this very simple rule is violated on four out of five sites. Why? Because people like to name things, and people like to be clever. So instead of calling our news section, "News," we name it "Currents" or "Talk of the Town."

Rather than tickle your user's tongue with alliterations and puns, focus on choosing labels that are short, simple, and specific. (See <u>why section names should be clear, not clever</u>, p. 126.)

choosing jargon-free names Every industry and every company has its own lingo—a specialized way of talking about its products and the world that make perfect sense to them and none to anyone else. There's nothing inherently wrong with jargon. But you have to keep it off your web site—that is, if you want anyone to understand it.

"Jargon is rampant inside companies," says Jesse James Garrett, an information architect who's consulted for companies large and small. "All kinds of companies have their own special language for products and features. There's the language they use internally, and there's the language they impose on external communications for marketing reasons."

Jargon often creeps on to web sites, because people are used to describing products in their own industry terms. Often, they don't even realize they're using jargon.

"One of the hardest transitions for people to make in any given business is from the mind of the seller to the mind of the buyer, and from the language of the seller to the language of the buyer," says online marketing expert Hunter Madsen.

The link, "My Chapter," lets users find a **Sierra Club** group near them. But the word "chapter" is confusing, because it has a more commonplace meaning.

His advice: "Go through your entire web site, identify every term that looks like an inside or category term, circle it, and ask if there isn't an easier word that you hear your buyers use—the improper term they use—for the phrase you would prefer. Then switch your web site's verbiage to fit the buyer's venacular."

What does "jargon" mean?

- **Acronyms** that aren't self-explanatory.

- **Code words** used in the company. "In large organizations, it's often easier to sell your work internally when you use the company's buzzwords, division names, and so on," said designer Jeffrey Zeldman. "But you pay a price for doing so."

- **Double entendres**, or words that have two meanings. "The classic example in computer science is the word 'default,'" says Professor Michael Twidale. "We all know what default means. But if you're building software for an accountant, they also know what 'default' means. And it means something completely different."

- **Formal or technical words** that real people don't use. For example, the Black and Decker site has a section, "Garment Care." But real people call "garments" clothes.

- **Industry terms** that customers may not know and would never use.

- **Marketing slogans** that you'd like your customers to learn. For example, the juice company Odwalla has a section called "Freshology."

- **Slang** that your visitors don't actually use.

What's at stake here isn't just comprehension, but also competition. If users have a choice between two sites—one that confuses them and one of that speaks plainly—they'll choose the one they understand.

As Jesse James Garrett says: "Users can adapt to jargon, but if they have a choice, they won't."

choosing consistent names

Consistency is one of the keys to an intuitive navigation system. The names on your site sections should be consistent, so users can quickly grasp the relationship between them. Granted, it's difficult to find names that are consistent in every way, but it's what we strive for.

factor		examples	
Part of speech	Section name based on a noun or verb.	Good:	Cars | Homes
		Bad:	Cars | Buy a home
Verb tense	Labels with verbs should all use the same tense.	Good:	Buy a car | Buy a house
		Bad:	Buy a car | Buying a house
Plural or singular	Labels should either all be plural or all be singular.	Good:	Artists | Authors | Musicians
		Bad:	Artist | Authors | Musician
Capitalization	The same words should be capitalized in each label.	Good:	Buy a car | Buy a home
		Bad:	Buy a car | Buy A Home
Language	Names of foreign languages should either all be written with the English word, or all be written with the native word.	Good:	English | Spanish | French
		Bad:	English | Español | French
Number of words	Labels should all have roughly the same number of words.	Good:	Create Profile | Edit Profile | Search profiles
		Bad:	Create a profile | Edit profile | Search all the profiles
Length of words	Labels should all be roughly the same length.	Good:	Buy a home | Buy a car | Buy an RV
		Bad:	Buy a home | Buy a car | Buy a recreational vehicle

a few good examples

1

2

3

4

5

1. **RedEnvelope** lets you choose gifts by the recipient, each of which is labeled, "for ____."

2. **The Guggenheim Museum** lets you find artwork based on six characteristics, each of which is expressed with a single noun.

3. **BBC News** lets you read articles in many languages—each of which Is listed in its own language and alphabet.

4. **BackRoads** offers many types of trips, each of which is labeled with an adjective and noun.

5. **Nerve.com** offers six ways to use their personals, each of which is labeled with two words: a verb and a noun.

why section names should be clear, not clever

We humans have an inexplicable urge to name things. We name our children, our pets, our toys, our cities, neighborhoods, and streets. We've been known, on occasion, to name our body parts.

Every industry, it seems, has a self-indulgent name game. Magazines come up with clever names for each section, column, and story. Car companies devise different names for makes and models. The cosmetics industry, for its part, has produced more names for nail polish than there are stars in the sky.*

For the most part, this is a harmless fetish. If you want to give a clever name to every clever column in your clever magazine, who will it hurt?

But on the web, it hurts both your users and your site. Using vague, obscure names for site sections leads to confused and frustrated users. The web doesn't provide enough contextual clues to help the user understand that "Thorn Tree" means "Discussion area." And if they don't know what's behind a link, they're unlikely to follow it.

"Following a link is like buying meat—packaged meat," laughs Martha Brockenbrough, former managing editor of MSN.com. "You don't want it to just say, 'MEAT.' You want it to say what animal it came from. You want to see the freshness date. You want to be able to see the product. You want to see: Does it have that rainbow hue? Or is it still looking good?"

The same is true on the web, she continues. "People don't click if they're not sure what they're going to get. That's why it's important to have very clear labels. Clear is better than clever, always."

This is a hard adjustment for editors who began their careers in print. Magazines and newspapers place a premium on puns and alliterations. But the wordsmith's approach is a recipe for failure online.

"On the web, you need a level of clarity that you don't need in other media," says Jim Frew, a designer who splits his time between print and the web. "For magazines, you can choose names that are stylized and kind of cryptic. But online, everything has to be totally clear. You can't call search 'Quest.'"

> **"Online, everything has to be totally clear. You can't call search 'Quest.'"**
>
> —*Jim Frew*

Of course, we didn't always know this. When HotWired launched, for instance, we used magazine-style section names like "Piazza" and "Signal." They were catchy, but they confused our users. Without any other clues, they didn't know what to do or where to click.

Needless to say, we learned our lesson. And we weren't the only ones. Producers all over the web were making the same mistake.

"I abused section names," Brockenbrough admits. "I named Joel Stein's humor column 'Lúser.' It's French, because he's supposed to be the everyday user. And Ha, ha. Funny pun on 'Loser,' but no one knew what it meant."

Her take-away? "Do not try to be smart. Do not try to be clever. Do not try to spin people. You can have a voice and elements of whimsy, but do it with something less critical than your navigation."

On a very clear night, in a very dark place, 8,768 stars can be seen with the unaided eye. If you count the nail polish colors on the make-up floor at Macy's, you'll see that it's higher…

strange names

All kinds of things go wrong when people sit down to name their site sections. The first problem is that they let their company's internal jargon creep onto their web sites. The second problem is that people love to name things, and they love to be clever. But vague, cryptic names lead to confused and frustrated users.

Clockwise from left: The names and icons that represent sections on the (1) **Lonely Planet** site are colorful but mystifying. What is a thorn tree? (It's the discussion area.) (2) **HotWired's** first front door (circa 1994) featured striking icons and clever section names that baffled users. (3) **Sierra Club** created clever names that are hard to decode and their grouping—which makes them appear related—makes matters worse. "Currents" means news. (Why not call it "News"?) "Zoomer" helps you find sites about local issues. (Why not call it "Local Issues"?), and "Lewis & Clark" is surprisingly literal. The section's actually about Lewis & Clark. (4) **Odwalla** uses marketing slogans as site navigation, with sections called "Freshology" and "People to Planet." (5) **360degrees** let technical jargon become site navigation, with a section called "Dynamic Data" that conceals some great interactive features, such as quizzes and polls.

2

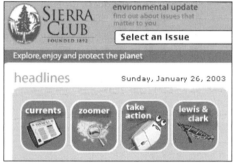

3

1

5

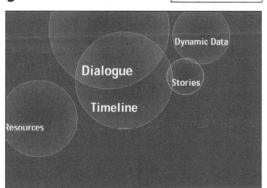

4

how will you name your site sections?

If you feel the urge to be creative or clever, channel that energy elsewhere. It's quite important to use simple, clear, boring section names that people can understand.

section names

Group 1

1._____

Is this: ❏ short ❏ clear ❏ jargon-free

2._____

Is this: ❏ short ❏ clear ❏ jargon-free

3._____

Is this: ❏ short ❏ clear ❏ jargon-free

4._____

Is this: ❏ short ❏ clear ❏ jargon-free

5._____

Is this: ❏ short ❏ clear ❏ jargon-free

6._____

Is this: ❏ short ❏ clear ❏ jargon-free

7._____

Is this: ❏ short ❏ clear ❏ jargon-free

8._____

Is this: ❏ short ❏ clear ❏ jargon-free

9._____

Is this: ❏ short ❏ clear ❏ jargon-free

10._____

Is this: ❏ short ❏ clear ❏ jargon-free

Group 2

1._____

Is this: ❏ short ❏ clear ❏ jargon-free

2._____

Is this: ❏ short ❏ clear ❏ jargon-free

3._____

Is this: ❏ short ❏ clear ❏ jargon-free

4._____

Is this: ❏ short ❏ clear ❏ jargon-free

consistency check

Do your sections names agree with each other in terms of

- ❏ Part of speech (verbs vs. nouns)
- ❏ Verb tense
- ❏ Capitalization
- ❏ Language
- ❏ Number of words
- ❏ Length of words

jargon check

Are you quite sure that none of these names are:

- ❏ Acronyms
- ❏ Code words
- ❏ Double entendres (words with double meaning)
- ❏ Formal words
- ❏ Industry terms
- ❏ Marketing slogans
- ❏ Slang

"You're supposed to correct my spelling, not criticize my use of symbolic imagery!"

usability testing

"Testing one user is 100% better than testing none."
- *Steve Krug*

Sooner or later, every web designer learns the same simple lesson: For a site to succeed, visitors must be able to use it. And this simple requirement is the driving force behind web design. Nearly every decision has to take usability into account.

"Forgetting about usability on the web is like forgetting about the plot in a movie," said designer Jeffrey Zeldman (www.zeldman.com). "If there's no usability, there's no site."

And while good designers always keep usability in mind, you can never know for sure how a site will be used, until you see people interact with it. That's where usability testing comes in.

Usability testing gives you a chance to see real people use your site in a way that simulates the user experience. As users navigate your site and attempt to complete a given task, you (or your tester) can ask questions: Do they understand what the labels mean, where the links lead, and what the buttons do? Does the interface work the way they think it will work? Can they complete a given task?

By watching volunteers attempt to interpret, navigate, and generally use your site, you get a painfully clear picture of what works—and what doesn't—in your design.

You'll find that nothing is as powerful—or as instructive—as watching real users struggle with your site. And struggle they will. No matter how good your initial design or how talented your product team, some aspect of your interface—be it the navigation system, the labels, or the sequencing of events—will invariably confuse your users.

Things happen in usability testing that you can never predict.

"Things happen in usability testing that you can never predict," says Doug Bowman, former design director for HotWired and Terra-Lycos. "What you think is so painfully obvious and clear might be the most difficult thing in the world for five users in a row to figure out."

5 types of usability tests

1. task-oriented tests

The standard usability test is a task-oriented test of a working site. Volunteers are given specific tasks to accomplish while an observer records their reactions and results.

2. over-the-shoulder observation

Rather than bringing volunteers to a test computer, it can be useful to observe people in their natural online environment—whether it's at home or in a cubicle. This is a more anthropological approach to user testing, one that gets you as close to the actual user experience as possible. You get a more complete picture, including the clutter on their desks, and the goings-on around them: phone ringing, baby crying, co-workers interrupting, and so on.

3. open exploration

Certain types of sites can benefit from less-directed user tests. Rather than giving volunteers a specific task, you simply set them down in front of your site and see what happens. This is most appropriate for immersive, entertainment-oriented sites like games.

4. eye tracking

Eye-tracking tests give you an extraordinarily detailed picture of how users scan web sites and where their eyes fall. Using special cameras pointing at the users' eyes, researchers can follow where users actually look—rather than where their cursor is or what they say they're looking at.

5. paper prototypes

Very early in the design process, it can be helpful to put simple paper prototypes in front of users. These early tests can help uncover user reactions to the site name and basic layout: Do people understand what the site is? Do they understand intuitively what they can do there, and how?

what you can learn from usability tests

The great advantage of usability testing is that it lets you see your site through someone else's eyes. And this helps you catch mistakes and pinpoint problems you can't see when you've designed the site.

Usability testing is "like a form of sensitivity training," says Michael Twidale, professor of computer science at the University of Illinois Urbana-Champaign. "It helps you figure out, 'What's this going to feel like for people who aren't me?'"

"The art of good usability design is that you can put on these spectacles," he says. "You can look at your design through someone else's eyes. Now that's very hard to do. But you can practice if you watch other people using the system."

And that's where usability testing comes in. "Sitting in on user testing sessions has changed my view of design,"says designer Doug Bowman. "It helps you with the design that you're testing, but it also gives you insight that you file away in your head. So when you're designing a site, you just automatically think about what you've seen in past user tests, and you know instinctively how a user behaves when they arrive on a page."

But no matter how many times you've designed and tested sites, you still need to test each interface. Because the longer you work on a site, the harder it is to distance yourself from it. And no matter how well-versed you are in user behavior, you'll always be surprised by what you learn.

"You do find surprises," agrees Greg Dotson, Chief Information Officer for Guru. "Usability studies are really good at finding simple things you've overlooked. And they're also good at confirming things you've done well."

"I can't imagine a scenario in design where usability testing is not helpful, period," says designer Doug Bowman. "Your perception of how someone's going to use your site is entirely different from what happens when a user actually tries to use it."

Sometimes, your findings will seem obvious: As Greg Dotson says, "After you conduct a test, you think, 'How could I have been so stupid?'" But sometimes, they're completely unpredictable.

"That's what's interesting," says Steve Mulder, user experience manager for Lycos. "Sometimes you just don't know *why* something doesn't work."

In any case, the most important takeaways from usability testing are precisely the issues you couldn't see on your own because you're too close to the work.

"User testing reveals problems that people who know the brand and the product and the Internet can't see," said Lance McDaniel, VP of Creative for SBI and Company. "And when you get those big surprises—that, to me, is a Godsend, because what you've done is avoid launching a site to ten million people with a problem that was obvious to the eight people who tested it."

What you can learn from usability tests:

- **Problems with site organization.**
  Sometimes a site will organize its content differently than the user might expect. This may slow the transaction down or even prevent the visitor from accomplishing what they set out to do. (See site organization, p. 98).

- **Problems with names or labels.** Often, users get confused by the names used for site sections and links. The features themselves may be perfectly usable, but if users can't understand the labels, they won't be able to find them—much less use them. (See naming site sections, p. 122).

- **Problems with placement.** Often, users will intuitively look for a button or link in one part of the screen (the "shopping cart" link in the upper-right corner, for example). If a user hesitates and scrolls around the page, he's probably having trouble finding what he wants. (See how people see web sites p. 86.)

- **Problems with grouping.** Users will intuitively expect related items to be grouped together. They may get confused if seemingly unrelated items are grouped together or if an item they view as related is set apart. (See navigation systems, p. 114.)

- **Problems with pacing or the order of events.** When users are completing a transaction, they have expectations about what should happen next. Some are negotiable, and some aren't. For instance, they usually expect to enter a credit card number last in a shopping transaction. If you add an additional step after the credit card is charged, they may never even notice it.

So, by putting your site in front of users early in the design process, you can validate your assumptions and catch significant problems early enough to correct them. Some of the problems—such as misleading labels—are easy to change. Others, however, may be more involved. Usability testing sometimes turns up problems that are more than skin deep. You may discover problems with your site's functionality or organization that force you to rethink your entire approach.

and what you can't learn...

Although usability testing is powerful, it's not a panacea. It can't solve all your site's problems or prevent all its pitfalls. And it can't substitute for the earlier rounds of user research.

"You have to make time to understand customers, and usability testing is only part of understanding customers," explains Mike Kuniavsky, author of *Observing the User Experience: A Practitioner's Guide for User Research.*

"By the time you're doing usability testing, you should know with a very, very high degree of confidence that you have the right audience, that you

🛒 **Buy this book!**

Don't Make Me Think!
by Steve Krug
A wise and witty manual on user-centered design and usability testing. Also one of the best books written about the web.

know what problems they're having, and that you have a solution they will want and they will use," he said. "The only thing usability testing does is check whether the solution you've created is actually usable."

And just because a feature is usable, it doesn't mean it will be used. "The discount bins in record stores are littered with records that everyone can use, but nobody wants."

This last point can be hard to get across, because many proponents of usability testing confuse user ability with user *interest.*

"It's amazing how many bad decisions have been made on web sites thanks to usability tests," says Adam Berliant of Microsoft. "Why? Because usability has nothing do with whether or not people actually use something. There's a big difference between the question, '*Can* you operate this coffee maker?' and '*Will* you operate this coffee maker?'"

"So when I'm prioritizing my research, my first first question is 'Will people use it?' If the answer is 'yes,' then I want it to be usable."

What you *can't* learn from usability tests:

- **Whether the features will be used.** In usability tests, you're guiding volunteers through a task that requires them to use your site features. From this, you'll learn whether the features can be used, but you can't conclude anything about whether they *will* be used.

- **Whether you've included the right features.** Usability testing will occasionally turn up clues about features you should have included (if a user is unable to complete a task, for instance). But it can't tell you whether you've chosen the right ones. "Usability testing is very good for seeing if someone is able to complete a task," said Jeffrey Veen. "And that's about it, really."

usability testing on the cheap

If you have a reasonable—or even a modest—budget for developing your web site, you should invest in professional usability testing, conducted by neutral, experienced usability experts in a lab-like environment.

But if your budget makes this unrealistic, you can conduct serviceable user tests on your own with a few hours and a few willing volunteers. Even this simple setup can reveal important insights into how users will see your site.

"Even a user test of one person reveals an awful lot," says University of Illinois professor Michael Twidale, who offered some of the advice that follows. And, as Steve Krug says in his excellent book Don't Make Me Think, "Testing one user is a 100% better than testing none."

1. set up your "lab"

The setting for your usability test can be as simple as sitting behind a co-worker at his desk and watching over his shoulder as he uses your new site. But to make your tests a bit more professional, you should look first to a setup in a real usability lab.

Most usability labs set up volunteers at a computer with a video camera pointed at them that records their facial expressions. Another camera records what they're doing on screen. This video is used in two ways: It's recorded to tape—for future use and study—and it's run through wires to an adjoining room, where observers can watch the test in real-time, seeing the user on one TV screen and a simulation of the web browser on another. (Some labs have the volunteer sit in front of a two-way mirror, through which they can be observed.)

equipment needed

- Computer with access to the Internet or just the site being tested
- Video camera or camcorder
- Adjoining room with video hookup (optional)
- Television for simultaneous playback of user monitor (optional)
- Second television for playback of user's face (optional)

usability testing (continued)

2. recruit volunteers

The type of volunteer you recruit will have an important impact on what you find. Professional usability labs usually draw from long lists of potential volunteers, solicited through phone calls or email by a professional screening service.

recruiting volunteers

If you're building a large-scale usability effort, you'll probably want to hire a professional recruiting service. But you can recruit volunteers on a less expensive and less formal basis by looking to the following:

- **Customers.** Existing customers are prime candidates for usability tests, because they're already familiar with—and interested in—your products. You can work from existing client lists or solicit volunteers through an ad on your site.

- **Co-workers.** Co-workers can make fine informal interface testers, provided they don't work directly on the product being tested. Keep in mind, though, that internal testers know more about the product than real users. Also, their responses may be politically motivated.

- **Friends and family.** There's nothing wrong with recruiting friends and family members to test new sites for you. Just know that they may not be entirely honest. Their comments may be more diplomatic than normal users. (Or less diplomatic, depending on your friends.)

screening volunteers

Your volunteers should match the profile of your target user as closely as possible:

- **Familiarity with content.** If your site is targeted to users with a specific interest, need, or area of expertise, your volunteers should share it.

- **Familiarity with technology.** Your volunteers should match your audience in terms of their comfort level and familiarity with internet technologies.

- **Familiarity with test computer.** Volunteers should be comfortable using the test computer and browser.

3. give them a task

Some user tests are open-ended, allowing volunteers to explore the interface and make of it what they will. This is fine for some sites and some purposes, but it's generally not the best technique.

Rather than have volunteers drift aimlessly about your site, you should give them one or more tasks to accomplish. This engages them more actively and also mimics real-world use more closely (because most users have a goal in mind when they arrive at a site).

first, reassure them

Volunteers inevitably feel a little nervous in user tests. When they're given a task to accomplish, they feel like they're being tested—as if they were back in school, being graded for their performance. Now, a nervous tester doesn't deliver realistic or helpful results, so it's very important to assure them that they're testing the system, not vice versa.

In fact, you might want to say just that. Mike Kuniavsky, author of *Observing the User Experience* and founder of Wired's usability lab, would always begin tests by reassuring volunteers: "Remember, you're testing the interface. The interface is not testing you. You can't do anything 'wrong.'"

lay out a clear task

Give the volunteer a plausible scenario about what she's trying to accomplish on the site—whether it's finding the location of a store, transferring money in a bank account, or finding a photo of the scarlet tanager. It's important that the volunteer understand what she's trying to accomplish, even if it's something she may not do in real life.

get out of the way

You must resist the temptation to show the volunteer what to do. This is difficult, of course, when you're testing a site you built yourself. (You'll want to explain it to them, or defend it, or show off its best features.) But you have to let the user struggle on her own, if you're going to get a clear picture of how people use your site outside of a usability lab.

4. observe

As your volunteer makes his way through the task you've assigned, the most important thing to do is keep quiet and watch. Some of the things to watch for include the following:

- **User path.** Mentally follow the user's path through the site, and notice where he deviates from the expected or recommended route. Pay attention to how he handles a "dead-end" situation: Can he find his way back and correct the mistake?

- **Hesitation.** Notice where the volunteer hesitates or falters, perhaps hovering the cursor over several links. This points to an ambiguous choice in the interface. Even if this user chooses correctly, another may get it wrong.

- **Searching and scrolling.** Pay attention when the volunteer seems to be searching for a link but not finding it.

- **Emotional reactions.** Notice when the volunteer registers surprise ("Whoa!") or frustration ("Arg!").

Ask questions. As you become more experienced with testing, you can ask questions to clarify the volunteer's thoughts. But take care with your phrasing.

- **Ask open-ended questions.** Don't ask, "Does this look like a link to the help section?" Instead ask, "What would you expect to find behind that link?"

- **Don't ask, "Why did you do that?** "People associate that with the classroom, says Prof. Michael Twidale. They may become defensive, or may invent an answer. "Instead of asking, 'Why did you do that?'—implying that it was the wrong thing to do—I might say, 'Why do you think the computer led you to do that?'" he said.

- **Just say "Hmm."** When you want to understand what's causing frustration or confusion, try prompting the volunteer by saying "Hmm." "It's very strange," Twidale says. "People will often elaborate when you say, 'Hmm.' If you say, 'Can you tell me what you're thinking?' that sounds scary. But if they just said something like, 'Whoa,' and you say, 'Oooh,' they'll start elaborating on what's going on."

5. pinpoint problems

By watching volunteers struggle with your interface, you can identify the major usability issues pretty quickly. Usually, a small test sample of three to five volunteers will uncover the major problems in a site's interface. By watching volunteers closely, you should be able to tease out not only the problem areas, but the underlying causes. Here are some of the things to watch for:

- Problems with placement

- Problems with labeling

- Problems with grouping

- Problems with pacing or the order of events

- Problems with the mental model

If you catch a clear, simple problem early on in the testing process (on the first volunteer, perhaps), you may want to fix it before the next volunteer begins. By removing an initial obstacle, you can focus on the other, less-obvious issues.

6. reward volunteers

If you're going to take up someone's time, you'll need to give them something back. In standard user tests, volunteers are paid with cash. But people are motivated by other things as well. Merchandise and "shwag" sometimes work (your company's products, or T-shirts, bags, mugs, etc. with your product logo. Gift certificates—especially for a free movie or meal—also go over well. If you're recruiting within your company, employees may respond to an offer of an extra day or afternoon off.

 Buy this book!

Observing the User Experience: A Practitioner's Guide to User Research
by Mike Kuniavsky (Morgan Kaufmann, $44.95)

how usability testing can go wrong

Usability testing may well be the best thing that happened to the web since—it may be the best thing that happened to the web, period. But it's not an undisputed force of good in the web universe. As designer Jeffrey Zeldman wrote in his book, *Taking Your Talent to the Web*, "There is good [usability] testing and there is worthless pseudo-science that promotes banality. Unfortunately... it's hard to tell until you're working at a web agency whether its testing practices are informative or a shortcut to hell."

If you want to stay out of hell, it helps to recognize the signposts. Here, then, are a few ways usability testing goes astray:

1. You don't know what you're testing for. It's important to decide up-front, before you begin a test, what aspects of the site you're testing. This helps focus the test, and also helps you to ignore unhelpful, extraneous input from the volunteer.

> **"It's really hard to trust the data, because you can take what you want from it."**
> —*Sheryl Cababa*

"One of the keys to testing is figuring out what information you want to know, because you do not get to control what the person comments on," says Lance McDaniel, VP of Creative at SBI and Company. Volunteers love, for instance, to talk about color. "The client says, 'Oh, they didn't like the color!' And you have to say, 'But we're not testing the color, we're testing the check-out process. And luckily for us, they actually *liked* the check-out process.'"

2. You test something that can't be changed. Many usability tests have been wasted because the volunteer or the tester focused on elements of the site or interface that couldn't be changed.

"The first thing you need to know, going in, is what can you change and what can't you change," says designer Jim Frew. "Like if your logo is green, and it has always been green, and it always will be green, don't ask if they think the logo should be red. It's never going to be red."

3. You test something that doesn't matter. Too often, usability tests go astray by focusing on the wrong things—aspects of the site's features or interface that don't really affect usability. Again, color is the major offender. People love to comment on color. And color does impact the user experience, but it rarely affects usability unless it renders the site illegible.

"People don't leave a web site because they don't like purple," says Lance McDaniel. "They leave a site because it doesn't load, or because they can't find what they need, or because there isn't anything on the site that interests them."

4. The tester hasn't prepared a good script. When you're running your own usability tests, you have to make sure your tester can clearly, succinctly, and non-judgementally explain to the volunteer what's expected.

"I've done user testing at the really bare-bones level—the pizza and beer level—and the in-house people doing the testing aren't always familiar with how to encourage people, how to direct the testing process," says designer Jim Frew. "So whole tests would go out the window because the person doing the test couldn't get the person he was testing to the right points."

5. The volunteer isn't a typical user. The whole point of usability testing is to get inside the users' heads and follow them through a typical experience on your site. But this goes wrong if your volunteer isn't representative of your user group. If your volunteer has fundamentally different attitudes, skills, or computer experience than your typical user—if she knows too much or too little about the subject matter, too much or too little about the web—you won't get valid results.

"Your research will be exponentially better as the users you talk to are closer to your audience," says Jeffrey Veen. "The more effort you spend on accurate recruiting, the better the testing will be. Always."

6. The results are misinterpreted. Like most things in life, usability tests are open to interpretation. And conclusions drawn from the same test can vary wildly, depending on the profession and personality of the person watching. A designer, an engineer, and a salesperson may have vastly different take-aways. And a good test poorly interpreted is worse than a bad test.

"When my product is up for usability testing, I try to go to every single test," said Sheryl Cababa, a product designer for Microsoft. "And then I see how the usability engineers sum up that data and what they glean from it. And it could be totally different from what I glean from it. It's really hard to trust the data, because you can take what you want from it."

7. You try to test whether a feature will be used. This is the classic problem with usability testing: People will interpret positive test results as confirmation that they're doing the right thing. But usability testing can't tell you this. All usability testing tests is whether you've designed a feature that people can understand and use, when prompted. It doesn't tell you whether they'd voluntarily decide to use it.

As Martha Brockenbrough, former managing editor of MSN, put it: "Usability testing can't test whether a feature will actually be used."

8. The tester—or the volunteer— has an axe to grind. When they fall into the wrong hands, usability tests—or their results—become a weapon in the pettily political battles so common in the workplace. The tester may lead the volunteer toward a particular conclusion, and the person interpreting test results may interpret them to suit his department or his own opinion. And the volunteers, too, can throw things off, if they have a particular beef with the company, the site, or the world.

> **"Usability is like spell-checking. Spell-checking doesn't make your essay better. It just makes it correct."**
>
> —*Jeffrey Veen*

9. It's expected to solve all your problems. "The biggest misconception my clients have is that usability is a solution," says Jeffrey Veen. "Usability is really like spell-checking. Spell-checking doesn't make your essay better, it just makes it correct. And usability is the same way. It's the final, last little step in a whole series of things that you should do to understand who your users are. And all it does is check that your assumptions are right.

chapter 7

visual design

The consensus among most web professionals is that a site must, above all else, be functional, usable, and clear. But that doesn't mean it can't have style.

"Most people agree that you have to have a functional site in order for your product to be successful, and that it takes a lot of skill and expertise to create a site like that," said designer Wendy Owen. "But I also strongly believe that if the experience of that well-functioning site is pleasurable, it's going to create a much deeper relationship with the customer and ultimately lead to a [more successful] site."

"We're such a pleasure-driven culture and such a visual culture, it seems pretty obvious that visual design has an impact, even if you can't quantify it that easily."

What visual design does for your site:

- **Brings the site structure to life** in a way that users can immediately grasp

- **Defines your brand** by making a visual statement

- **Tells the user what's most important** by giving greater visual emphasis to certain sections or page element

- **Creates a mood** through the use of color, type, imagery—and possibly animation, video, or sound

bringing the site structure to life   Job one for the visual design is simply to give form to the site's content, features, and navigation. The challenge here is to create a design that gets the job done without calling too much attention to itself.

"Design in its purest form should be completely invisible and transparent," said Doug Bowman, former Network Design Director for Terra-Lycos. "When you notice design, it can get in the way."

defining your brand   Whether you know it or not—whether *they* know it or not—your site's appearance will resonate with visitors on an emotional level, creating an impression that affects the way they think about you and act on your site.

> **Look and feel make a big difference in the initial brand impact. And since a lot of people do their initial research on brands online, it turns out to be deceptively important.**

As more and more people use the web—and use it as part of the purchase process—companies have to take the web more seriously as a communication outlet.

"Look and feel make a big difference in the initial brand impact," said Hunter Madsen, online marketing expert and former senior partner with the ad agency J. Walter Thompson. "And since a lot of people do their initial research on brands online, web presentation turns out to be surprisingly important."

telling the user what's most important   Using color, size, and placement, the designer can communicate what's most important and where the user should start. But a lot of sites overlook this step, offering many options of equal weight.

"More often than not, web sites aren't paying close enough attention to hierarchy," says Doug Bowman. "So when the user arrives on a page, they have no idea where to start. Or if they do, the hierarchy's reversed compared to what it should be."

creating a mood   Sight is our strongest sense, and humans respond deeply—on an emotional level—to their visual surroundings. So your site's design can impact the mood and behavior of people using it.

Derek Powazek, author of *Design for Community*, learned this the hard way. His site, Kvetch, originally had an all-black background. And he found the design colored people's comments, making the site's outlook rather bitter and bleak. "If you want dark, black thoughts, make a dark, black site," he said.

front door design

The central challenge of front door design is to communicate very quickly and clearly who you are. What kind of site is this? What can I do here? These are the immediate questions that users have upon arriving at your site.

But so many sites leave these questions unanswered. "As silly as it sounds, a lot of sites don't put their primary purpose on their homepage," said Mark Hurst, founder of consulting firm Creative Good. "Or it's there but it's obscured."

"On an insurance site, let's say, the great majority of customers who come there just want to get a quote," he explained. "But what does the homepage have? Oh, it's got the logo, and it's got the slogan, and it's got recent news, and it's got this new feature they just launched."

"Somewhere on a nav bar, on a secondary level, in a link that's not even underlined (because that would break the graphic design paradigm) there's something that says 'QuoteMaker™.' And that's the problem."

"The best counter example of this is Google," Hurst continued. "It puts its primary purpose first…What's Google? It's a search site. And I don't have to tell you that, because it's kind of hard to miss."

> **You have to quickly and clearly tell people who you are. But there are different ways to get the point across.**

Indeed, there's not a lot of room for subtlety on a website's front door. You have to explain who you are quickly, and in a very small space. But there are different ways to get the point across. You can choose a straightforward name and URL, or you can add a line of text that explains what you do. You can put your functionality front and center, or you can express your identity through images, color, or sound. Often, sites will combine methods to get the idea across.

6 ways to tell users who you are:

1. **Name and URL.** The name of your site or company is the first clue users have to your identity. Sites like partyplanning.com or HinckleyforHouse.com are readily understood. But if your name lacks intrinsic meaning (or if its meaning is unrelated to what you do, like "Amazon")—you'll have to work harder to help people understand.

2. **Tagline.** The simplest way to let people know who you are is to tell them: It's smart to include a short tagline—or introductory sentence—that succinctly explains who you are and what you do. Many sites err in one direction or the other: either offering no explanation when one would be helpful, or writing a long mission statement, which no one will read.

3. **Navigation.** The way you divide your site—and the names of the sections within it—can communicate a lot about what your site offers and how it works.

4. **Functionality.** Rather than just telling users who you are, you can show them—by displaying the tools or features they can use on your site.

5. **Color.** People respond on an emotional level to the colors in their environment, and the colors you choose go a long way toward both defining your brand and setting the mood for your site.

6. **Images.** On the web, pictures aren't quite worth a thousand words—because they don't communicate as clearly. But they can help users understand who you are by setting the mood, illustrating a point, or displaying a particular product.

Google has one of the simplest front doors on the web, and it works perfectly for them. It communicates who Google is by offering a **search box, and not much more than a search box.** The message sent? "We're a company that's focused on one thing: search." The **playful logo** (which occasionally changes) communicates "But we're not above having a little fun."

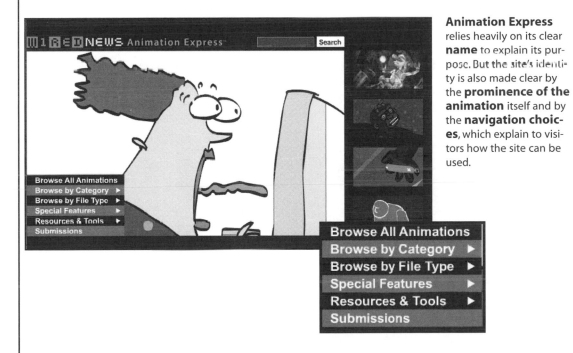

Animation Express relies heavily on its clear **name** to explain its purpose. But the site's identity is also made clear by the **prominence of the animation** itself and by the **navigation choices**, which explain to visitors how the site can be used.

Herman Miller—a design-oriented furniture company—lets visitors know who they are through a simple **tagline**, describing what the company does. But the company also communicates through the site's **design** (sleek and spare), its **product categories**—"Work Environments" and "Modern Classics"—and by **highlighting the Aeron chair** (top), for which they're well-known.

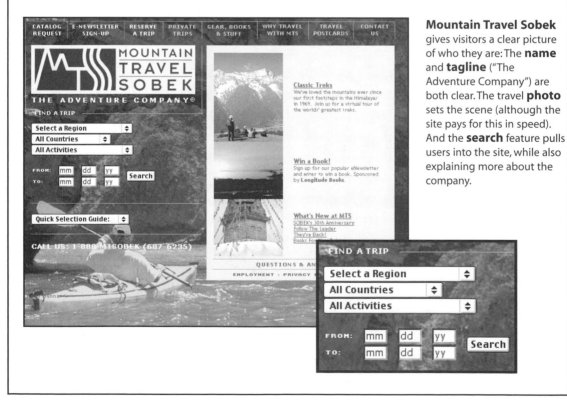

Mountain Travel Sobek gives visitors a clear picture of who they are: The **name** and **tagline** ("The Adventure Company") are both clear. The travel **photo** sets the scene (although the site pays for this in speed). And the **search** feature pulls users into the site, while also explaining more about the company.

8 design tips for non-designers

If you find yourself in the position of designing your site even though you know perfectly well that you're not a designer, these simple suggestions will keep you from doing too much damage.

1. create templates for pages

Rather than design each page individually, it's best—both for you and the user—if you create a few templates and base each page on one of them. This saves you time, because you don't have to approach each page as a brand-new design challenge. And it makes your site easier to use: When all the pages follow the same basic structure, people can move more fluidly around your site.

2. create a grid for each page

Most successful designs are based on an underlying (invisible) grid that gives the page structure. So don't just put things down willy-nilly. Plan out each placement based on a logical grid. (A pad of graph paper is a fun way to get started.) But try not to get too complex. The more rigid your design, the harder it is to actually build it using HTML.

3. pay attention to placement

Whether or not you realize it—whether or not *they* realize it—people draw a lot of meaning out of the arrangement of elements on your site. Make sure you're mindful of where you've placed each item and why. Similar things should be grouped together. Dissimilar things should be somewhat separate. And also pay attention to alignment: Everything on your site should sit on the grid lines (Remember the grid you're creating for each page?) to make sure the layout is easily navigable with the eye.

4. be consistent

Consistency is one of the keys to a usable site. As visitors move from page to page, they expect things to remain in more or less the same place. So don't move your navigation or page elements around. Pick a system, and stick with it.

5. emphasize what's most important

Before you start designing, you should decide which elements of your site are most important. There are techniques for getting these things seen. You can make them bigger. You can make them bolder. You can make them a brighter or darker color (more saturated colors are more visible). You can make them move (with animation). You can put them in the center of the page or the top-right corner. All of these things will help them grab attention.

6. carefully choose colors

Unlike most print projects, where color is expensive, web sites can use unlimited colors for free. This is liberating, but dangerous. It's hard to use a lot of colors well. The best approach is to keep it simple. Choose color combinations you've seen before (and know you like). And don't choose too many: 1–3 colors can go a long way. See color on the web, p. 146.

7. go easy on the fonts

Type choice is limited online, and that's a blessing in disguise: It keeps people from making too many mistakes. Amateur designers inevitably go font-crazy with their first designs. The rule of thumb in any graphic design is to limit yourself to two fonts: One serif font, one sans-serif font, and maybe—maybe—one accent font. See typography on the web, p. 150.

8. watch out for line length

It's hard to control line length on the web. But keep this in mind: When lines of text are too long, they become unreadable because it's too difficult to find the next line. The rule of thumb is that a line of text shouldn't be longer than two alphabets (or 52 characters). See typography on the web, p. 150.

5 raging debates in web design

1. to splash or not to splash?

A splash page is the introductory page—usually animated—that precedes the real front door to a web site. The animation plays, and then the user is automatically "pushed" to the next page (the real front door).

The debate: Designers are divided over when—and if—the splash page is a good idea. Proponents view splash pages as a chance to grab users when you have their full attention and submerge them in the world of your site (without bogging them down with all the navigation and practical functions of the front door). Detractors view splash pages as a poor imitation of TV and a huge waste of bandwidth and time.

A balanced perspective: "I like the theory of having a foyer—an entryway that provides a transition and establishes where you've arrived," says Nadav Savio, a principal at Giant Ant Design. "But not that many web sites can afford that transition. In the majority of cases, the purpose of a web site is to connect people to some kind of information, and a splash is often going to get in the way of that."

2. to Flash or not to Flash?

Macromedia Flash is a plug-in technology that brings animation and interactivity to a web page. When a large portion of the page is smoothly animated, Flash is usually involved.

The debate: It's hard for designers to reach an agreement about Flash, because it's enabled some of the most exquisite work on the web, and some of the most excruciating. At its worst, Flash promotes poor navigation, non-standard interfaces, annoying gratuitous promotions, and inaccessible content. At its best, Flash is used to create entertaining animations, wondrous art, engaging multimedia presentations, and interactive navigation systems that wouldn't be possible with regular HTML.

A balanced perspective: Like any technology, Flash should be used where it makes sense and where it best solves a problem: to animate, to show motion, to incorporate sound, and possibly to facilitate complex transactions within a single screen.

The site for **Def Poetry Jam** decided to splash and Flash: This animation—executed in Flash—introduced the site when Def Poetry Jam's Broadway show opened in 2002.

3. scrolling vs. paging

Frequently, you'll have more information to put on a single page than can possibly fit. Should you put all the information on one page and make users scroll down, or should you divide the content into multiple pages and make them click through?

The debate: There's a lot of disagreement about this question: How deep—or long—should a web page be? How far down should a reader be expected to scroll?

Some take the stance that pages can be endlessly long: That the goal is to minimize the number of downloads, and it's better to cram a lot of information on one page than to require users to click again (because users "hate to click"). Go ahead and pile it on: Let the users decide when they're tired of scrolling.

Another perspective favors shorter, more concise pages and multiple opportunities to click onward (because "users hate to scroll"). These page breaks are psychological as well as practical—they help mark users' progress and provide a needed mental and visual break.

A balanced perspective: As is so often the case, the best approach probably lies in the middle. Users will continue to click and scroll, so long as they're finding what they're looking for. A number of studies have shown, however, that users prefer to click. When given a choice, for example, between 10 search results per page and 50—they'll choose 10.

5. pop-up windows: friend or foe?

Pop-up windows are the small windows that pop up alongside the main browser window.

The debate: Pop-ups inspire strong feelings, largely due to the ads that normally appear in them. But they have other uses as well: help systems, maps, calendars, and notifications, to name a few.

A balanced perspective: "I think pop-ups can be used very effectively," says Wendy Owen. "And I get annoyed with people who say, 'No pop-ups ever.'"

4. to clutter or not to clutter?

Many web sites have a problem with clutter: More things need to go on the front door than can comfortably fit. Is It OK to clutter, or should you pare down?

The debate: Most graphic designers love white space. They like to leave breathing room around elements on a page. And the web-wide inclination to pile things on a site's front door runs counter to their best judgment.

"It's my opinion that most sites are just trying to cram too much on the page, too high above the fold," says Doug Bowman. "I think that's actually been to the detriment of the web."

"There's no white space on the web anymore," he continues. "Real estate is at such a premium that people don't think about using space to help set off certain elements."

But some site owners will tell you that clutter's effective—even if it is ugly. "We have this constant debate about clutter," says Adam Berliant, a group manager with Microsoft who has overseen both MSN.com and the WindowsMedia sites. "Less clutter is easier to look at. It's easier on the eyes. But that forces the web producer to try to come up with clever ways to make content available through fewer links."

"Suddenly, I need something that says 'Entertainment' to represent everything from games to entertainment news to radio," he says. "But if I just link directly to games, news, and radio, guess what? More people click. So while clutter is certainly not as attractive, it often means more usage. And that's why this web site exists. It exists to be used. It doesn't exist to be pretty."

A balanced perspective: The appropriate level of clutter seems to depend a lot on the site. One way to find the right balance is to test what happens on your site when you're pared down vs. cluttered up. Does your site use go up? Then it's probably a good thing. Does it plummet? Well, then, it's probably not a great idea.

color on the web

In most areas of design, the web is deeply constraining: You don't have a lot to work with in terms of fonts or formatting techniques. And the need for speed puts a serious limit on the images you use. But color is the one arena where you often have more options than you would in print.

Color's expensive in print, but free on the web, where sites can incorporate millions of colors at no additional cost. But abundance, too, has its price. It's difficult to use a full spectrum of colors well. And it introduces more complexity into the design.

3 key issues in web color:

1. **Choosing the right colors.** Pick the right colors for your site and your brand, and make sure you know what those colors say about you.

2. **Creating a color system.** Your hues should work together to send the right messages.

3. **Making color work on the web.** Screen colors are different from print colors, so matching can be a challenge. Also, web colors may be seen differently by users with different computers.

choosing the right colors

The colors you use on your site will say a lot about your organization. But what, exactly, will they say?

Different colors have different associations for different people, based on all kinds of cultural factors. So the wider spread of your audience, the more meanings you'll need to consider in choosing a color palette.

As Network Design Director for Terra-Lycos, a Spanish company that operates portals

the many meanings of color

Everyone agrees that color is meaningful, but there's no consensus on what each color means. Colors have different implications—strong implications—for different people around the world:

- **Color can mean action.** On the web, you have to think about what the user does, and "certain colors have action-related associations," says designer Jim Frew. "In the real world, green means go, red means stop. Online, blue means a link, and purple is recognized as a visited-link color."

- **Color can mean emotion.** Color can alter users' moods and conjure up color-specific emotions. Red is passionate, blue is tranquil, yellow is cheerful, and black is angry.

- **Color can mean brand.** Certain colors are associated with the brand that's claimed them. Yellow & red might mean McDonalds. Red & white might mean Coca-Cola.

- **Color can mean nationality.** Some colors conjure up national identity. Red, white, & blue might mean the USA. Or it might mean the UK, depending who you ask.

- **Color can mean sports teams.** Some people identify as strongly with their sports teams as they do with their nations. So specific colors can mean the home team—or the enemy.

- **Color can mean religion.** Blue & white might mean Judaism, red & green might mean Christmas, and red might mean Tibetan Buddhism.

- **Color can mean historical eras.** Thanks to changing fashions, certain colors are linked with specific time periods. Brown & orange may mean the 70s. Teal & mauve may mean the 80s.

throughout Europe and the Americas, Doug Bowman confronted more than his share of color conundrums. Often, they'd have to choose colors that would work for users in a dozen different countries, speaking three different languages.

"We had a lot of debates with international designers over the connotations of color, because it's different for different cultures," Bowman says. "For example, here, if we think of a finance site, we think green. But green doesn't inherently mean money. It's just the color of our dollar bills. In other countries, their bills are different colors."

Cultural connotations aside, it's always a challenge to choose colors, because they need to communicate about your brand, while also setting the mood for your site.

So the first thing to think about when choosing colors is the impression you're trying to make with them. What do you want them to say about you or your brand? What feelings do you want them to conjure up? How do you want your users to feel when they're looking at them?

Criteria for choosing brand colors:

- **What should the colors say about you?** Do you want to appear serious and sophisticated? Approachable and fun?

- **Who should the colors appeal to?** Are you reaching out to rugged outdoorsy types? Urban hipsters? Suburban moms?

- **How should visitors feel on your site?** Serious and reflective? Upbeat and energized? Outraged and ready for a fight?

Although these criteria are all subjective and emotional, they can provide concrete guidelines for a choice that might otherwise seem arbitrary.

6 tips on choosing colors

If you're in the position to choose colors for your site—and you're not in the position to hire a designer to help you—here are a few good methods for faking it:

1. Get ideas from other sites. By looking at other sites in your industry, you get a sense of what your customers expect. And by looking at sites with a similar personality, you can get specific ideas to work from.

2. Get ideas from other sources. Paintings, magazines, products—even nature—can provide inspiration for your choices. Find an artist, magazine, or brand you like, and borrow from them.

3. Get ideas from a color book. Idea books like *Color Harmony for the Web* (see subsequent listing) are great when you need inspiration, lack confidence, or both. The specific color combinations all work. You can just choose one that resonates with you.

4. Limit your choices. More isn't always better. Many people—including professional designers—feel overwhelmed by the choice of colors on the web. To limit your options, stick to the 216 colors in the web-safe palette.

5. Start with a single color. Once you've chosen a single shade that works, you can match others with it. The best way to find appropriate matches is by choosing colors with the same "value" (or darkness). Lynda Weinman shows you how in her book *<designing web graphics.4>* (listed later in this chapter).

6. Learn a little theory. By reading just a little bit about colors and color combinations, you can build your confidence and improve your chances of making a good choice. Again, Lynda Weinman's *<designing web graphics.4>* is a great place to start.

creating a color system

Designing for the web means you're not just choosing colors, you're creating a color system. Your hues have to work together to help the user understand your brand and your site.

"Designing for the web is more complex than print," says designer Jim Frew. "Color isn't just color—it's color systems. Once you have your corporate ID colors chosen, you need to think about colors for your navigation system."

You have to choose a color for your links—and perhaps different colors for followed links and "active" links (the color links turn at the moment the user clicks them).

Visitors will take cues about what to do based on your links and other elements on the page. So you have to think through the "action-related color implications," Frew says. "Certain colors have action-related associations: Green means go, red means stop, blue means a link, and purple is recognized as a visited-link color."

Your color system should include

- **Brand colors.** These are the colors you've chosen to represent your brand (See choosing the right colors, p. 146). They'll often include 1–3 complementary hues, which probably appear in your logo and may or may not be integrated throughout the rest of your site.

- **Background color.** The site's background is frequently left white—particularly on

commerce sites, where product pictures must blend into the page. But colored backgrounds are common on other kinds of sites, and they play a major role in the emotional impact of your site.

- **Text.** Most sites leave their text a basic black. But you can change it up a little, so long as you choose colors with sufficient contrast to be read.

- **Headline colors.** Will they be the same as the text or a different shade?

- **Link colors.** You'll need a color for regular links (which will be blue, unless you specify something different). But you'll probably want to choose a visited-link (vlink) color and an active-link (alink) color as well. "Your link, alink, and vlink all need to play nicely together," says Jim Frew. "The link should pop forward, and the followed link should sit back."

- **Section navigation colors (optional).** You may choose to color-code your sections, which adds another layer of complexity to the design. "If you really want to make it hard on yourself, you'll have a color-based organization to your site—where section a is blue, section b is green, section c is pink, section d is lime," says Jim Frew. Note, however, that it's not wise to rely on color for site navigation. Users tend not to notice it.

Buy these books!

<designing web graphics.4>

By Lynda Weinman

If you want to learn about web color, make better decisions about color combinations, or ensure that your colors of choice appear correctly on the web, this is the best resource out there. Serves both the novice and professional designer (New Riders, $55).

Color Harmony for the Web

Cailin Boyle

Need inspiration? This book offers an excellent selection of color combinations, both bold and subtle. Includes colors' RGB and hex equivalents (Rockport Publishers. $30).

RGB vs. CMYK color

Colors are created differently on screen than they are for print. So every color can be described two ways: Its CMYK value describes how it's created for print, and its RGB value describes how it's created for the screen.

CMYK stands for Cyan Magenta Yellow blacK— the colors that are added to the **printed page** to produce a full range of colors.

RGB stands for Red Green Blue—the colors that are removed from **light-based media** (like computer screens) to create a full range of colors.

making color work on the web

Whether you're choosing colors for your site or matching your corporate colors to the web, there are two issues at play.

2 issues in making web color work:

1. **Matching print colors to screen colors** so they appear as similar as possible

2. **Choosing web-safe colors** that can be viewed by people on different platforms, browsers, and monitors

matching print colors to screen colors Print colors and screen colors appear differently, because they're created differently. Print colors are created by adding four colors—cyan, magenta, yellow, and black—in different quantities to white paper. But light-based media, like TV or computer screens, create different shades by removing colors (red, green, and blue). The different methods create colors with different qualities.

So print and screen colors will always look slightly different. But some colors won't translate at all. Metallic colors—silver, gold, bronze—that shine on the page will look dull on the screen. And some of the vibrant colors you see on screen (like the "Wired" colors—electric pink, acid green, video blue—cannot be reproduced on paper using the normal (CMYK) color process. They can only be replicated on a printing press by using a special PMS color.

Knowing the differences between print and web color can help you choose a palette that translates. This is especially important if you're starting from scratch, and you plan to promote your product in different media. "You need to look at the big picture when you're starting a logo system," says Jim Frew. "Design for your primary medium, but be aware that some things won't translate."

understanding hex color

Every color that appears on the web is described by a hexadecimal (hex) code. Hex codes are just a way to specify colors in a way the browser can understand (just as Pantone numbers are used to describe precise colors in print).

A hex code is always six digits long, and it combines numbers and letters. (A nice bright purple is #6600CC. A pale pink is #FFCCFF.) This code is actually a translation of the color's RGB values, or the percentage of red, green, and blue that must be used to achieve the specific shade. You can use software to translate a desired color into its hex code, or you can look at a hex chart and choose a color.

A hex chart can be found online here: http://www.lynda.com/hexh.html.

choosing web-safe colors When the web was first developed, most computer monitors could display only 256 colors. So the browser creators had to decide *which* 256 colors a web browser would display. Since different browsers chose differently, and since colors display differently on the Mac and the PC, only 216 colors can be reliably displayed on any monitor and any platform. These 216 colors are known as the web-safe color palette.

Fortunately, computer systems have improved over the last 10 years, and the vast majority of U.S. Internet users can now view millions of colors on their monitors. This frees designers to choose any color they'd like. Even Lynda Weinman, the web graphics guru who made the existence of the web-safe color palette known—no longer follows it.

But if your users are on older systems—in libraries or schools, or in countries that haven't upgraded as widely—or if you want to play it safe or limit your options, it's a good idea to stick with the web-safe palette. You'll find it online at http://www.lynda.com/hex.html.

typography on the web

The art and science of typography offers different challenges in different media: Type choices for a brochure will differ from those for a highway billboard or a television commercial. And the web presents its own set of challenges.

6 challenges of web typography:

1. **Font availability.** On the Web, you must use fonts that your users have installed on their computers. Otherwise, your site won't look the way you designed it. The problem is: Most users have only the limited choice of fonts that came with their computer.

2. **Screen legibility.** Most digital typefaces were designed to print well on a page; not much attention was paid to on-screen legibility. As a result, most fonts are hard to read online, especially at small point sizes.

3. **Cross-platform inconsistencies.** Different fonts come installed on the Mac and the PC, and fonts with the same name may display differently on the two platforms, making precision typography difficult.

4. **Lack of precise positioning.** HTML is a ham-handed tool for type placement. This has improved greatly with the advent of stylesheets, but advanced effects—like overlapping letters or text wrapped around an image—can be maddeningly difficult, if they're possible at all.

5. **Larger type size.** Type must be relatively large on screen to be readable. This eats into the available real estate and restricts design options.

6. **The failure of classic typefaces.** Typefaces that appear beautifully on the printed page often break down on the screen, appearing broken and fuzzy.

So typography on the web is a severely constrained art. The fonts used on most web sites can be counted on one hand, and many of the most popular sites employ typographic "techniques" that make designers cringe.

No, precision typesetting isn't the web's strength. The web offers cross-platform distribution, flexible displays, and user control—all of which run quite counter to the goals of typographic artistry. So what's evolved is an aesthetic of constraint—one that highlights usability and readability.

choosing a typeface

In the early days of HTML, type choices were massively restricted…in that you didn't have any choice at all. *Users* controlled the font displayed on their browsers, but most users didn't even know they controlled them. As a result, most people saw web pages written in the default font, Times New Roman, which is a sub-optimal choice, at best.

Thankfully, times have changed, and HTML now allows the designer to specify the font used for any particular page or word or headline, if she so desires. But the choices are still restricted to those typefaces your users have installed on their computers.

And since most users stick with the small number of system fonts that come bundled with their computers, and since different fonts come with the Mac and the PC, and since very few of those fonts are appropriate for on-screen reading, your choices are limited indeed.

---

serif vs. sans-serif fonts

Serif fonts like Garamond (left), have small strokes—called serifs—embellishing the end of the character's major lines.

Sans-serif fonts like Helvetica (left), have blunt edges, without serifs. Just so you know: Sans means "without" in French.

on-screen legibility

In any medium, from TV to billboards, the legibility of text (or the ease with which it can be read) is affected by many factors: the size, weight, and color of the type; the background color; the spacing between letters, words, and lines; the number of words per line; the distance of the reading material from the eye.

But computer monitors introduce a few quandaries all their own:

■ **Typeface.** Not many typefaces are available for web use. Of those, it's best to choose one that was designed to be read on the screen.

■ **Type size.** At small point-sizes, characters (especially bold and italic) lose their shape, becoming blurry blobs that are difficult to read. So type generally needs to be larger on screen than on paper.

■ **Type color.** On the screen (as on paper), you need sufficient contrast between the text and background colors for text to be readable, and dark text over a light background is preferred.

■ **Line Length.** The rule of thumb—in print and on screen—is that a line of text should be roughly the length of two alphabets (52 characters). Too short and readers grow weary; too long, and they can't find the next line.

recommendations for on-screen legibility

Typeface	Verdana, followed by Arial, Times, and Georgia.
Type color	Dark text against a light background, providing sufficient contrast.
Type size	12-point for body text. Though older people prefer text even larger (around 14-point).
Line length	Roughly two alphabets (52 characters).

To find a font that's both available to most users and acceptably readable, your options are generally limited to Verdana, Arial, Helvetica, Times, Times New Roman, and maybe Georgia. The best choice is Verdana (see Verdana: the web's first font, p. 152), which was designed from the ground-up to be read on screen. Traditional typefaces, such as Helvetica and Times, were designed for the printed page, with the screen fonts coming as an afterthought.

As a result, Verdana is more readable on screen than any other font (thought usability tests show Arial and Times are also quite readable). And while there are more and more typefaces designed for the screen these days, Verdana is the most ubiquitous.

Many designers who migrated to the web from print (which is to say most designers) have a hard time letting go of their favorite typefaces. And you can't blame them: Centuries of typographic design inform the elegance of **Garamond**, the bold simplicity of **Gill**, the downright goofiness of, say, Mister Frisky.

Although you can't take full advantage of the bountiful, beautiful fonts available in print, you need not abandon them entirely. There are two options for integrating non-standard typefaces: using an image of the type or downloading a font with the page.

2 ways to use non-standard fonts:

1. Using an image of the words

2. Downloading a font with the page

using an image of the words The simplest way to integrate non-standard fonts into your web page is to make an image of the word (displayed in the font of your choice) and integrate that image into the web page.

Although this is appropriate in some cases—logos, of course, and also some display copy—it raises several serious problems:

Problems with using images of words:

- Images of words **aren't searchable** and can't be cut-and-pasted.

- Images of words **download much slower** than the words themselves.

- Images of words **can't be read by the screen-readers** on which blind users depend. (This is particularly problematic if the image-words are part of the navigation.)

- The words **can't be read if the image doesn't download or display**.

So this approach, while tempting, should be used in moderation. My personal guideline is that nothing longer than a sentence should be placed in an image.

downloading fonts This is the holy grail of web typography: the ability to download a font, along with a web page, so the page design can make use of the font. To make this dream a reality, several different techniques have been proposed over the years, but none have yet caught on. The basic problem is download time: It just takes too long to transfer and install the font. At some point, however, it will be possible—most likely with stylesheets.

🛒 **Buy these books!**

Typographic Design: Form and Communication
Rob Carter, Ben Day, and Philip Meggs (Wiley, $55.00)
Designing with Type
James Craig (Watson-Guptill, $39.99)

Typography on the web

Fonts.com
http://www.fonts.com

Counterspace
http://counterspace.motivo.com

ABC Typography
http://abc.planet-typography.com

Adobe Type Library
http://www.adobe.com/type/

MyFonts.com
http://www.myfonts.com

Verdana: the web's first font

Most typefaces are a holdover from the days when print ruled the roost. They looked lovely on paper, but the screen fonts were mere placeholders: fuzzy shadows indicating how the text might look, once it's printed. With the advent of the web, people are reading more and more from the screen. We need fonts that are legible, not just presentable, online. Enter Verdana!

Verdana was the first typeface designed specifically for screen display. Microsoft commissioned typographer Matthew Carter to design the system font for Windows 95. So he designed Verdana from the ground up to be readable on screen, especially at small point sizes.

Verdana was the first typeface designed specifically for screen display.

To accomplish this, Carter reversed the usual approach to type design. Normally, a designer draws an outline of the letters, then creates a bitmap that matches the shape. (The bitmap determines the way pixels are used to represent the letter on screen.) But Carter began with the pixels—creating a bitmap that would allow exceptional legibility even in bold and italic at small point sizes (where limited pixels are available to represent the shape). He then drew an elegant outline to define the letters.

Verdana's legibility comes from its bitmap-derived shape, and also its loose spacing and very **bold** bold. Care was taken to distinguish between similar characters like j, i, l, I and 1, and to ensure that letter combinations, such as fl, don't touch.

It's lovely, legible, and actually pleasurable to read on screen.

formatting text

With the advent of stylesheets, it's become possible to exert control over text on a web page in ways that were impossible just a few years ago. Stylesheets let you specify the precise size of the text (in any number of ways: pixels, point size, you name it) as well as the leading—the vertical space between lines.

This is a giant leap for web design, but an admittedly small step for typography. Type treatment on the web is still quite primitive. Relatively simple type treatments—such as overlapping text or wrapping text around an image—can only be achieved with difficulty. And the control that typographers crave—setting precise line length and page depth—just isn't possible.

In truth, it's difficult to control anything with absolute precision online. The web just doesn't work that way. Sites must display on a wide range of platforms, browsers, screen resolutions, and browser window sizes. So the page design must adapt to fill the space available.

Typographers *hate* this. Many designers push back against it, producing contorted web pages with restricted widths and forced line breaks that are supposed to display exactly the same way in every monitor. But alas, these overly controlled designs frequently fail. There's almost no way to reliably ensure that your text will lay out exactly the way you hoped. And the sooner you come to terms with that, the better your web designs will be.

What you can control:

- **Font size.** With stylesheets, you can set the size of your text, based on point size, pixels, and other measurements. However, you should provide users a way to adjust it.

- **Font color.** Using stylesheets, the font tag, or even just the body-text color tag, you can dictate the color of text with reasonable accuracy.

---

is it a font or a typeface?

A **typeface** is a design for a set of characters, usually including letters, numbers, and punctuation. (Helvetica is a typeface.)

A **font** is a printable and displayable version of a particular typeface in a specific weight and size. (10-point Helvetica Bold is a font.)

In the digital age, however, **the two are used interchangeably.** I wouldn't sweat the difference, unless you're in very persnickety company.

- **Link color.** The color of links and followed-links can also be customized with stylesheets or the body-text tag. Otherwise the browser will default to the standard blue underlined links.

- **Font weight.** You can reliably change the weight of a given word, using tags for bold or italic text.

- **Leading.** Stylesheets allow you to set the leading, or vertical space, between lines.

chapter

8

understanding design technologies

"This one is at the absolute cutting edge of obsolescence."

don't miss ...

As web designers quickly learn, the way your site looks and acts depends very much on the technologies you use. The choices may at first seem overwhelming: Names and buzzwords are thrown around without much context. But once you sort out which technology does what, you'll be better prepared to make decisions.

Design technologies include

- HTML & XHTML
- Stylesheets
- Plug-ins
- JavaScript
- Server-side scripts

html & xhtml

HTML, or Hypertext Markup Language, is used to define the structure of a web page. Every page on the web uses HTML (or its close cousin, XHTML) to tell the browser what the page contains and how it should be laid out. See building your first web page, p. 196 and understanding xhtml, p. 158.

HTML features include the following:

- **Tables** allow the page to be creatively subdivided. See understanding tables, p. 160.
- **Frames** allow the web page to be divided into multiple, independent, scrollable sections. See understanding frames, p. 161.

stylesheets

Stylesheets (or cascading stylesheets) work alongside HTML to define how a page should look. HTML defines the structure; stylesheets define the appearance. See understanding stylesheets, p. 162.

plug-ins

Plug-ins are add-on technologies that blend seamlessly into the browser, bringing audio, video, or multimedia capabilities into the page. However, users must have the particular plug-in installed (and installed correctly) to benefit from them.

Plug-ins include the following:

- **Flash** is a multimedia player from Macromedia, which brings animation, sound, and interactivity into the site. See understanding flash, p. 166.
- **QuickTime** is an audio and video player from Apple. See choosing a format for online video, p. 215.
- **RealMedia** is an audio and video player from RealNetworks. See choosing a format for online video, p. 215
- **WindowsMedia** is an audio and video player from Microsoft. See choosing a format for online video, p. 215.

client-side scripts (javascript)

Client-side scripts are small programs that download with the web page and bring interactivity to the site. JavaScript is the main client-side scripting language, and it's used for features like image rollovers, image maps, and collapsible menus. See understanding javascript, p. 164.

server-side scripts (asp, php)

Server-side scripts connect the web page with a database or application, allowing you to customize your site for different users and serve dynamic pages. Scripting options included ASP, JSP, PHP, ColdFusion, and CGI scripts. They all live on your site's server and rely on its processing power. See understanding php, p. 168.

java applets

Applets are small, custom-made programs that download with the browser and play or function in the user's browser. Programmed in Java, these applications are more robust than JavaScript programs, but they also take longer to download and play. For more on Java, see other programming options, p. 165.

how'd they get that look?

Just looking at a site, you can't always tell how it was built; different technologies can sometimes create similar effects. Here's a selection of eye-catching designs and how they were achieved.

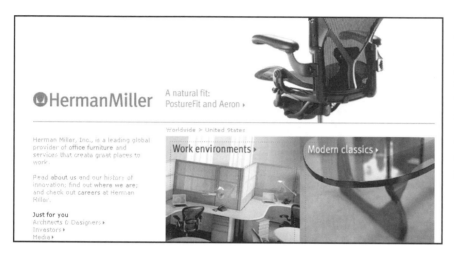

Herman Miller
The layout is done with **tables**—to align page elements and create white space between them. The logo, tagline, and chair are all in one image. The text on the left is written in plain HTML text and formatted with **stylesheets**.

Nantucket Nectars
The layout here is done with **tables**. Large images are sliced and placed in adjoining table cells, so they appear continuous. When you mouse over the bottlecap logo, it "flips" over, revealing the trademark quote inside the cap. This image swap, or rollover, is done with **JavaScript**.

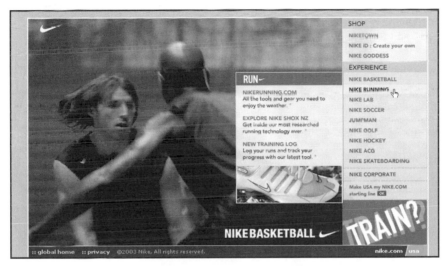

Nike

The layout is done entirely in **Flash**. The background image remains static, while the image on the lower right animates and changes. When you select from the cascading menus, a "click" sound confirms your choice.

Happy Cog Design

The layout is done with **stylesheets** and **<div>** tags. When you select an image, a corresponding text block appears below the image grid. This design is 100% XHTML-compliant.

understanding xhtml

Over the last few years, a massive transition got underway from the old way of designing and building sites to the new. The old way was improvised and based entirely on the site's appearance. (HTML tags were used in ways that were never intended…read <u>understanding tables</u>, p. 160, for a good example). The new way is structured and logical. And while it limits some of your immediate design options, it builds your site to last.

XHTML—which will replace its close cousin, HTML—is at the crux of this transition. The purpose of XHTML is to create a web that's more standardized and more compatible with other systems that might want to display the same content, such as screen readers for the blind, older backend database systems, and new upcoming technologies like handheld computers or web-enabled cell phones.

To achieve full compatibility with these (and other) systems, the ideal language is XML (extensible markup language), a flexible customizable markup language. But an immediate transition from HTML to XML is impractical, considering the billions of documents written in HTML.

This is why the W3C (the industry standards body) introduced XHTML, a transitional language similar to HTML that can pave the way to future.

html & xhtml: what's the difference?

To the untrained eye, XHTML looks exactly the same as HTML. In fact, XHTML *is* almost the same as HTML. It was designed to follow the grammar of HTML as closely as possible. The differences, you'll find, are in the details.

5 differences between html and xhtml:

1. **XHTML is case-sensitive.** All tags must be written in lowercase. Certain declarations must be in uppercase.

2. **XHTML is persnickety about closing tags.** All tags must be closed—even those, like <img>, that lack closing tags in HTML.

---

what you need to know about xhtml

what it is

XHTML (extensible hypertext markup language) is a modified version of HTML that is compatible with XML-based systems. XHTML takes web pages beyond the web browser, allowing them to be interpreted by a wider range of applications and systems.

how it's used

Like HTML, XHTML is used to create web pages. But this newer markup language structures the text and elements so they can be displayed in a browser *and* understood by other applications.

why it's loved

XHTML makes web documents readable and usable by a wide range of other applications, including old content systems that pre-date the web, specialized display systems like screen readers for the blind, and future technologies—including those in handheld computers—that are just evolving.

why it's hated

XHTML is persnickety and precise, requiring more documentation and specific formatting than HTML.

- XHTML is unforgiving of small mistakes. A tiny error can make a document invalid.

- It's time-consuming to convert existing HTML documents to XHTML.

- XHTML relies on stylesheets for design (instead of tables or font tags). And stylesheets don't work as well with certain types of designs.

Transitioning to XHTML?

A List Apart's XHTML tutorials
http://www.alistapart.com/stories/indexHTMLXHTML.html
New York Public Library's XHTML style guide
http://www.nypl.org/styleguide/

Buy these books!

HTML & XHTML: The Definitive Guide
By Chuck Musciano & Bill Kennedy
(O'Reilly, $34.95)

Designing with Web Standards
By Jeffrey Zeldman
(New Riders, $34.95)

3. **XHTML is persnickety about nested tags.** All nested tags must be closed in reverse order to how they were opened. The tag opened first must be closed last.

4. **XHTML is persnickety about attribute values.** All attribute values must be placed in quotes (such as <link color="blue">), and all attributes must have values

5. **XHTML uses slightly different declarations** to open the document.

As you can tell, XHTML is more picky and less forgiving than HTML. It introduces some new rules and rigorously enforces the existing ones.

transitioning to xhtml

For some sites, the transition to XHTML is straightforward. It may be the simple (if time-consuming) matter of revising your current HTML to follow the new rules more exactly.

But not all sites have it this easy. If your site design depends heavily on tables and font tags, there's no quick fix. You'll need to revamp the structure of the pages and learn how to accomplish visual effects using stylesheets. You may find that your existing design simply doesn't translate.

In this case, you may want to make a gradual transition: First converting from HTML to XHTML, but keeping a tables-based layout. Or you may decide to jump in all the way with a complete redesign, as Wired News did in late 2002.

So depending on your site, the transition to XHTML may be a bit painful. New shoes always hurt, as they say. But the transition is inevitable. And the benefits of converting far outweigh the inconvenience of change. So if you're experiencing a lull in development or launching a brand new site, take the opportunity to make the transition. Sooner or later, you're going to have learn the new way.

For a complete transitional guide:
"Better Living through XHTML" by Jeffrey Zeldman: http://www.alistapart.com/stories/betterliving/

converting html to xhtml

The transition from HTML to XHTML need not be as painful as you'd think. It's all in the details:

- **Close every tag.** In HTML, you can leave certain tags, like <p>, unclosed. In XHTML, all tags must be closed—in this case, with a </p> tag.

- **Close even "empty" tags.** In HTML, certain stand-alone tags—like <img>— lack closing tags. But even these tags must be closed in XHTML by inserting a space and a slash into the tag itself: <img />.

- **Use only lowercase letters.** HTML lets you write tags in capital or lowercase letters (<IMG> or <img>) but XHTML tags must be lowercase.

- **Assign a value to every attribute.** In HTML, some attributes don't take values, like the frames attribute noresize. In XHTML, they must. You simply repeat the name: noresize="noresize".

- **Use quote marks around values.** In HTML, the quotes around value attributes (color="blue") are optional. In XHTML, they're required.

- **Avoid non-standard tags.** HTML documents can include proprietary tags, like <font>, but XHTML documents can't.

- **Add new introductory "declarations."** HTML documents start with the <html> tag. But XHTML requires a little more explanation. You'll need an XML declaration, which identifies the version of XML used, a <!DOCTYPE> declaration, which identifies the markup language, and a modified <html> tag. A page that uses XHTML 1.0, in English, with the Western Roman alphabet, will start like this:

```
<?xml version="1.0" encoding="UTF-8">

<!DOCTYPE html PUBLIC "-//W3C//DTD
XHTML 1.0 Transitional//EN"
"http://www.w3.org/TR/xhtml1-
transitional.dtd">

<html
xmlns="http://www.w3.org/1999/xhtml"
xml:lang="en"  lang="en">
```

understanding tables

The HTML tags that create tables have become the workhorse of many web designs. They were designed to display rows and columns of data, but have been used instead to creatively subdivide the page, creating grids for interesting layouts.

Over the years, tables have been combined and contorted to make way for any number of creative web designs. Tables can be used to create columns of text or lovely patchworks of color. And graphics can be chopped up and divided among table cells to achieve the illusion of a continuous image.

The problem with tables is that the HTML code gets very complex. And this complexity slows down your site: Embedded tables—and mistakes within complex ones—are a major culprit behind slow web pages.

There's another big problem with tables: Data in a table is structured simply to look good in a web browser—there's no deeper meaning in its use of rows and columns. This renders the page unreadable to other types of applications, such as handheld computers (which have a smaller screen) and screen readers for the blind (which rely on a logical structure to translate pages into verbal explanations).

For this reason, many designers now use stylesheets to lay out their pages. Stylesheets (combined with <div> tags) allow you to format the page visually without confusing the page structure. (See understanding stylesheets, p. 162, and building your site to last, p. 184.)

learning to use tables

The trick to using tables is translating the visual design you want into a series of table "cells" (of varying width) within rows (of the same width). All the content that appears in the table must be contained within one of the cells.

You'll find good tutorials on tables on the site Webmonkey (see the listing on this page) or in most HTML reference books.

---

what you need to know about tables

what they are

Tables are an HTML feature that allow you to divide the page into columns and rows.

how they're used

Although they were designed to contain columns and rows of data, tables are actually used as the workhorse of web page layout. Designers use them to creatively subdivide the page into sections that contain different background colors, images, and/or text.

why they're loved

Tables made advanced layout on the web possible. They allowed designers to create the illusion of columns, to stagger images and text around the page, and to create complex interfaces.

why they're hated

Many feel the time of tables has passed, and that designers should be moving toward stylesheets as a presentation tool. Also:

- Tables are overused and misused. Many sites rely unnecessarily on an intricate grid of tables embedded within tables.

- Complex, poorly specified tables slow pages down.

- Pages built in tables are very specific to the web browser. They can't be displayed by other systems, like handheld computers or other future devices.

- Pages built in tables can't be easily interpreted by screen readers for the blind.

- Sites built with tables don't comply with web standards. See why you should follow web standards, p. 186.

Learning to use tables
Webmonkey table tutorials
http://www.webmonkey.com/authoring/tables/

understanding frames

Frames allow you to divide the browser window into several independent, scrollable areas, each of which displays a different, unique HTML document. So you're actually displaying several different web pages within one interface.

Frames allow more complex interactions to take place within the window of the browser, without completely reloading the page. One area of the page can remain static while another reloads, creating a more consistent visual environment. This same-page environment makes more complex interactions possible and helps prevent the disorientation so common on the web.

But frames have fallen out of favor over time. Their decline can be attributed partially to the evolution of other, more elegant methods of interactivity (involving JavaScript or Flash), and partially to their drawbacks: They require a lot of careful production work, in which it's easy to introduce errors. Also, the pages in a frames-based site lack unique web addresses, so users can't bookmark them, other sites can't link to them, and search engines can't always index them.

learning to use frames

The first thing to learn about frames is this: The HTML document for a frames-based page won't contain any actual content. It will merely describe the structure of the page (the frameset), and point to the web pages that should appear within each individual region (or frame).

A frames-based page can be divided into as many regions as you care to make. You can describe the page in terms of columns or rows, and size the frames based on a percentage of the overall browser window or a precise value—in pixels.

You'll find good tutorials on frames on the sites Webmonkey and A List Apart (see listings on this page) as well as most HTML reference books.

what you need to know about frames

what they are
Frames are a feature of HTML that let you subdivide the browser window into two or more independent, scrollable sections.

how they're used
Frames can increase interactivity and aid navigation by allowing one area of the web page to stay stationery while another reloads. This creates a consistent visual environment (one that doesn't entirely disappear as information refreshes).

why they're loved
They rely wholly on HTML, can be created by non-programmers, and are supported by all major browsers in use today.

why they're hated
Creation and troubleshooting can be a real production nightmare. It's easy to make mistakes that cause pages to load in the wrong area of the window. Also:

- The pages in a frames-based site don't have unique web addresses, so other sites can't link to them and users can't bookmark them.

- Because they lack unique web addresses, the pages also can't be searched by users or indexed by many search engines.

Learning to use frames
Webmonkey frames tutorials
http://www.webmonkey.com/authoring/frames/
A List Apart Frames tutorials
http://www.alistapart.com/stories/frames/

understanding stylesheets

Stylesheets work alongside HTML to define what a web page looks like. The HTML marks up the document *structurally*—indicating what bits of content are headlines, body text, lists, etc., while the stylesheets describe how the headlines and other elements should *look* in the web browser.

If you've worked with a page-layout program (like PageMaker or QuarkXpress), you're probably familiar with stylesheets. They allow you to specify how particular types of words—headlines, for example—should appear throughout a document.

So every time you write a headline, you simply mark the words as a headline (or "apply the headline stylesheet") and they take on the appearance of other headlines in your document. It's easier and more efficient to use a stylesheet than it would be to customize the text every time you wrote a headline.

Stylesheets work similarly on the web. With stylesheets, you can create a document using simple, traditional HTML tags—<p> for a new paragraph, <h1> for the largest headline—but redefine how those elements should look. Want your headlines to appear in gray, 72-point Helvetica Bold?

Before there were stylesheets, designers had to individually customize every chunk of text in a document by listing its point size, type face, color, and so on. But stylesheets eliminate all that fuss. With stylesheets, you describe what a headline looks like once, then every headline in the document takes on that appearance.

Let's take a moment to appreciate how cool that is. Before stylesheets, you had to decide between structure and appearance: You could either use the <h1> tag—which properly labels page elements—and get a generic-looking page created by the default browser styles. Or you

what you need to know about stylesheets

what they are
Stylesheets—or Cascading Stylesheets—work alongside HTML to define how a web page looks. The HTML defines the structure of the page (This is a headline. This is a list) while stylesheets describe how each element looks.

how they're used
Stylesheets are primarily used to specify how text looks. Increasingly, they're also used for page layout.

why they're loved
Stylesheets help you build a site in compliance with web standards. Also:

- They separate content from presentation, letting you create a site that's both structurally sound and visually attractive.

- Pages designed with stylesheets load faster than those designed with font tags and tables.

- Pages designed with stylesheets are more accessible to the blind.

- Stylesheets make it faster and easier to make changes.

why they're hated
Although stylesheets sound great on paper, they present some practical problems:

- They aren't supported by older browsers.

- They're supported differently by different browsers and require a lot of trouble-shooting.

- They require designers trained with tables and font tags to learn a new way of designing.

Learn to use stylesheets
Webmonkey stylesheet tutorials
http://www.webmonkey.com/authoring/stylesheets/
A List Apart stylesheet tutorials
http://www.alistapart.com/stories/indexCSS.html
CSS Central on DevEdge
http://devedge.netscope.com/central/css/

could use the font tags—which let you customize appearance—but your document would have no structural integrity. With stylesheets, you can have it all.

The benefits of stylesheets:

■ **Control.** Stylesheets let you boss around text in ways that were impossible before, giving you greater control over appearance.

■ **Efficiency.** Rather than define and redefine the font tags for every chunk of words on your web site, stylesheets let you define them once for an entire document or even an entire site. (Headlines look like this. Paragraphs look like this.) This is particularly useful when you have to make changes.

■ **Speed.** Web sites designed with stylesheets load faster than those designed with tables.

■ **Separation of content and presentation.** Stylesheets define how your page appears visually, leaving the structure to the HTML tags. This allows your content to be viewed on other devices, beyond the browser. (See building your site to last, p. 184.)

■ **Standards.** Stylesheets help your site comply with web standards. (See why you should follow web standards, p. 186.)

The drawbacks of stylesheets:

■ **Lack of support in early browsers.** Stylesheets weren't supported in early browsers, still in use by roughly 5% of web users.

■ **Inconsistent support in browsers.** Stylesheet features are supported differently in different browsers. So designs that work in one browser might fail in another. But there are workarounds, says designer Jeffrey Zeldman. "Once the workarounds are known, problems of browser difference largely vanish."

■ **Re-training required.** To work effectively with stylesheets, designers have to rethink a many of their assumptions about building for the web. And this takes time.

learning to use stylesheets

Whether included in HTML or delivered on their own, stylesheets have a particular structure they follow, which looks something like this:

```
h1 { color: white; font-family:
verdana; font-size: 16 pt }
```

The stylesheet above redefines the <h1> headline tags so that all <h1> headlines on the page will appear in 16-point Verdana, colored white. Once this definition is included, the designer can simply label headlines <h1>, rather than reiterating each time that the text should be 16-point white verdana.

There are four different types of stylesheets.

4 kinds of stylesheets:

1. **Global stylesheets** are incorporated in the top of an HTML document and apply to all the content within that particular page. They're also called embedded stylesheets.

2. **Local stylesheets** are integrated within the body of the HTML document to control the appearance of a specific word, sentence, or area of the page. They're also known as inline stylesheets.

3. **Linked stylesheets** are small, independent text documents separate from the HTML file. Also known as external stylesheets, they control the appearance of multiple pages. So instead of embedding stylesheets into each page, you create one stylesheet document and link it to all your pages.

4. **Imported stylesheets** are similar to linked stylesheets, but they allow you to combine stylesheet methods.

More reasons to use stylesheets
designing for speed, p.92
building your site to last, p. 184
why you should follow web standards, p. 186

understanding javascript

JavaScript is a programming language that's built into your web browser and lets you manipulate the images, text, and other objects that appear in the browser window.

JavaScript is responsible for many of the dynamic elements in today's web's sites. Some, like image rollovers, are visible to the user. And others work behind the scenes to detect, for example, what type of browser the visitor is using and customize the page accordingly.

The real power of JavaScript is that it's a *client-side* programming language, which means it can perform all sorts of functions within a web page and without help from the server. Once a page with JavaScript appears in a browser, it has everything it needs to perform lightweight programming functions, such as calculating totals, swapping images, or expanding and collapsing menus. So these tasks can be completed without a new page loading.

The benefits of JavaScript:

- It's **built into the browser**, so it can manipulate the words and images in the window more easily than other programming languages.

- It can **interact with the user's computer**, gleaning basic information about the user's environment (platform, browser, etc.).

- It's relatively **easy to learn**—more difficult than HTML, but much easier than complex programming languages like Java or C++.

- JavaScript programs are generally **short and sweet**, and they can be integrated right into the HTML document.

- JavaScript code can be **shared easily** among developers. You can cut and paste a script from one HTML page to another.

- JavaScript programs are **self-sufficient**. They run in a user's browser, without relying on the site server for help.

what you need to know about javascript

what it is
JavaScript is a programming language built directly into the web browser. It's a relatively simple language that's easy to learn and integrate.

how it's used

JavaScript is used to add interactive elements—including image rollovers and image maps—to a web page. It's also used for launching small pop-up windows, running a "ticker" along the browser frame, gathering information from forms, expanding and collapsing menus, and detecting the user's browser and platform.

why it's loved
JavaScript was the first—and still one of the most accessible—ways to bring interactivity to otherwise static web pages.

- It's relatively easy to learn.

- It's easy to steal and customize scripts.

- It adds interactive elements with relatively little programming work.

- It doesn't put a strain on the server.

- It allows easy access to the elements on the web page.

why it's hated

People love to hate JavaScript because:

- Different browsers support JavaScript differently. So a program that works in one browser might crash another.

- Inexperienced programmers create buggy scripts that don't work consistently.

- Some common applications—like ticker tape or pop-up windows—are overused and annoying, but they just don't go away.

Like most technologies, JavaScript is a double-edged sword. Its powers can be used for good or evil. Most of the problems with JavaScript stem from its overuse or misuse.

The drawbacks of JavaScript:

- Different browsers support JavaScript differently. A program that works effortlessly in one browser may choke in another.

- The accessibility of JavaScript means there are many novice programmers producing buggy, inconsistent code.

- Because JavaScript can be shared so easily among sites, many non-programmers integrate JavaScript into their sites without understanding what they're doing or why.

learning to use javascript

JavaScript programs are integrated directly into the HTML document (in the header area at the beginning of the document) and are sandwiched between the <script> </script> tags.

The code for a Javascript alert box will look like this:

```
<script language="JavaScript">
alert("Here's something you can do with
JavaScript"),
</script>
```

And will appear on screen like this:

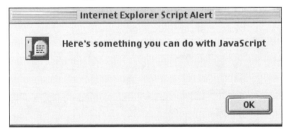

This example is very simple. And that—again—is the beauty of JavaScript: You can easily learn to do some simple tricks just by copying another site's code. But if you really want to learn JavaScript, it's best to take a more structured approach.

other programming options

VBScript Developed by Microsoft, VBScript is similar to JavaScript and serves the same purpose: to let programmers easily manipulate the object in a browser window. But VBScript only works on Microsoft's Internet Explorer browser, running in Microsoft Windows. This makes it a poor choice for most sites.

Server-side scripts These can accomplish many of the same things as JavaScript, but they rely on the site's server to get things done. They're primarily used to pass information between the user and a database or application. See <u>understanding php</u>, p. 168.

Java Although they sound related, Java and JavaScript have little in common. Java is a full-featured, object-oriented programming language, similar to (though simpler than) C++. It was developed by Sun Microsystems as an agnostic language that works across all platforms. It's used (among other things) to develop small web-based applications ("applets") that download with a web page.

Learning JavaScript is a dual process:

- Learning to think with the structural logic of an engineer

- Learning JavaScript itself

Learning a programming language is a lot like learning a real language. You have to learn both the words (called "variables") and the grammar (or "syntax") used to string the words together. The best place to start is Webmonkey's JavaScript tutorial, written by web veteran Dave Thau. His book *The Book of JavaScript*, is a great follow-up.

Learn JavaScript
Webmonkey JavaScript tutorials
http://www.webmonkey.com/
programming/javascript/
A List Apart JavaScript tutorials
http://www.alistapart.com/
stories/indexJavaScript.html

🛒 **Buy this book!**
The Book of JavaScript
By thau!
(No Starch, $29.95)

understanding flash

Flash is a "plug-in" technology that allows you to integrate multimedia files (animation, navigation, etc.) directly into a web page. In order for users to see your Flash file, they must have the Flash player installed, in addition to a web browser.

Flash is a creation of Macromedia, and it's attracted an almost cult-like following in the web design community, because…well, largely because it's so much fun. Flash allows you to create effects that you couldn't accomplish—not even close—with HTML and could only otherwise produce with great technical effort and mixed results.

Technically, Flash seems too good to be true. The animations are quite beautiful, with smooth transitions, rich colors, and perfectly synced sound. Flash "movies" (as they're usually called) can be stretched to fit different size browser windows and still retain the original look and feel. All this, and they download pretty quickly, too.

No doubt: Flash has a lot going for it. But in truth, it's drastically overused on the web today. Most sites, in reality, don't need animation. So while it's perfectly suited to some sites, it's just a distraction on others. As with all technologies, you should know what Flash is good for, and only use it when it makes sense. (See to flash or not to flash, p. 144.)

The benefits of flash:

- **In-page interactivity.** Flash allows you to create highly interactive experiences without reloading the entire page. This often improves the speed of transactions and minimizes the disorientation people experience when transitioning between steps.

- **Smooth animation.** Flash is by far the best tool for online animation.

- **Large installed user base.** As a proprietary plug-in technology, Flash isn't accessible to everyone online. But the number of users is vast and growing, because the Flash player is now bundled with each Internet Explorer browser.

what you need to know about flash

what it is
Flash is a so-called "plug-in" technology from Macromedia that lets you create animations or interactive, multimedia presentations and integrate them into a web page.

how it's used
Flash is the most popular platform for online animation and is also commonly used to create interactive experiences within a web page.

why it's loved
Flash vastly increases the options available to the web developer—bringing animation, interactivity, video, and sound to the web page.

- It's efficient and downloads relatively quickly.

- It works with vector-based graphics, so it's scalable: The same "movie" can appear in different size windows.

- Although it's a plug-in technology, it ships with most browsers and is now in use by a wide majority of web users.

why it's hated
Flash is often over-used in places that don't require animation or in-page interactivity. Also:

- It isn't universally accepted, and some users have problems managing versions.

- Flash-based content isn't searchable or indexable.

- Flash-based navigation systems are frequently non-standard and hard to use.

- Vector-based graphics tend to look stylistically similar, so there's a specific "Flash" look.

Learn how to use Flash
Webmonkey Flash tutorials
http://www.webmonkey.com/authoring/stylesheets/
A List Apart Flash tutorials
http://www.alistapart.com/stories/indexFlash.html

■ **Fast downloads.** Thanks largely to its use of vector-based graphics, Flash files compress remarkably well and download more quickly than you might expect. Also, Flash files can begin playing before the entire file is loaded (increasing their perceived speed).

■ **Scalable size.** Thanks again to vector-based graphics, Flash files can stretch to fill the space available in a browser window. This makes it easier to design effectively for different-sized monitors.

The drawbacks of Flash:

■ **It's not universal.** Although most people have some version of Flash installed, they don't all have it properly installed. Also, different versions are in use.

■ **It's not searchable.** The text in a Flash-based site can't be searched by the user and can't be indexed by most search engines.

■ **It's not linkable.** Individual pages within a Flash file cannot be "bookmarked" or linked to individually.

■ **It's not inter-operable.** The text and images in Flash files cannot be interpreted or displayed in other environments beyond the web browser.

■ **It's often unnecessary.** Flash animations are often gratuitous; they frequently appear on sites that really don't need animation. And in some cases, they duplicate what could be done nearly as well and complication-free in HTML.

■ **It's often nonstandard.** Interfaces built in Flash often ignore web design conventions, forcing users to learn a new system. This can be fine if you're creating an immersive site that's entertaining or educational, but counterproductive if you're building an information resource or an online store.

■ **Visual techniques are limited.** Because Flash makes use of vector-based graphics, the range of visual techniques is limited. Most Flash animations have that smooth-lined, flat-colored, "Flashy" look.

learning to use flash

The hard thing about using Flash isn't the developer software itself, but the skills it takes. Great Flash designers are skilled at animation, navigation, and scripting. Not an easy combination.

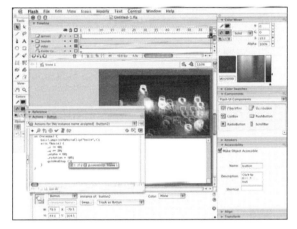

The Flash developer software acts as both a graphics program and a movie editor, so it combines the tools you'd expect in both types of programs.

The Flash software looks like this:

All Flash files are given names ending with the .swf extension. You can include them in a web page by placing a few lines of code within the HTML. So a Flash movie named "coolflashthing.swf" would be integrated like this:

```
<object width="300" height="300">
<param name="movie"
value="coolflashthing.swf">
<embed src="coolflashthing.swf"
width="300" height="300">
</embed>
</object>
```

🛒 **Buy this book!**
Flash to the Core: An Interactive Sketchbook
Joshua Davis (New Riders, $45.00)

understanding php

PHP is a scripting language that helps you create dynamic web sites. You can think of PHP—and any "server-side" scripting option (ASP, JSP, etc.)—as a go-between. It transfers information (such as a search query) from the user to the back-end database or application; it then takes the results from the application and turns them into a web page.

For instance, some sites serve personalized information to returning customers ("Welcome back, June! The weather in New York is still awful!") Server-side scripts, like PHP, make this possible. They grab information about the user who requested the page, and pass it to the back-end application, which runs on the server. The application decides what to do, based on what the script told it (Print the text: "Welcome back June!"), and the script translates that into a web page. All this usually happens in a matter of milliseconds.

Like all "server-side" scripting languages, PHP uses the power of your site's server to create these dynamic elements. It has many applications.

php is used to

- Gather user information from forms.

- Detect the user's browser and platform, and serve dynamic pages or elements.

- Serve dynamic pages based on user input.

- Serve randomized images or ads.

- Track users through the site.

- Reuse a single page template throughout the site.

PHP will work on any site whose server has the (free) PHP software installed.

Learn PHP

Webmonkey PHP tutorials

http://www.webmonkey.com/programming/php/

---

what you need to know about php

what it is

PHP is a scripting language that helps you create dynamic web sites. The commands are integrated into normal HTML files, but it uses the server's power to perform the tasks.

how it's used

PHP is most often used to link a database with a web site, drawing dynamic elements into otherwise static pages. It's also used for collecting user information from forms, generating dynamic page content based on user input or other factors, detecting the user's browser and platform, and tracking users through the site.

why it's loved

- PHP is free!

- It's intuitive, accessible, and relatively easy to learn—even for non-programmers.

- PHP is open-source, so it's developed by a software community (not a company) and the source code is freely available.

- It's compatible with nearly every server.

- It's compatible with a wide range of databases, including Sybase, Oracle, Informix, and the free, open-source MySQL.

why it's hated

Well, hate is a strong word. But PHP doesn't serve everyone's needs.

- Integration with other systems isn't always as efficient as with commercial scripting options.

- Other scripting options offer easier solutions for common procedures.

- Other scripting options offer professional technical support (though you can get tech support for PHP through Zend: www.zend.com).

php vs. other server-side scripts

Of all the server-side scripting options (see the accompanying sidebar), PHP is the most talked-about. Not because it's the most powerful or because it's the best choice in every situation (it isn't), but because it puts the power of dynamic publishing in the hands of people who couldn't otherwise afford it.

PHP, you see, is an open-source technology. The needed software is available for free, so any site—regardless of size, scale, or income—can use it. All you have to do is install the free PHP software on your server (it works on nearly every operating system).

If you combine PHP scripts with a free, open-source MySQL database and free, open-source Apache server software, you can create a very affordable infrastructure for a very sophisticated site.

That said, PHP isn't the right choice for every site. Large-scale sites often choose one of the other options (ASP, JSP, ColdFusion, etc.). These scripting options will cost you more, but the benefits may be significant: They integrate more elegantly with other systems; they let you re-use code from other applications; and they offer easier solutions for complex, but common procedures, like integration with commerce engines. Plus, they offer professional technical support.

learning to use php

PHP commands can be incorporated directly into the HTML file that creates the web page (though the file should be renamed with the .php extension instead of .html.) The scripts appear in the file wherever they'll appear on the page and are always sandwiched between <?PHP and ?>.

If you have a simple PHP script like this:

```
<?php print ("Behold the power of PHP!"); ?>
```

The server creates an HTML page with this code:

```
<p>Behold the power of PHP!
```

Which appears on the web page as:

Behold the power of PHP!

other server-side scripting options

PHP is popular, sure, but it isn't the only game in town. There are a lot of good options for server-side scripts; your choice depends on your taste, your technical requirements, and, of course, your budget.

ASP, or Active Server Pages (a Microsoft product), are dynamic pages, created on-the-fly by the server. Many application-based sites—search engines, commerce sites—deliver results in ASP. To create ASP (.asp) pages, you combine HTML with scripts (usually written in VBScript). To serve ASP pages, you need a Windows server or a Unix server enabled for ASP. One great advantage of ASP is that it allows developers to reuse software components, written in Visual Basic or Visual C++. This makes integration easier.

CGI scripts are the oldest scripting option on the web, and they're commonly used to provide the functionality behind forms. CGI scripts are usually written in the programming language Perl, and they'll run on any web server. Their biggest drawback is inefficiency: They require a lot of processing power from the server.

ColdFusion, a Macromedia product, was designed to help businesses link their databases with the web browser. To create ColdFusion (.cfm) pages, you combine HTML tags with ColdFusion scripts. Unlike other scripting solutions, which rely on existing languages like Visual Basic, ColdFusion uses its own scripting language, CFML (ColdFusion Markup Language) developed specifically for this purpose. You can serve ColdFusion pages from any server with the software installed.

JSP, or Java Server Pages (a Sun Microsystems product), are dynamic pages, created on-the-fly by the server. Many commerce sites deliver pages in JSP. To create JSP (.jsp) pages, you combine XML tags with small programs (called servlets) written in the programming language Java. JSP is very powerful, very fast, and viewed by many as the best choice for large-scale systems.

building

your site

chapter

building for the web

MY BODY IS A NATURAL, BEAUTIFUL THING...

SECURE WEB SITE

don't miss ...

For many site owners, building is the most intimidating step in starting a web site. The plan they can read; the design they can see. But the building process is shrouded in mystery. They know it happens, but they have no idea how.

It's natural, actually. As Arthur C. Clarke famously said, "Any sufficiently advanced technology is indistinguishable from magic." And the magic that makes your web site work can be confounding indeed—obscured as it is in acronyms and buzzwords.

But even if you don't know HTML from the ACLU, you could build a simple site in a day. The basic technology is easy to learn (Start with how web sites work: a primer, p. 190). Of course, things quickly get more complicated. You'll need experienced engineers, designers, and production specialists to build a site of substance.

But even if you're working on a complex, commercial site, you can still contribute to technological decisions. And you must. While it's good to recognize your limits and trust the people you hire, you have to stay involved. (See how to work with engineers, p. 236)

"Looking back, I would have asked more questions," said Randi Shade, founder and CEO of CharityGift. "And I would have stayed involved even if the engineers said I shouldn't—because the things I brought up really were important to the product."

Confidence is key here. You can't allow yourself to be intimidated, even if the technology is new to you. "It's important not to be afraid to sound stupid if you don't understand what someone's talking about," said Tim Ziegler, founder of FamilyAlbum.com. "The critical thing is to ask questions."

So as you build your site, keep your wits about you. Don't be razzle-dazzled by the technology—just focus on what you know. Be clear about your priorities. Keep your eye on the end product. Hire good people, set reasonable deadlines, invest in testing, and don't forget to throw a party when you're done.

---

the well-built web site

Every site owner should know how to assess the workmanship on her site, even if she couldn't build one herself. Here's what to look for:

The well-built web site is

1. **Fast.** This may be the only thing that matters. You could do everything else right, and still fail if your pages load too slowly. See building for speed, p. 221.

2. **Compatible.** People will use your site with a wide range of computers, browsers, monitors, and connection speeds. Your site doesn't have to look the same in all browsers—it doesn't even have to look good in all browsers—but it should work for the vast majority of your users. See building for compatibility, p. 176.

3. **Reliable.** Customers expect your site to work consistently and reliably, just as they expect their TV to turn on or their newspaper to be delivered. Your site should always be available, the pages and images should always load, and the applications should return correct results. See building for reliability, p. 179.

4. **Accessible.** What's true in the real world is true online: It's good business to make your site accessible to the disabled. You should offer a coherent, if not equivalent, experience to users who are sight- or hearing-impaired. It's nice. It's smart. And in many cases, it's the law. See building for accessibility, p. 182.

5. **Built to last.** When you bring your company online, it should be an investment in your future. Your site should be built to function not only in today's web browsers, but future devices as well. To ensure longevity, build the site in compliance with industry standards. See building your site to last, p. 184

Not sure where to start
how web sites work, p. 190.

building for speed

I am, by nature, a cluttered person. My tiny apartment is about as densely packed with books, magazines, CDs, photographs, electronics, and shoes as is practically possible and socially acceptable.

Living in such a small apartment keeps me disciplined. I'm constantly evaluating my decisions about what I keep and what goes out on the street. Do I *really* need 15 Avengers videotapes, which take up a cubic foot? Should I buy the DVDs instead? Or toss them altogether? These are the sorts of questions I ask myself regularly.

You have to bring the same kind of rigor to your web site. Web pages have a tendency to expand over time, with more and more links and promotions piling on. And as sites get more sophisticated—with dynamic elements and complex applications—it's more difficult to keep them running quickly.

Speed is crucial to site success, but it's easy to let it slip.

Speed is crucial to site success, but it's easy to let it slip. This is why every person on your team needs to evaluate every aspect of the site that they touch. So many things affect speed—the backend code, the design, the features you include, the servers you buy—that everyone's role offers opportunities for speed savings—and waste.

"You need everyone to come together and work on site speed," says Pamela Statz, former production manager for HotWired and Lucasfilm. "You can't do it alone."

Speed affects all web disciplines, including

- Design
- Engineering
- Production
- Infrastructure

top 10 reasons your site is so stinkin' slow

1. **Pages are just too big** and take too long to transfer. Too many graphics, too many scripts, and too much multimedia add up to a long wait for users.

2. **Images are too big** and take too much time to transfer. They should be cropped and/or compressed to reduce K-size.

3. **Nested tables** in the HTML code confuse the browser, preventing it from drawing—or forcing it to re-draw—the page.

4. **"Rich media" ads** that use Java-based programs take too long to load.

5. **Too many ads** on the page slow it down—because of their size and sometimes because of the scripts that pull them in.

6. **Width and height** aren't specified for images and tables. This forces the browser to either wait for every element to load before drawing the page or to "guess" how much room to leave. If it guesses wrong, the entire page must be redrawn.

7. **Site isn't compatible** with all common platforms and browsers, causing the site to sputter and choke for some users.

8. **Servers lack the strength** needed to quickly generate results for many simultaneous users. Increasing both the number of servers and their processing power can help.

9. **Bandwidth is insufficient** for the number of visitors you're receiving, especially during peak hours.

10. **Inefficient backend code** puts way too much strain on the servers, especially for application-based sites like retail stores, banking centers, or even database-driven news sites.

design and site speed   More than any other factor, the need for speed has shaped what it means to design for the web. There are many constraints on web design: It must be usable, it must be compatible with different browsers and platforms, it must be technically feasible with HTML.

But it's speed, more than anything, that has shaped design aesthetics for the web. Download times put a sharp limit on the number and size of images (or animation or video) a site can use. And certain types of images are smaller and faster than others.

So the best web designers have adapted their style to the medium, using skinnier graphics and other speed-friendly techniques (color, words, placement, pacing) to convey meaning and emotion within a site that's also usable and fast. (See designing for speed, p. 92.)

engineering and site speed   Unlike designers, who think of speed only when they're designing for the web (and not, for instance, when they're designing a magazine), engineers are always thinking about speed.

Speed is always on the engineer's mind, because it's important in all kinds of software. Lag-time is never suffered gladly by users, so the aegis is always on engineers to make programs run faster. A wasted second is a problem to be solved.

It's important to bring engineering in early when you're talking about site speed. In fact, you should bring them in early on all product development, because they can identify (among other things) where time can be saved.

Engineers almost always think about speed when they're evaluating a product proposal, according to Noah Mercer, former CTO of Nextdoor Networks: "We'll look at a product specification and say, 'Well, this feature's going to be really inefficient or really slow. So can we do without it? Can we change it? Are there other ways the product could function that would make it happen faster?'"

Sometimes, there's a solution, Mercer says. But sometimes there isn't: "If the answer is 'No. It absolutely has to be this way,' then you look at what it's going to cost you to support that functionality for a specific number of users. And it becomes a business decision at that point."

production and site speed   Efficiency is the name of the game in web production. Production managers are always thinking of ways to save time—both for themselves and the user.

> **The best web designers have adapted their style to the medium, using speed-friendly techniques to convey meaning.**

Production-wise, templating is perhaps the best way to improve speed. "Plan your web site in terms of what can be templated," says Pamela Statz. "Can you use the same design page after page? Can you reuse assets?"

If you reuse images, animation, and stylesheets throughout your site, the user's browser will only have to download them once. So subsequent pages will load much faster, even though they have the same elements.

infrastructure and site speed   The servers that host your site, and the bandwidth available to them, have a direct impact on the speed of your site. So for large-scale sites, especially, it's smart to have a capacity plan in place before you start designing or coding. You should know how many concurrent users you expect at launch, and how you'll scale up.

But don't get too far ahead of yourself. Scaling up too quickly can waste money and time. "As Donald Knuth said, 'premature optimization is the root of all programming evil,'" laughs Greg Dotson, Chief Information Officer of Guru. "Left to our own devices, engineers think, 'This isn't gonna be fast enough if I have a million users!' But you're never going to have a million users! And if you do, you can always throw another server at the problem. Hardware is cheap."

Speeding up your site?
designing for speed, p. 92
preparing images for the web, p. 208
improving site speed, p. 218

building for compatibility

Compatibility is perhaps the most vexing problem faced by web developers. Users have different computers, different browsers (and different versions of the same browser), different monitors, different color capabilities, and different connection speeds. All these factors affect the site—its speed, its functionality, and especially its appearance.

The good news is that the differences are less pronounced than they once were. There are fewer browsers in use, and they're more similar than they once were. Monitors have improved in both color capacity and screen resolution, and fewer and fewer people are on truly slow connections.

That said, you still need to think about compatibility: "It's an issue," says designer Nadav Savio. "It's still a terrible issue."

Compatibility problems arise from

- Platform
- Browser
- Plug-ins
- Monitor
- Color capability

platform   People use the web on just about every computer (and every operating system) ever made, including Windows, Mac, Unix, and the odd NeXT box. This affects both the functionality (certain programs—especially Java or JavaScript-based—may not work cross-platform) and the appearance (colors and fonts may vary).

Check your compatibility
NetMechanic
http://www.netmechanic.com

browser   Users view the web through many different versions of many different web browsers. Not to mention cell phones and braille browsers for the blind. This may affect the site's appearance, as different browsers support different design features. Inconsistent support for stylesheets is the biggest problem today; it varies even between different *builds* of the same browser.

plug-ins   Not everyone has plug-in technologies, like Flash, installed properly. So if your site uses plug-ins, not everyone will be able to see it. Because of installation problems, it's hard to estimate how many people you're excluding. (See understanding flash, p. 166.)

monitor   People use monitors of different sizes and resolutions, and this dictates how much space you get on their screen. See where's the fold?, p. 91.

color capability   There are slight differences in color on different platforms. And older computer systems don't display the full range of colors See color on the web, p. 146.

planning for compatibility

If you want your site to be compatible with different systems, you should start thinking about it before you start the development process. Although it may seem counter-intuitive, the best way to approach compatibility is to choose a *single* browser/platform for which you're designing, (these days, it's usually Internet Explorer 6.0 or 5.5 for Windows) and then adapt your work.

1. **Identify your audience.** Before deciding which browsers and platforms you'll support, find out which are most popular among your users. This information is stored in your site's log files, which you can access using traffic-analysis software. (See measuring traffic, p. 245.)

2. **Develop toward a single browser.** After examining the make-up of your audience, choose a single platform/browser combination to develop toward.

3. **Research the differences.** Make sure you're aware of the differences separating your target browser and the rest of the web world. Sometimes, small changes in approach make the difference between your site working for many browsers or only one.

4. **"Degrade gracefully."** Your pages should be designed and built to "degrade gracefully." This means they still function and display reasonably in earlier browsers.

5. **Create a secondary design.** Sometimes your primary design just won't translate to other browsers or platforms. In this case, you'll probably want to create a secondary design for other browsers. But it's best to limit yourself to these two: One design for the target browser; one for everyone else.

6. **Test! Test! Test!** No matter how well you've researched browser and platform differences, you'll always be surprised—and probably frustrated—by what testing reveals.

compatibility testing

No matter how much you research and plan, you can never anticipate all the problems that might arise when your site is used on different browsers and platforms.

So creating a site that displays acceptably and performs reliably across all these systems remains at least a full-time job, if not a lifelong obsession.

The most important thing to remember is that browsers don't work exactly as they should. Each version introduces new bugs along with new features. You have to keep testing to keep up.

Ready to set up your own compatibility testing station? The site A List Apart has a great tutorial: http://www.alistapart.com/stories/xplatform.

Set up a testing station
A List Apart tutorial
http://www.alistapart.com/stories/xplatform

an industry snapshot

People access the web using a wide range of computers, browsers, and monitors (to say nothing of web-compliant cell phones). But the popularity of different systems is always shifting. Here's an industry snapshot, as of January 2003:

Platform
▼ **91%** Windows
▼ **4%** Mac
▼ **1%** Linux
▼ **4%** Other
Source: Google Zeitgeist.

Browser
▼ **52%** Internet Explorer 6.x
▼ **39%** Internet Explorer 5.x
▼ **1%** Netscape Navigator 4.x
▼ **1%** Netscape Navigator 5.x
▼ **1%** Internet Explorer 4.x
▼ **6%** Other
Source: TheCounter.com.

Monitor resolution
▼ **46%** 800 x 600
▼ **40%** 1024 x 768
▼ **4%** 1280 x 1024
▼ **3%** 1152 x 864
▼ **2%** 640 x 480
Source: TheCounter.com.

Colors
▼ **43%** 32-bit (millions of colors)
▼ **43%** 16-bit (65,000 colors)
▼ **9%** 24-bit (16 million colors)
▼ **3%** 8-bit (256 colors)
Source: TheCounter.com.

For updated industry statistics, try
The Counter: http://www.TheCounter.com/stats
Google: http://www.google.com/press/zeitgeist

how will you make your site compatible?

An essential issue in site building is ensuring your site can be seen by everyone—or at least everyone that matters to you. First, figure out what systems your visitors use. Then decide which to focus on.

what setup will you design for?

What browser will you develop for?

❏ Internet Explorer   version _____   Mac | PC

❏ Netscape Navigator   version _____   Mac | PC

❏ Other _____   version _____   Mac | PC

What size browser window will you design for? (In other words, "Where's the fold?")

❏ 640 x 480   ❏ 800 x 600   ❏ 1024 x 768

❏ Other _____   ❏ What?

How many colors will you use?

❏ 256—I'll restrict myself to the "browser-safe" palette.

❏ Millions—I'll use any colors I want, since most of my users can handle it.

what set-ups will you test?

Outside of your target, what other browsers/platforms/monitors will you test?

_____

_____

_____

what do your visitors use?

Using traffic-analysis software, determine what kinds of systems are used to access your site. If you can't access this information, use <u>industry statistics</u>, (p. XXX) for an estimate.

Platform

____ %   Windows

____ %   Mac

____ %   Unix

____ %   Other

Browser

____ %   Internet Explorer 6+

____ %   Internet Explorer 5+

____ %   Internet Explorer 4+

____ %   Netscape Navigator 6+

____ %   Netscape Navigator 5+

____ %   Netscape Navigator 4+

____ %   Opera

____ %   Other

Monitor resolution

____ %   800 x 600

____ %   640 x 480

Colors

____ %   Millions of colors (24-bit color)

____ %   256 colors (8-bit color)

building for reliability

It's a simple fact: People expect your site to work. And they expect it to work the same way it did the last time they used it. But a lot of sites struggle with reliability, especially as they grow.

There are a lot of reasons why a site may not work (or may not work as expected). It may have grown quickly, it may have failed to invest in equipment, it may not have been tested properly, or it may have been built poorly.

An unreliable site may suffer from

- Traffic overload
- Bandwidth blackout
- Browser incompatibility
- Buggy code

traffic overload When sites—or applications within them—"go down," the culprit is often traffic. The site may have outgrown its infrastructure, or it may be experiencing a sudden surge of user requests that it's unequipped to handle. (Unexpected spikes can bring down even well-established sites.)

There are two factors limiting a site's capacity: the bandwidth and the servers. The bandwidth determines how much data can be transferred from your site at once. So if you're serving large files, like video, you're likely to get bottlenecked. The server determines how many users can log on simultaneously and how many requests can be processed at once. An overloaded server will have to turn away visitors and may end up crashing (and serving no users at all).

bandwidth blackout Sometimes, your hosting service may experience a service outage, where user requests can't get through to your servers. Even established internet providers may experience blackouts, but they're never acceptable. Follow up with your provider, and make sure it's addressed.

compatibility failure Sometimes a site that appears unreliable may actually be incompatible with a particular browser or platform. An application that performs perfectly on a PC may perform erratically on a Mac, or not at all. Mac-only users would think the site is broken, while users who switch between platforms would see it as unreliable.

> **It's the double-edged sword of web success: More users mean higher costs.**

buggy code Sometimes unreliability is caused by bad code. A program may have a bug that causes it to function erratically, or a web page may have errors that cause it to fail under certain conditions.

improving reliability

As you can see, good planning is really the key to a reliable web site. And while you can't exactly go back and start over, there's a lot you can do to make your site more reliable, even once you're up and running.

- **Test your site thoroughly.** Errors in code and in compatibility can be uncovered in the QA process—if you have a QA process, that is. It's essential for any site that takes itself seriously to make every effort to identify—and repair—site errors (including those that only emerge in highly specific situations) before its users do.

- **Increase server capacity.** If your site is growing, and you're seeing large increases in traffic—or if you've begun serving large files, like audio or video—you need to think about adding server capacity, either by increasing the number of servers or their individual processing power.

- **Increase bandwidth.** As you grow, you'll need to add more bandwidth to support your users. This is the double-edged sword of web success: More users mean higher costs.

fixing a broken site

The problems you observe on your site can have a wide range of causes—from limited servers to faulty code to a poorly chosen name. So next time you say, "This doesn't work," you can suggest a solution.

the problem you see	the likely cause	prevention/cure
Links are "broken." When you follow a link, you get an error message. (It probably reads, "Error 404 File Not Found.")	Either the link was written incorrectly, or the page it links to was moved or taken down.	▨ Check the site regularly for incorrect or "dead" links. ▨ Use a link-checking tool. Your HTML editor may have one, or try http://www.netmechanic.com. ▨ Make sure to change links and provide "redirects" when you move a page on your site. ▨ Customize the error message. Instead of just saying, "Error," offer a site index or a search box.
Links don't lead where you expected. When you follow a link, you end up someplace completely foreign or different from what you expected.	Possibly an error in the link, but more likely an error in the design, or in the labeling of the link. If the user's path is misleading, the problem could be as simple as a poorly named link or as complex as a misunderstanding of your user's goals.	▨ Make sure all the site's links go to the right place. ▨ Make sure all the section names and labels on your site are clear. (Don't be clever. Don't by coy. Don't use jargon.) See naming site sections, p. XXX. ▨ Test the site with users to make sure it's structured in a way they understand.
Pages don't load. Some pages spin endlessly without loading.	Possibly server overload. If more people are visiting your site than your server can handle, it may choke on delivery. Alternately, it could be a technical problem related to a script, an application, or a "rich-media" ad.	▨ Evaluate server and bandwidth capacity. Coming up short? Consider investing in more, to handle your site's growth. ▨ Test, test, test your site—and the ads on it!—on different platforms and browsers.
Pages partially load. A new page appears, but some of its elements don't. The browser just spins. Your screen may freeze.	Likely a technical problem related to a single element—a script, an image, an ad, or even a poorly constructed piece of HTML.	▨ Again: Test, test, test your site on different platform and browser combinations. ▨ Don't forget to test on the Mac! Please!

the problem you see	the likely cause	prevention/cure
Images don't load. The pages load, but the images don't appear. All you see is a little broken picture or an "X."	Either the images are misnamed, or they aren't where they're supposed to be, so the browser can't "find" them.	▪ Find the images. Link to them correctly. ▪ Make sure you've named the images correctly. ▪ Remember for next time: Every time you move images around, you have to make sure you're linking to them correctly.
You can't find anything. You know what you're looking for, and you know it's on the site, but you can't for the life of you find it.	This is a problem with either site design or search. Navigation should lead users almost effortlessly toward their goals. And if that fails, the site search should take them there directly.	▪ Integrate a better search mechanism. Try the one offered by Atomz: http://www.atomz.com. ▪ Customize search results for the most popular searches. Pick the pages on your site that best match what the user is probably looking for, and lead with those. (You site search should let you do this. If it doesn't, get a new search tool.) ▪ Rethink the site's organization and navigation. Does it really address user goals? User testing might help you pinpoint the problem.
Nothing makes sense. You can't figure out how to accomplish your goal, or even how to get started.	This is a big problem.	▪ Review the product plan: What, exactly, is your site supposed to do? If you don't have a product plan, you've found the problem. ▪ Make sure your front door clearly explains who you are and what users can do on your site. ▪ Make sure your front door highlights the things most users are looking for.
Your computer crashes. As a new page loads, your screen freezes, the application quits, or your whole computer crashes.	Clearly a technical problem—most likely with a script, ad, or application within your site.	▪ Once again: Leave plenty of time to test your site on different platform and browser combinations. ▪ Don't forget to test on the Mac! Please!

building for accessibility

Compatibility, as you've read, is a major theme of web production. In order to reach the widest possible audience, you have to build a site that will display appropriately on computers with different platforms, browsers, and connection speeds.

But along with technical disparities, it's important to consider the different physical needs of users. There are millions of sight- and hearing-impaired people online, who customize their browsers to compensate for their disabilities. With just a small amount of thought and effort, you can make your site accessible to them.

it's not just nice—it's smart

In the real world, modifications made for the disabled usually help everyone. The ramps cut into curbs, for instance, make city sidewalks navigable for people in wheelchairs. But they also help bicyclists, rollerbladers, scooter-riders, suitcase-draggers, and pram-pushers get around with ease.

Similarly, the modifications you make to your site to help people who are blind or deaf will serve your entire audience and your bottom line. Most of the needed modifications involve improving annotations (such as offering short text descriptions of images) or structuring your site in a more logical manner, so it can be analyzed by a browser for the blind.

But these changes not only help disabled users, they also help ensure a clear, logical experience for everyone. In the process, they also make your site more accessible to search engines (important for building traffic) and more compatible with future applications, beyond the browser.

and in america, it's the law

If your site is for a U.S. government agency—or an organization that receives government funds or contracts—you're actually required by law to make it accessible to those with disabilities. In 1998, the Rehabilitation Act was amended, requiring federal agencies to make their information technology (including web sites) accessible to people with disabilities.

The implications are explained here: http://www.section508.gov.

accommodating disabled visitors

In order to make your site accessible, there are two main user groups to consider:

- **Sight-impaired users** who navigate the web using a screen-reader (which reads the page aloud) or a braille browser (which prints out each page in braille).

- **Hearing-impaired users** who make use of close-captioning technologies to translate audio material into text captions.

sight-impaired users   The web poses obvious challenges for people who are sight-impaired. It's almost exclusively a visual medium, providing few tactile or audio clues to aid understanding. However, internet tools for the blind are quite sophisticated. By reading a page aloud—or printing it out in braille—they allow people to use the web without the benefit of sight. Unfortunately, there remain a few barriers to effective use.

3 challenges for the sight-impaired:

1. **Interpreting images.** Images are often used to replace words on web sites. And if the site doesn't provide text equivalents for these images—especially the ones used in navigation—it can't be understood by a blind person. "The first rule for accessibility is providing a text equivalent for everything that's visual," says Matt Margolin, who's writing a book on the subject. "It's simple, but it takes time."

Making your site accessible?

'Bobby' (checks your accessibility)
http://bobby.watchfire.com/

Web Accessibility Initiative
http://www.w3.org/wai

IBM Web Accessibility checklist
http://www.ibm.com/able/accessweb.html

2. **Understanding page structure.** Many sight-impaired users navigate pages with a screen reader, which calls out the headlines and subheads that divide a page. However, not all sites use headline tags to structure their pages; some rely on purely visual cues (like the font tag or images) and ignore document structure. These unstructured pages are difficult to interpret—both by screen readers and other applications.

3. **Reading small text.** Designers are often tempted to use a small font, because it saves space on the screen. But many people (not just the blind) struggle to read the tiny text on these sites. This can be addressed by using larger type or giving users different size options.

hearing-impaired users   The web is still primarily a text-based medium, but as bandwidth and audio-compression have improved, some sites have moved toward a richer multimedia experience. If your site incorporates audio information, you should of course consider the needs of hearing-impaired users.

This is especially important in the arena of online learning, where audio and video often figure prominently into the educational experience.

2 challenges for the hearing impaired:

1. **Understanding what's being spoken** in audio soundtracks or videos. They can't rely on reading lips, because the person speaking isn't always pictured, and poor video quality distorts mouth movements. This problem can be addressed by subtitles.

2. **Understanding non-verbal clues**, such as a siren or the sound of a door slamming, in audio soundtracks or videos. These can be explained with captions (e.g. "A door slams in the background.")

---

5 easy fixes to make your site more accessible

1. Offer a text description of each image. Every image on your site should have a brief text description of what's pictured (This is known as "alt" text.) Lots of images? Focus first on those used in navigation.

2. Offer text-based navigation. What's true for regular images is especially true for navigation: Make sure you have a functional text equivalent for every navigational clue, including nav bars, image maps, icons, and buttons.

3. Use stylesheets, not font tags. Both font tags and stylesheets can be used to change the appearance of words on a web page. But stylesheets also allow you to indicate what kind of text it is: Headline? Sub-head? Body text? And this context helps blind users navigate the page.

4. Let users change the font size. To help people (especially seniors) read your site, offer the web-equivalent of a large-print edition. This is easier than ever, with stylesheets.

Text Size: A A A A

Above: **Wired News** readers can choose between different sized text. Left: **Tupperware.com** offers a large-print version.

5. Provide subtitles for audio. This is labor-intensive, but a do-it yourself captioning tool, called MAGpie, can help. It's offered for free by the National Center for Accessible Media: http://ncam.wgbh.org.

To evaluate how accessible your site is, try the free service, "Bobby" (http://bobby.watchfire.com). Margolin also recommends viewing your site with a text browser, like Lynx. "If your pages can be rendered in text, chances are really, really good they can be rendered using a braille browser or a screen reader."

building your site to last

For many organizations, the web is a big leap forward: an opportunity to communicate in a new way with customers, employees, investors, and the media. Your web site, then, should be an investment in your future.

But most sites are built to work exclusively in web browsers—this year's web browsers. And that's short-sighted. At some point (perhaps sooner than you think) you're going to want your information to appear in other display systems, like handheld computers, or to integrate with backend databases. You may want it to work on screen readers for the blind or on future applications we can't anticipate.

> **Most sites are built to work exclusively in web browsers—this year's web browsers. And that's short-sighted.**

At first, this may not seem relevant to you—after all, you're building a site for the web and may not have long-term plans for it. But—especially for large institutions—it's important to take the long view. If you're going to the trouble of building a site, and spending thousands—or even millions—of dollars on it, you should think about all the ways you might eventually want to use the information.

Ideally, your site should work with

- **Past, present, and future web browsers**

- **Older "legacy" databases** and content systems that predate the web (think of the databases you search at the library)

- **New technologies with different types of displays**, like handheld computers and web-enabled cell phones

- **Display systems for the blind**, including screen readers and braille browsers

This may seem like a pipe dream. But in fact, it's possible, even today, if you follow web standards.

Developed by the industry group, W3C (World Wide Web Consortium), standards lay out a set of guidelines for how sites should be built. They don't dictate how a site should look or work—only how the pages should be structured. The goal is to both standardize web production and improve compatibility with past, present, and future systems.

why standards are needed

To understand the need for web standards, it helps to review how sites are currently built—and why.

During the rapid commercial development of the web—from 1994 to 2000—web designers and builders didn't have the luxury of standards. The web was expanding so quickly and so dramatically that the technology couldn't keep up. Developers had to do their best with the limited technologies available to them.

So they stretched and bent HTML to do things for which it wasn't designed and spent substantial portions of their time developing elaborate hacks and workarounds just to make their pages work.

The result is that most web sites are built using a mish-mash of HTML directives, all aimed at producing a site that *looks* a certain way in today's browsers. The commands in HTML are used in ways that bears little resemblance to what they were designed for. (For example, designers frequently use the HTML tag <ul>—which is meant to set off a list—to indent text and create a margin.)

The problem with this visual orientation is that the HTML code gets very complex and very *specific*: The data is structured to look good in a web browser—and only a web browser—and this renders it useless to other types of applications.

The madness that is web-page markup was necessary at the time, because there weren't any other options. But now it's short-sighted. With the advent of standards—and the support of new technologies—it's possible to create sites with a logical structure and a much longer shelf-life.

how web standards work

The theory behind web standards is that sites should be built in a more standardized way, to improve compatibility with past, present, and future systems. This would make sites more accessible in the short term, and more durable in the long term.

To accomplish this, web standards propose an important shift in the way sites are built. They call for a change in the basic language used to mark up web pages—from HTML to XHTML—and recommend designing with stylesheets rather than tables or font tags.

Standards recommend that sites

- **Use XHTML to structure pages** instead of HTML. The two are very similar, but XHTML is more precise and more portable. It can be understood by other systems and software, beyond the web browser.

- **Use stylesheets for design** instead of font tags, tables, and other assorted tags. This makes the page structure logical and fast, and allows it to be interpreted by other systems.

The reason web standards are effective is that they separate content from presentation. XHTML is used to identify each element within the content ("This is a headline." "This is a paragraph.") Stylesheets define how each page element should *look*. ("A headline looks like this." "A paragraph looks like that.")

Because content is separated from presentation, different systems can display the same content differently. When content is pulled into a device other than the browser, its presentation can be redefined. A screen reader may read it aloud, beginning with site sections and headlines. A Palm Pilot may put all the headlines in a tiny little list. But they can both work from the same content.

so what's the hold-up?

There are a lot of persuasive arguments for following web standards. (See why you should follow web standards, p. 186.) But designers and developers have been slow to get on board. Why?

Why sites are slow to adopt standards:

- **They haven't found time to retrain.** Standards redefine how sites are built, and web professionals have to learn the new way. But it's hard to find the time when you're always scrambling to hit deadlines.

- **Stylesheet support still isn't perfect.** It can be time-consuming and frustrating to get a stylesheet-based design to work. "Browser support for stylesheets is good, but not perfect," says designer Jeffrey Zeldman, author of *Designing with Web Standards*. "So some designers get frustrated and give up—especially if they're detail-oriented. But there are (standards-compliant) workarounds for browser differences, and members of the design community are great at sharing these workarounds with each other. Once the workarounds are known, problems of browser difference largely vanish."

- **Some designs don't work in stylesheets.** Designs that are based on a strong grid are better suited to tables. So some designers have taken a transitional approach, using stylesheets for text and tables for layout.

- **Some designers don't consider their site a long-term investment.** They don't care whether it will work three years from now.

- **Some designers don't care about accessibility.** They don't mind if their site doesn't work in voice and braille browsers

- **People don't like change.**

lesson from the trenches

why you should follow web standards

The question's been debated for several years now: Should web developers be expected—or even required—to build sites in accordance with industry standards?

Web standards, established by the W3C (World Wide Web Consortium), call for a fundamental shift in the way sites are designed and built (using XHTML rather than HTML, and stylesheets rather than tables or font tags).

Many site owners have resisted the standards, but others needed no convincing. Carrie Bickner, for example, immediately saw that standards ensured a longer lifespan for digital information. Because standards-compliant sites are built using XHTML, they'll be more compatible with both older database systems and future devices we can't yet anticipate.

As a librarian and webmaster with the New York Public Library, Bickner understands the importance of preservation.

"My first job at the New York Public Library was at the reference library," she explains. "The collections there range from the latest scholarly material to rare special collections. And so I handled a lot of things that were very old—some of them in good condition, some of them not. And I always had to think about how to strike a balance between providing access to an item now and preserving it for the long run."

"So someone would ask to photocopy a book. And I'd have to look at it and say, 'Boy, this binding is already cracked. I'm sorry, I can't let you photocopy this. But I'd like you to have access to the information, so maybe we can take photographs of it.'"

"So, I was always balancing those two concerns: access now versus preservation over the long term. And I see the same exact thing happening with the web. We want our pages to look great now on the current generation of browsers. But I'd also like these pages to look good three years from now—or five years from now—on whatever device we're using then. I'd like them to look good on a Palm Pilot, I'd like them to read well on braille browsers and audio browsers. So I've got this big picture view that I feel responsible for keeping."

> **"You should use web standards—whether the client requests it or not—as a matter of professional integrity."**
>
> **—Carrie Bickner**
> **New York Public Library**

Longevity is a major concern for libraries and other institutions with large digital archives. But the investment in your future isn't the only reason to follow web standards. Great-looking, fast-loading pages are another.

Standards call for a stylesheet-based design, which is a departure for many designers. And many are skeptical about its potential. Not Jeffrey Zeldman.

Zeldman, who just wrote the book *Designing for Web Standards* (New Riders), is one of the most prominent proponents of standards-compliant, stylesheet-based design. All the sites he creates for clients are now standard-compliant—and the rich-looking, but fast-loading sites always get an "I can't believe it loads so fast!" response.

"Clients are always impressed by how well the site works, how quickly it loads, and by the fact that they can update content without worrying that in so doing, they'll accidentally destroy the layout."

"My philosophy is 'Show, don't sell,' Zeldman said. "The most persuasive argument for standards is a good site."

Dig Deeper
building your site to last, p. 184.

lesson from the trenches

But Zeldman has other arguments, as well. Standards, he says, improve web sites on many different levels. And the arguments against them are outdated. "Too many designers and developers still think each browser or device requires unique markup and its own set of stylesheets," Zeldman says. "This misguided belief results in pages that weigh too much and take too long to load, and that fail for many users."

Still, web developers have been slow to adopt standards. And many blame their clients, saying they don't care—or haven't heard—about them. But Bickner doesn't buy this argument. It's the responsibility of the consultant, not the client, she says, to learn the industry's best practices.

"If I hire you to put in a wood floor in my apartment, I don't care what kind of preparation you do," she explains. "I just want the wood floor to look good and wear well. And it shouldn't be up to me to think about how you did it. Same with web standards. If you want to give a client a site that's going to work now and for at least the next three years, you should probably use web standards—whether the client requests it or not—as a matter of professional integrity."

8 reasons to follow web standards

1. It's an investment in your future. Sites that follow standards will be easier to adapt to future browsers, databases, handheld computers, and other devices we haven't thought of yet.

2. It saves a lot of production time. You may have to invest time in learning XHTML and stylesheets. But you'll make it up later. Stylesheets make production far more efficient, allowing for quicker markup and easy changes.

3. It looks great. Loads fast! Sites built using stylesheets can be gorgeous and eye-catching, making use of typographic treatments you

can't otherwise achieve. But thanks to a clean structure—no messy tables, no need to repeat and re-repeat style for text—the pages load much faster, and work more consistently. The savings in speed and bandwidth can be staggering. ESPN, for example, cut 50K off each page when it converted to a stylesheet-based design. With 40 million pageviews/day, they saved an astounding 2 terabytes in bandwidth per day (1 terabyte is a million megabytes!).

> **"My philosophy is 'Show, don't sell.' The most persuasive argument for standards is a good site."**
>
> —*Jeffrey Zeldman*
> *Founder, A List Apart*

4. It makes your site more searchable. Sites designed with stylesheets are structured logically and can be more easily interpreted by search engines. This can improve your search rank, and therefore visibility.

5. It makes your site accessible. If you design your site with stylesheets—instead of tables and font tags—it will be more accessible to sight-impaired users.

6. It may help you comply with the law. Don't make me bring up section 508! If you're a U.S. government site—or if you receive funds from the federal government—you're required by law to make your site accessible to those with disabilities. Standards help.

7. Your site will work on any browser or web device. Sites that follow the XHTML spec will work in earlier web browsers. They may not look good, but they'll work. And that's more than you can say for most non-standard designs. "With simple, correctly authored, structural markup, you can serve every browser and Internet device—from Internet Explorer 6 to an old Newton hand-held," Zeldman says.

8. It's good for the industry. As Zeldman says: "The medium shouldn't evolve with duct tape." Following standards can be your contribution.

building the backend

When launching a new site, you have to make decisions about its technical infrastructure: What kind of hardware and software will support your site?

Smaller sites usually sidestep these decisions by working with a web-hosting service like Earthlink or Yahoo Stores. In this case, the hosting service makes most of the technical decisions for you. They own and control the servers, and dictate what can and can't be done on the sites they host.

But larger companies, which own and operate their own servers, have choices.

Backend technologies include

- Server hardware

- Server operating system

- Server software

- Database

- Programming language (for any applications developed)

- Server-side scripts

Now, it's only in rare cases that you have a clean slate for these decisions. Usually, they'll be forced by the company's previous choices and existing technical infrastructure. In those rare but lovely instances when you do have all your options open, your decisions will be framed by the constraints of time, money, and people—and the needs of the site itself.

Factors affecting technical decisions:

- **Existing infrastructure.** What servers or operating systems are currently in use? Do you need to integrate with a backend mainframe or legacy software?

- **Familiarity with technologies.** There's always an argument for sticking with what you know. It takes time—and sometimes money—to learn new systems.

- **Available developer pool.** Especially when choosing a programming language, the ability to hire experienced developers is always a priority.

- **Cost of systems and support.** Decisions are always framed by what you can afford—both in terms of equipment and support.

- **Scale of site.** Your technical needs may change depending on the amount of data managed by your site. A commerce site with 200 items, for example, will have different needs from one with 20 or 20,000 items.

- **Traffic to site.** Similarly, technical needs change as a site grows more popular, particularly if the users are placing orders or using applications.

- **Cost of failure.** A question you must ask yourself: What happens if the system fails? For most sites, it's an inconvenience. In some companies, it could mean your job. But in extreme cases—like a stock-trading site—it could mean a criminal investigation.

- **Risk tolerance.** Different organizations have different attitudes toward risk. Some are willing to try new technologies; others won't stray from the tried-and-true. Witness the IT maxim that goes: "No one ever got fired for buying Microsoft."

a note on open-source technologies

As a site grows, its backend infrastructure becomes more expensive: You need more servers and more bandwidth to meet the needs of a growing user base.

One way to keep costs manageable is to use open-source technologies, which are free (or nearly free). The operating system Linux, the web server software Apache, the database MySQL, the server-side scripting language PHP, and the programming language Perl are all excellent, low-cost options on which many sites, large and small, depend.

sorting out backend technologies

technology	what is it?	what are your choices?
Server hardware	This the actual computer from which the site is served.	Choices include Sun, Compaq, Dell, Silicon Graphics, Hewlett Packard, and others.
Server operating system	This is the basic system software running on the server.	Choices include Windows NT, Windows XP, OS2, Mac OS X, Linux, Solaris, and other types of Unix.
Web server software	This is the software that's installed on the computer to convert it from an ordinary machine to a web server.	Web server software includes Windows IIS, Mac, and Apache.
	Application server software runs complex web applications, like those for online stores or banking sites.	Application server software includes Weblogic, iPlanet, IBM Websphere, and Microsoft.
	Streaming server software is specialized to serve "streaming" audio or video files.	Streaming server software includes WindowsMedia, RealMedia, and QuickTime.
Database	This is the software that stores, organizes, and provides access to large collections of data, such as the products sold in a store or the articles served on a news site.	Choices include Informix, MySQL, Oracle, Sybase, IBM, and others.
Applications	These are the computer programs that power all the web's complex functionality, like banking systems or search engines. These programs are installed on the server. See adding applications to your site, p.226	No generic choices here. There are many different types of applications, from shopping cart software to search engines to content-management systems.
Server-side scripts	These are small computer programs that connect the application to the web page. See understanding php, p.168	Choices include ASP, JSP, PHP, ColdFusion, and CGI Scripts.

how web sites work (a primer)

"My computer is completely down—I seem to have gnawed through the wires again."

don't miss ...

how web pages are built

Although web sites may seem enormously complex (and some of them are), the underlying technology is relatively simple. If you're comfortable using a computer, you could learn the basics in a day.

Every page on the web is created and delivered as a plain text document, containing the words that will appear on the web page, as well as instructions for how they should appear, and what else should appear with them.

> **HTML tags are like stage directions. They tell each element on the page when to appear and what to do.**

These instructions—about where the page elements should be placed and what they should do—are written in HTML, or Hypertext Markup Language. HTML uses a collection of "tags" (words or abbreviations sandwiched between angle brackets < >) to give the browser directions about how the page should look. You can think of these tags like stage directions: They tell each element when to appear and what to do. (To visualize how an HTML file translates into a web page, see picturing how html works, p. 194.)

Most HTML tags are relatively simple. A <p> tag creates a new paragraph. A <b> tag makes text bold. <img> brings in an image. And <table> creates—you guessed it—a table.One thing to know about HTML tags is that they come in pairs. There's an opening tag, like <b>, and a closing tag, with a slash, like </b>

So if you have the sentence: "I love sesame chicken from Mama Buddha." And you want the word "love" to be bold, your HTML would look like this:

```
<p> I <b>love</b> sesame chicken from
Mama Buddha </p>
```

And the words will appear like this on the web page:

I **love** sesame chicken from Mama Buddha

<p> </p> started and ended the paragraph. <b> </b> started and ended the bold text.

As web pages grow more complex, they pull in other things: images, animation, audio, video, even interactive multimedia and small applications. But at its core, the web is still based on HTML.

creating an html document

Since HTML documents are just text documents, they can be created with any text editor, like SimpleText, Notepad, or Microsoft Word. But there are other ways to create a web page, and they don't all require you to know HTML.

3 ways to create an HTML document:

1. **With a template-based system** like the ones offered by web-hosting services. You just choose a design template, and don't worry about the HTML

2. **With an HTML editor** like Dreamweaver You decide how the page should look, and the program creates the HTML.

3. **With a text editor** like Notepad. This method is often called "hand-coding" because you craft the HTML yourself.

Learning HTML?
The Webmonkey Teaching Tool
http://www.webmonkey.com/teachingtool/

3 ways to build a web site

Depending on your staff, your budget, and the complexity of your site, there are three approaches you can take.

	1. use a template	**2. use an html editor**	**3. use a text editor**
how it works	Many web-hosting services offer simple template-based systems for creating a site. You just choose one of several designs and add your own words and images. You don't have to learn HTML; it's all done for you.	HTML editors, like Macromedia Dreamweaver, let you create web pages in a visual environment. You can push text and images around, specifying how the pages should look. The program invisibly creates the needed HTML (which you can tweak).	With a plain text editor, like SimpleText or Microsoft Word, you can "hand-code" an HTML page by entering all the HTML tags yourself.
who should use it	Small businesses or individuals who want a web site, but don't have a lot of time or money.	Most organizations investing in a custom web site, who want control over its appearance.	Individuals who want to learn HTML and are creating a small, simple site.
advantages	**Speed.** If you're throwing up a web site, nothing is faster than this. It combines the creation and posting of the web site all in one. **Cost.** You don't have to hire a consultant or train yourself to use HTML software. **Ease of use.** This is a very simple approach to web-site creation.	**Control.** You can customize exactly what your page looks like. And the better programs let you customize the HTML as well. **Efficiency.** Most HTML editors let you create your own templates, which you can re-use throughout your site. They also eliminate a lot of tedious typing. **Accuracy.** It's easy to make mistakes when you hand-code pages—and hard to figure out where they are. HTML editors automate a lot of steps to avoid errors and help you identify problems when they arise.	**Control.** You can—and indeed you must—very precisely control every single element on every single page. Training by doing everything on your own, you really, really learn how web sites work. **Cost.** You can use the text editor that came on your computer. No need to buy software. **Street Cred.** You get to say that you "hand-coded" your site. Which, admittedly, is pretty cool.
disadvantages	Very little control over appearance or functionality.	Takes time and effort to learn the intricacies of web production. It can be—and for many people, it is—a full-time job.	Outrageously time-consuming for all but the smallest sites.
	▉ BigStep ▉ Yahoo Stores ▉ Most web hosts	▉ Macromedia Dreamweaver ▉ Microsoft FrontPage ▉ Adobe GoLive	▉ Notepad (Windows) ▉ SimpleText (Macintosh) ▉ Microsoft Word

what makes good web design?

1. Simplicity. "For me, as a user, the simpler the better," says Jeffrey Zeldman, author of *Designing for Web Standards*. "So I carry that through in my design. It's all about simplicity."

"I think for many designers—especially those with a graphic design background—web design is about crafting many subtle visual elements: little decorative flourishes that are repeated through the site," Zeldman said. "For me it's not that at all. For me, web design is about removing everything extraneous."

"Good design, to me, is like rock and roll. If you can do it with one guitar, that's better than two guitars. If you can do it with one guitar without an orchestra, that's better than guitar plus orchestra. The best rock and roll is stripped down, minimalist."

> **"For me, as a user, the simpler the better. So I carry that through in my design."**
>
> *- Jeffrey Zeldman*

2. Clarity. "As silly as it sounds, a lot of sites don't put their primary purpose on their homepage," said Mark Hurst, founder of consulting firm Creative Good. "The best counter example of this is Google. It puts its primary purpose first. What's Google? It's a search site. And I don't have to tell you that, because it's kind of hard to miss."

3. Empathy. "Emotional empathy, I think, creates good design," said Derek Powazek, author of *Design for Community*. "You need empathy for the user."

As you design, you should ask yourself, "How does this page feel? When I look at it, before I've read anything, what feeling is it communicating? Is it welcoming or threatening? Is it giving me all the answers or is it holding a little back to pull me in? Is it creating an experience or is it dispensing information? Is it a utility, like a phone book, or is it a cafe? Is it a tool or a story?"

The key to communicating effectively, he said, is "totally understanding what the person on the other end of the computer is feeling, thinking, why they're there."

"I talk about feeling so much, and it makes me sound like such a Californian," Powazek laughs. "But it's true. People puff themselves up, and talk about usability, but what they're really saying is: 'I don't like this website, because it made me feel stupid.' That's the same thing as saying, 'User testing shows that 70% of people when confronted with blah, blah, blah.' It's saying the same thing in an emotional language."

4. Functionality. "A good website is one that works," consultant Janice Fraser says simply. "That's really it."

5. Effective use of technology. "I still believe that good web design exploits the medium," says Jeffrey Veen, author of *The Art & Science of Web Design*. "So any designer who says they're limited by HTML and by the fact that they don't have control of fonts—they don't get it. They don't understand web design."

The key, he said, is learning the technology. "You've got to exploit the medium," Veen says. "You have to understand it inside and out. I just don't think you can do good web design without knowing HTML—without getting deep into it."

6. A good idea. "Great design is always based on a great idea," says Barbara Kuhr, the celebrated Creative Director of HotWired, who had previously co-founded *Wired* Magazine. "If you have a good idea, and you can express it simply and beautifully, you'll achieve great design."

picturing how html works

Structuring an HTML document

The HTML document is divided into two sections: The head and the body.

The HTML tags

<html> </html> creates an html document. Every web page must begin and end with these invisible tags.

The Title

<title></title> creates a title, which will appear in the browser's title bar.

The **head** contains background information about the web page, such as its title.

The **body** contains all the elements that will appear on the page itself, as well as instructions about how they should look and what they should do.

The Headline

<h1></h1> creates the largest possible headline.

The Paragraph

<p></p> creates a paragraph, preceded by a line break.

The List

<ul> </ul> creates an unnumbered (bulleted) list.

<li> </li> surround each item on the list, indicating where the line breaks and where the bullet points go.

The Link

<a href=""> </a> creates a hyperlink—in this case to the National Geographic site. The link will appear in blue underlined text, unless you specify otherwise.

The Image

<img src="" border=0> pulls in an image—in this case, "ostrich.jpg"—and makes it borderless (no frame).

the HTML document ➡

```
<html>
<head>
<title>Africa's Big Five</title>
</head>

<body>
<h1>Africa's Big Five: A new list</h1>

<p>When you go on an African safari, every-
one wants to see the so-called Big Five --
buffalo, elephant, leopard, lion and
rhino -- the big, aggressive, impressive
creatures that give you bragging rights.</p>

<p>I, however, preferred a less-celebrated
five.</p>

<h3>My big five: </h3>
<ul>
<li> Giraffe </li>
<li> Zebra </li>
<li> Waterbuck </li>
<li> Warthog </li>
<li> Ostrich </li>
</ul>

<p>Ugly, awkward, unimpressive, and/or
relatively common, they're not exactly
<a href="http://www.nationalgeographic.com">
National Geographic</a>
material! But they won me over, all the
same!

<p align="center"><img src="ostrich.jpg"
border="1"></p>

</body>
</html>
```

picturing how html works (continued)

 **the web page**

building your first web page

If you lived in New York, you'd probably know the motto of this AM radio station:"1010 WINS: You give us 22 minutes, we'll give you the world."

I'll make a similar promise: Give me 22 minutes, I'll give you a web site.

00:00 getting started

You'll create your first web page using a text editor. If you're on a PC, use the program Notepad; if you're on a Mac, use SimpleText.

If for some reason you can't find these programs (They ship with every computer; they should be there somewhere—probably in the Applications folder), you can use any word-processing software, like Microsoft Word or WordPerfect.

You might want to start a new folder for your web pages. To make things simple, name the folder "web."

02:30 open a new text document

Within your text editor, start a new document and type the following:

```
<html>
<head>
<title>
My 22-minute web page
</title>
</head>

<body>
<h1>Who cares about the
web?</h1>
<p>Well ... <b>lots</b>
of people. </p>
</body>
</html>
```

Be sure to transcribe it exactly; don't add any extra spaces or slashes.

05:00 save the html file

If you're working in SimpleText or Notepad, all you have to do is select "Save" and then name the document (see below). But if you're working in Word or WordPerfect, you'll need to think about how to save it.

An HTML document must be saved in a "text only" format, so it can be read by any computer, on any platform. Programs like Word add a lot of junk to a text document to make sure it appears with all your fancy fonts and margins. But web browsers get confused by all this junk. So you have to save your document as "text only." To do this, just select the command "Save as" from the "File" menu, then choose "Text" or "Text only" from the formatting choices.

06:30 name the html file

When you save your document, you also have to name it. In the "Save as" dialog box, enter a name for your web page. One good name would be 22minutes.html But you can actually name the file anything you want, as long as you follow three rules.

3 rules for naming HTML files:

1. **Name has no spaces.** HTML documents must be named as one continuous word, with no spaces. So 22seconds.html is okay, but 22 seconds.html isn't.

2. **Name ends in .html.** All html documents must have the extension .html or .htm at the end of the file name.

3. **Name should be all lower-case.** Web page names are case-sensitive, which means it matters whether the letters are uppercase or lowercase. Hungry-June.html is different from hungry-june.html. It's best to stick with lowercase.

09:30 look at the web page

I left a generous $3\frac{1}{2}$ minute gap there for you to name your page, because if you're like most people, you spent way too much time thinking of a clever little name. (I urge you to break this habit: See naming site sections, p. XXX.)

Back to business: To see your first web page, launch your web browser (probably Internet Explorer). Under the "File" menu, select the command, "Open File." Select your new page from the dialog box that pops up.

11:00 do you see it?

If you've followed all the directions above, you should see your modest (but exciting!) little web page in the browser. Your title should appear in the very top of the browser; the headline should be biggish and bold, and the paragraph should be in normal text. Overall, it should look something like the image above.

But what if it doesn't?

Well, this is the first important lesson in web development: Things don't always work the way you think they're going to work. That's why we left 22 minutes for what could have been an 11-minute job. 11 minutes to build, and 11 minutes to make it work. Sounds about right.

12:00 you don't see it?

If you don't see the web page, you're in luck! You'll get to not only build a page, but troubleshoot it. Let's think about what might be wrong:

■ **The page is showing gibberish instead of words?** If so, the page isn't saved right. Go back and re-save it as "text-only."

■ **The words appear, but they aren't formatted?** Check the filename. Make sure it has the extension .html on the end, and make sure it doesn't have any spaces.

■ **All the words look like headlines?** You probably forgot to close the <h1> tag with an </h1>. Make sure the second </h1> has a slash in it and no spaces between characters.

■ **The headline is missing?** You might be missing the first <h1> tag, or you might have mistyped the tag as <h1 or h1>.

17:55 do you see it now?

I'm pretty confident that your page is displaying properly by now, so we'll spend the final four minutes examining what it all means.

17:55 understanding your web page

Let's take a look at each element of your HTML document, starting, as all HTML documents do, with <html>.

<html> The first thing on this—and every—web page is the <html> tag. All HTML documents begin with the tag <html> and end with </html>. (It's the document's way of saying "Curtain up!" and "Curtain down!")

<head> The first section of the HTML file, between the <head> and </head> tags, is called the header. It contains all the background information about the page, such as the title. Nothing that appears in the header will show up on the web page itself.

<title> Every web page should have a title, which identifies its main purpose. The title doesn't appear in the page proper. It's displayed at the top of the browser window, in the frame around the page.

</title> You've probably noticed by now that HTML tags almost always come in pairs. Sweet, isn't it? So remember to finish what you start. With very few exceptions, every opening tag, like <title> needs a corresponding closing tag: </title>.

<body> Begins the body, or the visible portion of the web page.

<h1> Headlines are marked off by the tags <h1>, <h2>…<h6>, with <h1> the biggest and <h6> the smallest. If you're feeling cocky, you can experiment with your page now: How does the headline look in <h2>?

</h1> Closes the headline. All subsequent text will be the default body text, unless you specify differently.

<p> Begins a new paragraph by skipping a line.

**** Creates bold text.

**** Ends the bold text; returns to normal text.

</p> Ends the paragraph.

</body> Ends the body, or the visible portion of the page.

</html> Ends the HTML document.

22:00 celebrate!

Believe it or not, you now know enough to build a web site. Once you understand how to create and save an HTML document, the rest is a cinch.

So don't stop now! Learn everything else about HTML at Webmonkey's Teaching Tool: http://www.webmonkey.com/teachingtool

---

Don't stop now!

The Webmonkey Teaching Tool can teach you everything else you need to know about HTML:

■ Links

■ Images

■ Background colors

■ Text formatting

■ Tables

■ Frames

■ Forms

■ Stylesheets, and more

http://www.webmonkey.com/teachingtool/

how web pages turn into a web site

So every web page, we've learned, is created as a simple text document, incorporating HTML commands. There are four steps to turning web pages into a web site: Naming pages, organizing pages, and transferring them to your server.

4 steps from web page to web site:

1. **Naming pages** correctly

2. **Organizing pages** efficiently

3. **Linking between pages**

4. **Transferring pages** to a server that's connected to the Internet

naming web pages

Each page on your web site will have a unique web address (or URL), based on the name of its corresponding HTML file. There are a few rules about how web pages (and thus HTML files) should be named.

4 rules for naming web pages:

1. **Names should end in .html or .htm.** This identifies it as an HTML file.

2. **Names may not contain spaces.** A page called lucky duck.html will not appear in the browser. If you want to create the illusion of a space (for easy reading) try an underscore: lucky_duck.html.

3. **Names are case-sensitive.** A page called LuckyDuck.html is different from a page called luckyduck.html. You can mix uppercase and lowercase letters, but the convention is to stick with all-lowercase.

4. **The home page is named index.html.** The browser will automatically look for a file called "index.html" when someone accesses your site.

If you're developing a site with many pages, you'll want to create a system for naming them—so you can organize and identify them more easily. Different people have different methods. For instance, if you have a page on your website with publicity information and press releases, you might name it press.html or company_press.html. It depends on what other pages you're naming and what feels right to you. Once you've decided on a system, though, you should stick with it. Your site will be more logical and manageable if your file names are consistent.

organizing web pages

The pages that make up your web site will be stored in a collection of files and folders similar to those that appear on your desktop computer (though perhaps more rigorously organized).

The placement of any particular page within the hierarchy of folders and files will dictate its web address, or URL.

So a web page whose URL appears like so:

http://www.beardedman.com/beard_types/ goatee/index.html

comes from a file called "index.html," placed in a folder called "goatee," which is in another folder called "beard_types," which lives on a server called "WWW," which is registered to the domain "beardedman.com."

Folder names follow similar rules as the individual files: They can't contain spaces, and they're case-sensitive—so you have to pay attention to whether you're using uppercase or lowercase letters.

The folder and file names on the server become part of the URL. So the file and folders above would appear as http://www.beardedman.com/beard_types/goatee/ index.html.

Now, if you have a simple site with just a few pages, you can put all the pages (including the front door) in one folder. But if you have a more complex hierarchy of site sections and subsections, your directory structure, too, will be complex.

The folders that contain your web pages (also known as your site's directory structure) should be organized to reflect your site's structure. So if you have five main sections on your site—dogs, cats, birds, snakes, and hamsters—your pages should be organized into folders with those names.

For an overview of how to organize your site, try this Webmonkey tutorial: http://www.webmonkey.com/html/96/45/index2a.html.

linking between pages

Normally, when you're linking to another page on the web, you include the complete URL of the page to which you're linking. (For a review of URLs, see <u>understanding web addresses</u>, p. 34. But if you're linking to a page on your own site, you can use a partial, or relative URL.

- **Complete URLs** show the file's full web address, domain name and all: http://www.localbooks.com/readings.html.

- **Relative URLs** show part of the address: readings.html.

Relative URLs are easier and more efficient. Rather than giving the full address, they describe the location of the page in relation to the current page.

So if you're linking from the front door of your site to another page that's in the same folder, you can just include its file name, like readings.html.

For a complete explanation of relative URLs, try this Webmonkey tutorial: http://www.webmonkey.com/99/39/index3a_page3.html.

transferring web pages

Once you've created your pages, named them, and organized them into folders, you're ready to put them on the web.

The task is pretty simple: You have to move the files from your computer to a server that's connected to the Internet. (See <u>how web pages are served</u>, p. 200.) The process will vary a little, depending on where your server is.

If your company has its own server, you can transfer the pages on your local network. In most cases, you'll move the files to a "staging" server, and someone else—the system administrator or the production director—will move them to the live site.

If you use a web host, you'll transfer the pages over the Internet and into your site's directory on the server. You'll do this with an FTP program (On the PC, try CuteFTP. On the Mac, try Fetch).

FTP—or file transfer protocol—is a simple way of transferring files over the Internet. Basically, you choose the files on your computer that you want to move and specify the server you want to move them to.

Before you can FTP your files, however, you'll need the server address and a user name and a password—all of which your web host will supply.

To learn more about FTP, try these Webmonkey tutorials:

FTP basics
http://www.webmonkey.com/02/36/index4a.html

FTPing with CuteFTP
http://www.webmonkey.com/98/42/index2a.html

FTPing with Fetch
http://www.webmonkey.com98/41/index4a.html

how web pages are served

Once a web site is created, it's placed on a server so anyone on the web can access it. Like buildings on a street, every server has a unique web address (or domain name), so it can be located by browsers. And—like apartments in a building—every page on a server has a unique address within that domain.

When a user follows a link or types your URL (web address) into his browser, the browser sends out a request, trying to find first the server, and then the specific page indicated in the URL.

If the server and page are located, the server sends the page—in the form of an HTML file with any accompanying images—across the Internet to the end user.

Now, in order for a server to send a web page to a browser, the two computers must "converse" in a common language. That language, or protocol, is usually HTTP (HyperText Transfer Protocol).

This interaction is called a "client-server" relationship, in which the browser (or the person using it) is considered the "client." (Like a client in a store, the browser is requesting things from the server.)

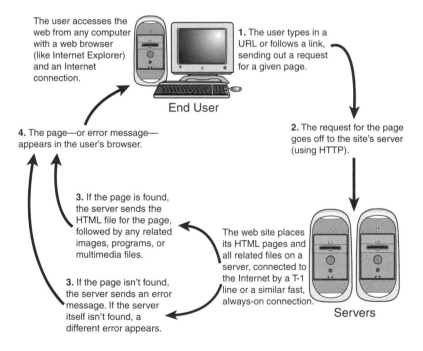

The user accesses the web from any computer with a web browser (like Internet Explorer) and an Internet connection.

End User

1. The user types in a URL or follows a link, sending out a request for a given page.

2. The request for the page goes off to the site's server (using HTTP).

4. The page—or error message—appears in the user's browser.

3. If the page is found, the server sends the HTML file for the page, followed by any related images, programs, or multimedia files.

3. If the page isn't found, the server sends an error message. If the server itself isn't found, a different error appears.

The web site places its HTML pages and all related files on a server, connected to the Internet by a T-1 line or a similar fast, always-on connection.

Servers

serving "dynamic" pages

On simple sites, the server's role is pretty straight-forward. It stores a lot of web pages, waits for a request, and sends the selected page off to the web user.

But few sites are so simple anymore. Rather than just serving pre-packaged "static" pages, many sites are serving customized "dynamic" pages—which may say things like, "Welcome back, Jennifer! Check out the new Erasure CD!"—and which require a lot more work on the part of the server:

- **Static pages** are created in HTML, placed on a server, and served in the exact same format to every user.

- **Dynamic pages** are created on-the-fly by the server and may appear differently to each incoming user.

What makes a web page dynamic isn't the content itself, but how it's created. A dynamic page is created on-the-fly by the server, once it's requested by the user. This gives the server a chance to make last-minute revisions, based on who's asking for the page. The level of customization varies. Depending on the site, the server may have to perform calculations before creating the page; it may have to draw information out of a database; or it may just chose from among several pre-packaged pages.

Dynamic content may be based on

- **The user's profile.** Returning visitors may be automatically served personalized information, like their local weather.

- **The user's input**. Visitors may receive customized pages, based on something they did —like a search.

- **The user's browser or platform.** Visitors on a Mac may see a different version of the site than those on Windows

- **Date, time, location or other factors!**

Dynamic pages are generally made possible by scripts (like those written in PHP or ColdFusion) that reside on—and rely on—the server. (See <u>understanding php</u>, p. 168.)

---

understanding the server

A server is simply a computer that's connected to the Internet and can receive requests from—and send web pages to—other computers.

Any computer can be used as a web server, once you've installed server software (and connected it to the Internet, of course). Now, servers are usually high-performance computers connected to the Internet by a high-speed T-1 line. However, sites can be delivered from less-powerful machines with less substantial connections. They'll just deliver pages more slowly.

Variations on the server:

- **Web servers** store and deliver the elements of web pages. Most sites are stored on basic web servers.

- **Application servers** run specialized Internet applications, like commerce engines. They're customized to process requests and deliver dynamic results.

- **Streaming servers** deliver audio or video to the end user in real-time.

- **Secure servers** are web servers that encrypt data before transmitting it, to prevent electronic eavesdropping. They're commonly used for credit-card purchases and other financial transactions.

- **Staging servers** are used to preview web pages before they're moved to the public web server.

- **Mail servers** send and receive email.

- **Name servers** are specialized servers that serve as giant directories of web servers: they keep track of all of the world's registered domain names.

preparing images & multimedia for the web

"Granted, it does hold more data, but the phone book still looks more impressive."

don't miss ...

The challenge of preparing images—or any kind of media—for the web can be summed up in two words: size and speed.

Everything that appears on your web site has to be transferred across the Internet before it appears on the user's screen. The bigger the images and files, the longer they take to send, and the less likely your viewers are to wait around.

So the goal is to get files—all files: images, audio, video, animation—as small as possible while retaining their artistic integrity. And whatever medium you're dealing with, the steps will be similar.

4 ways to make a file appear faster:

1. **Edit or crop the file** so it's smaller or shorter. With time-based media, like audio or video, you can make the clip shorter by editing out material you don't need. With images and video, you can make the picture smaller by reducing its dimensions.

2. **Choose a file format.** Before you can place any kind of media on the web, you have to convert it to a file format that works in the web browser. For images, you might make a JPEG or GIF. For music, it might be WindowsMedia, MP3, or several options.

3. **Compress the file** so it shrinks to a smaller size while maintaining reasonable quality. Each file format has its own compression technique. So when you save an image as a JPEG, the JPEG compression is applied. When you convert a music file to an MP3, the MP3 compression is applied. The compression technique, then, is what makes an MP3 an MP3 and a JPEG a JPEG.

4. **Deliver the file** over the Internet. With time-based media (audio, video), you have the option of streaming it over the Internet, so it's delivered in "real-time," rather than being downloaded all at once.

Step 1: Crop!
The easiest way to save space is by cropping images (and shortening audio or video). The larger photo has a nice symmetry, but you get the same content in the tighter image (left), and It's half the K-size.

understanding compression

The goal of compression is to reduce the amount of space a file takes up, while keeping it as close as possible to its original form. Some compression techniques permanently shrink the file. Others shrink it temporarily   while in storage or transit —and expand it once delivered. (Think of stuffing big items in a small suitcase and unpacking them on the other end.)

2 kinds of compression:

1. **Lossless** compression squashes a file in a way that allows it to completely recover, with no information or quality lost.

2. **Lossy** compression also squashes a file down to size, but some information is lost in the process. Once lost, it can't be restored.

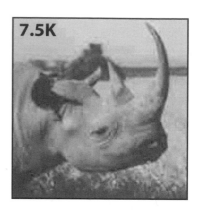

JPEG compression produces different results depending on the level of compression. The more you compress, the smaller and rougher your image will be. The original image (a TIFF file) was 53K. **Image 1 is 35K.** This image was saved at level 12 for "Maximum" quality. It's nearly identical to the original. **Image 2 is 15.8K.** This JPEG was saved at level "8." It lost a bit of detail, but looks good, considering it's half the size. **Image 3 is 7.5K.** This JPEG was saved at level "1" for "Low" quality. And it shows.

So, lossless compression re-creates the original file exactly as it was. And lossy compression reinterprets it, producing an approximation of the original.

Lossless compression is the ideal we're striving toward. But right now, lossy compression is often the only choice. For video production in particular, there's just no way to deliver (or even work with) the extra-extra-large files without it.

how compression works

In any medium, compression programs try to find extraneous information that can be eliminated, or repetitive information that can be blurred, fudged (that's a technical term), or combined with something else in a way that won't drastically alter the overall file. The methods vary, depending on the media type and the specific compression algorithm.

Image compression generally works by finding similarities within the picture—mostly based on color—which can be blurred or combined. This is why heavily compressed images appear, well, blurry. The detail has all been sucked out. You can see this in the pictures above: The heavily compressed rhino has lost all its wrinkles; the JPEG compression smoothed right over them.

This is also why cluttered images tend to compress poorly: When there's a lot of unrelated visual content, the compression algorithm has a hard time finding ways to save space. And its efforts to do so are usually clumsy and obvious, leaving the image badly scarred.

Video compression works in a similar way, but it looks for similarities not just within a single frame, but between frames. It also has to consider both audio and visual elements. Since choppy audio is more disruptive to the viewer than choppy images, most codecs will preserve sound quality at the expense of video.

Audio compression looks for patterns as well, but better techniques (like MP3) also try to eliminate sounds we can't hear or won't notice. This reduces the file size without significantly damaging the sound quality.

For example, certain tones are outside the range of human hearing, so those will be removed. And certain sounds we're less likely to hear. For instance, if two sounds play simultaneously, we would normally hear only the louder sound. So audio compression might remove the softer one.

understanding memory

Memory issues come up all the time in web production. Designers and engineers are constantly wringing their hands over the size and speed of their pages, which directly correlates to how much memory—or storage space—they take up.

Although you don't need a degree in computer science to know your site is slow, it's helpful to understand the basic principles behind computer memory and networking—just in case.

The first thing you should know is that everything on your computer has to be stored: your software programs, your files…even the sound file that plays when you turn on your computer. All these things take up space—or "memory"—on your computer's hard drive.

measuring the size of a file

Computer memory is generally measured in bytes, so every single item on a web page—or a computer for that matter—can be described by the number of bytes it takes up. A single byte, however, is rather small. So items are usually measured in kilobytes (1,000 bytes), called "K" for short, or in megabytes (1 million bytes), called "Meg" for short.

Although it rarely comes up in the context of web sites, it's helpful to know that each byte can be further broken down into 8 bits. A bit is the smallest possible unit of memory, containing one of two values: 0 or 1, on or off.

measuring the capacity of a computer

When it comes to memory, all computers are not created equal. Depending on how they're built, they differ widely in how much information they can store and how much they can process at once.

memory: more, more , more!

Byte	8 bits
Kilobyte	1,000 bytes
Megabyte	1,000,000 bytes
Gigabyte	1,000,000,000 bytes
Terabyte	1,000,000,000,000 bytes
Petabyte	1,000,000,000,000,000 bytes
Exabyte	1,000,000,000,000,000,000 bytes
Zettabyte	1,000,000,000,000,000,000,000 bytes
Yottabyte	1,000,000,000,000,000,000,000,000 bytes

2 kinds of memory:

- **ROM (read-only memory)**, which stores files, but can't do anything with them. This is better known as the hard disk.

- **RAM (random access memory)**, which actively processes the files you're using at any given moment.

The hard disk provides permanent storage for files. This type of memory is relatively cheap and plentiful, but it isn't active. Things on the hard disk are in deep storage. And that's where RAM comes in. RAM is the more active, short-term memory. It's constantly shuffling things back and forth to the CPU—your computer's processor—for, um, processing. So the whole time you're using your computer—opening and closing files, calculating, completing tasks—the RAM is fetching things from permanent storage and handing them off to the CPU as fast as its little legs can carry them. The more RAM you have, the more legs it has to transport things, and the faster they can run.

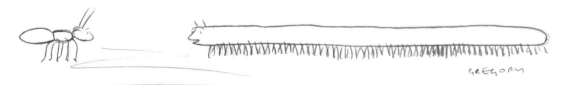

GREGORY

"I was a millipede, but I upgraded to gigapede."

images on the web

The most basic way to breathe life into your web site is by incorporating images. But images also have their price. Even small images add up, when it comes to K-size. If you're not careful, they can slow your page to a crawl.

Artistic instinct, technical knowledge, and restraint are all keys to effective use of images online. You have to know visually when a graphic is needed, technically how to produce the smallest possible file, and instinctively (or politically, in an office environment) when enough is enough.

2 types of images on web sites:

- **Inline images**, which are pulled into the web page along with the text and graphics.

- **Background images**, which are like wall-paper. They're the bottom layer over which all other elements of your site will be laid.

1. inline images These are your basic, run-of-the-mill images on the web. They may be used for logos, buttons, navigation bars, or editorial elements. There are two common ways to enhance images: with image maps and image rollovers:

- **Image maps** let you link from a single image to multiple web pages, depending on where you click.

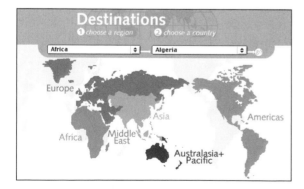

The image map on **LonelyPlanet** (www.lonelyplanet. com) lets you select the corner of the world you want to visit, and brings up the appropriate travel guide.

The logo on Nickelodeon's website (www.nick.com) splatters when you mouse over it, thanks to a rollover. It also makes a "Bwaaap!" sound which kids love.

- **Image rollovers**—or "mouseovers" as they're often called—are images that change when you mouse over them, revealing a second image.

2. background images aren't used as often as inline images. Most sites just work with a background color. But there are a few interesting uses of background images, which can be produced two different ways:

- **Full-screen backgrounds** fill the browser window with a single image, stretched to fit. The most important thing to remember here is file size. Images large enough to fill the browser window can grow quite large in terms of how much memory they require. One smart strategy is to use a small, low-resolution graphic, and stretch it to fill the space available.

- **Tiled backgrounds** fill the browser window with rows and rows of the same image, laid one next to the other. The image must be square or rectangle in shape, but it can be any size (as small as a single pixel).

choosing an image file format

All digital artists can rattle off a long list of image file formats—PICT, TIFF, JPEG, GIF. There's a time and place for each of them. But only two—GIF and JPEG—can be reliably displayed on the web (PNG is still up-and-coming). So any web image must be converted into one of these file types.

Image type	GIF	JPEG	PNG
Pronunciation	Either "Jiff" or with a hard G, like "give."	Jay-peg.	Ping!
What it stands for	Graphic Interchange Format.	Joint Photographic Expert Group.	Portable Network Graphic.
What it's good for	Illustrations and graphics. Also animation.	Photographs. Also graphics with colors that blend or fade.	Everything GIFs do: Graphics, illustrations, animation.
What it's not good for	Photo-realistic images with colors that blend: They'll appear broken and jagged.	Pictures—either graphics or photos—with large areas of a single color.	Photographs.
Colors	1-bit to 8-bit color (256 colors).	24-bit only (millions of colors).	8-bit, 24-bit, or 32-bit color.
Animation	Yes.	No.	Yes, with MNG.
Transparency	Yes. A single color can be transparent.	No.	Yes. Plus 256 levels of partial transparency.
Compression	Lossless.	Lossy.	Lossless.
File size speed	Images can be reduced to truly tiny file sizes, but compression isn't as good as it could be.	File size tends to be larger than GIFs, but excellent compression almost makes up for it.	Compression is excellent (better than GIF).
Advantages	▪ Tiny images. ▪ Animation. ▪ Transparency. ▪ Almost universally supported.	▪ Excellent color retention. ▪ Excellent compression allows large images to load quickly. ▪ Simple compression process.	▪ Excellent compression with no loss of quality. ▪ Suitable for a wide range of images. ▪ Excellent cross-platform viewing.
Disadvantages	▪ Complicated optimization process. ▪ Certain visual effects (such as glowing light, feathered edges, and vertical stripes—of all things—compress poorly.	▪ Not much control over compression process. ▪ Larger file size. ▪ No transparency. ▪ No animation.	Not widely supported.

preparing images for the web

1. scan. sketch. snap. steal.

First, find or make the image you plan to use. Then get it into your computer by one of the following means:

Scan. You can digitize an existing photo or graphic by scanning it into your computer. You'll need access to a scanner, of course. (Most copy shops and computer centers have them; you can also buy one for under $200.)

Sketch. You can create a new image of your own, using image-creation software like PaintShop Pro or Illustrator

Snap. You can take pictures with a digital camera and easily transfer them to your computer.

Steal. The web is designed so you can easily pinch graphics off neighboring sites. Just right-click on any image (on the Mac, you click and hold), and select "Download to Disk." The image will be saved to your desktop. But remember: Just because it's easy, that doesn't mean it's legal.

Equipment needed:

■ Scanner, or

■ Image-creation software like Paintshop Pro, or

■ Digital camera

On the web

Webmonkey Graphics tutorials

http://www.webmonkey.com/design/graphics/index.html

2. crop

Crop the image tightly, using Photoshop or similar image-editing software. Remove extraneous elements and cluttered backgrounds. This will reduce the file size, and therefore the download time, of the image.

By the way, this isn't just good web advice, it's good visual advice. A closer, tighter shot is almost always more effective. As the photo-journalist Robert Capa said, "If your pictures aren't good enough, you're not close enough."

Equipment needed:

■ Image-editing software, such as Adobe Photoshop. (See choosing software for web design, p. 89.)

3. pick a file format

Every image has to be saved in a format appropriate for the web. To keep matters simple, there are only two real options: GIFs and JPEGs.

GIF. In general, graphics and line illustrations with solid, flat color should be saved as GIFs.

JPEG. In general, photographs— or images with colors that fade and blend—should be saved as JPEGs. See choosing an image file format, p. 207, for explanations and exceptions.
Note: Before saving an image as a GIF, you must convert it to "indexed color." Before saving an image as a JPEG, you must convert it to "RGB" color.

🛒 **Buy this book!**

<designing web graphics.4>
Lynda weinman (New Riders, $55)

An excellent overview of image production techniques, serving both the novice and professional production artist.

4. compress

Compression is the most important part of image preparation, and the one most unique to the web. In print media, it doesn't matter how big an image file is. But on the web, size is everything. Images must be as small as possible in order to download quickly.

So this is where the real work comes in. Images must be strategically altered and then shrunk to the smallest possible size that retains their original look and feel.

The process is different for GIFs and JPEGs.

JPEGs are easy to compress. There isn't much detail work or even much choice. You simply choose a level of compression, from 1 to 12 (12 is the highest quality image with the largest file size), and observe the trade-offs in size to speed.

Fat images, saved with "maximum" compression, will be beautiful and terribly slow. Slimmer images, saved with "low" compression, will be fast and rough. The challenge is to pick the sweet spot in the middle.

GIFs are more complicated than JPEGs, but they give you more control over the compression process.

The main way to shrink a GIF is by reducing the number of colors in the image. You can do this with any image-optimization program.

The trick is to reduce colors without dramatically altering the picture's appearance. As Luke Knowland wrote on Webmonkey, you have to "stealthily suck the color out," being selective and strategic.

Reduce colors in a GIF by:

- **Creating a custom color palette.** Colors that won't be missed are removed; only essential colors remain.

- **Dithering the image.** Colors are strategically clustered together, creating the illusion of additional colors.

- **Banding the image.** Intermediate shades are removed; you get dramatic rings of flat color instead of a gradual fade.

- **Setting a transparent color.** You can mask out a color, so the image blends into the web page. This reduces the number of colors by one.

Equipment needed:

- Image-optimization software, like Equilibrium's DeBabelizer, or

- Image-editing software, like Adobe Photoshop.

5. post!

Once your image is digitized, cropped, and compressed, you're ready to integrate it into your web site.

Images are brought into a page using the <img> tag, which lets you identify the image's name and location, height and width, and border size. It also lets you incorporate a short text description (called "alt" text), which describes the picture.

The HTML would look something like this:

```
<img src="rhino.gif"
height="100" width="100"
alt="Photo of a wrinkled
rhino" border="0">
```

audio on the web

The topic of audio on the web presents a real quandary for web developers. It's wildly popular —when you're just talking about downloading MP3 files—and it has loads of potential (to create atmosphere, invoke emotion, etc.). But due to cost constraints and user resistance to automatic sound, it can be hard to find the right approach.

Uses for online audio:

- **Short sound clips integrated into the page.** These are especially useful as instructional or explanatory devices. (For instance, language sites can incorporate sound clips of native speakers pronouncing words.)

- **Longer audio files (like MP3s) placed on a page.** The web is mainly used for distribution—not playback—of MP3s. They're downloaded from the web page and played back on an MP3 player (or burned to a CD).

- **Streaming audio programs with radio-style programming.**

- **Live webcast of a concert or event, delivered using streaming audio.**

- **Sounds used as interface elements.** Sometimes, sites will integrate audio to emphasize a user's navigation choice. When you mouse over an image—or click on it— the page will tick or bleep or bong at you to let you know you hit a hot spot and that clicking will cause some action. Generally, it's smart to give the user feedback on a choice. But after a while, these cute interface noises can get annoying. And if your users are in a work environment, they may not appreciate it.

- **Background music.** A technique that's not recommended. (See the accompanying sidebar.)

why background music can backfire

The overwhelming lack of sound on the web is a common lament among media professionals. Many believe sound is the most powerful way to create an environment or manipulate emotions.

And while it's easy to get caught up in the idea of the environment you're creating on the web, you should never forget the actual environment of your user. Unexpected sounds, remember, are startling, and they shatter the feeling of privacy or control. In many ways, they're a violation of personal space.

Nonetheless, many web sites toy with the idea of integrating audio—to set a mood, to punctuate an action, to brand the site, etc. The urge to integrate sound—ambient sound, sound that plays automatically—into your site may be very strong. Resist.

 If you integrate background music, make sure users can turn it off (without leaving your site). This symbol, from a card on **American Greetings.com**, does the trick.

The inclusion of sound on web sites— whether as ambient mood-setter or interface punctuater—almost always turns users off. Especially when they can't turn the sound off.

There are exceptions, of course. Certain types of sites are expected to have sound, like online greeting cards, for instance. But they always let the user turn it off.

So if you decide to include audio that plays automatically, be sure to follow their lead: Provide a prominent "On/Off" switch (like the one pictured previously), so users can lose the music without leaving your site. And watch your log files: If traffic drops off, you'll need to rethink.

choosing a format for online audio

	Streaming audio	Non-streaming audio
File formats	▓ RealMedia ▓ WindowsMedia ▓ Streaming QuickTime ▓ Streaming MP3	▓ MP3 ▓ MID ▓ .aiff ▓ .au ▓ .wav
How it works	Audio is "streamed" over the Internet and played in "real time" on the user's computer. Playback begins shortly after streaming starts. No files are downloaded or stored on user's hard drive.	The audio file is either played within the browser window (.aiff, .au, .wav) or downloaded in its entirety to the user's computer, where it can be played on the desktop, burned to a CD, or downloaded on to an MP3 player (MP3).
What it's good for	▓ Live webcasts of concerts or news events. ▓ Extended programs of pre-mixed music or interviews.	▓ Distributing individual songs. ▓ Integrating sound clips as on a language instruction site.
Download time	Seems to load quickly, because playback begins almost immediately.	Varies with file size, but file must download in its entirety before it can be played.
Playback quality	▓ Playback quality varies, depending on connection speed, available bandwidth, and other factors. ▓ Sound quality unpredictable.	▓ Playback quality consistent and smooth, though download size restrictions may necessitate lower quality recording.
Equipment required	Requires special streaming servers (most of which are rather expensive, though some—like IceCast—are available free).	No special server required.
Advantages	▓ Listener gets instant gratification. ▓ Allows for longer programs. ▓ Doesn't save to user's hard drive (good for saving memory and preventing intellectual theft).	▓ Industry standard for independent musicians. ▓ MP3 players are ubiquitous and free. ▓ Control over sound quality. ▓ No special server required. ▓ Can be saved to hard drive. ▓ Can be emailed or transferred on disk.
Disadvantages	▓ Cost and maintenance of streaming servers. ▓ Unpredictable playback quality. ▓ Not everyone has streaming audio players installed.	▓ File size somewhat limited. ▓ Download time can be prohibitively long.

preparing audio for the web

1. record or find

Record. The first step toward integrating audio into your site is to record—or find—the audio you need. If you're creating original content, you can record it on any medium you'd like, analog or digital.

"We're at an interesting time in terms of recording technology," says Tim Ziegler, founder of the music marketing service, Lost Rock. "There are a million ways to record an album right now. Some are very affordable, and some of them aren't. But all of them are good."

So you can record to any medium you choose: mini-disc, analog tape, Hi-8 tape, whatever. And while many musicians now record straight to digital, some are sticking to analog formats, Ziegler says, because the sound is "warmer."

For voice, it's easiest to record directly into the computer, using a microphone.

Find. You can also use "found" sound from just about any audio source: CDs, tapes, vinyl, etc.

Equipment needed:

This varies with the recording medium, but in general:
- Computer with lots of RAM (random access memory), and hard drive space.

- Microphone (or other input device)

- Speakers

- Recording/editing software

2. digitize

The next step is to convert your audio file from its current format (DAT, 8-track, CD, whatever) to a digital file on your computer. This is a job for the analog-to-digital (A/D) converter on your sound card.

If your source material is on CD, just insert it in your computer's CD drive. You can use just about any audio-editing software (or an MP3 "ripper") to convert the file to a .wav file (On the Mac: .aif. On Unix: .au).

Otherwise, plug in your tape deck, mixer, or stereo to the "audio in" port of your computer. Then use audio-editing software to convert it .

As you digitize, you'll have to pick your sampling rate, which partially determines sound quality.

The sampling rate in audio is similar to the frame rate in video: It measures how much information (per second) is captured from the original file. To create a digital file, the computer "samples" an audio track, taking snapshots of individual moments that will be laid together.

The sampling rate is the number of snapshots taken per second. The higher the sampling rate, the better the sound, and the bigger the file. CD-quality sound requires a 44.1 KHz sample rate, which means the computer takes 44,100 samples per second, recording 16 bits of data each time.

Equipment needed:

- Player for source material (e.g. tape deck or CD player)

- Mini stereo jack or similar cable

- Sound card

- MP3 ripper or other audio-editing software to convert files

3. edit

Once your audio is digitized, you can edit it in all the ways that traditional recording studios do: Setting and mixing tracks, rearranging song sections, adding fades, reducing noise, correcting pitch. You name it.

Let's reflect on how cool this is: "Fifteen years ago, if you wanted to make a record, you had to come up with $10,000, and you had to go into a recording studio, spend a lot of that money and record it," says Matt Margolin, a web producer who also plays a mean guitar. "Then you had to find someone to make the records and do the artwork. It was really a complicated process. It was expensive, it took a long time, and it was hard to do. There was a huge barrier to entry."

Today, those barriers are eroding. "Now, you can set up a home studio for a couple thousand dollars, and make your own CDs," Margolin says. "You're basically your own record label."

Equipment needed:

- Audio-editing software, such as Macromedia's Soundedit16 or DigiDesign's ProTools. Cheaper options include programs like CoolEdit and SoundEffects.

4. choose a format

MP3 is the industry standard for distributing music online. But not all audio is music, and not all music is best-suited to MP3.

Depending on your project and your budget, other options may better suit your needs. See choosing a format for online audio, p.211.

The best tool for the job:

- **Song files: MP3.** MP3 offers great compression and playback quality, and it's currently the industry standard.

- **Live events: Streaming formats.** To broadcast—or webcast—a live event, you'll need a format that can be streamed.

- **Radio-style programs: streaming formats.** Longer, radio-style programs require a streaming format, even if they're pre-recorded. Otherwise, they would take too long to download.

- **Sound clips: QuickTime or a simple format (.aiff, .wav, .au).** To embed a short (under one minute) sound clip in your web page, you'll want a format that integrates well with the browser and which most users can play.

- **Background music: Flash or a simple format (.aiff, .wav, .au).** If you want ambient music to play when people view your site (a risky strategy: See why background music can backfire, p. 210), a simple format can work, but Flash might be better. It lets you synchronize the audio to user actions.

5. compress

The final step in preparing your audio as in any media file—is to compress it, so it can be transferred more quickly and easily across the Internet. Although audio compression is enormously complex, the process for you is simple enough.

To compress your audio:

- Select the appropriate encoder.

- Select the level of compression.

Select the appropriate encoder. Each audio format has its own method of compression, which is accomplished through software called an encoder. So if you're saving your sound file as an MP3, you'll use an MP3 encoder to compress/encode it. And if you're streaming your audio with RealMedia, your encoder will be the Real Producer software.

Select the level of compression. Whatever format you choose, you'll have to select the level of compression—also known as the encoding rate. With MP3s and other static files, you'll weigh the trade-offs between sound quality and file size. With RealMedia, the file is compressed at different levels to serve visitors on different speed connections.

Equipment needed:

- The encoder for your chosen file format. For MP3, this could be a combined ripper/encoder

- Audio-editing software will include other, non-proprietary codecs

6. deliver

Once your audio is recorded, digitized, edited, and encoded, all that remains is to deliver it.

Two choices about delivery:

- Static or streaming files?

- Embedded window or pop-ups?

Static, stand-alone files are delivered in their entirety and must be downloaded completely before they're played. They may be emailed as attachments or embedded in a web page. They're generally higher quality than their streamed counterparts but take up more disk space.

Streaming audio is delivered and played in "real-time" on a user's computer and will begin to play moments after the download is initiated. Playback is erratic and sometimes rough, but the format can handle long programs that would be unrealistic as static files. You'll need a dedicated streaming server to deliver streaming files.

Embedded window or pop-up?

When you add audio to your web site, you can sometimes determine how the player should appear on your web site: either as a window within the page, or as a separate pop-up window.

video on the web

For as long as I've been working on the web, there's been talk of "convergence"—of the broadband future in which video will stream into our computers as seamlessly and beautifully as it does into our television sets, but with the added perks of interactivity.

Don't hold your breath.

Like so many futures, this one's been a long time coming. The basic problem is bandwidth. Video files are huge, and hard to deliver over Internet connections. We just don't have the infrastructure to support it.

But thanks to improvements in compression rates and the growing number of Americans with high-bandwidth connections, online video is finding its legs. As of December 2002, 33.6 million Americans had broadband connections at home (Nielsen NetRatings). And while that's still less than ⅓ of online users, it's a start.

"The quality of video that can be shown on the Web is so much higher than it was a few years ago," says Jasin Wishnow, founder of the New Venue (www.newvenue.com), the first site to showcase online film. "The film companies are now putting out really lush, high-bandwidth, 20-Mg video files, which look great."

This is a big change from just a few years ago, when web movies were primitive, postage-stamp sized productions. "When I started the New Venue, my requirement for showing a film was that it be no more than 5 MB in size," Wishow said.

And as video has become more sophisticated on the Web—loking more and more like TV—new outlets, like cell phones and hand-held computers, have emerged for "micro-movies," as Wishnow calls them.

The micro-movies we're now seeing on hand-held computers are not so different from the types of movies you saw on the web five years ago, or on any computer 10 years ago, or in a kinetoscope 100 years ago," Wishnow said. "The micro-movie has always been the same type of movie."

Movies have come a long way since W.K.L. Dickson shot "Record of a Sneeze" in 1894. And web video has come a long way since the tiny QuickTimes we watched in the '90s. Top: "Record of a Sneeze" from the Library of Congress (http://www.loc.gov). Bottom: "Coin Laundry" by Jerome Oliver, shown on NewVenue (www.newvenue.com).

Uses for online video:

- **Distance learning** which lets "virtual" students attend classes.

- **"Webinars"** (web-based seminars) aimed at the corporate audience.

- **Video clips** of news events or news stories, often accompanied by video ads.

- **Trailers for feature films** distributed to promote the movie or video online.

- **Short independent films** distributed online, as well as through other venues.

- **Webcasting of concerts** and corporate events (for employees in other regions).

choosing a format for online video

	Streaming video	**Non-streaming video**
File formats	▪ RealMedia ▪ WindowsMedia ▪ QuickTime	▪ QuickTime
How it works	Video is "streamed" over the Internet and played in real time on the user's computer. Playback begins shortly after streaming starts. No files are downloaded or stored on user's hard drive.	The video file is downloaded in its entirety to user's computer, where it is then viewed using one of several video players.
What it's good for	▪ Videos over three minutes. ▪ Live broadcasts of concerts, news events, or corporate presentations.	▪ Videos under 3 minutes. ▪ Low-budget projects. ▪ Movies requiring absolute control over image quality.
Download time	Seems to load quickly because playback begins almost immediately.	Potentially slow downloads with nothing to entertain you while you wait.
Playback quality	▪ Playback quality varies, depending on connection speed, available bandwidth, and other factors. ▪ Frame rate erratic. ▪ Image quality unpredictable.	▪ Playback quality is consistent and smooth, though download size restrictions may necessitate lower quality video. ▪ Image quality and frame rate are determined in editing process.
Equipment required	Requires special streaming servers, which are expensive both to buy and to operate because they use so much bandwidth (although some are available free).	No special server required.
Advantages	▪ Instant gratification. ▪ Allows for longer video. ▪ Doesn't save to user's hard drive (good for saving memory and preventing intellectual theft).	▪ Control over image quality and frame rate. ▪ No special server required. ▪ Can be saved to hard drive. ▪ Can be emailed or transferred on disk.
Disadvantages	▪ Cost and maintenance of streaming servers. ▪ Cost of bandwidth. ▪ Unpredictable playback quality.	▪ File size and movie length are limited. ▪ Download time can be prohibitively long.

preparing video for the web

1. film or find

The first step toward integrating video into your site is to film—or find—the footage you'll use.

Film. If you're creating original content, you can shoot it with any analog or digital video camera (or even a movie camera, if you have a preference—and the budget—for film).

As you film, you should always keep the final online product in mind and emphasize those filming techniques that lead to better compression. For tips and tutorials, try the film site New Venue (http://www.newvenue.com).

Find. Rather than filming it yourself, you can use "found" footage from films or videotapes, if you can obtain the rights. You can also use photographs or other still images, which can be scanned into the computer and integrated—slideshow-style—into the video.

Equipment needed:

- Video camera or camcorder
- Analog or digital video tapes
- Microphone (optional)
- Tripod (optional)

2. digitize

If your film is shot using analog (normal) video, you'll need to convert it into a digital format. The process varies depending on your source material, but your computer will need a video capture card.

Digital video can usually be transferred directly from video camera to computer, using a specialized cable called "FireWire."

Equipment needed:

- Firewire or other high-speed cable (if shooting digital video)
- Computer with a Firewire port
- Video capture card (if shooting analog video)

3. edit

If you're really old-school, you might still edit video on the traditional (and expensive) Avid workstation. Otherwise, you'll look to the new generation of video-editing tools, all of which were designed for editing digital video on a desktop computer.

When editing digital video, you have to make a few choices that don't come up in TV or film. Namely:

- **Frame rate.** Frame rate measures the number of still images (or frames) that appear each second in a video, creating the illusion of continuous motion. Rates are standardized in film (24 frames per second) and TV (25 or 30 fps), but they are still an open question in the digital world, where a slower frame rate means a smaller file size and a faster download. Typical rates are 10, 12, or 15 fps.

- **Picture size.** For obvious reasons—based on their respective screens—TV and film both have standardized picture proportions. TV is, well, TV-shaped, with a 4:3 aspect ratio, while films are wider (1.85:1 or 2.35:1). No standard has emerged for online video, but the most common window sizes (320 x 240, 240 x180 and 160 x 120 pixels) all preserve TV's 4:3 aspect ratio.

  As you edit, you should emphasize those editing techniques that lead to better compression.

Equipment needed:

- Video-editing software, such as Final Cut Pro, Adobe Premier, or Media100 CineStream.

4. pick a format

There are several different formats for online video, and your choice will depend on your project and your budget.

The basic choice you'll have to make is between streaming and non-streaming (static) video. There are several choices for streaming video (Windows, Real, and QuickTime) but QuickTime is the only choice for non-streaming.

See <u>choosing a format for online video</u>, p. 215.

The best tool for the job:

■ **Live video: Streaming formats.**
If you're "webcasting" an event as it happens, you'll have to use a streaming format.

■ **Long videos: Streaming formats.**
Videos longer than three minutes should be streamed. Otherwise, they take too long to download.

■ **Short video: QuickTime.**
Videos under one minute should probably be static.

■ **Video on the cheap: QuickTime.**
Streaming video has many advantages, but cost is not one of them. It's expensive not only to buy the streaming servers, but to operate them. (You need a lot of bandwidth to serve streaming video!) So QuickTime is the way to go for low-budget projects.

5. compress

Your compression technique (called a codec) will be dictated by the file format you choose. And all the standard codecs come bundled with video-editing software. So you can simply export from your editing suite to the final format. However, most video professionals invest in a specific compression suite, like Media Cleaner or Sorenson Video.

Final decisions. When encoding your video, you'll have to give final answers on the following questions:

■ **What video format?** QuickTime, Real, Windows?

■ **What delivery medium?** Web? DVD?

■ **What delivery method?** Normal or streaming?

■ **What frame rate?** 10, 12, 15 frames per second?

■ **What window size?** For example, 240 x 180 pixels.

■ **What connection speed?** 56K modem? DSL? T1?

Equipment needed:

■ Video compression suite like MediaCleaner (terran.com), or just video-editing software.

6. deliver

Once your video is recorded, digitized, edited, and encoded, all that remains is to deliver it.

Two choices about delivery:

1. Static or streaming files?

2. Embedded window or pop-up?

Static, stand-alone files are delivered in their entirety and must be downloaded completely before they're played. They may be emailed as attachments or embedded in web pages.

Streaming video is delivered and played in "real-time" on a user's computer and will begin to play moments after the download is initiated. Playback is spotty, and it requires a dedicated streaming server, but the format can handle long videos that would be unrealistic as static files.

Embedded window or pop-up?
When you add the video to your web site, you determine how the movie should appear on your web site: It can either be embedded within the page or served in a separate pop-up window.

"I'm afraid we're going to have to put your son in a class for children with slower modems."

improving site speed

"Remember that time is money."
- Benjamin Franklin

In Hollywood, it's said that one can never be too rich or too thin. But on the web (where most professionals are neither as rich nor as thin as they once were) only one such maxim applies: You can never be too fast.

Speed is the single most important factor for any web site, regardless of its audience, focus, or goals. For all web users—from the clueless newbie to the cranky veteran—have one thing in common: They hate to wait. They expect the web to move as fast as their desktop applications—as fast as their minds work, really—and even a few seconds of lag time can set them on edge or send them packing.

"Something about the web has just made my attention span shrink," says Noah Mercer, former CTO of Nextdoor Networks. "It's measured in hyper-seconds. If a site's slow, and I don't need it, I either abandon it or find another site that does the same thing. So for that reason, I think speed is very, very important."

Indeed, slowness is the number one complaint of web users. And it affects a site's success in more ways than one.

Speed affects

- Traffic to the site
- Sales generated from web customers
- Pacing of the user experience
- Cost of running the site

Traffic   It's a fact: The longer users have to wait, the more likely they are to leave. Just ask Omar Wasow, founder of BlackPlanet.com.

As traffic to BlackPlanet grew, they had to increase their capacity—adding more and more servers to handle the rising tide. Every time they began to hit their limit, the site slowed down under the strain, and traffic dropped off.

"When traffic plateaued, it wasn't because interest had diminished, but because we'd basically hit our capacity," Wasow said. "The site was getting so slow that people weren't spending as much time on it. When we threw more hardware at it, all of a sudden it would start to grow again."

Sales   Just as speed affects traffic, it also impacts sales. "Speed is more important to commerce sites than content sites," says Jim Morris, former Director of Software Engineering for Fogdog Sports, now GSI Commerce, Inc. "On content sites, you're clicking and reading, clicking and reading. But on commerce sites, you're clicking through pages at a faster rate."

> **All web users—from the clueless newbie to the cranky veteran—have one thing in common: They hate to wait.**

Quick clicking makes customers more aware—and less tolerant—of lag-time. So transactional sites are often held to a higher standard. And the stakes are also higher. Content sites may profit from visits of any length (because revenue is based on the number of ads served) but visits only matter to a commerce site when they result in a sale.

Pacing   For some sites, timing is everything. The order and pacing of events can impact user understanding on transactional sites and even content-based sites. It's hard to dictate timing with any precision, says Wendy Owen, principal of Giant Ant Design. "But by thinking about speed—image size, download time—you take more control over pacing."

Cost   The main reason to focus on speed is its impact on traffic and revenue. "But speed is also important from a cost perspective," says Noah Mercer. "If a site is running slowly, it's often because it's using a lot of machine or network resources. It's expensive to add more resources to make it run fast. So from that perspective, it's a good idea to have things run as efficiently as possible, and that's usually connected to speed."

why sites are slow

There's no single factor that slows down a site. Between the moment a user clicks on a link and the moment the page appears on her screen, a lot of things have to happen, and they all slow you down.

A web page seems slow when

1. **The page is generated slowly.** After receiving the request for a page, the server must find— or generate—it. Simple, static pages area easy, but it takes longer to generate a dynamic page, like a search result. The speed with which pages are generated depends largely on the servers: how many there are, how powerful they are, and how many user requests they can handle simultaneously. But the application itself can also affect the speed; code can often be rewritten to use the server more efficiently.

2. **The page is transferred slowly.** Once the page is located, it's sent across the internet to the user's browser with all its accompanying files (images, movies, scripts) in tow. The transfer speed depends on three factors: your site's bandwidth, the user's connection speed, and—especially—the size of the files you're transferring. If the page has a lot of images—or if those images take up a lot of memory—the page will transfer very slowly.

3. **The page is drawn slowly.** Once the files are transferred to the user's computer, the browser draws (or "renders") the page. This should be a straightforward process, but often is not. The browser may have to wait for all the elements to load before it can draw anything at all. And the browser may get bogged down by contradictory commands in the HTML, which cause the screen to be redrawn.

how slow is too slow?

Site speed is usually measured in the seconds it takes a single page to load over a given internet connection (56K modems are usually the lowest-common denominator). This speed is then translated into a rough K-size, so the production team can stick to the guidelines without speed-testing every page.

A good rule of thumb is that your pages should load in less than 12 seconds for users on a 28.8K modem (that's about 8 seconds on a 56K). But every site has to decide for itself how fast its pages should be. Sites aimed at utility—search engines, for example—need to be whip-fast. While online magazines and art galleries can afford to be a bit slower.

> **Between the moment the user clicks on a link and the moment the page appears on her screen, a lot of things have to happen. And they all slow you down.**

Expectations will often vary even within a single site. The home page is expected to be the fastest (though often it isn't), so you can pull visitors into the site. Subsequent pages can be a bit slower—since users are more engaged and more likely to wait.

Now, that isn't to say users won't wait for anything. If you have an interactive game or a short film, users will expect to wait longer. But even then, you need to get them in the door first. Once they understand your site's content, and decide it's something worth waiting for, that's when you can hit them with a long download. But not before.

Check your speed
NetMechanic
http://www.netmechanic.com

a speedy site in 6 steps

1. reduce page size

Every single thing you put on a web page—text, images, scripts—adds up. If you're serious about speed, you'll have to tighten your belt.

Reduce the number of images. Images are the most common offender on slow web sites, and the easiest to fix.

- **Eliminate unnecessary images.** By paring down your images, you create a more focused user experience and a faster loading site.

- **Replace images of words with words.** Avoid using pictures of words: They're slower than regular text and can't be searched.

- **Repeat images through the site.** If you re-use images throughout your site, the browser will store them so they don't have to be downloaded a second time.

Reduce the size of images. Techniques may vary, but every image on your site—without exception—should be compressed. See preparing images for the web, p. 208.

Remove unnecessary multimedia. Audio, video, and animation force the user to stop, look, and listen. If the message isn't crucial, it's a distraction.

Remove unnecessary scripts. JavaScript programs and other scripts can slow down your site. At least take the time to improve the code.

Lose the link farm. The text on your site is usually the least of your speed troubles, but long lists of links will slow the browser down.

Evaluate banner ads. If your site accepts ads, you'll need a strict evaluation process. Ads that are too big—or that use "rich media" technologies—can slow your site to a crawl and cost you more in customers than you gain in revenue.

See designing for speed, p. 92
understanding memory, p. 205
preparing images and
multimedia for the web, p. 202

2. increase bandwidth & server capacity

Sometimes your speed issues are caused not by your pages or your scripts or your ads, but the system that serves them. As a site grows in size and popularity, its backend also needs to scale upward. You need sufficient server capacity, and sufficient bandwidth, to handle all the requests pouring in, particularly at peak hours. You should be able to get reports that tell you what capacity you're running at.

- **Number and capacity of servers.** Only a limited number of people can access your site from a single server at any given time. So if your site's traffic is taking off, you should consider adding more (or more powerful) servers.

- **Bandwidth.** Internet hosts only allot a certain amount of bandwidth for each client. And if you're traffic is on the rise, you may have outgrown your allotment. You should consider options for increasing bandwidth—possibly through sharing—at least during peak hours.

See building the backend, p. 188
building for reliability, p. 179

3. overhaul the html

When it comes to speed, size isn't the only thing that matters. Even small pages—with minimal graphics and no scripts—can be painfully slow. The main culprit here is poorly constructed HTML.

HTML tells the browser what a page should look like. (See picturing how html works, p. 194.) But sometimes it leaves out important details, such as the size of an image. When this happens, the browser has to wait for the big, fat image to load before it can draw anything at all. Worse, it may begin drawing the page, then "realize" it's made a mistake (e.g., the image is too large for the space it allotted). The browser will then clear the screen and re-draw the page, to the dismay of the user.

To avoid HTML speed traps:

▓ **Specify height and width of images.** Every image on your site should be described by dimensions. This saves the browser a lot of thinking and your users a lot of waiting.

▓ **Specify height and width of tables and table cells.** Like images, tables—and the cells within them—should be described by their height and width. This helps the browser draw them accurately…on the first try. See understanding tables, p. 160.

▓ **Avoid nested tables.** To achieve complex designs, designers often nest smaller tables within larger tables. But too many nested tables can bog a browser down: It has to calculate too many things before it can even begin drawing an image.

▓ **Switch to stylesheets.** Many sites still use font tags to control typography. But font tags—which have to be repeated again and again throughout the site—waste a lot of bytes and a lot of your time. A switch to stylesheets means faster-loading, faster drawing of pages, and—bonus—a lot of saved production time.

See designing for speed, p. 92
building your site to last, p. 184
understanding stylesheets, p.162

4. overhaul backend code

If your site is application-based (like a search engine or a commerce site), the code itself could be holding you back. Engineers are constantly working on ways to optimize code, making it run faster and putting less strain on the servers.

There are a lot of ways code can contribute to site speed: sometimes the code is inefficient and steps can be combined or skipped altogether. Sometimes a procedure is more processor-intensive than it needs to be. Sometimes the ordering of events can impact the load on the server. Sometimes code can be pre-compiled rather than generated on the fly. And sometimes server-intensive (read: slow) features just need to be taken off the site.

See adding applications to your site, p. 226

continues

a speedy site in 6 steps (continued)

5. test cross-platform

The concept of cross-platform and cross-browser testing is old hat for most web production gurus. There are so many different browsers, and each has different versions for the Mac and the PC, not to mention Unix.

The focus is usually on visual display: How do the pages look in each browser? But cross-platform speed tests are also important—particularly when your design uses a lot of HTML hacks, nested tables, or add-on technologies.

See designing for different systems, p. 90

building for compatibility, p. 176

6. show important things first

As a final note, let's talk about the power of perception. Sometimes what we perceive is more important than what is. For example, most CEOs believe their company has very efficient tech support—because the tech support team always responds quickly to the CEO's concerns. (They're no dummies, the tech support guys). Support for the rest of the company may in fact be abysmal; but the CEO would never know it, and his perception is what matters most.

How does this relate to you and your web site? Well, you, too, can be manipulative. You can manipulate the user's perception of your site's speed by manipulating which items on the page load first.

Users don't really care how long it takes to load an entire page. They only care about the things they came for. Visitors to a news site want to see the headlines; visitors to a search engine want the search box. So, if you manipulate your page to ensure the key elements appear first, you can vastly improve the perceived speed of your site without doing another thing.

Pages generally load top to bottom, left to right. But this order can be manipulated using stylesheet positioning (Jeffrey Veen explains how in his book, *The Art & Science of Web Design*). And if you manipulate the order so users immediately see what they came for, well, that's a big savings in speed without making a single tough decision.

how will you improve site speed?

You could build the world's most brilliant and user-friendly web site—one that elegantly fills an unmet need for the entire online population—and still fail miserably if your site is too slow. So what are you going to do about it?

send the page faster

strategy	done	not doing it
Decrease overall page size	❏	❏
Remove unnecessary images	❏	❏
Repeat images throughout the site	❏	❏
Replace pictures of words with words	❏	❏
Replace image maps with text navigation	❏	❏
Crop images more tightly	❏	❏
Compress images more completely	❏	❏
Remove unnecessary Flash files	❏	❏
Remove unnecessary multimedia files	❏	❏
Remove that JavaScript ticker!	❏	❏
Remove unnecessary scripts	❏	❏
Reduce the number of banner ads	❏	❏
Set stricter policy on the size of banner ads	❏	❏
Eliminate rich-media ads, or at least test them	❏	❏
Eliminate unnecessary scripts	❏	❏
Increase bandwidth, at least at peak hours	❏	❏
Remove multimedia files; serve them on a separate page	❏	❏

generate the page faster

strategy	done	not doing it
Overhaul code to lessen strain on servers	❏	❏
Check for code inefficiencies	❏	❏
Add more servers	❏	❏
Add servers with greater processing power	❏	❏

draw the page faster

strategy	done	not doing it
Overhaul HTML; replace troublesome code	❏	❏
Specify height and width of images	❏	❏
Specify height and width of tables	❏	❏
Make sure height and width are correct	❏	❏
Avoid nested tables	❏	❏
Check JavaScript for errors	❏	❏
Check all scripts for "grammar" errors	❏	❏
Test site cross-platform and cross-browser	❏	❏
Create illusion of speed with priority loading	❏	❏

chapter

adding applications to your site

don't miss ...

At some point, almost every commercial web site will need more advanced technology. The technology may appear on the site, like a shopping cart for an online store, or it may be used behind the scenes to send email newsletters or manage content. Whatever it is, the site faces the essential question: Build or buy?

If you build your own application from scratch, you'll get a product custom-made to your own needs. But you'll have to invest the time and engineering effort to create—and maintain—it. If you buy a third-party product, you may not get everything you hoped for, but you'll get it a lot faster.

Nine times out of ten, it's more sensible to buy a technology than to develop it yourself.

In the early days, of course, we didn't have this choice. Site developers had to build everything—from the features on their site to the software behind it—themselves. But the most common needs are now addressed through commercial products. And you should use them. If at all possible, you should use them. Nine times out of ten, it's more sensible for companies to buy a technology than to develop it themselves.

Using third-party products saves you time, money, and frustration, and lets you focus your efforts on those aspects of your site that matter most. That said, you shouldn't expect to find a turn-key solution to every problem. In most cases, you'll be choosing among several imperfect solutions. And it may take a real effort to make them work for you—and with each other.

"I came to the web thinking you have to build everything yourself, because when I started, you did," says Dave Thau, an industry veteran who wrote *The Book of JavaScript*. "Now I'm kind of amazed by what you can buy…and also how hard it is to get things you buy to work together."

Whether you're buying a commercial application or building your own, there are always trade-offs to be made. And it's smart to consider them before choosing a direction.

3 ways to add a new technology:

1. **Build your own application** from scratch.

2. **Buy a flexible application** that can (and must) be customized.

3. **Buy a ready-to-use technology** that can be used straight out of the box.

building your own application   The advantage of designing and developing your own product is obvious: You get something custom-made for you and your needs. But there are serious drawbacks: It takes time and money to develop software. And it doesn't end when the program's up and running. You still have to document and maintain what you've built. "The word 'maintain' may sound innocuous, but there's a lot hiding behind that word," warns Noah Mercer, former director of software development for *The New York Times* and *The Washington Post*. "You have to evolve the software to keep pace with your business, integrate it with other software you buy, and update it as the underlying infrastructure changes."

buying a flexible product   Many third-party technologies can be customized to suit your particular needs and can evolve as your organization grows. These applications are more like a toolkit than a finished product: They let your engineers *build* a product that meets your specific needs. The flip-side to this flexibility is the work it takes to customize. You'll need to devote staff—or hire consultants—to adapt the software to your needs. This can be expensive and time-consuming.

buying a ready-to-use technology   Some off-the-shelf products can be installed and used immediately after they're purchased, with only minimal configuration. They're fast and fuss-free, but you may outgrow them. A few months or a few years down the road, you may find that your your site has grown or your needs have changed.

choosing the right technology

To make a good decision on technology (to make a good decision about anything, really), you have to know what you want. If you know what you need from a product and how much time, money, and effort you're willing to invest in it, you're more than halfway toward the right decision.

Before you choose a new technology:

1. Know what you need.

2. Know what you can live without.

3. Think about how you'll grow.

4. Get technical advice!

know what you need   This may sound simple, but it's the most common mistake people make when choosing technologies. Your first step shouldn't be assembling a line-up of products, but figuring out what you would need from one.

"Start with your need," says Dave Thau. "You don't want to go into a store not knowing what you need, because you're going to end up getting something you don't want."

And the same goes for web technologies. You should know exactly what you need from an application before you go looking for it. Otherwise, you may snap up an expensive product that doesn't actually make sense for your site.

know what you can live without   You probably won't find a product that precisely matches all your needs. So it's a good idea to know beforehand what might be negotiable. Which features are pertinent, and which are preferred?

"Focus on what you really need," says Pamela Statz, former production manager for HotWired and Lucasfilm. "And don't get starry eyed, thinking you need more."

think about how you'll grow   Although it's essential to remain focused on your key needs (and not get carried away), you should also keep an eye on the future. Your site will grow and evolve, and you may need the product to grow with it. Audience size alone could change your technological needs. Will your audience grow? Will you expand the scope of your site? Will you partner with other sites? All these changes could alter what you need from the technology and how well it can serve you.

It's important to have foresight when you choose a technology, because it can be hard to change course later on. "Once you start with a system, it's almost impossible to undo it," says Tim Ziegler, founder of FamilyAlbum.com. "You can't put the toothpaste back in the tube."

get technical advice   "Make sure you get technical advice on technical products," advises Lance McDaniel, VP of Creative at SBI and Company. It's a simple suggestion, sure. But "it's a good one, and it seems not to be followed much."

avoiding potential pitfalls

What kind of problems might you have with the technologies you buy? Well, to quote the wise witch in the musical *Into the Woods*: "They disappoint, they disappear, they die…but they don't."

The Witch was talking about parents, actually. But web sites have the same problems with their chosen technology partners:

Potential problems in buying technology:

- The technology doesn't live up to your expectations.

- The vendor doesn't provide adequate support.

- The vendor goes out of business.

You can't always predict or prevent these problems, but you can do your best to avoid them by asking the right questions before you buy. See <u>evaluating a new technology</u>, p. 229.

evaluating a new technology

You'll need someone technical to help you evaluate potential technologies. But most of what you need to know has less to do with technology and more to do with business.

What you want to know	What you should ask (or look for)
How good is the product?	▥ How long has the product been in development? ▥ How many customers does it have? ▥ Is the technology currently used in any working sites?
How well does the product fit your company's needs?	▥ Who are their other customers? ▥ Does it have other customers with needs like yours? Are they the most important customers? ▥ Is its marketing material geared toward you? (If not, that's a bad sign.)
How hard will it be to integrate the product with your existing systems?	▥ Will the product integrate with your existing system? ▥ Will the integration require custom work? ▥ How long will the integration take?
If customization is required, how difficult will it be?	▥ What is the development environment like? What programming language does it use? Are your staff engineers familiar with it? ▥ Does the development environment require special training? if so, are there consultants available to help with customization?
Will the company stay in business?	▥ How long has the company been around? ▥ Who is the management team? What's their track record? ▥ How many employees does it have? ▥ How was the company funded? ▥ How many customers does it have? ▥ How many paying customers does it have?
What is the company's commitment to the product?	▥ What other products does the company produce? ▥ What is its biggest money-maker? ▥ What products are promoted on its web site?

10 questions to ask
before choosing a new technology

Before you buy a new technology for your site, make sure you know what you need.

1. What will this technology do for you?

_____
_____
_____
_____

2. What are your specific needs?

_____
_____
_____
_____

3. What can you live without?

_____
_____
_____
_____

4. Will your needs change as your site grows?

_____
_____
_____
_____

5. What kind of scale are you talking about? (Number of users served, emails sent, products or documents in the database, etc.)

_____
_____
_____
_____

6. Does the new tool need to work with any other technologies you use?

7. What is your budget?

$ _____

8. Who will work on implementation?

❑ I have a full staff of engineers to customize it for my needs.

❑ I have some limited resources to install and perhaps customize it.

❑ Implementation?!? No one said anything about implementation!

9. Taking all your answers into account, is it more important for this tool to be flexible or ready-to-use?

❑ **Flexible.** My site's going to grow and change, and the software needs to grow and change with it. I don't mind waiting awhile before I get to use the new technology. And yes, I have the engineering support to make this happen

❑ **Ready-to-use.** I need to use it right away, and my site's needs will probably remain the same over time. Besides, I don't have the staff, time, or money to work on customization.

10. Answer this, and be honest: Are you hoping this technology will solve a non-technological problem? (Like getting people to follow office procedures or write documentation or play more nicely with each other?)

❑ No.

❑ Yes. And here's how I should solve that problem instead:

_____
_____
_____

developing software for your site

When you can't find a commercial application that suits your needs—or when you want to build a tool that will differentiate you from your competitors—you'll find yourself developing software for your site. Whether it's a tool for your users (like a search engine) or the site creators (like a content-management system), the development process is the same. And it's a challenge.

You'll need a product manager, an engineer, and a designer to come together and design the application. And even when team members are skilled, motivated, and focused on the same goal, they face enormous hurdles: They don't think the same way, they don't work the same way, and they don't even speak the same language. And that, as they say in Engineerese, is "non-trivial."

So it helps to begin this process with a mutual understanding of what you're trying to accomplish, and how you plan to get it done.

4 keys to application development:

1. Clearly define the problem.

2. Limit the scope.

3. Let the application evolve.

4. Collaborate.

clearly define the problem Before you begin work on a software application, you have to define the problem it will solve—and be specific. Some of the saddest stories in software development began with a vague, open-ended product idea which the engineer had to interpret.

"An ill-defined product makes me extremely nervous," says Noah Mercer. "An ill-defined product with no one around to define it makes me more nervous. An ill-defined product with someone around to define it—who doesn't have the time or the skills to do it—makes me want to run away in panic."

So the first challenge is to nail down the specific problem you're trying to solve with the application. Then sit down with the engineer (and a designer), and work through the details.

"What most engineers like is definition," Mercer explains. But that doesn't mean writing a description of a product and asking them to build it. "Engineers often like—and should be involved in—the definition phase," he says. "So don't just go off and define the product and hand it to them. That's not a good idea. But it's a *terrible* idea to go off, *halfway* define it, then hand it off without involving them. That's a recipe for disaster."

> **This is your nightmare: The engineer delivers a product that cleverly solves the wrong problem.**

The problem with handing off a vague request is not only that it annoys engineers, but it prevents them from doing their jobs well. For starters, they can't give you a reasonable estimate for time or costs on a product that's only partially described. "You're going to get back an estimate that doesn't take any of the details into account," Mercer says.

The other problem is that the engineer can't read your mind. He won't necessarily know how to interpret your impressionistic request. And if you're not clear about what you want, you may get something you don't need.

Mercer offers an example of how this process goes wrong: "Let's say you want an application that will organize your grocery list, so that when you go into the supermarket, you can go through aisle 1, 2, 3, 4, 5, 6, 7, then checkout—instead of aisle 1, aisle 3, aisle 2, aisle 7, aisle 5, aisle 3, aisle 1."

"A really bad product definition would be, 'Hey, I just need something that organizes my grocery list so I can go through the aisles and pick up the stuff I want.' Literally, some people do that. They give the engineer this simplistic description of what they want, and expect to get back a finished product."

"This is fine," he says, "as the beginning of a collaboration. But it's not sufficient on its own." The devil, as they say, is in the details.

"The programmer starts digging into it, and he realizes, 'Well, we've got a few problems here. Do you want it to work with multiple grocery stores or do you have one grocery store in mind? Aisles are sometimes numbered differently—there might be aisle 7A and 7B—how do you want us to handle that? What about the row at the back where the dairy and the meat are, which isn't really an aisle? Do you want me to divide that up into the aisles that lead into it or should I assign it an arbitrary aisle? How do I handle that one?'"

"And so the person who thought that they were going to type their grocery list, and hit 'go' suddenly finds they have this 63-page web application with admin tools for setting up grocery stores and SKU product numbers for inputting item data."

This, you see, is your development nightmare: The engineer delivers a product that cleverly solves the wrong problem.

limit the scope   One of the biggest mistakes software teams make (even teams of experienced developers at well-known companies) is trying to solve too many problems at once.

To prevent your project's scope from creeping endlessly outward, it helps to focus on a particular user facing a particular problem. Your goal, says engineer and usability expert Indi Young, is to "form a mental model of what the user is trying to get done."

> # The biggest mistake software teams make is trying to solve too many problems at once.

"But before you can form a mental model, you have to figure out the scope of what the user is trying to accomplish," she explains. "You can't form a mental model about really large things, just like you can't form communities around really vague topics."

Sometimes, a project's scope expands because team members can't make up their minds or don't agree on who the primary user is. But "scope creep" can also result from overzealous planning.

You'll pay the price for this kind of ambition. If you define a problem too broadly, you may create something that's too complex to finish and too complicated to use, or that doesn't quite solve anything for anyone.

"Software that's extremely flexible is often unusable," says Jim Morris, former director of software engineering for Fogdog sports, an early e-commerce company. "It's also really hard to launch. It's hard to finish it."

let the application evolve   It's the most common mistake that rookies make: Launching a finished product.

The web gives you unprecedented opportunities to observe how an application is used and apply that learning to future versions, which can be released in quick succession. And if you over-design at the beginning, you may paint yourself into a corner, limiting your ability to change direction or improve upon what you have.

"You should design your system to evolve," explains Greg Dotson, Chief Information Officer of Guru. "A good application development company is constantly getting feedback from real users and incorporating that into the site. Feedback between users and the system is key."

This can be a hard adjustment for some product managers, who like to think through all the details before development begins. Dotson himself says he had to make that transition:

"I went through a phase in my career when I thought specifications were the best thing, because you do everything up front," Dotson explains. "It's always easier to identify an error up front than it is downstream."

"But what I've learned is that no matter how much you think about a problem, there are always things you don't consider. Business needs change. The world around you changes. There are so many

building the right team

To build a successful application, you first have to build the right team. Technical projects are best produced by a small, collaborative team with a clear objective and the authority to make product decisions.

This team should include the producer (or product manager, depending on your terminology), the lead engineer, and the designer or usability expert. Depending on the project, one or two other team members may be appropriate.

However, if this team isn't small, isn't collaborative, or isn't empowered, you're going to run into trouble. A team that's too big will have trouble scheduling meetings, maintaining consistent communal knowledge, and making decisions.

If the team isn't small, isn't collaborative, or isn't empowered, you're going to run into trouble.

A group that isn't collaborative will move too slowly, miss opportunities, and risk building a product that's completely off the mark. Location is one of the keys here. So try to assemble a group that works in the same place. The farther apart a team is geographically, the harder it will be to stay in sync. Even co-workers in the same office benefit from getting closer: You can set up a common workspace for the duration of the project. (See how to encourage collaboration, p. 330.)

Finally, a group that isn't empowered will waste a lot of time making decisions that will later be overturned—resulting in lost momentum and ruined morale. Be sure that company stakeholders give their input early on. They should communicate their priorities, set clear goals for the project, and then get out of the way.

things you can't anticipate. So a powerful benefit of developing on the web is that you can consciously plan to iterate on those things you didn't anticipate."

collaborate   To create a successful web application, you need every team member—engineers, designers, product managers (or business users)—to bring their knowledge to the table in a way the others can understand.

> ### "In my experience, the only successful applications have happened when there was mutual respect between the engineering department and the creative department."
>
> *—Janice Fraser*

But communicating across disciplines is a challenge. So the process works best when team members work closely, communicate openly, and consider each other partners in the development process.

"In my experience, the only successful applications have happened when there was mutual respect between the engineering department and the creative department," explains Janice Fraser, a partner with Adaptive Path. "The most disastrous happened when those two groups had animosity toward one another."

The goal, she says, is "to bridge the gap, and to develop tools so the two groups can communicate effectively in language that the other understands."

Managing a cross-disciplinary team?
setting goals for a company site, p. 14
managing a web team, p. 328
how to encourage collaboration, p. 330
how to run a brainstorming session, p. 326

developing the application

Once you've assembled a team and defined the problem your solving, you're ready to sit down and design the application.

But the actual process of software development varies widely from company to company. Some are very structured, following rigid rules and producing formal documentation. Others (usually smaller, younger companies) seem to make it up as they go along.

But most teams center the initial development process (sometimes called the definition phase) around creating two—or sometimes three—documents.

Software documentation:

- **The functional specification** explains—in plain English—what the product will do and who will use it.

- **The technical specification** outlines how the problem will be solved technically.

The functional specification—also known as the "product definition" or the "requirements document"—is written by the producer or product manager, while the technical specification is written by the lead engineer. Sometimes a design specification is produced as well; it would come, of course, from the designer.

But the documents themselves don't matter as much as the decisions they document. So rather than just pass documents back and forth—or present dueling PowerPoint presentations—the best approach is to just sit down and talk through what, exactly, this application will do. Get your (small) team together, sit down in a room—for a few hours, or a few days, or even a few weeks—and hammer out the product definition together.

"The key is to sit down with the engineer, and go through all the details," says Noah Mercer. "Define everything in as much detail as you possibly can. And then write it down."

documenting how it works

When developing an application, you should produce two parallel documents, which together outline the task at hand:

Functional Specification	Technical Specification
a.k.a. "product definition" or requirements document.	a.k.a. "design document."
Explains what the application does, and who it's for.	Explains how the application works from a technical standpoint.
Authored by producer, with consultation of lead programmer and designer/usability expert.	Authored by lead programmer. Uses the functional spec as a guide.

One way to help things along is to break out of formal structures. Product managers are often asked to write "specs" (or specifications) for the application. But they don't know where to get started, or what, exactly, is expected of them.

To jumpstart the process, Jeffrey Veen discards the spec altogether. "I just have someone tell me a story about how the application should work," he says. "Because people know how to tell stories. They don't know how to write specifications."

the functional specification Also known as the product definition or the requirements document, the functional specification offers a detailed description of what the product will do and how it will work, from a user perspective.

These functional diagrams shouldn't be confused, however, with the final design.

The functional spec should include

- High-level description of the product, covering what it is and who will use it

- Description of users, with any needed detail

- Task-by-task description of functionality

- Screen-by-screen diagrams, showing visible functionality

- Flow chart, diagramming the user path

- Complete listing of input fields, with acceptable variables

- Potential user errors, and how they'll be handled

To produce the functional spec, the team often starts off with a high-level overview of the product's purpose and intended audience. They then walk through the program task by task, following the basic flow of the user experience and detailing all the functionality.

Many teams find it helpful to move page by page (or screen by screen) through the application. Some document everything in writing, some create paper prototypes, and others actually build HTML mock-ups on the fly, so they have a clickable prototype when they're done.

In any case, they would account for all the decision points users have, the input fields with which they'll be presented, and all the variables they'll accept. Ideally, they'll anticipate every possible user error and decide how each will be handled.

The functional spec can be delivered primarily in writing, but it's most effective when accompanied by flow charts diagraming the user's path through the tool and schematics showing roughly how the features will appear on the web page. These elements are sometimes broken off into a separate design spec, and in some cases they replace the written spec altogether.

It's important to note that these functional diagrams shouldn't be confused with the final design. Their purpose is to visualize functionality and express the relationships between different features. They may be produced by the designer, who will later create the actual interface, or they may be handed off to visual designers, who will collaborate with the team on the final product.

the technical specification Also known as the design document and often called the "tech spec," the technical specification outlines the product's high-level technical architecture and provides details on how it will be executed. Its intended audience is the other members of the technical team, including programmers, QA specialists, and the company's technical director. It's also important to future members of the technical team, as it provides both an outline for understanding the product's structure and a rationale for choices made.

Producers should note—perhaps with relief—that this document isn't for them. They probably won't understand it at all. And that's okay. That's why you created the functional spec. As long you have a functional spec in place, you can leave the engineering team to translate it into a working product. For more on writing technical specs, try "Anatomy of a Design Document" by Tim Ryan: http://www.gamasutra.com/features/19991019/ryan_01.htm.

how to work with engineers

One of the biggest challenges of web development is bridging the gap between technical and non-technical team members. Here's a guide to get you started.

1. Bring them in early. This applies to all collaborative projects, and holds true here: You should consult engineers early in the development process, when the product is still being defined. If you don't, you risk both charting an impossible course and alienating your engineer.

2. Present a specific problem to be solved. Engineers are natural-born problem-solvers. They usually produce their best work when presented with a problem to solve (rather than a solution to implement).

3. Collaborate, don't dictate. It takes at least two minds to create a web application. You may understand the user problem you're solving, but the engineer understands the technical problem. You need each other. In order to produce a successful site, you must find a way to work collaboratively. (See how to encourage collaboration, p. 330.)

4. Be clear about what you need. You must have a clear mutual understanding of what a requested feature has to do and what it doesn't have to do. So don't ask for vague or ill-defined features. Go over every aspect of the product in painstaking detail, in order to avoid misunderstanding. "The key thing to do is to sit down with the engineer and go through all the details," says Noah Mercer. "Define everything in as much detail as you possibly can. And then write it down."

5. Be decisive. Think through needs and priorities before development starts. Nothing causes engineers more pain than "flip-flop" project managers who can't make up their minds, says Jim Morris. A change in plans usually means you've wasted their time and energy. "Every feature change feels like a stab of a knife to an engineer."

6. Prioritize. Every new feature added to the list pulls resources. Don't request a new feature without explaining where it falls in the priority list. Be explicit about what's most important, and what should be completed first.

7. Set clear goals for the project. The better you articulate the goals, the more effective your engineers can be. "If it's ingrained in them—what the goals of the project are—then they have a measure by which to make some of the micro-decisions, even when you're not around," says Greg Dotson. "Then they don't have to involve you in every micro-decision, and they feel empowered."

> **"The key thing is to sit down with the engineer and go through all the details. Then write it down."**
>
> **—Noah Mercer**

8. Think in versions. The first released version of your application will not be the last. Web software development involves constant iteration, so you have to get out of the mindset of producing a grand, perfectly executed product all at once.

9. Ask questions. As producer or designer, you need not understand the intricacies of the site's system architecture or object model, but you do need to understand what's going on.

"You have to ask questions," says Lance McDaniel. "Non-technical people get thrown off in technical conversations by acronyms and jargon. But once you get caught up on the terms, the conversation is not unreasonable to follow."

And there's another benefit to asking questions. "People like to be thought of as experts," says Greg Dotson. "So asking lots of questions that appeal to their knowledge—and listening to the answers—are good keys to opening up a dialogue and building rapport."

10. Learn the language. As intrepid travelers always learn: It helps to speak the language. Or at least understand a few words. Brush up on the terms you hear engineers throw around. (You can look up any word on Google and have a definition in seconds.) But don't just throw buzzwords around—make sure you understand words before using them yourself.

11. Ask about implications. It's hard for non-engineers to know whether a given task is easy or difficult. So it's important to ask: "How much time will this take? Will it jeopardize other projects?" Cate Corcoran, former Director of Online Communications for PeoplePC, says, "One thing I would do is just admit that I didn't understand the magnitude of certain requests. It's almost like a two-step request process. First I'd ask, 'If I requested this, what would it mean?' Then I'd say, 'OK, I'm requesting it.' Or, 'OK, I'm not requesting it.'"

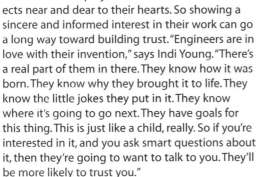

12. Show some interest. Many engineers hold their projects near and dear to their hearts. So showing a sincere and informed interest in their work can go a long way toward building trust. "Engineers are in love with their invention," says Indi Young. "There's a real part of them in there. They know how it was born. They know why they brought it to life. They know the little jokes they put in it. They know where it's going to go next. They have goals for this thing. This is just like a child, really. So if you're interested in it, and you ask smart questions about it, then they're going to want to talk to you. They'll be more likely to trust you."

13. Convince them it was their idea. "There's a lot of judo involved in working with engineers." said Jeffrey Veen, author of *The Art & Science of Web Design.* "You know, you use the force of your attacker against them."

He explains: "Last week, I spent, literally, an hour going in this huge circle with an engineer until he decided to do the thing I wanted to do in the first place…That's the judo you use with engineers. Let them decide to do the right thing, by directing them toward it."

"Of course, designers are just as bad," he laughs. "They're both equally stubborn."

14. Find a good mentor. It's hard to find an engineer who can patiently explain technical concepts in non technical terms. When you find such a person, don't let them go! Get them on your team whenever possible. And even if they aren't working on the same project (or in the same company), hold on to them! Ask them questions; take them to meetings with you; remember their birthdays; buy them coffee. They are very, very important to your success.

> **"Engineers are in love with their invention. If you're interested in it, they'll be more likely to trust you."**
>
> —*Indi Young*

15. Don't forget to say thank you. "It's really important to give people positive feedback, and to thank them for the things they do," says Cate Corcoran. "A lot of times, engineers will act like they don't need your praise. When you thank them profusely for working all weekend, they'll act like you're a dork. But I wouldn't believe that message."

16. Smile and nod. There's nothing wrong with faking it every once in a while. As designer Jeffrey Zeldman writes in his book, *Taking Your Talent to the Web,*" You might hear [developers] talk about Perl, Java, ASP, PHP, SSI, XML, ColdFusion, and other technologies. Just smile and nod as if you get it."

17. If all else fails, quote *Star Trek.*

maintaining

your site

chapter

monitoring & evolving your site

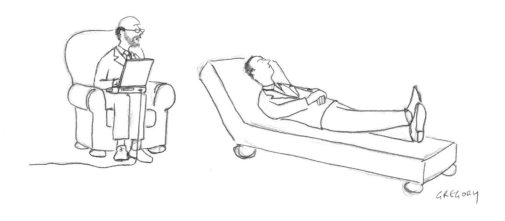

GREGORY

"One of the people logged in to my web site has a question."

don't miss ...

Once your site is planned, designed, built, and launched, you may feel a sense of accomplishment (and you should). But don't confuse a launch party with a finish line. Your work's only just begun.

It's only after you've launched your site that you can begin to learn what works and what doesn't. Successful web development is an iterative process: You launch the site, study how it's used, and make continual changes to improve it.

This is the advantage of the web over other media: Everything can be measured, and then changed to reflect what's been learned.

The web is more measurable than

- **Magazines.** Editors can't know which stories are most widely read, or which headlines are most effective at drawing readers in. But web site editors can.

- **Stores.** Store managers can't know how many customers leave without making a purchase or what they looked at before they left. But web site managers can.

- **Software applications.** Engineers can't know for certain which features are widely used and which are ignored. And they can't change a product once it's in use by the customer. But web engineers can.

The measurability—and flexibility—of the web proves important to just about every industry, because it helps businesses understand their customers and better serve their needs.

"Quantitative research on the Internet is so luxurious," says Adam Berliant, a group manager for Microsoft, and previously a lead product planner for MSN.com. "I cannot pick up an issue of *Newsweek* and tell you which article was read the most. Or how much time people spent on each article. Or which headline was the most effective. I can't do that. On the Internet, I can! I can tell you what 100% of the people who used this site did."

But Berliant's interest isn't just academic. The purpose of studying your site is to figure out how to improve it. "I can run experiments and see which headline does better," he says. "I can take the same photo and run it with different headlines, or take different headlines and run them with the same photo—or whatever combination of things I want to test."

The advantage of the web is that everything can be measured—and changed to reflect what's been learned.

"You end up with this ever-building cumulative picture of what works and what doesn't work on a particular web site," Berliant continues. "And the beauty of the web over software is I can take that learning and act on it tomorrow."

In fact, this seems to be the beauty of the web over everything. Magazines, software, stores—they all benefit from this immediacy. "There's enormous potential in the flexibility—and constant changeability—of the web site," said Hilary Billings, chairman of RedEnvelope and former VP of Pottery Barn. "The cement is always wet on the web, which is very different from stores and direct mail."

"We have the ability on the web to rotate products all the time," Billings explained. "We can constantly change the environment, which in a store, you just can't. It's a lot of logistics to change a store. And the catalog, once it's printed, it's done."

Continual improvement, it seems, is the secret behind so many sites' success. The big players, like Amazon and MSN, are always evolving. And smaller sites, too, benefit from this approach.

But it's a big transition for many site owners. "In almost every other area of business—certainly in technology—the focus is on the product," says Andrew Anker, Internet pioneer and a partner at August Capital. "But on the web, it's really the *process*. The easy part is getting the product out. The real challenge is to figure out what you did right and wrong, and change quickly."

Put plainly, Anker says, "The biggest mistake you can make on the web is thinking you're done."

studying your site

If there's one thing all successful web sites have in common, it's this: They pay close attention to what's happening on their sites. By watching what people do—where they come from, where they click, how long they linger—they learn what works on their sites, and how to provide more of it.

And unlike other industries, where data analysis is an arena for specialists, web companies spread this work throughout the product team so that everyone—designers, editors, engineers, producers—has the tools to make and analyze decisions.

"In a lot of companies, this kind of analysis ends up isolated in marketing," says Kris Carpenter, former VP of Excite. "The product team is handed some of the data, but they're not expected to be in the logs everyday. But when you have a product that's active and available online, suddenly the whole team needs to be familiar with the data."

And perhaps the most important thing a site owner can do is make this data available to their staff. This was always a priority for Beth Vanderslice, former president of Wired Digital (and the author's former boss). "I was always so passionate about traffic reports—and usability testing, and customer feedback," Vanderslice said. "Because if we weren't creating something that people wanted to use—or could use—then what's the point?"

"So the first thing I did was create a distributed reporting system, which allowed everyone in the company to log on and see how their sites were doing," Vanderslice explained. "I wanted to get that information into the hands of people who could use it—the designers, the engineers, the editors—so they could see for themselves what was working and what wasn't."

3 ways to study your site:

- Traffic analysis

- Usability testing

- Customer feedback

traffic analysis   The first step toward understanding your site is studying your traffic. How many visitors do you have? Where do they come from? How long do they stay? This information—and much more—is stored in your site's log file, but must be analyzed by software to produce meaningful numbers. (See choosing software for traffic analysis, p. 247.) You can quickly move beyond the basics—getting a feel not only for how many people visit, but where they go, what they do, and why.

usability testing   If traffic analysis tells you how your site is used, usability testing helps you understand why it's used that way. A typical test would involve watching a user as he performs a given task on your site. By watching what he does—does he know where to go? Can he correct mistakes?—you get a sense for how real users interact with your site. (See usability testing, p. 129.)

customer feedback   Although it may not always feel this way, customers pay you a big favor when they give you a piece of their mind. Email, letters, and phone calls offer valuable insight into who your users are, and what they want from your site.

Of course, people are more likely to write when they're angry than when they're delighted. So feedback tells you more about what frustrate users than what pleases them. When you do get positive feedback, it's a strong indication that you're doing something right. Keep in mind, however, that positive feedback doesn't always correlate with popularity. The things that inspire people to write a letter aren't necessarily the things that inspire use.

"The things we get the most email about are not the things that are most popular," says Esther Drill, co-founder and editor of gURL.com. "We get thousands of emails a day about some of our features. And they're definitely popular and they elicit contributions, but they're not the things that drive the traffic, not even close."

evaluating how people use your site

What you want to know	Where you can find the answer
How many people visit my site?	**The log file** (think of it as a guest book) can usually tell you the number of visitors. But accuracy varies, depending on the software you use.
How do people find my site?	**The referrer file** tracks the origin of each user who comes to the site. It reveals which sites sent you the most traffic, and how many users find you on their own (without following a link from another site).
Where do people enter my site?	Most traffic-analysis software can issue a **Top Entry Pages** report.
What part s of my site do people use?	**The log file** keeps a running list of each page served from your site. Most traffic-analysis software will issue a **Most Visited Pages** report. And many will let you view pageviews by section.
How long do visitors stay on my site?	If your site is application-based—and requires users to log in—you should have a **log file** that captures the length of each user session, in minutes. If your site (like most sites) doesn't require a log in, you'll have to estimate the length of visits by the number of pages each visitor viewed.
How often do visitors return to my site?	Again, if you have a site that requires users to log in, the **log file** should reveal great detail about repeat visits. Other sites can track repeat visitors by setting cookies but this method is less precise.
Where do people leave my site?	Most traffic-analysis software can issue a **Top Exit Pages** report.
What are my visitors really looking for?	**Surveys or focus groups** can ask people their motivations. But the best way to **measure** what people are looking for is through a **keyword or search report**, which tells you the most popular search terms on your site. Also look at **log files** and **clickthrough reports** to see where people are clicking and where they're spending the most time.
Where do people click? And why?	A **clickthrough report** (available through some reporting systems) can track the number of people who click on any given link. Experimentation will tell you what factor (wording vs. color vs. placement) inspired the click. No one can exactly tell you *why*.
Why aren't customers buying?	Sorry. I don't have all the answers.

Who to ask

If you work for a large company that manages its own web servers, ask your system administrator what logs or reports are available. Otherwise, your hosting service should provide them. If your hosting service doesn't provide any traffic-measurement utilities, consider switching!

sources of traffic to your site

When a new store or restaurant opens, the owner will often ask, "How'd you hear about us?" This is an informal way of testing their marketing program: Should they advertise in the local paper? Or is the Yellow Pages enough? Is word-of-mouth what counts? Or is location, location, location all that matters?

Web site owners don't need to ask, because their log files already tell them what they need to know. There are a limited numbers of ways people can arrive at your site.

Users can reach your site by

- Following a link on a search engine

- Following a link on a web site

- Following a link in an email

- Clicking on an ad banner or paid link

- Typing in your URL

- Adding your site to their "Favorites"

- Making your site their Start Page

links on search engines   When people are looking for a particular type of web site, they'll often turn first to a search engine to find it. And this is how many visitors will find their way to you—by searching on a related topic and following a link to your site. See <u>improving your search rank</u>, p. 309.

links on other web sites   For most sites, search engines and portals are the most important sources of traffic. But don't discount the little guy. You'll be surprised how much traffic you can get from smaller sites that link your way. See <u>linking strategies</u>, p. 290.

email links   Email yields mixed results as a source of new users, but it's an *essential* tool for encouraging repeat customers. In fact, email newsletters and updates are the single most important source of traffic to many sites. Content sites,

in particular, rely on email to bring in up to 50% of daily traffic. But every site—regardless of focus—should use email to keep existing users coming back. See <u>email strategies</u>, p. 282.

ad banners and paid links   The staple of online marketing, ad banners are an admittedly blunt tool for increasing traffic. But they do work, and—combined with their simpler cousin, paid links—they're probably the best "buyable" tool for raising awareness and attracting new users. See <u>online advertising</u>, p. 294.

typed-in URLs   There's nothing better than someone who knows exactly what he wants—and it's you. Or your site, anyway. A good portion of users will arrive after simply typing your URL (or web address) into their browsers. Maybe they heard about your site in a newspaper article. Maybe a friend recommended it. Or maybe they just thought to themselves, "I wonder if anyone has the site, bananabread.com? Whatever the motivation, enjoy it when it happens.

"favorites" lists   It's always nice to be someone's favorite. But the best thing about being added to someone's "Favorites" list (which is integrated into the Internet Explorer browser) is that it gives them a slightly better chance of remembering your site and a much better chance of finding you, once they decide to return.

start pages   When a user makes your site her start page—meaning the first site that appears on her browser every time she starts it up—it's a great coup. It means a guaranteed pageview for your site every time she goes online, and a great chance that she'll use your site for her immediate online needs.

getting to the source

You can learn the source of your site's traffic by looking at the referrer log, which displays the name of the referring page for each user that visits. Users that come on their own—by typing in your URL or following a bookmark—will appear as a "null" referral.

measuring traffic

The first step toward understanding your site—and therefore evolving and improving it—is measuring your traffic.

Measuring traffic is as important as counting money to a web business. Unfortunately, it's a little harder. There are several different approaches to counting and tracking users, and—I'm sorry to say—none of them is exactly accurate.

It's always best to decide how you're going to measure traffic before you launch your site—partially because your decision may affect site structure and partially because you'll want to have traffic reports from the beginning. Collecting these initial reports allows you to do a full comparison as your site grows (it's not usually possible to do retroactive reporting).

If your site is already launched, don't wait for a redesign to put a measurement system in place. Choose a system, and begin running reports as soon as you can—preferably on an ordinary month, so you can establish a baseline comparison for any future changes.

how traffic data is collected

To explain how traffic is measured and analyzed, we need to first review some basics: When you visit a web site, your computer sends a message to the site's server, requesting the page and any accompanying graphics or scripts that appear on it. This message, or request, is usually called a "hit."

> **Traffic measurement is inexact. One visitor may be counted as 10, and 10 may be counted as one.**

When you visit a web site, the site's server log (think of it as a guest book), will usually record some data about you, or rather, about your computer: the computer platform and browser you're using, the domain you're accessing from (such as earthlink.net or berkeley.edu) and—most importantly—the IP address that uniquely represents your computer. (Note: IP addresses are *temporary*

---

key advice on measuring traffic

1. **Choose a method before you launch.** You'll want to have traffic reports from the very beginning. And your decision may affect site structure.

2. **Stick with the method you choose.** Your method must be consistent, in order to get a sense of both scale and growth over time.

3. **If your site has already launched, begin measurement on an ordinary month—well before any major redesign.** This way you'll have baseline numbers to help you understand the impact of any changes you make.

---

identifications assigned to each user during each session; they don't stay with you over time.)

In addition to the IP address, the server may place or look for a "cookie" on your computer. A cookie is a cute code name for a unique tag, which a site may leave with your browser, so it can identify you when you return.

The IP address and/or cookie will help the site's server track you through the web site. By the time you move on to the next site, the server log will have documented your visit, including the number and order of pages viewed.

The server log, however, contains only raw data. This data must be analyzed with software (like WebTrends' Log Analyzer) in order to return meaningful statistics, like unique visitors or pageviews per visit. (See choosing software for traffic analysis, p. 247.)

an inexact science

It's important to realize that traffic measurement (like vote-counting in U.S. elections, apparently) is not an exact science. You can never know exactly how many users come to your site. No one can.

The sites with the most accurate numbers are those that require users to log in before entering the site or using key areas.

But this kind of tracking isn't feasible for most sites; they'd lose their users if they required them to log in. So the best bet for the rest of us is to count the individual computers—as opposed to users—that log on to the site. The limitations of this approach are obvious: If one person logs on from 10 different computers over the course of the month, she'll be counted as 10 *different* visitors. Conversely, if 10 people access your site from a single computer (in a public library, for example), they'll be counted as a single visitor.

The uncertainty doesn't stop there. One of the basic and vexing questions (for sites that don't require log-ins) is how to track users as they make their way through the site: Are you receiving multiple hits from the same user, or single hits from multiple users? This is the question the server log asks thousands of times each day. Because there are so many ways to count and track users, no two systems will turn up exactly the same numbers for the same site. That's why it's important to choose one system and stick with it.

The differences between reporting systems also make it difficult to compare numbers between companies. It's very difficult to ensure an apples-to-apples comparison. So your best best is to use the estimates reported by industry analysts Media Metrix or Nielsen Net Ratings. They both use a consistent methodology on all participating sites, ensuring a level playing field. Bear in mind, however, that the ratings will inevitably differ from your in-house measurements.

Learning the Lingo

"Hits" vs "Pageviews"

A **pageview** is a single viewing of a single page on your site, by a single visitor.

A **hit** is a single request made for a single item on a page. To view a page, a user's computer must fire off many "hits" to your server—one for the page, one for each image, one for each ad, and so on.

So **sites log far more hits than pageviews**. Nonetheless, the two terms have become blurred. People often say "hit" when they mean "pageview." And that's okay in casual conversation. But if you're structuring a business deal, be clear about which term you're using, and what you mean by it.

how the rating systems work

For web sites—like TV shows and beauty contestants—ratings matter. Advertisers, investors, reporters and, in some cases, users all flock to the top-ranked site in any given sector.
But how do the rating systems get their numbers? How do they know the top-ranked sites are really the most popular?

There are two top research services that measure site popularity: Nielson/Net Ratings and Media Metrix. Both arrive at their numbers by observing a sample population, and calculating projections for the rest of the country.

Both Nielsen NetRatings and Media Metrix mainly study Internet users at home, not at work.

Both services recruit large panels of volunteers—Nielsen has 65,000 in the U.S.—through random-digit dialing (thought to be the most neutral recruiting method). Volunteers agree to have software installed on their computers, so their Internet use can be monitored. The software then tracks their every move—every site visited, every link followed, every purchase made—and feeds it into a giant database of user behavior that can be studied every which way.

Based on these sample groups, analysts create estimates for overall Internet use, including the number of visitors to each individual site.

These popularity projections are powerful, but there's one limitation you must keep in mind: Both services primarily study Internet users at home, not at work.

Since it's believed that most U.S. Internet use is conducted at work, and that web use is different at work than at home, the ratings may be skewed toward sites with strong at-home audiences.

Nielsen/NetRatings:
http://www.netratings.com
Media Metrix: http://www.comscore.com

choosing software for traffic analysis

	1. services from your web host	2. desktop software	3. server-based software
what it is	Software—offered through your web host—that analyzes your site traffic. Usually provided at no extra charge.	Software—installed on your desktop—that analyzes your site's traffic. Logs are downloaded to a local computer to be analyzed.	Powerful software—installed on your site's servers—that analyzes your site's traffic.
who should use it	Most small sites will find their needs met by these basic tools and reports.	Sites that use hosting services, but need more reports than their host can provide. Medium to large sites that are hosted on their own servers.	Companies with very large, complex sites that are hosted on their own servers.
advantages	Low cost and simplicity. The program will come packaged with services you're already paying for. No need to install software or customize your site.	Powerful analysis tools that go beyond the basics. Interface is usually intuitive. Reports are standardized for ease-of-use, but some can be customized.	Highly robust, powerful analysis tools. Custom reports can reflect your site's specific structure and reporting needs.
disadvantages	Limited functionality may not provide all the information you want. Very little customization.	Can be deathly slow and processor-intensive. Options are limited by computer platform.	Expensive. Slow. Requires a lot of computing power. Labor-intensive. Options limited by server platform.
cost	No added costs. Included in web hosting package.	$100–$1000. Some freeware is available.	$1,000–$20,000.
choices include	Most web hosts offer traffic-analysis services.	WebTrends Log Analyzer, Quest's Funnel Web Analyzer, Analog, Webalizer, Mach5 FastStats Analyzer, NetGenesis NetAnalysis, SurfStats Log Analyzer, Maximized Software FlashStats, ThinWEB's WebCrumbs, W3Perl.	WebTrends Enterprise Reporting Server, Urchin, Media House LiveStats.

creating a traffic report

The traffic report may be the single most important document for monitoring the health of your site. Your success is dependent on your users, and traffic reports give you a brutally honest picture of how users are behaving on a day-to-day basis.

Whether delivered daily, weekly, or monthly, traffic reports keep you up to date on the metrics that matter most to your site. The metrics you watch will depend both on your site's focus (what's fascinating to one site producer will be meaningless to another) and the limitations of the system you're using.

Every traffic report should include

- Unique visitors over the period covered

- Daily visitors

- Daily pageviews or transactions

- Average visit length (or time spent on your site—measured in minutes or pageviews)

Traffic reports are most useful when combined with relevant financial reports, such as ad revenue, product sales, paid subscriptions, or other successful transactions. Taken together, traffic and revenue data deliver a complete picture of site performance.

what to look for

When analyzing traffic reports, the first thing you should look for is big disparities: Is one section of your site more popular than others? Is your site busier on certain days than others? By getting a feel for these disparities and watching numbers fluctuate week-to-week, you develop an understanding of how your users behave, and—quite possibly—what they want.

You should always keep an eye out for big, dramatic changes, like a sudden surge or drop in pageviews. And when you notice a change—even if it's only a one-day blip—you should immediately investigate, and keep notes on what you learn.

But to recognize these big shifts, and—more importantly—to understand what they mean, you

---

what to look for

As you familiarize yourself with your site's traffic, important patterns will emerge.

traffic patterns

- How many people visit your site?
- How do people find your site?
- Where do people enter your site? Through the front door, or an interior page?
- What parts of your site are most popular?
- How long do visitors stay on your site?
- How often—if ever—do visitors return to your site?
- Where do people exit your site?

traffic spikes and dips

- When do traffic levels usually rise or fall? Which months are busiest? Which days?
- When do you see sudden spikes in traffic? After sending an email? Right before the weekend?

purchase patterns

- How many visitors make a purchase?
- What's the cost of the average purchase?
- How many items are purchased at once?

clickthrough patterns

- Do users click on a certain part of the page?
- Do users click on certain words or pictures?

registration patterns

- If users register for your site—or your newsletter—when do they sign up? Where?
- Are there certain features that inspire registration?

searching or browsing patterns

- What percent of visitors use your search engine?
- What do they search for?
- If they don't search, how do they navigate the site?

---

must have a baseline familiarity with your site's traffic patterns. Toward this end, I recommend looking at your numbers daily and compiling weekly and monthly traffic reports to discuss at staff meetings. This way, the entire team becomes aware of your site's traffic trends.

a sample traffic report

Traffic reports are as unique as the sites they monitor. The structure of your report will mimic the structure of your site. And the metrics you track will depend on what matters most to your site and your business. Below is a sample report to get you started.

My Sister's Garden
Monthly Traffic Report: April 2003

Site Section	Pageviews	High PV day	Daily PVs	Daily Users	PV/visit	Unique Users	Subscribers
Annuals A-Z	1,275,903	57,654	42,530	5,078	8.4		
Perennials A-Z	983,520	41,908	32,784	4,872	6.7		
Shady gardens	222,894	25,678	7,430	3,467	2.1		
Sunny gardens	223,406	12,301	7,447	3,193	2.3		
Container gardens	98,106	8,675	3,270	1,345	2.4		
Garden Equipment guide	75,603	9,043	2,520	2,024	1.2		
TOTAL	2,879,432	155,259	95,981	10,452	9.2	127,460	75,629

Most Visited Pages
1. Front Door
2. Annuals A-Z Front Door
3. Perennials A-Z Front Door
4. Pretty petunias!
5. Shady gardens front door

Top Entry Pages
1. Front Door
2. Annuals A-Z
3. Perennials A-Z
4. Sunny gardens front door
5. "How to grow roses"

Top Exit Pages
1. Front Door
2. Error 404
3. Garden Equipment Guide
4. Pretty Petunias!
5. Begonias page

Notes
1. Link from AOL drove traffic to "Annuals A-Z" on April 21, leading to record pageview
2. Front door promotion for "Pretty Petunias" feature very popular!
3. Redesign of Garden Equipment Guide launched. Pageviews declined slightly. Not sure why ....

Metrics you may want to include

- Unique visitors
- Daily visitors
- Daily pageviews
- Pageviews per visitor
- Session length
- Section-by-section breakdown of pageviews
- Most visited pages
- Top entry pages
- Top exit pages
- Number of registered users
- Number of subscribers
- Number of paying customers
- Number of items purchased per order
- Average cost per order
- Most popular search terms
- Most common error messages
- Busiest days and times

investigating changes

When something significant affects your traffic—causing it to either spike or dip dramatically—it's important to get to the bottom of it as quickly as possible (preferably within a few days). The longer you wait, the less people remember, and the more of a mystery your traffic reports become.

To investigate a fluctuation in traffic, ask

Did something happen on your site?

- Did you launch a new feature or ad campaign?

- Did a single article or headline prove popular?

- Were users searching on a particular keyword?

- Did your servers go down?

Did something happen in the world?

- Was there a major news event?

- Was it a national or school holiday?

Did something happen on the web?

- Did an ISP, like Earthlink, have a blackout?

- Did a major site link to you?

As you investigate a change in traffic, it's a good idea to ask coworkers—perhaps in the staff meeting—for help. You may not get to the source of all your traffic fluctuations, but by recording events when they happen, you'll be in a much better position to analyze cause and effect. Hopefully, you'll uncover enough clues to form a theory on the source of the traffic change. And with any luck, you'll be able to learn something from it.

For instance, if you lost traffic due to a server crash or service blackout, try to develop systems or purchase equipment that prevents it from happening again. If your traffic spiked because of a new initiative—an ad campaign, an article, a site

---

what makes traffic spike?

Sudden spikes and slumps in traffic can be mystifying, but there's usually an explanation.

traffic spikes occur when

- A new feature or section is introduced.
- A new promotion scheme—ad campaign, link campaign, etc.—goes into effect.
- An effective email update is sent to users
- The site is promoted in a newsletter, mailing list, news story, or elsewhere on the web.
- A great sale, compelling story or sexy headline pulls readers in.
- A major news event drives people online. This effect isn't limited to portals and news sites; all sites may get a lift.
- A news event or TV show drives interest in a topic related to your site.
- A portal, news site, or "site-of-the-day" feature spotlights your site.
- You add the words: " Free," "New," "More" or "Sex" to your front door.
- Seasonal fluctuations kick in, especially in January and September.

traffic slumps occur when

- One or more of your servers goes down.
- You experience a bandwidth black-out.
- A major ISP experiences a service outage, keeping many subscribers off-line.
- A national holiday keeps people away from work, and therefore off the Internet.
- A school holiday keeps students out of school, and therefore off the Internet.
- Seasonal fluctuations kick in, such as the summer slump.
- It's the weekend.
- An application or ad on your site is crashing users' computers.

---

feature—try to repeat the success. And if the traffic fluctuation was completely out of your control—caused by a holiday or news story or another remote event—well, just chalk it up to experience. Next time, you'll be ready.

typical traffic patterns

Traffic can seem like a supernatural force—the work of a capricious god, who withholds when your site needs it most and floods you when you least expect it.

But traffic levels need not take you entirely by surprise. Like commuter cars on a highway, web traffic ebbs and flows. And like its automotive counterpart, it's both predictable and inexplicable. (Sure, you can expect delays during rush hour, but bumper-to-bumper traffic on Highway 101 at midnight? On a Tuesday! Why? WHY?)

Traffic patterns vary from site to site, depending on popularity, user base, and offerings. But there are many consistent patterns that show, in broad brush strokes, how people use the web.

> **Traffic drops sharply on weekends. Most people access the web from work, on work days, during work hours.**

So how *do* people use the web? Well, in a nutshell: They use it at work. Most people access the web from work, on work days, and during work hours. (Take a moment to consider the implications.) So traffic drops sharply—30% or more for many sites—on weekends and holidays. Since most visitors to most U.S. sites are American or Canadian, daily traffic is clustered during North American work hours, with another bump mid-evening from home users.

And the annual cycle is also predictable (See <u>a year's forecast</u>, p. 252), peaking in January, stagnating over the summer, and dipping in December.

There are exceptions, of course. Depending on your site's content and audience, your traffic patterns may vary.

Dig Deeper
<u>take action! increasing traffic</u>, p. 267.

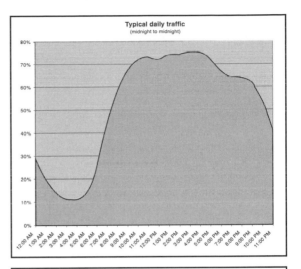

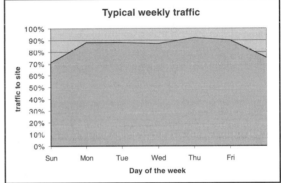

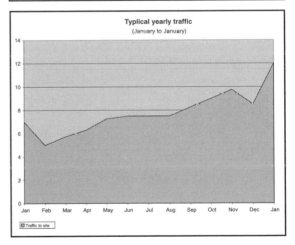

Source of top two images: Nielsen/Net-Ratings.
Web traffic has become more predictable, if not entirely explicable, over the years. It's no surprise that U.S. Internet use is heavy during work hours on weekdays. But why is there such a tumble of traffic every January? No one knows.

a year's forecast

In the U.S., web traffic over the course of the year is surprisingly predictable—assuming (and this is a big assumption) that your site's audience is increasing at roughly the same rate as the web. But even if your site isn't growing at all, you'll still see the same annual cycle play out.

Although it's hard to separate them, several key factors seem to affect seasonal traffic swings:

Seasonal traffic factors:

- **Climate.** Web use increases during cold, wet winter months and decreases during warm summer months.

- **School schedule.** Web use increases when schools are in session and declines during breaks and holidays.

- **Holidays.** Web use declines over major holidays. In the U.S., the biggest decline sets in from Thanksgiving (late November) to New Year's Day, though retail and travel sites may see a surge of use during that same time period.

The yearly forecast that follows is based on traffic to American sites. But other countries will see similar traffic patterns, if they share the same climate and major holidays.

So ready or not, here they come: The January surge, the summer slump, the December dip…. Learn to love the web's traffic patterns, or at least live with them.

the january surge

This we know: January is a busy month on the web. Users flood back online after New Year's, producing record-high traffic levels. But we don't really know why.

No one can quite explain the January surge, since it doesn't happen in other media. (There's no noticeable increase in TV use or magazine sales in January. And it's a slow month for stores.) The leading theory is that the spike comes from new users, testing out the brand-new computers they received as holiday gifts. Another theory is that the increased use reflects the reinvigoration—a getting-back-to-work—that accompanies the end of the holidays and the start of the new year (or perhaps it's explained by the procrastination that inevitably accompanies this "reinvigoration?")

Whatever its cause, the January surge is cruel to sites that run ad banners, since it coincides with the seasonal dip in advertising dollars. As in other media, January is the weakest month for ad sales online. Most ad budgets are blown in November and December, in anticipation of the holidays. So when traffic on a site is strongest (January), the pages are worth the least. And when traffic is weakest (December), they're worth the most.

> **Ready or not, here they come: The January surge, the summer slump, the December dip…. Learn to love the web's traffic patterns, or at least to live with them.**

Traffic drops off in February, but it will generally remain higher than it was the year before. And it continues to grow throughout the spring, with a possible dip in April for Spring Break.

the summer slump

And then comes summer, when nothing happens. Summers are stagnant online. Traffic levels across the web—and at most individual sites—remain unchanged from June to August. So if you've planned for steady month-to-month growth, just know you'll have a lot of catching up to do, come September.

Why doesn't traffic grow over the summer? That's an easy one. School's out, and the weather's great. Who wants to use your stinkin' web site when they can be at the beach? So go ahead and enjoy the summer yourself; there's very little you can do to break its spell.

autumn growth

In September, it's back to business as usual. Vacations end, schools reopen, and traffic takes off. Everyone breaks out their web browsers, along with their wool sweaters and corduroy pants. Throughout the fall, traffic should grow at a good clip. Until Thanksgiving, when everything goes to hell again.

the december dip

December will almost always be a weak month for non-retail, non-travel sites. Thanks to holiday parties, gift exchanges, and final exams, hardly anyone's surfing the web, unless they're shopping. Retail sites generally see a surge—in both traffic and orders—from Thanksgiving to Christmas. (If you don't, that's bad.)

So December offers two types of hell: Retail hell and Content hell. Retail Hell involves overloaded servers, back-ordered merchandise, unfulfilled orders, angry customers, and frazzled employees (unless the turn-out is disappointing, which results in a different variety of hell). Content Hell involves eager-beaver advertisers and sales reps, straining to meet quotas and failing to fulfill orders with the meager pageviews your audience is turning out.

So good luck to you. And hey, Happy Holidays.

exceptions to the rule

Although most sites see some seasonal fluctuation, they don't all follow these patterns. Travel sites peak with regional tourism seasons; religious sites peak with holidays (the timing of which depend on the religion). And baby sites will buzz year-round, because pregnancy knows no season.

Unusual circumstances can also overpower the normal, seasonal cycle. September 2001, for example, was no ordinary month. Web traffic went off the charts for several days after September 11th, but fell off precipitously for the rest of the month, as the U.S. (and the world) reeled from the disaster.

In fact, big news events always affect online traffic. Any time a big news story breaks, Internet traffic spikes—not only on news sites, but across the web.

And of course, these seasonal patterns aren't the only factors that move the needle. Your site affects its own destiny as well. And any time you have a big promotion—a sale, a popular article, national publicity—you can expect a spike in your traffic logs. No matter what month it is.

evolving your site

Successful site owners know that close attention to user behavior—coupled with incremental changes—can have an enormous impact on the user experience, and the bottom line.

You can see this purposeful evolution in action on most leading sites. The portals, like Yahoo and MSN, experiment with headlines, and subtly change the placement of links. Amazon slowly phases in new features—altering, for example, the way the site recommends related products or cross-links among departments.

Of course, these large sites have both the staff to make changes, and the tools to measure them. But even small sites with minimal resources can benefit from this approach. As long as you have a system for measuring traffic, the time to make changes, and the discipline to follow up, you can move mountains for your web site, one boulder at a time.

time.com—small changes, big impact

Like most web pioneers, Josh Quittner's earliest web ventures were perhaps more educational than profitable. When he launched "The Netly News" for Time, Inc. in 1995, it was the company's first foray into original independent online content.

While the site was widely read and admired, it didn't prove financially sustainable. "Virtually everything we did was wrong," Quittner laughed. "We learned so much about what not to do, it wasn't funny."

But those lessons came in handy when Quittner (now the Editor of Business 2.0) revamped *Time Magazine*'s site in 1997. The first thing he did was ask: Who's using this site? And when?

"When I took over Time.Com, there was one big data dump that occurred every day at 7 p.m. It was the top-15 stories, written as one endlessly scrolling page," he said. "It was about as wrong an approach as you could have designed."

The mistake, he said, was not considering the users. "They had all this data about who was using the site—and when they were using it—which they ignored."

But Quittner did his homework. "If you looked at that data, it told you that people started coming to the site between 9 and 10 a.m. Usage peaked around noon—when Californians were getting up and New Yorkers were having lunch—and it started to tail off around 3:00. By 7 p.m.—when they would put the day's news up—there was nobody online."

> **After examining traffic logs, Time.com made simple changes that increased traffic sixfold.**

Quittner made some immediate changes: News would be posted at 9 a.m. And—since their revenue was based on pageviews—stories would be broken out on to separate pages. "I said, 'Instead of having 12 stories on one page, we're going to have 12 stories on 12 pages—actually 14 pages. Let's have an introductory page, too, which summarizes them.'"

These simple changes brought dramatic results, taking the site from 150,000 to a million pageviews per week. And the technique that worked for Quittner will work for any site owner who takes the time to study his site. "Listen to what the data tells you," Quittner says. "This is a medium that tells you who's there, when they're there, and how long they stay there. It tells you what they're interested in, and what they're not interested in."

"Anyone who doesn't look at that stuff may as well be selling shoes—because that's the strength of this medium. It gives you a huge amount of information about who wants you."

testing your theories

Different sites evolve in different ways. Sometimes, as with Time.com, changes are dramatic: A redesign completely changes how a site is used. But evolution is usually a slower process, involving small day-to-day changes that add up over time.

4 steps to evolving your site:

1. Focus on things that matter

2. Learn what's working

3. Experiment with changes

4. Follow up

focus on things that matter The first step toward evolving your site is choosing a direction. Too many sites waste time on redesigns with fuzzy goals, and site "improvements" that don't measurably improve anything. Don't make changes just for change's sake. Every time you redesign or launch a new feature, you should have clear goals for what you're trying to achieve.

"When we go into a project, the first thing we do is identify the metrics," says Mark Hurst, founder of consulting firm Creative Good. "Is it a revenue-generating site? Is it a site with a conversion rate? Or is it pageviews they care about? Maybe it's not a revenue-generating site, maybe it's a site that generates cost-savings. Or maybe it's an intranet that has operational efficiencies that you can measure."

Whatever the site, Hurst wants to know how they define success. "We need to know that, so we know what metrics we're trying to improve."

From there, Hurst and his team study traffic logs and conduct usability tests (which they call "listening labs"), but all with an eye on moving those metrics. "If you improve 'usability' on the site, but the business doesn't grow, and you can't measure any tangible success, who cares?"

learn what's working If you spend even a few minutes with your site's traffic logs, you'll see some strange patterns: One section of your site may be more popular than others. Traffic may spike on a particular day and time.

When you see a pattern that's working in your favor, find out why it's happening—and see if you can repeat the success. (See the case studies on MSN p. 256, gURL p.260 and Webmonkey p. 258)

experiment with changes After studying your site for any length of time, you'll probably hatch some theories about what's working and why. The next step is to test them.

At HotWired, for example, our email newsletters brought in up to 50% of daily visitors. So we were always looking to build our subscriber lists. I wondered: Why did some subscriber lists grow faster than others? Did the sign-up rate relate to the site's content? Or did it depend on the placement of the sign-up form? I thought it was placement.

After taking a closer look, I found sign-up rates were much higher on sites that offered a sign-up form—which could immediately be filled in as opposed to a link that said "Subscribe." This jibed with what I knew about the Web: That people like to engage with the page, and not just look at it. So on one of our sites, I replaced the link that said "subscribe" with a fill-in form. The results were immediate and dramatic: Sign ups increased by nearly 1000% in a week—all because of a small change in the interface.

follow up It's always hard to predict how a given change will affect the way people use your site. So you have to pay strict attention to what happens after you redesign a site or launch a new feature.

"Every time we add a new feature to the site, it completely changes the shopping patterns of customers," said Hilary Billings, chairman of specialty gift store RedEnvelope.

"So after each change, you ask, 'Did that improve the site, or did it not?' And you make totally different decisions about the new set of features you're going to implement based on what you've learned from the old."

"It's always a surprise."

how MSN got people to click (a million times over)

If you were creating a game show just for web producers (and if any of them had time to watch) you might call that game, "Who wants a million clicks?"

All producers try to draw users into their sites. And Martha Brockenbrough, former managing editor of MSN.com, seems to know the siren song that lures them. When she became editor, she was tasked with creating a space for 'programmed editorial' (headlines and the like). Within just a few months, the programmed spot went from getting 250,000 clicks to more than 1 million per day. They soon beat 2 million, and then passed the 4-million-click mark.

Her secret? A near obsession with traffic reports, and a willingness to experiment.

"We went from 250,000 to 3 or 4 million by evolution," she explained. "By asking ourselves, 'What words work? What voice works? What mix of content works? What types of images work?' And we just kept building, and building, and building on what we learned."

"It's like being a chef," Brockenbrough explained. "You take a recipe for something, and you say, 'This is good, but what if I changed that?' And you keep changing one thing at a time until you come up with something that's the best in its class."

Constant experimentation—and rigorous analysis—was key here. Adam Berliant, a group manager at Microsoft (who then supervised MSN) said they constantly test different apparoaches—different headlines and images in different combinations—to see how each fares. "You end

> **"The reason we got there was because we had a specific, concrete goal: 'Get a million clicks!'"**
> —*Martha Brockenbrough*

up with this ever-building cumulative picture of what works and what doesn't," he said.

So a gradual evolution improved the MSN home page. But there's a second secret to MSN's rapid rise in clicks: A very specific goal.

Shortly after she was named editor, Brockenbrough challenged her staff. The brass ring? Get 1 million clicks per day off MSN's home page.

"What I did with my team was set goals," Brockenbrough explained. "I said, 'All right. We're starting out at a quarter of a million clicks a day. Let's break a million.'"

"And everyone said, 'No way! A million? It will never happen.' But we kept getting closer, and then, boom, we broke a million. The next week, we did it again. Then the next month, we did it five days in a row. And so, I bought a cake, and we celebrated."

"And the reason we got there was because we had a specific, concrete goal.," she explained. "It wasn't just 'Get a lot of clicks!' It was: 'Get a million clicks!' It was a crazy goal, but it was measurable and we experimented with different ways of achieving it."

By setting a group goal, Brockenbrough also allowed different team members to bring their skills to bear. "You define the goal, and then let people use their talents," she said. "Whether it's the page downloads more quickly, or the art is more compelling, or the language is more clear, or the design is more elegant and effective and gets people there quicker. It's using whatever tools you have ... and then having cake when you're done."

so what made people click?

So that's how MSN got users to click. but one can't help but wonder: What, exactly, do people click on?

people click on:

- Timely news stories

- Clear, compelling headlines (not clever, vague headlines they don't understand)

- Pictures of happy topics, cute animals, cute people (not distressing news photos)

- Red and bold links

- The words free, downloads, hot, sexy, and games

- A link that says More!

> **"You end up with this ever-building cumulative picture of what works and what doesn't work."**
> —*Adam Berliant*

So subject matter, word choice, and page design all matter.

Both Berliant and Brockenbrough (who are married) started their careers as newspaper reporters, so they're no strangers to editorial decisions. But their conclusions about what works online often flies in the face of their news training.

Newspapers, for example, consider bad news "real news," and happy news "fluff." Maybe so, says Brockenbrough. But people prefer to be happy. "People are much more interested in happy news, happy photos," she says. "If an image is disturbing, people will avoid it."

"So there's always a balance between what's popular and what's important," she continued. "But just because a twister flattens a mobile home in Alabama, it doesn't mean people want it in their faces. They'd much rather find '5 Tasty Soup Recipes.'"

"Timeliness also matters," Berliant says. "If it's happening today, it works better than something that's happening all the time or something that happened yesterday."

"So 'Stock Market Down Today' is more interesting than 'This Week's Stock Review.' And 'This Week's Stock Review' is more interesting than 'The Basics of Stocks.'

"But if I were going to run this week's stock review, I would say, '50 Hot Stocks Now'" Brockenbrough added. "Because it's concrete."

And the words you choose also make a difference. "Some words are incredibly appealing," Berliant says. "Downloads, free, hot, top, games …"

"And 'sexy,'" Brockenbrough added. "If you run

'5 Red Convertibles' vs '5 Sexy Red Convertibles,' the sexy convertibles will do better."

Another thing people click on: A simple link that says "More." 'More' is a beautiful word," Berliant said. "You know who wants more? The browsies— the people who click around."

And color is another way to get attention: If a link is turned red, it's more likely to be clicked. "What a surprise, right?" says Berliant. "But what's encouraging is that after it goes back to its original color, the usage stays up."

"So you can see on MSN, we rotate links in red for that reason." And other colors also work. "We've tried bold. We've tried blue. We've tried various colors," Berliant said. "They all had the same effect."

Over time, MSN has built a pretty complete picture of where users click, and why. Still, there are always surprises.

"On WindowsMedia.com we found out last week that blond Shakira did better than brunette Shakira," Berliant laughed. "Same headline, same content. We just used a different photo. Blonde Shakira did 30% better than brunette."

how webmonkey became a (profitable) library

You don't hear the words "profitable" and "library" together all that often. But it was the transition from magazine to library that pushed Webmonkey into the black and kept it there.

"When we first launched Webmonkey, it was more like a publication than the resource library it is today," explained Kristin Windbigler, the former executive producer, who led the site through its transition (and into profitability).

Although the site was updated daily—like most news sites—the traffic logs had sobering news: "Even our most devoted users weren't visiting the site every day," Windbigler revealed. "In fact, most people were coming once or twice a month. It was completely logical: They were coming when they needed to learn something new."

Like all web producers, Windbigler was eager to improve traffic to the site. On an advertising-driven site, pageviews equal revenue. And she wanted a way to boost both, while remaining true to Webmonkey's users.

Sensing that the audience craved help in greater depth than they were providing, Windbigler assigned Wired's senior scientist Dave Thau to write an in-depth introductory tutorial on JavaScript. The piece was posted over several days, and each day's lesson was divided into multiple pages.

As Windbigler points out, "This was a tougher decision than it might seem today." Although most content sites now divide long articles into several pages, it was less common then. So the staff had to think through the implications for their users.

"We knew most of our users accessed Webmonkey over modems," Windbigler said. "We didn't want to give them more pages to download." But the complex content demanded it.

"In the end, we decided that if the content was worth waiting for, they wouldn't mind."

Apparently, they didn't. The JavaScript tutorial received four times as many pageviews as the rest of the site combined. "People were nuts about it," Windbigler said. "Our readers were happy. Our sales team was happy. We were happy," Windbigler said.

> **"It was time to throw out our old publication model, and reorganize the site as a library."**
>
> *- Kristin Windbigler*

But what came next was perhaps more intriguing. Most Webmonkey articles were popular when they first posted, and then faded into obscurity once they moved into the archives.

But the JavaScript tutorial continued to draw more traffic than anything else on the site. Weeks—even months—after it was removed from the front door, people continued to visit in droves.

The staff had to wonder: How did they even find it? The site's archives were a tangled mess. "Even we were having trouble finding information on the site, never mind our users," Windbigler said.

The traffic, as it turns out, was coming from links people had built to the tutorial, and from people who had bookmarked it. They were already using Webmonkey as a library—without any help from the site.

Windbigler realized then it was time to make a major change in how Webmonkey worked. "It was time to throw out the publication model we'd used for years, and reorganize the site as a reference library."

lesson from the trenches

Over several months, the Webmonkey staff underwent a major undertaking of re-classifying and reformating all their old articles (discarding some in the process), and organizing them into web development topics.

This was great for users and also advertisers: By segmenting off site content, the sales team could book advertisers more easily. Companies like Adobe and Macromedia were eager to advertise in "Design"; others, like IBM, lined up for "E-Business."

It was a major undertaking, but one that paid off. "When the redesign launched, it set Webmonkey on a course for enormous traffic growth," Windbigler said. By the end of the year (the tutorial had posted in January), traffic—and revenue—had increased three fold, making Webmonkey a very profitable library, indeed.

The secrets of Webmonkey's success:

1. Watch how people really use your site. Don't assume, for example, that because you're changing your site daily, people are visting daily. Use traffic logs to learn how the site is really used.

2. Understand your site's role in users' lives. Webmonkey recognized that its readers used the site as a library—not a magazine—and made changes to help them.

3. Introduce changes gradually. Windbigler suspected that her audience wanted in-depth tutorials and a library-style format. But she tested these theories bit by bit, instead of springing a new design on them all at once.

4. Look for ways that everyone wins—your users and your business. Webmonkey's library structure helped users find what they needed, and this led to greater pageviews (and therefore more ad revenue). But it also helped the sales team attract new advertisers.

Top: Webmonkey's news-oriented front door, circa 1997. **Center:** The JavaScript tutorial (by Dave Thau), whose success led to the site's reorganization. **Bottom:** The Webmonkey front door, circa 1998, reorganized to serve more easily as a reference library.

how gURL.com learned what girls want (games!)

It's an age old question: What do girls want? But if you ask Esther Drill, co-founder and editor-in-chief of gURL.com, she'll give you a definitive answer: Games.

gURL.com is the web's number-one site for teenage girls, and it didn't get there by accident. From the time the site launched as a student project in 1996, its founders have paid close attention to what their visitors wanted and evolved the site to give them more of it.

"Traffic has absolutely molded our priorities," Drill says, explaining that the site launched as an informational resource, and become more interactive over time.

"When we started, we were really an online magazine with games," Drill explains. "Then we were an online magazine with games and a community. Now we're a site that really focuses on games —games and quizzes for teenage girls."

> **"When we looked at our traffic, it was obvious that the things girls could play with were the things that were successful."**
> —*Esther Drill*

The evolution was based not on what Drill liked, or on what she thought girls might like, but what girls actually did on the site.

"When we looked at our traffic, it was obvious that the things girls could play with and interact with were the things that were successful. We're going with games because that's where we see the growth and that's what girls want."

But games and quizzes weren't a complete departure for the site, which has always incorporated interactivity, and a serious sense of fun. When the site launched in 1996, it had a game called Paper Doll Psychology, which continues to this day and remains one of the most popular

features. Fashionistas of all ages can piece together an outfit from various separates and then have their choices analyzed.

"Girls love it," Drill says. "And it's always at the top of our traffic."

The success of Paper Doll Psychology started sparking ideas in the gURL staff and shifting their ideas about their site's focus. They experimented over the years with new interactive features and games, and watched their audience grow. In February 2001, they hit the bull's eye with a game called Make Your Own Boy Band. "It was the biggest thing we ever did," Drill says. "It got huge traffic—around one million pageviews a day."

So in keeping with their tradition, the gURL team quickly applied what they'd learned and began making other, similar games—like the Valentine's Day special, Make Your Own Sweetheart and Make Your Own Reality TV Show—many of which went on to dwarf their initial success stories.

But gURL's games haven't stopped evolving. They're now developing ways to make the games more social. For example, after girls make their own rock band, they can invite friends to hear them 'play.' "The more we do games, the more we're trying to incorporate other people, and bring other people to the site," Drill says.

So what comes next for the web's most popular girls' site? Esther's not saying, but you can guarantee the inspiration will come from the girls themselves.

The secrets of gURL's success

1. Pay attention to traffic. gURL's creators learned that girls loved games by watching their traffic logs and paying attention to the features that proved popular.

2. Build on good ideas. The gURL team turned good ideas into great ideas by continually improving on the things that worked.

3. Remember that people love to play. The gURL team quickly learned that teenage girls respond best to those features they could interact with: polls they could take, games they could play. But this doesn't apply just to teenagers or just to girls. Everyone likes to interact with the screen, and the more engaging you make your site, the longer visitors are likely to stay.

The secret of their success.

Interactive games are at the heart of gurl.com's popularity. But the number-one site for teenage girls didn't stumble into success. The site creators paid close attention to what girls liked—as measured by what they were using—and found ways to give them more of it.

how BlackPlanet got users to register (and pay)

When BlackPlanet launched in 1999, it wasn't exactly voted Most Likely to Succeed. The site got a decidedly dismal reception from the media, which didn't see a big future in targeting African Americans online. "From a business perspective, they're doomed," one analyst said.

"We were launching at a time when people thought community was crazy, ethnic community was really crazy, and black ethnic community was just insane," says founder Omar Wasow.

But three years later, BlackPlanet has emerged as the number-one destination for African-Americans online, according to Nielsen NetRatings, with an audience of 1.5 million monthly visitors and its first profitable quarter behind it.

Wasow bet right on two big gambles—the growing number of blacks online and his company's ability to earn revenue from them. But he doesn't credit his vision with BlackPlanet's success.

"What kills a lot of companies is they get really excited about big ideas.," Wasow says. But the key to online success is actually in the details: "You can't focus enough on boring day-to-day execution."

"We're constantly paying attention to what works and what doesn't," Wasow explains. "We look at where the traffic is on the site. We look at what kind of feedback we get from our members. And we look at what other sites are doing."

They then take what they learn and apply it toward the site, on an almost daily basis. "We're constantly refining the site and its individual features."

Last year, this emphasis on continual improvement helped BlackPlanet clear one of its most critical hurdles: Getting users to register and pay for services—in this case, their matchmaking site, BlackPlanetLove.

After launching the personals site in 2002, BlackPlanet faced a dilemma. A lot of people were trying the service and filling out profiles, but too few were committing. "We were having a hard time converting those folks to paid users," Wasow says.

Wasow and his team wondered what separated those who registered from those who didn't. And—as usual—they looked to their traffic logs for an answer. "We stumbled on a statistic that told us users were far more likely to sign up if they already knew someone was interested in them—

"Users were far more likely to sign up if they already knew someone was interested in them."

—Omar Wasow

if someone had already sent them a note saying, 'I'd like to talk to you.'"

The challenge was clear: They had to encourage users to contact each other, in order to boost registration and get the system going. But how?

The BlackPlanet team looked outside their site for inspiration, and they found it in an unlikely place: a quirky homespun web site called "Am I hot or not?" where people could post their photos and get rated by other visitors.

"Am I Hot or Not? was hugely popular for about six minutes and spawned all kinds of knockoffs," Wasow says. "A lot of fun, very addictive, but not a business unto itself."

But by integrating an Am I Hot or Not?–like tool into their own dating service, BlackPlanet found the key to converting new users.

Using this new tool, "Users can go through a list and say 'I think this person is cute. I don't think this person is cute. I'm interested in this person. I'm not interested…' and very quickly plow through a whole bunch of people," Wasow explains. "Then all those people get alerted that someone thinks they're cute. But the only way to find out [who's interested in you] is to join the service."

Not surprisingly, this high-tech ice breaker has been a significant driver of registrations. It works for the site because it works for the user. As Wasow says, "It's facilitating matchmaking in a way that's easy for everybody."

In retrospect, these insights seem smooth and logical, but in reality, they involved "experiments and trials and errors," Wasow says. But incremental changes are the only way to move a site forward.

"It's really important to focus on continuous improvement," Wasow says. "That's hard for smaller companies, because they can't afford to have people focused every day on adjusting minutiae of the web site. But that's really been one of the things that has allowed us to succeed."

The secrets of BlackPlanet's success

1. Look to your site for answers to vexing questions. When Wasow's team wanted to understand why users weren't registering, they looked first to their traffic logs for answers. This worked, because they were in the habit of monitoring their site and had a sense of what to look for.

2. Look to other sites for inspiration. Part of BlackPlanet's solution came from a goofy independent site, "Am I hot or not?" So you never know where the winning ideas will come from. "We look at what other sites are doing," Wasow says. "There's lots of inspiration to be had just surfing the web."

3. Consider your site a work in progress. Make a habit of making constant small changes, and don't be afraid to make mistakes. "In the early days of the web, people would have these signs up saying 'This site is under construction,'" Wasow says. "But you don't need to have that sign up, because your site is always under construction. It's never going to stop being under construction."

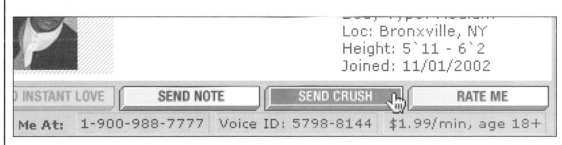

how is your site used?

Site evolution and growth begins with an understanding of how your site is used. Use these pages as a starting point to get to know your site. It could be the beginning of a beautiful friendship.

Where do your users come from?
__ % Search engines
__ % Email promotions
__ % Ads or paid links
__ % Type in URL
__ % Other sites (list)

What sites refer the most traffic to yours?
1.
2.
3.
4.
5.

How many sites link to yours?

Google says:

HotBot says:

Alltheweb says:

Where do users enter your site?
__ % Front door
__ % Other sections (list)

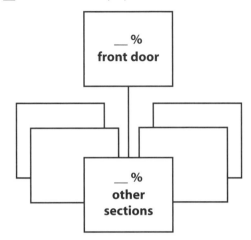

Where do users exit your site?
__ % front door
__ % check-out page
__ % error message
__ % other sections (list)

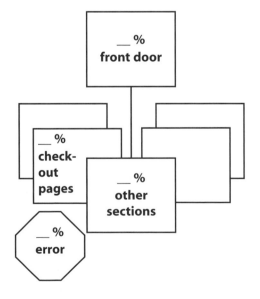

how is your site used?

Graph your traffic during an average weekday:

Midnight   Noon   Midnight

Graph your traffic during an average week:

Sun Mon Tues Wed Thu Fri Sat

Graph your traffic during an average year:

Dec Jan Feb Mar Apr May Jun Jul Aug Sep Oct Nov Dec

How much traffic do you get?
Unique monthly visitors _____
Daily visitors _____
Daily pageviews (weekday) _____
Daily pageview (weekend) _____

How long do visitors stay on your site?
Avg. length of visit (in minutes) _____
Avg. pageviews/visitor _____

What are the most popular sections of your site?
1. _____
2. _____
3. _____
4. _____

What are the most popular pages on your site?
1. _____
2. _____
3. _____
4. _____

What links do your users click on?
1.
2.
3.
4.
5.

Where do these links appear, on your front door?

VISIT OUR WEBSITE AT:
WWW911.COM

GREGORY

increasing
traffic

"If you should put even a little on
a little, and should do this often,
soon this too would become big."
- *Hesiod*

Whenever I'm confronted with mystical forces that seem beyond my control, I become exceedingly rational. I break down problems, prioritize goals, make lists, and take frequent breaks for important tasks like reorganizing my bookshelves.

Multi-faceted problems, like increasing your site's traffic, benefit from this uptight approach, because it's hard to get your head around all the issues at once. Traffic, you see, isn't merely a function of your site's popularity or marketing budget. Many symbiotic factors influence the final numbers. Fortunately, the problem can be broken down into four basic objectives. Yes, just four:

To increase traffic to your site:

1. Attract new visitors.

2. Keep visitors around longer.

3. Bring visitors back more often.

4. Improve site speed.

The relative importance of each step varies from site to site, but they all make a difference. Most sites place too much emphasis—and waste too much money—on acquiring new users, while giving little thought to retaining the ones they have. It's important to build an audience. But to sustain growth, you have to keep people coming back.

So focus first on increasing traffic from existing users, getting them to return more often and perhaps use more of your services. And if, on each visit, you can increase the length of their stay, then everyone wins. You get increased pageviews, increased revenue, and a chance to build a deeper relationship with the customer. And the user's been engaged enough to warrant an extended stay. Of course, visit length isn't directly correlated with user satisfaction. A long *frustrating* visit doesn't do anyone any good.

The final factor related to traffic may be the most important. You could do everything else right, and still fail, if your pages load too slowly. It's the speed, stupid.

---

5 quick traffic tips

1. **Know your user.** The more you know about your users, the easier it is to find and keep them.

2. **Respect your user.** Stupid schemes to trick users into visiting—or rack up extra pageviews—always fail in the long run.

3. **Work as a team.** Traffic development is not just a "marketing problem."

4. **Speed it up.** If your site is lagging, you're sabotaging your own efforts.

5. **Get in the In-box.** Email is the best tool you have for attracting repeat visitors. Use it.

---

getting started

Let me start by saying: This is not just a "marketing problem." Though customer acquisition (or audience development, depending on your industry) is typically the marketing department's domain, this quest is interdisciplinary on the web. The strategies used to increase traffic touch almost everyone in the organization.

It's possible—and often useful—to assign ownership of the sub-goals to different organizational departments: Marketing can bring in new users and remind them to return, design can increase the length of visits, and engineering and production can speed the site along. Meanwhile, the producer can develop product strategies that influence all these factors.

But don't use this as an excuse not to communicate. Compartmentalized solutions rarely work on the web, and each of these sub-goals requires a cross-disciplinary approach.

It's a good idea to have a single person responsible for coordinating traffic-development efforts. This probably isn't a full-time job, but it's an important cross-disciplinary task for someone who communicates well.

50 ways to increase traffic

attract new visitors

1. Get site listed in directories, such as Yahoo!.

2. Get site listed in all major search engines.

3. Improve ranking in search engines by:

    4. Targeting the right keywords.

    5. Targeting different keywords for different pages of your site.

    6. Including these keywords in page titles, headlines, and meta tags.

    7. Placing keywords near top of page.

    8. Considering a more relevant URL.

    9. Getting popular sites to link to you.

10. Let offline customers know about your web site.

11. Collect email addresses from offline customers; send them promotions for your web site.

12. Solicit links from complementary sites.

13. Join a web ring or link exchange with related sites.

14. Buy keyword-based ads (or paid links) on relevant sites or search engines.

15. Run ad banners on related sites. Strong offers and relevant placement produce the best results.

16. Reward users for "telling a friend."

17. Let users email site content (articles, product reviews, itineraries) to a friend.

18. Create an affiliate program so other sites can promote your products.

19. Post site information to related discussion groups.

20. Enter your site in relevant contests.

21. Promote your site to the press, especially web-based operations.

22. Send targeted email to a list of potential customers. But beware! Unsolicited mail may anger recipients.

23. Try cross-media marketing: direct mail, in-store promotions, TV, and print ads.

keep visitors around longer

24. Test what works best for your site: Watch your traffic logs and run experiments to see what gets used and why.

25. Experiment with headlines to see what words and content users respond to.

26. Improve site speed so users don't leave in frustration.

27. Improve site search so users can find what they came looking for.

28. Improve site navigation (this produces more successful visits, which may be longer or shorter).

29. Keep your home page fast and simple to get users in the door.

30. Remove the audio soundtrack from your home page—immediately!

31. If you must have audio on your home page, give users a way to turn it off!

32. Break articles or features into multiple pages.

33. Encourage participation, through bulletin boards or user-gener-ated reviews.

34. Integrate searchable databases.

35. Offer related links or products.

36. Add polls and quizzes, with results leading to related content.

bring visitors back more often

37. Create mailing list with email addresses.

38. Place "enter email" solicitation on every page of site, including the front door.

39. Set up one or more email newsletters.

40. Experiment with different newsletter formats to see what works best.

41. Offer customers specialized newsletters, addressing their personal interests.

42. Update site more frequently, giving users a reason to come back.

43. For stores, run sales and promotions.

44. For stores or service sites, send a confirmation email with each transaction.

45. For content sites, launch an ongoing series. Supplement with a newsletter.

46. Add participatory features, so users feel part of a community.

47. Encourage users to make your site their personal home page.

48. Encourage users to add your site to their "Favorites" list.

49. Distribute content to handheld electronics (Palm Pilot, cell phones, etc.).

ask your mom

50. Hey, if all else fails, and your mom isn't too busy...Click, Mom, click!

attracting new visitors

The most intuitive—though not necessarily most effective—way to increase traffic is to attract more people to your site. If you're launching a new site, this is of course the place to start.

These strategies focus on attracting qualified users—those with a genuine interest in your site and an inclination to become repeat customers. They specifically avoid those tricky tactics (like misleading ads or browser hacks that "force" people on to your site) that temporarily bloat your numbers, but do little for your business over the long run.

Dig Deeper

1. existing (offline) customers

If you already have a business (or organization, or publication, or band) that exists in the real world, the smartest place to start is with your existing customers (or members, or readers, or fans).

Let them know you have a web site. The first step is the simplest. Just get the word out!

Get the word out:

■ Promote the site in your store, at your events, or in your publications.

■ Put the URL on your receipts, your menus, your shopping bags.

■ Put the URL on your ads, your posters, your stickers.

■ Put the URL on your personal correspondence: your business cards, your business stationery, the signature file in the emails you send.

Collect their email addresses. This is probably the single most important way for existing businesses to promote their sites: Collect email addresses from existing customers and then follow up with promotions for your site—or whatever it is that's most important to you: your events, your sales, you new issue, whatever. (See email strategies, p. 282.)

2. free links from other sites

A site's popularity is often proportional to the number of links leading to it. If sites all over the web, and all over the world, are linking to your web site, there's a good chance that people will follow them, providing your site with a steady stream of new users.

Search engine listings. If someone out there is looking for a site like yours, she'll probably turn first to a search engine to find it. So your goal is to make sure your site is indexed in all the major search engines and appears in the results for keywords relevant to your site.
See improving your search rank, p. 309.

Directory listings. Directories—like those on Yahoo and About.com—can also be key sources of traffic, as they too attract mass audiences. But directories differ subtly from search engines; they offer hand-selected lists of web sites, which are chosen by individuals with a specific area of expertise.
See getting listed in directories, p. 311

Links on other sites. Search engines and portals are important, but they're only part of a comprehensive linking strategy. You'll also want to drum up links from smaller sites similar to yours.

Headlines on other sites. Rather than just having another site link to you, it can be more effective to place actual content—headlines or bite-size content, like tips—on the other site.

3. word-of-mouth

"Tell-A-Friend" programs. "Tell a friend" is one of the oldest marketing tricks in the book, but it's been reinvented for the web. Sites add all sorts of innovative features to let customers spread the word.

Users can tell their friends by

- Polling their friends

- Inviting their friends

- Emailing their friends

- Faxing their friends

- Showing their friends photos

These programs succeed because they work for both the user and your site. They give visitors a fun, easy way to stay in touch with the people in their lives. And they give your site a steady stream of new, qualified users.

Affiliate programs. Affiliate programs can help commerce sites raise awareness and draw traffic. The idea is straightforward: Other sites link to yours, and you pay them a bounty for each customer they send your way (or a percentage of the customer's purchases).

Piggyback messages. If users are using your services to contact their friends and family—through free mail, for example—be sure to attach your message to theirs. Free mail services, such as HotMail and Yahoo! Mail, always attach their own, short promotional messages to the bottom of each outbound email. And no one seems to mind too much. After all, it's a small price they pay for an otherwise free service.

4. email marketing

Email is the undisputed king of online marketing. It's cheap, it's direct, and it works. It's best used for drawing back repeat customers, but it can also be effective at recruiting new ones. The key here is targeting potential customers with a genuine interest in and need for what your site has to offer.

The advantages of email marketing:

- Fast, low-cost production & delivery

- Fast response rate

- High response rate due to ease of follow-up

The disadvantages of email marketing:

- Angry responses to unsolicited "spam"

5. advertising— online…

If the sites you've targeted for free links have turned you down, don't despair. We all know how to open those doors: Just talk to the advertising department. Once you become a paying customer, as opposed to a comrade or competitor, all the rules change.

3 keys to a successful online ad:

- Contextual placement

- A good offer

- Rigorous analysis

As in any medium, you need to get the right message in front of the right people at the right time. But the web offers extraordinary opportunities to capture an audience at the decisive moment, and an unsurpassed capacity to measure success.

See <u>online advertising</u>, p. 294.

…and off-line

Many web producers long to promote their sites in the "real world." They covet TV ads and billboards and bus-side banners that will give their site the aura of legitimacy— and the traffic the boost it so rightly deserves.

But every online marketer will tell you: It's hard to get people to jump media. The fastest, most frictionless way to attract new users is through the web itself. Nonetheless, there are some terrestrial tactics worth exploring. See <u>cross-media strategies</u>, p. 305.

keeping visitors around longer

Another way to increase traffic is to encourage your guests to stay longer. By increasing the length of each visit—or making your site more "sticky"—you can maximize your return from each visitor (while simultaneously maximizing what they get from you).

On its surface, a long visit has excellent implications: The longer visitors stay with your site, the more they learn about you, the more ads they view, and the more likely they are to make a purchase. Cha-ching! But beware: A long visit isn't necessarily a good visit. If users linger on your site because they're lost or because they can't find the darn thing they were looking for…well…a long, frustrating visit doesn't do anyone any good.

1. pay attention to traffic logs

If you want to learn what makes your users stick around, all you have to do is pay attention. By watching your traffic logs, you can learn almost everything you want to know about how visitors use your site: where they come from, where they click, where they linger, and when they leave.

What to watch for:

- What days and times do you get the most traffic?
- What parts of your site are most popular?
- What pages do users exit from?
- When do you see traffic spikes and dips?
- Where do users click?
- What do users buy?
- When do users register?
- Do your users browse or search?

Test what works. By running experiments—and watching the results—you can figure out what exactly keeps your users around, and what turns them away.

2. improve site design

One simple way to keep visitors around longer is to make sure they're aware of everything your site has to offer and can find what they want.

To improve site design:

- **Make choices intuitive.** If users don't understand their choices—or can't figure out how to get where they're going—they're likely to give up before completing their tasks.

- **Don't bury site features.** Site features often go undiscovered, because they're buried deep within the site or hidden behind unclear links. Make sure you let users see their options: Label site features clearly, and bring features up to the top level whenever you can. For example, if you have a search feature , don't bury it behind a link that says "Search." Integrate the search form directly into the front page—or all the pages, for that matter. This encourages immediate action: The search form almost begs to be filled in.

- **Make navigation consistent.** If users have to learn a new interface and navigation scheme every time they click, they'll soon tire of trying.

- **Thoroughly test site with users before launch.** You should perform extensive user testing to insure you're providing intuitive choices.
  See usability testing, p.129.

Dig Deeper
understanding user needs, p. 60.
organization sites, p. 98.
usability testing, p. 129.

3. add muti-page features

For content sites, which earn money based on the number of pages—and therefore ads—their readers view, it's helpful to break long articles or exhibits into multiple pages.

The benefits of multi-page articles:

1. **Your site gets credit** for how long the reader stays on the site. Rather than lingering on a single page for 20 minutes, he clicks through several pages, while reading the article.

2. **Readers get a break** from absorbing endless fields of text. By breaking articles down into more manageable chunks, you're offering readers a psychological break between sections.

3. **Editors see what works**, or at least what people read. By breaking up the article, writers and editors can see just how far readers get into each article. (A 50% drop-off between pages is typical.)

The downside of multi-page articles is that they're exceptionally annoying when poorly implemented. To avoid irritating—and losing—your users, follow these tips:

- **Offer a single-page option** for readers, which they can use to read—or more importantly, print—the article in its entirety.

- **Provide a list of article pages**—with sub-headings for each—so users can skip around.

- **Don't overdo it** by creating 1,000 super-short, linked pages.

4. offer "more"

From time to time, web developers have to think like store owners. This is one of those times. You learn in Retail 101 that any time you have a customer interested in an item, you should offer them something related: "Want fries with that, sir?" "Matching socks for that sweater?" It's known as "filling the basket."

Now the leap from The Gap to gap.com isn't too great. Retail sites, like retail stores, can obviously benefit from offering customers "more." But the concept applies just as easily to content and service sites.

- **News sites** can offer articles on related topics or other articles by the same journalist.

- **Retail sites** can offer complementary products, matched by category (ski goggles offered with the parkas, or female vocalists displayed with each purchase of a Sheryl Crow CD), or more sophisticated matches. Amazon, for instance, displays products that were purchased by other people who bought your book.

- **Any site** can offer clusters of related links and products when a user completes a given task.

5. let them search

There are two types of web users: browsers and searchers. Browsers will navigate through your site sections and hierarchy, absorbing their choices and trying to navigate their way to what they want. Searchers, on the other hand, will simply enter what they want into the Search box and skip (hopefully) to the page they need. To accommodate searchers as well as browsers, make sure your site search is integrated into every page, and that it works—returning useful, relevant results for at least the most common queries.

6. improve site speed

Simple fact: Pages that load quickly and consistently are more likely to be seen than those that sputter and choke. Web users are an impatient lot. Generally speaking, they know what they want and they want it fast.

To keep your visitors coming back, and to keep them longer while they're there—you'll need to speed things along.

See <u>improving site speed</u>, p. 218.

bringing visitors back more often

Although most site owners focus on the *number* of users they attract, it's important also to consider how often they return. Visit frequency is a great indicator of customer loyalty. And it helps you understand how people are using your site.

To bring users back to your site, you have to first give them a reason to return. Site quality is of course the most important factor here. But updated content and seasonal promotions sure help.

Then, you have to remind them. And this is where email comes in. Have no doubt, email is the single most important tool we have for building traffic. There *are* other solutions. But you shouldn't waste a minute thinking about them until you've exhausted every possible email opportunity.

1. emphasize email

Email is by far the best way to draw repeat traffic to your web site. You can use email to tell customers about new products, promotions, or content. You can use it to announce upcoming events, promote a seasonal sale, offer helpful tips, or just remind customers that you exist.

It takes some experimentation to hit on the right email strategy, but its worth the trial-and-error. Email is the most important tool you have for promoting your site, and you should use it for all its worth.

6 successful email strategies:

1. **Newsletters** update visitors on what's new on your site or in your organization.

2. **Targeted newsletters** address topics of specific interest to the user.

3. **Headlines** of news articles can be delivered to users via email, offering them a link that leads to the full story.

4. **Customized reports** give users updated information on specific topics of their choosing. Financial services, for instance, may send end-of-day reports on specific stocks; news services may alert users when articles on a specific topic appear.

5. **Announcements** are perfectly suited to email. Whether you're announcing a rock concert, an end-of-season shoe sale, or an activist campaign against drilling in Redrock canyon, email gets the word out quickly and cheaply.

6. **Bite-size content**—like tips or jokes or horoscopes—can be delivered daily.

It's important to remember, however, that not all sites are destined to become regular destinations. Many sites are visited strictly on an as-needed basis. Your challenge, then, is to help people remember you exist so they think of your site next time they need its services.
See email strategies, p. 282.

2. fill a need

The sure-fire way to bring visitors back to your site is to create something they need. It's simple, but true. Most users are task-oriented online; they're trying to get things done. So the best way to fit into their day is to get on their to-do list. So long as you're filling a recurring need in your users'—whether you offer free email, a reference library, or a party-planning service—you'll keep them coming back.

3. update more often

One way to bring people in more often is by keeping your site fresh. Content or informational sites can keep people coming back by offering new articles or features. The updated content need not be extensive—something as simple as a daily morsel or tip can do the trick. Commerce sites can also make this work for them by highlighting new products or running promotions (below). But remember: Updates are effective only if your users know about them. Use email to keep them informed, and promote new items on the front door.

4. run promotions

People are more likely to return to your site when you give them a reason—preferably a time-dependent, financially attractive reason. Every direct marketer knows that a sale will bring customers back into a store, even if the items they buy weren't part of the sale. This rule holds in the online world.

5. involve the user

People are more likely to return to places in which they feel personally involved. This involvement can take many forms—writing product reviews (a la Amazon), participating in discussions (a la SlashDot), or taking part in a marketplace (a la EBay). Even an indirect involvement—responding to a survey or submitting a recommendation and getting a personalized response—helps build a sense of belonging.

6. be the home page

Perhaps the best way to ensure visitors return often to your site is to encourage them to make your site their "home page"· the site that first appears in every new browser window. This guarantees they'll visit—or at least see—your site every time they go online. It's hard to get users to make this switch, but a great coup if you can. So why not encourage them?

how will you increase traffic?

Wish you had more traffic to your web site? Well stop whining and do something about it. This methodical approach—attracting new visitors, increasing the length of visits, and bringing visitors back more often—works every time.

attract new visitors

Get your site listed in search engines and directories:

task	done?
Submit site to Google and other search engines	❑
Submit site to Yahoo! and other directories	❑
Revise site as needed to improve search rank	❑

Try other strategies:

strategy	did it	not gonna do it
Solicit links from other sites	❑	❑
Advertise online	❑	❑
Advertise in other media	❑	❑
Start a "tell-a-friend" program	❑	❑
Buy an email list	❑	❑

bring visitors back more often

Craft an email strategy to bring users back:

task	done?
Start collecting addresses	❑
Integrate email sign-up form on home page	❑
Send first round of email messages	❑
Experiment with approaches to email	❑*

*That was a trick question. You're never "done" experimenting.

What are your other strategies?

strategy	did it	not gonna do it
Update site more often	❑	❑
Run promotions & sales	❑	❑
Add community features	❑	❑
Become the user's home page	❑	❑

increase length of visits

Improve site design

task	done?
Make choices intuitive	❑
Make navigation consistent	❑
Un-bury site features	❑
Clearly label site features	❑
Integrate site search	❑
Make sure site search returns good results	❑
Test site with users	❑
Test site with users other than Mom	❑

What are your other strategies?

strategy	did it	not gonna do it
Encourage participation	❑	❑
Break articles into multiple pages	❑	❑
Give "more" (suggest related links)	❑	❑
Integrate site search	❑	❑

improve site speed

	true	false
I have read and understood	❑	❑

improving site speed, p. 218.

promoting your site

"You know what's wrong with this commercial? It's too commercial."

don't miss ...

It's a familiar problem—one that's faced by every company, every product, every TV show: How do you get the word out?

The challenge is no different for web sites. "You should treat your web site the way you'd treat any other kind of destination point in the marketing process," says online marketing expert Hunter Madsen.

That said, the old rules don't always apply. First of all, the best place to promote a web site is on the web itself—or at least through email. Online, no one is more than a click away from your site. So the barriers to entry are astonishingly low, and memory isn't an obstacle. But other media—like direct mail or print ads—are less immediate, and therefore less effective.

Second, the role of the news media is diminished. A bad review can make or break some products, like packaged software, for example. But news coverage and reviews have little impact on the fate of web sites. "Peer-to-peer recommendations drive popularity on the web," says Adam Berliant of Microsoft. "[*Wall Street Journal* columnist] Walt Mossberg had nothing to do with the success of eBay."

And if reviews mean little to web sites, celebrity endorsements mean even less. "When we were first raising money for BlackPlanet, we had an opportunity to bring on some celebrity investors," says Omar Wasow, the site's founder. "But it was clear to me that the way to win was by delivering a better customer experience, not by having a celebrity spokesperson. This wasn't going to be a conventional marketing war."

The key to winning this war, it seems, is to take advantage of the web's user-centered properties, rather than fighting them. Many traditional promotional techniques try to change consumers' behavior by interrupting them, distracting them, or changing their minds. But people are singularly focused online. A promotion scheme that goes head-to-head with the user's own intentions will almost always lose.

6 keys to promoting your site

1. Focus your efforts online. Online promotions are far more effective than traditional media, like direct mail or print ads. "There's less friction and lower costs if you stay in the medium," says Hunter Madsen. "Getting people to jump media is extremely difficult."

2. Emphasize email. Email is by far the most effective way to lure repeat visitors back to your site. And it's not a bad way to find new customers either—so long as you choose your lists carefully. See email strategies, p. 282.

3. Find users when they're looking for you. Context is the key to effective marketing, and the web lets you reach customers when your site or product is most relevant—as they're searching on a related topic or completing a related task. See linking strategies, p. 290 and online advertising, p. 294.

4. Get users involved in site promotion. It's good for any business to get referrals. But web sites, especially, have much to gain when customers tell their friends. See word-of-mouth strategies, p. 280

5. Encourage immediate action. As Rabelais said so many years ago, "You must strike while the iron is hot." Whether you're sending an email or placing an ad, always spur users toward immediate action—clicking, buying, registering—while it's fresh on their minds.

6. Be clear, not clever. Funny, punny slogans and whizzy, fizzy graphics may work in other media. But web users want to know what they're getting when they click on a link or an ad. The last thing they need is more surprises. See why section names should be clear, p. 126.

However, when marketers work *with* users instead of against them, the results can be spectacular. If you find users when they're already looking for you; if you help them accomplish their task at hand; if you let them help you spread the word—you can reap remarkable results.

word-of-mouth strategies

Never, in the history of the world, have so many people held so many microphones, with so many others listening. The Internet makes it easier than ever for people to share ideas: Using personal web sites, bulletin boards, chat rooms, instant messaging, and email, people can communicate quickly and cheaply with friends and strangers alike.

So it makes sense that the most powerful promotional strategies are those that tap the web's grassroots potential. "The Internet is a social medium," says Omar Wasow. "People are constantly talking to their friends. So a good site will generate great word-of-mouth, and by extension, new members and customers."

Wasow should know. BlackPlanet grew to 1.5 million monthly users in only three years, becoming the leading site for African Americans. How? According to Wasow, the members like to talk. "The reason our sites have been successful is that our members love our sites and they tell their friends. We've built all sorts of tools to encourage this word-of-mouth."

BlackPlanet rewards members for referring friends. But other sites take a more aggressive approach, turning users into recruiters, whether they like it or not. HotMail, for example, offered its members free, anonymous email accounts, and made sure people knew it. Each message sent from a HotMail account included a promotion for the service. This turned each HotMail user into a promotion vehicle, who spread the word to everyone he knew.

Grassroots initiatives like these are generally inexpensive and efficient, when they take off. Of course, there are also drawbacks. These people-powered programs are inherently uncoordinated. They're hard to force, and difficult to control, once begun.

affiliate programs

The idea behind affiliate programs is straightforward: Other sites link to yours, and you pay them a bounty for each customer they send your way (or a percentage of the customer's purchases).

If this sounds like small potatoes, you should remember that Amazon's early success was often linked to its affiliate program, the first on the web. Thousands of sites integrated Amazon's "Buy a book" link into their pages. The sites promoted books they liked and got a cut of sales from users who followed the link. Amazon reeled in thousands of new customers and got its name splashed across the web.

Affiliate programs are great for commerce sites, and they can work for other sites as well. Be warned, however: You'll need a reliable tracking system to match incoming users to the site that referred them. Don't even consider an affiliate program if you can't back it up with the resources necessary to make it work.

tell-a-friend programs

It's one of the oldest marketing tricks in the book. Customers are urged to tell a friend, and rewarded when they do. These schemes have stood the test of time, because they really work. And on the web, they've been given a new life.

Users can tell their friends, or

- Poll their friends
- Invite their friends
- Email their friends
- Fax their friends
- Show their friends photos

These programs succeed because they provide a genuine service: People want to stay in touch with friends and family, and these programs let them do it in a way that's quick, easy, and fun.

News sites, for example, let users send articles to friends, and stores do the same for product descriptions. The variations are endless: You can send your friends greeting cards, show them your photos, or poll them about a pressing question, like potential names for your baby. Don't laugh. Okay laugh, but bear in mind: These programs bring thousands of new customers to sites like Snapfish Photos and BabyCenter. If it works for them, it could work for you.

clever ways to "tell-a-friend"

"Tell a friend" is one of the oldest marketing tricks in the book. But on the web, it's given a new twist. Users can tell their friends. But they can just as easily email them, fax them, invite them, poll them, or share their photographs with them.

News sites let users send articles; commerce sites do the same for product descriptions. And clever sites like BabyCenter let visitors poll their friends on important topics like potential names for their baby.

With a little creativity, you can make this idea work for you. And your users. And all of their friends....

Share the story. No news site is complete without a "Send this to a friend" feature—or four. The New York Times (below) incorporates a Starbucks sponsorship. Wired News (above) invites you to email the article, or sync it to your Palm Pilot.

Show and tell. No matter how old they are, people like to show-and-tell. Why not help them? BabyCenter (top) let's users poll their friends for help with baby names. gURL.com (middle) lets readers invite their friends to see—and hear—the band they create. And Snapfish (bottom) lets customers create photo albums and share them with their friends (who can order prints, of course).

email strategies

The basic challenge web sites face is that of human memory. People come back to your site only when they remember to. And usually, that isn't often. Unless your subject matter gives you top-of-mind awareness, your users won't return as often as you'd like them to—or even as often as they'd like to.

So the challenge is to remind them…as often and as persuasively as possible, without crossing the line into harassment. Email is the way. It's the most effective way to promote your site—and quite possibly your company.

The reasons are straightforward: Nearly everyone online has a personal email account, and nearly everyone uses email nearly every time they go online. In fact, 95% of Internet sessions include checking email. What better way to reach people?

Email can be used to find new customers (See should you buy a list? p. 286), but its real power is in bringing customers back. In fact, email updates containing links to current articles account for up to 50% of daily traffic to many news sites.

For commerce sites, the direct impact of email—on sales and site visits—is often less dramatic. But it's still seen as an important tool.

"Email is only about 7% of our sales," says Hilary Billings, chairman and chief marketing officer of specialty gift store RedEnvelope. "But even though it's not a big part of our business, we think it's a valuable one. It lets us keep in touch with our customers more frequently, and it also allows us to expose smaller holidays (like April Fool's) that aren't big enough for us to market to in a catalog."

And email has another advantage: It can easily be shared. So sites often find that customers forward their newsletters to friends—giving them great publicity and bringing in new customers. "The newsletters are our number one source of referral offline (or 'viral marketing')" says Lara Hoyem, senior marketing manager for Baby-Center. "They give users a reason to share their love of the site with others."

6 things email can do for you

1. Remind people that you exist. People only return to your web site when they remember to. So half the battle is just staying on their radar screens. An occasional appearance in their In-Boxes ensures that you won't be forgotten.

2. Drive traffic to your site. Ask any successful site owner: Email is the single most effective way to drive traffic to your site. Whether you're selling shoes, sharing opinions, or matching vacation homes with prospective renters, it's email—more than anything else—that keeps them coming back.

3. Increase sales. Through seasonal sales and online promotions, email can help you move merchandise.

4. Build awareness. Email can alert your users to new features, products, articles, and events. Even if a customer doesn't follow up on every email, she sees the message in her In-Box, and makes a mental note.

5. Build trust. Email should be used not only to reach out to customers, but also to follow up. Online shoppers have come to expect confirmation emails after an order is placed or shipped, or when something else significant happens (a shipment is delayed, etc.). These messages build a sense of comfort, trust, and predictability in what can otherwise be an alienating sales process.

6. Build a sense of community. Receiving email from an organization reinforces the idea that a person belongs to a community, whether it's based on interests, location, or affiliation. Even if she does nothing more than glance at it, the regularly received emails build a bond.

But the power of email extends beyond the web site; it can help build your off-line business as well.

"Email is a really overlooked tool," says Omar Wasow. "I'm amazed by how many small businesses I touch that don't ask me for my email address. Every business should be building an electronic mailing list. It's a missed opportunity if you don't."

choosing an email strategy

Your approach to email—like your approach to your web site—should be dictated by three main factors:

1. **What you need from your users.** Think about what kind of action you want to inspire: Do you want people to visit your site? Or attend an event? Buy a Mother's Day gift? Or sign a protest letter? Your goals should guide your approach.

2. **What your users need from you.** If you're sending a message to a customer's In-Box, there has to be something in it for them. Ask yourself: What value can you bring to their lives through email?

3. **What you can afford.** It takes time to write effective emails, technology to target them, and money to support the systems. Don't bite off more than you can chew: Start simple, and be realistic about your means.

For a site that does email right, look to BabyCenter, which caters to pregnant women and new parents. In 2002, they had 1.6 million subscribers to their newsletters, which brought in 40% of site visits.

Their big winner is "My Baby This Week," a newsletter that tells parents about their child's development on a week-to-week basis. Women give their due date when they subscribe, so the updates are customized just for them.

"Parents love them," says Emily Simas, the product manager who oversaw BabyCenter's email programs from 2000–2002. "We know they wait eagerly for them every week, because if they don't get them at the exact time, they'll tell us!"

And BabyCenter loves them, too. They've found email builds loyal customers. "The newsletters really hook our users on BabyCenter, and get them engaged and coming back," said Lara Hoyem. "Without them, we really wouldn't have the traffic."

collecting email addresses

No matter what your business, the first step of an email strategy is always the same: You have to build a list.

So before you decide what you're going to write in your emails, who you're going to send them to, or how often you're going to send them, you've got to start gathering addresses. **You should start building your email list as soon as your site launches, or as soon as you can.** Start now. Really. Right now. It's that important.

Commerce sites can collect email addresses during the check-out phase, but other sites have to try harder: Integrating a sign-up form into the site (preferably on the home page) and offering some incentive to lure users into signing up.

And if your site is built to support an off-line organization (a store or gallery or band or sports team), you can also collect email addresses the old-fashioned way: On a clipboard, at your next event.

web design do:

web design don't:

What a difference a form makes. By integrating an "enter email" form (like the one from mommychronicles.com, top) on the front door of your web site, you can increase email newsletter sign-ups by up to 1000 percent. No joke. A simple link (like the one from guggenheim.org, bottom) won't perform as well. The form seems to encourage immediate action.

choosing an email strategy

There are a lot of different ways to use email. Some sites send occasional chatty emails and others deliver automated, personalized stock portfolios several times each day.

Your strategy will vary greatly depending on your site's focus and goals. But whatever the level of invest-ment, email delivers. When done correctly—with respect for the user, attention to detail, and a willingness to experiment—email can work wonders just short of a miracle for your site.

1. newsletters

If people were interested enough to come to your site once, they may want to stay informed over time. Whether you're a choreographer for a hip-hop dance troupe or a scientist researching mating practices of pan-das in captivity, there are people out in the world who care about what you do. That's why they visited your site in the first place.

Email newsletters are a great way to build a sense of belonging: By receiving news from your organiza-tion, people begin to feel more and more invested in the community. Even if they only give it an occasional glance, its appearance in their In-Box reinforces the bond.

basic newsletters   The most basic newsletter simply updates recipients on the goings-on in your organiza-tion or web site, pointing them to where they can learn more. The fre-quency of the newsletter depends on how much you have to say and how much your members care. Most peo-ple won't require a daily (or even weekly) update on your progress, but a simple newsletter—distributed monthly or quarterly—can help build a dedicated audience (or customer base, or research community) for your organization.

targeted newsletters   Targeted newsletters add extra value to users by addressing the topics of specific interest to them. BabyCenter, for instance, sends specialized weekly newsletters to expectant mothers, telling them what's happening at each stage of their baby's develop-ment, based on their due date.

2. headlines

Used primarily by news (and other content) sites, headline emails give subscribers a summary of the day's news, with links leading back to each full story on the site.

While basic, these mailings are exceptionally effective, delivering up to 50% of daily traffic to many news sites. They're especially economical, because they can be generated automatically from most content-management systems and require little, if any, individual attention once they're created.

3. bite-size content

Another approach to email is to send bite-size content: jokes, tips, recom-mended sites, excerpts from discus-sion boards, or anything else that can be divvied up into tempting lit-tle tidbits and delivered to some-one's In-Box each day.

4. customized reports

Customized reports go one step further on the value chain. They deliver subscribers highly targeted, timely information on specific topics.

Customized reports include

- **The stock portfolio.** The most common example of a customized report is the stock portfolio. Most finance sites allow you to create a custom portfolio that tracks your stocks. Each day, at market's close, you receive a report showing how your stocks did that day and even tallying the value of your portfolio.

- **The news tracker.** Some news sites, like *The New York Times*, let you create custom news-trackers (sometimes called agents or bots) that notify you via email whenever an article on a certain topic appears.

- **The shopping bot.** Many commerce sites will send you alerts when a particular product becomes available or prices begin to drop on an item you want. Christie's auction house offers an email service that notifies collectors whenever a piece by a particular artist comes to auction— anywhere in the world. And used bookstores will notify users whenever a desired book is located.

5. announcements

Whether you're announcing a rock concert, an end-of-season sale on gas grills, or an activist campaign against exploratory drilling in Red Rock canyon, email gets the word out quickly and cheaply.

Announcements include

- **Event updates.** Email is a great tool for announcing upcoming events, reminding people as the date nears, and letting them know about last-minute changes. Email updates are now a staple among independent musicians, who often collect addresses at live gigs and let fans know when they're coming back to town. But it isn't just for indie bands. All sorts of organizations— from local libraries to professional sports teams—use email to announce events.

- **The "sale!" email.** A direct descendent of direct mail, the "sale!" email does just what it says: Informs the user about sales or discounts available on the site. As in traditional retail, the goal is to bring the customers back in and encourage them to buy the sale items and other full-ticket products as well.

- **The activist alert.** Now a tried-and-true staple among the activist set, alert emails go out to concerned, like-minded people whenever a critical issue arises. The power of email is not just in getting the word out (which it does—quickly and cheaply) but giving armchair activists easy and immediate ways to take action: By emailing a politician or company, forwarding an email petition, printing and sending a letter, or following a link to a web page.

6. many-to-many lists

All the other email strategies mentioned here are "one-to-many" (or in some cases, one-to-one) mailing lists. As the site and list owner, you send information to the recipients, but they only have limited ways to talk back to you. And they can't talk to each other. Which, frankly, is just the way most site owners want it.

But at some time or another, many site owners catch the "community" bug, and decide to launch a many-to-many list to build community around their product or organization. But I'd think twice about this, if I were you. Many-to-many mailing lists are tremendous as a cultural force and information source, but there are very few happy stories about their use as a marketing medium. Most mailing list communities take on a life of their own. They don't take kindly to being marketed to and often wish to distance themselves from the group that gave them their start. There are a few successful stories of developer lists and users groups within the software industry. Apple and Adobe, for example, have very successful user-to-user help systems. But most other stories I've heard have ended in tears.

setting up an email list

Setting up an email list need not be a complicated process. In most cases, the basic tools will already be at your disposal.

Most medium-to-large companies will already have a system for managing email lists. But even a small organization on a shoestring budget can do it. It's just a matter of scale. You can get started by using your normal email software and slowly develop more sophisticated systems as your mailing list—and list-management needs—grow.

For small sites, the simplest approach to list management is often the best. Just collect email addresses (on paper or through the web), and add them by hand to an ongoing list. Any time you want to send a mailing, just paste the names into an email using your current email software, hit send, and that's it.

As your mailing list grows or your mailings become more frequent, you may need more help managing your list. The mailings may take too much time or server power, and the process of subscribing and unsubscribing people may become too big a hassle to do by hand.

If you outgrow your normal email program, you'll probably want to invest in list-management software, which helps organize addresses, schedule mailings, and automate subscriptions and "unsubscriptions."

This software comes in two basic forms: server-based and web-based. Server-based programs—like ListProc and Listserv—are the smart choice for large organizations with separate IT departments or for individuals with access to their own mail server (and confidence in their ability to work with it).

But most small organizations will be better served by web-based services, which are simpler and often more economical. (See choosing software for email newsletters, p. 287.)

should you buy a list?

Email is best used for building relationships with existing customers. But it can also help you acquire new ones. By purchasing targeted email lists and sending straightforward solicitations, you can acquire new customers at a fraction of the usual cost.

"Targeted outbound email was the most effective tactic we used at ImproveNet," says online marketing pioneer Hunter Madsen, former VP of Marketing for ImproveNet. "We could get our cost of acquisition down to as low as $30, which was—for our products—very good."

The advantages of email marketing are obvious: The cost of the outbound mailing is very low, and it's easy for customers to follow-up: All they have to do is click on a link. Compared to other tactics, the turn-around time is quick, and you can immediately track the response rate.

"People don't like spam. But spam is defined by the person as anything that's preposterously irrelevant to them… Offers that are relevant do get read."

—Hunter Madsen

The trick, of course, is avoiding the wrath of recipients who consider unsolicited email "spam."

"We know that people in general don't like spam," Madsen says. "But spam is defined by the person as anything that's preposterously irrelevant to them, and therefore annoying."

But if you target effectively, make a good offer, and avoid being overly solicitous, you'll see results: "Offers that are relevant do get read."

choosing software for email newsletters

	1. regular email programs	2. web-based software	3. server-based software
What it is	Normal, desktop email—the kind you use to send and receive personal email.	Services, offered through a web site, that manage your email addresses and simplify the mailing process.	Specialized software, installed on your company's mail servers, that manages addresses and mailing schedules.
Advantages	▪ No technical skill needed. ▪ No access to servers needed. ▪ No special software needed. ▪ Complete control over addresses. ▪ Control over email appearance.	▪ No technical skill needed. ▪ No access to servers needed. ▪ Easy to manage. ▪ No demands placed on servers.	▪ Complete control over addresses. ▪ Complete control over email appearance.
Disadvantages	▪ Labor-intensive and time-consuming: Everything is done by hand. ▪ List management is a hassle. ▪ Can only send emails to limited number of addresses at once.	▪ Free services may not guarantee privacy of addresses. ▪ Free services may place ads in emails.	▪ Requires knowledge of server administration. ▪ Somewhat labor-intensive. ▪ Can be server intensive. Must often run at night.
Cost	Free.	Fee-based services from $40/mo. Some are free.	Software cost varies. ($100s to $10,000s.)
Choices include	▪ Eudora ▪ Outlook Express	▪ bCentral's ListBuilder ▪ BigList ▪ Boomerang ▪ ListChannel ▪ ListManager (Lyris) ▪ Mail-list.com ▪ PatronMail ▪ Topica ▪ Yahoo! Groups	▪ Majordomo (Shareware. primarily for many-to-many lists) ▪ Listserv (from L-Soft) ▪ Listmanager (from Lyris.com) ▪ eNewsletter Pro ▪ ListProc (Listproc.net)

12 secrets of successful emails

You may have hammered out the details of your site's email strategy—figuring out what kinds of email you'll send and to whom. But your work isn't done yet. Small, tactical decisions—about when to send messages and what, exactly, the subject line should say—can make or break an email campaign. Here are some lessons we've learned the hard way.

1. Set a schedule and stick to it. Decide on the frequency with which you'll send emails—whether it's daily, weekly, monthly or quarterly. Set a schedule for the mailings, and stick with it, even if it seems arbitrary. Most people won't notice when it arrives, but some will. And a regular schedule will help make the mailings more manageable for you and your team.

2. Send mailings early in the week. People are most likely to read and respond to email received earlier in the week. "After Wednesday, we get a much lower click-through rate," says Emily Simas of BabyCenter, which sends millions of newsletters each week. "It's the end of the week. People aren't reading as much. They're not in the office. They'll start reading again on Monday."

3. Send mailings overnight. Many people read their email first thing in the morning. Your message should be waiting there for them. The added benefits of overnight mailings are less stress on your server (since employees won't be mailing at the same time) and less traffic on the Internet, which means speedier delivery.

4. Offer both plain-text and HTML emails. HTML emails—which look like a web page—get much higher response rates than plain-text (or ordinary) email messages. However, not everyone can receive HTML emails, so it's best to give an option. And if you're sending HTML-based email, be sure to keep the code as simple as possible.

Many HTML editors insert a lot of extraneous code into the message, which can bog down the user's email program.

5. Use the words "free" and "new" You can laugh, but it's true: Certain words grab the reader's attention. "People respond to email with the same psychology that they respond to everything else in the marketing world," says Hunter Madsen. There are certain words and approaches they gravitate toward. To brush up on your advertising theory, Madsen recommends the old standard, *Tested Advertising Methods* by John Caples. "Not a very dramatic title," Madsen concedes. "But his conclusions were decisive and the industry has followed them ever since."

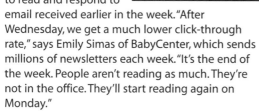

> **"People respond to email with the same psychology that they respond to everything else in the world."**
>
> **—Hunter Madsen**

6. Offer seasonal advice. Rather than send the same-old "Sale!" email, offer readers something they can use—right now. "Often, sites have specialized knowledge that their users need," Madsen says. "At ImproveNet, we'd send seasonal tips—like 'It's Fall: Here's how to get leaves out of your gutter'—that were relevant to homeowners." Even if your email just covers gift ideas for Mother's Day, its' more likely to be read than the same old "free shipping" promotion you've sent before.

7. Provide full URLs. If you're inviting users to click through to your site, always offer the full URL (including http://) and place it on a separate line. This avoids common errors and ensure users can click through.

8. Couple each headline with a URL. A convenient way to structure plain-text emails is to couple each headline with its corresponding URL. This creates one stand-out headline unit that is both readable and clickable:

New! The Congo Gorilla Forest
http://www.congogorillaforest.com/

9. Include unsubscribe Instructions. Always include easy-to-follow instructions on how to unsubscribe in every email you send. No need to place it at the top of the email—the bottom is just fine—but always include it.

10. Create a privacy policy and make it visible. Once you start collecting email addresses, it's critical to put a privacy policy in place that explains what you plan to do with your users' information: Will you share it? Will you sell it? It's common practice for magazines and stores to sell customer lists. But this is more controversial online. And—take note—it's illegal in many countries outside the U.S.

11. Hide the distribution list. If you're using email-list management software for your mailings, the recipients' addresses will be automatically concealed (so no one else can access them or create a duplicate list). But if you're emailing on your own—with a basic email program—you can still extend this courtesy, by using the :bcc (blind carbon copy) field. Place your own address in the "To:" field, and list the other recipients under :bcc. They'll each receive the email, but they won't know who else did.

12. Don't overdo it. Although you may never tire of writing about the daily trials and small triumphs within your organization, your audience may soon tire of reading about them. Says Madsen: "If you're trying to develop an elaborate scheme for intimate bonding with your customers, and for creating close day-to-day relationships between them and your shoe company (or whatever it is you're selling) you'll be disappointed. And they'll be annoyed!" Respect your members' time, and show some restraint with your mailings.

How much is too much? The answer depends on your relationship with the user. News sites may send multiple messages each day, while some organizations may email only yearly. Experiment with frequency to find the answer for your site. Better yet—let your users decide: "At ImproveNet, we were either sending emails out too infrequently for people to retain a vital link to the brand, or so often that we irritated the receivers," Madsen says. "Ultimately, we gave people a choice, and that seemed to work well."

> **"After Wednesday, we get a much lower clickthrough rate. It's the end of the week. People aren't reading as much."**
>
> **—Emily Simas**

linking strategies

Hyperlinks (or just "links") are one of the defining features of the web. The ability to leap effortlessly from one page to another creates a world of possibilities. Within our own sites, we can link users back and forth between services, we can suggest related products or stories, we can point them toward related web sites, and we can help them find the check-out stand or story archive with ease. We can also confuse the hell out of them.

But that's not my point right now. My point is this: Links are important. And every marketing strategy should take full advantage of them.

A site's popularity is often proportional to the number of links leading to it. If sites all over the web, and all over the world, are linking to your web site, there's a good chance that people will follow them—providing your site with a steady stream of new users.

But links don't usually blossom on their own. It's going to take some work on your end to get things going. You may want to start by targeting the five different types of links you can acquire:

Types of links:

- Search engine listings
- Directory listings
- Links on other sites
- Headlines or "tips" on other sites
- Paid links or ad banners

links from search engines

Search engines are by far the most important source of traffic for many small sites. If someone out there is looking for a site like yours, she'll probably turn first to a search engine to find it.

These general, navigational sites attract a large, mass audience—and are therefore the best place to target the largest number of people in one swoop. They're also often the best place to find the right visitors, because they help users find the niche sites they're looking for.

Why links matter (3 times over)

When people link to you, your site reaps triple rewards:

1. **Links attract** new users to your site.

2. **Links raise awareness** of your site, even if people don't follow the link.

3. **Links improve your search ranking** on sites like Google, which determine a site's relevance by the number of sites that link to it (among other factors).

Getting listed in search engines is fairly straightforward—it's essentially a matter of submitting your site's address. But rising through the ranks—so you appear near the top of the list for any given search—can be the challenge of a lifetime. See improving your search rank, p. 309.

links from directories

Directories—like search engines—are another big, important source of traffic for small sites. Unlike search engines, however, directories are compiled by hand. So there's a human who decides whether and where your site gets listed.

Getting into directories requires a bit more strategy than search engines: You have to choose the appropriate category and write an accurate description. It also helps to pay the expediting fee, which ensures your site will at least be considered. See getting listed in directories, p. 311.

links from other sites

Search engines and portals are important, sure. But they're also hard to break into. Especially if you lack the funds to pay an expediting fee, it can take a long time to even appear on sites like Yahoo! So it's important to also attract links from smaller sites that share your focus. These grassroots links can prove every bit as effective as a listing on one of the big dogs.

Now, a smart linking strategy is a focused linking strategy. You should zero in on the sites that are most likely to link to you and most likely to send qualified users.

Focus on sites that

- Attract a similar audience
- Cover similar topics
- Seem to have a linking program in place

To choose the right sites, you need to focus, once again, on your users. What are their interests? What other sites do they visit? Where are these potential visitors who haven't found your site yet?

As usual (when on a budget, or even when you aren't), the highly scientific method of, um, guessing should be your first approach. So if you're promoting a recipe site, you need to think about the mentality of the cook. Where can you find her? Well, surely you can find cooks on other cooking sites. But sites that complement yours—rather than compete with it—are generally more willing to share links. So you could try, for example, gardening sites (Promote your recipes for garden-fresh tomatoes) or party-planning sites (Promote "10 Crowd-Pleasing Punch Recipes"), or sites that sell cookware or gourmet foods.

Although guessing is always your best first bet, sites with deep pockets can validate their assumptions about where their users are. Research services, like Nielsen's NetRatings (See p. 246), can determine the approximate overlap in audience between any two sites.

Once you've identified a set of sites that your kind of users frequent, half your linking strategy is complete. Now you just need to get on those sites—one way or another. There are a few ways you can go about this: One is to join a web ring or link exchange, through which a group of related sites agree to link to each other—often using a common navigation bar. Another is to initiate an affiliate program—or other incentive program—through which sites receive financial incentives to link to you.

Alternatively, you can drum up links the old-fashioned way: Ask for them.

types of links: top-level and "deep"

Assuming you're on a tight budget, your first approach will be to look for free links. There are two basic kinds:

- **Top-level links** simply list your site and link to its front door.
- **Deep links** connect directly to an interior page on your site, showcasing a particular article or product.

top-level links   Top-level links will generally be offered by directory-style sites and the "related resources" page on smaller content-specific sites. The way you get these links is pretty straightforward: You ask for them.

Simply email the site owner, explain what your site is about, request a link, and wait. Keep in mind, however, that most free links aren't exactly free: They'll link to you, if you'll link to them. And these lists of links can become quite unwieldy, if you don't manage their appearance and upkeep. It's a good idea to have an out-linking strategy in place before you begin your solicitations.

> **Bear in mind: Most free links aren't exactly free. Sites will link to you…if you'll link to them.**

Web Rings are the natural outgrowth of mutual linking strategies. Often, groups of related sites will band loosely together to form a mutually beneficial network. The alliances are usually loose:

How many sites link to you?

Gauge your progress by searching for links to your site. You can search several search engines at once through Siteowner.com, now part of Microsoft's bCentral.

The Tool Box

Link Finder Results

For: http://www.webmonkey.com

Search engine	Links	Click to view
AltaVista	0	Check results
Google	13,900	Check results
AllTheWeb	77,818	Check results

Try another site or page:

http://   [Find Links]

Otherwise independent sites simply agree to link to each other, sometimes placing a standard button or navigation bar on their sites.

"Web rings are a low cost way to get people to click from one site to another," says Hunter Madsen, principal at H Marketing. "But usually you get what you pay for. My experience is that they don't work very well. People tend not to click on the web ring bars."

As the agreements between web rings become more formal, the arrangement might be called a network, as it is in the more corporate web world. Networks of sites may or may not be owned by the same corporate parent, but they generally share some type of navigation scheme, as well as an advertising sales force.

deep links The other free linking strategy involves so-called "deep linking," which is less dangerous (and less interesting) than it sounds. Deep linking sends traffic to interior pages on your site, rather than the front door. So a site may be linking to a particular service you offer or a particular product you're featuring.

This type of focused linking strategy is the smartest linking strategy. It forces you to think regularly about the content or services your site offers and who might be interested in them. If you've published an article on Apple products, for example, be sure to notify the Apple fan sites and discussion groups. If you have information on, say, rescuing retired racing dogs, then let the people who run Greyhound and Whippet sites know.

Also consider permanent partnerships with sites that provide complementary services. If you sell ergonomic keyboards, for example, then perhaps you should be partnering with sites that discuss work-related injuries. Or if you run a catering service in Portland, Oregon, think about partnering with a local florist, and printer—so you can cover the whole suite of party-planning needs for Portlanders.

headlines on other sites

Sometimes, it's a hard sell to get other sites to link to yours. Most large-scale sites aren't interested in simple link exchanges; they're looking for something more in their linking strategies. One of the things most sites are looking for, however, is content.

Many sites—especially portals—are looking for ideas on how to integrate subject-specific content into their sites. Content is valuable: It keeps users on a site longer (rather than just searching and clicking away, as is often done on portals), and—equally important—it allows them to charge advertisers higher rates, based on premium content. So if you're a specialized content site, you should consider generating headlines (or tips or any other small, bite-size morsels of information) for distribution on larger, more general sites.

paid links

If all else fails—or even if it succeeds—you may want to bring some paid links into your repertoire. Paid links can be a smart way to enter into advertising, without paying astronomical prices. They're also the best way to place your link exactly where you want it.

Although informal deals can be worked out with individual sites, there are several large-scale linking programs in place, including Google AdWords, Overture, and Sprinks.

paid links on search engines One of the best ways to spend a small advertising budget is placing text-based ads on search engines, where they can be targeted to specific keywords. These text ads aren't flashy, as ad banners are; they simply inform the user of your site's existence, which is exactly what you need them to do.

Search engines with paid links include

- **Overture** sells the actual search engine listings—so you can pay for your site to rank well for any given search. Pricing is based on an auction system: Whoever pays the most, wins the top spot.

- **Google** sells text-based ads, which are targeted to any given search. These text links are the only ads on Google. They don't sell banners.

- **Other search engines** sell a mixture of text links and banners, targeted to individual searches.

paid links on other sites Many other sites accept what are usually called "sponsored links." These can be purchased individually through sites or through a large-scale program, like Sprinks, which uses an auction model similar to Overture's and places links on many different sites.

"Don't just stand there—email an ambulance!"

On the web

Paid-link programs
Google AdWords
http://www.google.com
Overture
http://www.overture.com
Sprinks
http://www.sprinks.com

online advertising

If you're serious about promoting your site, and you have a budget—even a small one—to back you up, your first promotional dollars should go to online advertising, where you have the best shot at increasing traffic and the greatest ability to track results.

When planning an online advertising campaign, first think about your goals: What are you trying to accomplish with this ad campaign? Are you trying to increase awareness? Drive traffic? Increase sales?

"Where advertisers need to spend the most time is thinking about their objectives," says Internet advertising pioneer Rick Boyce, who's considered by many the father of the ad banner. "The medium is so infinitely flexible, you can do almost anything. So we always counsel people to really think about what they want to achieve."

But this crucial first step is often skipped, Boyce says, as advertisers jump ahead to tactics: where the ad will appear or what it will look like. "As in many businesses, sometimes the least amount of thought goes into strategy. No one ever answers the question, 'What the heck are we trying to achieve here?'"

crafting a successful campaign

Once you know what you're trying to achieve with your ads, you can craft a campaign aimed at meeting your specific needs. Whatever your aspiration, there are five key factors that help your ad succeed.

5 keys to a successful ad campaign:

1. Contextual placement
2. A good offer
3. Clear language
4. Compelling visuals
5. Rigorous analysis

contextual placement   The greatest strength of online advertising is its ability to put the right message in front of the right user at exactly the right time. At any given moment, web users are researching and reading and *doing* just about everything online. Your goal is to reach them at moments when your site or product is most relevant.

"Contextually relevant placement is a key factor in successful campaigns," says Peter Naylor, VP/GM of advertising sales at iVillage. "If you're selling mortgages, for instance, you want to be in the finance area of a site, and more importantly, the real estate area."

Search engines provide the most obvious example of contextual placement, because people use them when they're actively seeking a site or solution. A company that makes, say, devices that repel rodents, will always want to appear on the results for "mousetrap."

But it's important to look beyond the obvious, Naylor says. Sometimes an indirect approach works best: "If you're Glaxo Smith Kline and you're marketing Paxil [an anti-anxiety drug] your first instinct will be to advertise in the Health, Anxiety, and Depression areas on a site."

"But the users in these areas are already self-diagnosed," Naylor explains. "What you need to do is target topics that *cause* anxiety. You need to be in the work area, because people are anxious about their careers. You need to be in the relationships area, because people are anxious about their relationships. You need to be in the fitness area, because people are anxious about being overweight."

a good offer   The best way to capture the attention of web users is to make an offer they can't refuse—either because it perfectly meets their needs at the time or because it's too good to pass up.

Remember: Web users tend to be single-minded. At any given moment, they're focused on a particular task, and determined to get it done. If your ad doesn't further their goal—or give them a compelling reason to wander off-task—they're unlikely to follow it.

So ads promoting immediately relevant services are the most likely to get attention. But less-relevant ads can also get noticed if they play their communication cards right.

clickthrough isn't everything

The great promise of online advertising is its measurability: You can measure response to an ad because you can measure exactly how many people saw it, and how many clicked through.

But there's more than one way for an ad to be effective. And by focusing solely on response rate, advertisers risk missing the point.

"All people talk about is 'How many people saw the ad? How many people clicked on the ad?'" says Rick Boyce." The click rate became the determinant of success: Ads that had a high click rate—and the sites on which they ran—are considered successful, and those that had fewer clicks are considered less successful."

"So unfortunately, every advertiser on the Internet now thinks like a direct marketer, whether they are or not," Boyce says. "And that just makes no sense."

A successful ad, he explains, isn't measured by response alone. Ads shape brand perceptions and drive purchase decisions in more subtle ways than just inspiring a click. And the Internet works as well as other media in meeting these goals: "You can use the web to build awareness of your brand," Boyce says. "Or to add frequency to a TV or print campaign. Or to reach an audience you're not getting adequately in other media forms."

But still advertisers obsess over clickthrough.

"No one is ever going to click on a tomato sauce ad," Boyce says. "And that's okay. The user doesn't need to click to get the message. But nevertheless, mark my words, if there are tomato sauce companies advertising online, they are evaluating their success by how many people clicked on their ad."

"Generally, there are two things that make people click—the creative and the offer," Naylor says. So if your goal—like most advertisers—is to inspire clickthrough, you'll need either eye-grabbing visuals or a great sale to both draw users' interest and inspire immediate action.

But how good does the offer need to be? "If you're offering me free shipping or two-for-one, that's a good offer," Naylor says. "But if you're only offering free shipping for orders over $100 or 'Buy six, get one free,' well, that's less appealing. So the specific offer has a lot to do with whether or not a user clicks through."

clear language In ads—as in everything else online—I offer you this advice: Be clear, not clever. Web users don't like surprises. They usually want to know what they're getting before they click. So you're more likely to lure them in with a clear, straightforward offer than a clever riddle. (See naming site sections, p. 122.)

compelling visuals Although relevant, clearly described services are most likely to draw the user's attention, other ads *do* get clicked. Why? Usually the answer lies in the "creative," as it's called in the advertising world: The words, images, and sometimes sounds that make up the campaign. Provocative questions, cute animals, addictive games—all of these can draw in users who would otherwise have little interest in the product being sold.

And the ad type and placement can also help. "These days, the golden rules are that bigger is better," Naylor says. "People like bigger ad units. They like rich media, not GIF media. They like interactivity, as opposed to just flat. And clutter is bad. In the old days, we'd run five banners on page. Now advertisers want to be one of two ads, or the only ad. Share of voice is important."

But remember, there's a fine line between grabbing someone's attention and driving them crazy. As Steve Mulder, user experience manager for Terra-Lycos, says: "Intrusive ads are not the way to begin a long-term relationship with a customer."

rigorous analysis Like everything else online, the success of web ads can be measured—and measured to death. You can track how well each ad performs and how well each does on each site. If you view this as an ongoing challenge, you can build an increasingly clear picture of which ads succeed and why: Certain images, words, or colors may draw your users' attention. Certain promotions may prove persuasive. Certain ad types or placement may be more effective than others. All this, you can learn. And you should.

steal these ideas

6 ads that get noticed

1. contextual ads

Contextual ads get noticed because they reach the right user in the right place at exactly the right time. In some cases, the ad offers information or services that are at the top of the user's mind. In others, they offer a relevant service at a relevant moment, as in the following American Express ad, which was integrated into the check-out phase on Expedia.com.

American Express ad on Expedia. This simple promotional message—just a logo and some text—was perfectly positioned on the Expedia check-out page, just as users were asked for their credit card. A perfect example of contextual messaging. There's no better time to mention a product than when you're reaching into your wallet. And if that product's a credit card, then better yet.

2. compelling ads

Compelling ads get noticed because they catch the users' eye—either with images or words. Some things that draw the user in: Images of cute animals or people. The words "free" and "new." And, of course, anything they happen to be looking for at the moment (See contextual ads, previous.)

Bronx Zoo ad on The New York Times. This baby gorilla is the best possible salesman for the Bronx Zoo. Even if you don't like zoos, even if you don't live in New York, this ad gets you thinking about paying the little fella a visit. And monkeys don't work just for the Zoo—pictures of animals seem to do well across the board in ad banners.

3. entertaining ads

Entertaining ads get noticed because they look fun, and they engage the user. These ads usually make use of some form of "rich media," which makes it possible to embed complex animation or simple interactive games. The downside is that they're expensive for the advertiser and slow-loading on the site. So users may not wait long enough to see what the fuss is about.

MSN ad on The New York Times. This animated ad invites users to take aim at the moving ducks. Each time you hit one, it exposes the name for one of the Microsoft Network's sites and describes the target audience you'd find there. Target practice…target audience…Get it? Very clever. But more important: Fun.

4. functional ads

Functional ads get noticed because they offer the viewers a useful tool they can immediately put to work, like a search form or a scrolling menu. Even if the tool's purpose wasn't one the viewer particularly needed, they may be drawn in by its functionality. People like to play, after all, and if a tool beckons to them, they'll often take the bait. It's worth noting that these ads don't always have completely working parts. They may provide just an image of a tool to draw the user in. In these cases, the advertiser should be sure to actually offer the real tool on the page to which you link the user. That is, if you hope to keep them.

eDiets ad on iVillage. The pull-down menus in this ad draw users in, urging them in to choose their height and weight…and think about diets, of course.

5. deceptive ads

Deceptive ads get noticed because they trick you into believing they're part of the normal interface—by flashing a fake error message or dialog box. These ads work—in that people click on them, alright. But none of the users who click will stay on your site. They'll curse and mutter and go back to where they came from. Needless to say, this is not the kind of audience response most sites are looking for.

Ad on HotBot. This ad grabbed my attention, because of its warning sign and dialog-box appearance. But I knew better than to click through, having made that mistake several years before. It's a trick that only works once.

6. no-nonsense ads

No-nonsense ads get attention not by standing up and screaming and calling attention to themselves, but by very quietly and subtly offering the user precisely what he was looking for. These ads achieve the best—at times remarkable—results on search engines like Google, where they can be targeted to specific user searches.

> **40 million used books**
> Buy used and out of print books
> from over 40,000 booksellers
> www.bookfinder.com/
> Interest: ▬▬▬▬

Bookfinder ad on Google. This ad grabbed my attention because it was exactly what I was looking for when I searched for "used bookstores." I wanted used books, and I found them, by golly.

annoying ads

Annoying ads get noticed because they don't give you any choice but to look at them. Either they pop up in a new window and obscure your work, or they mesmerize you with seizure-inducing flashiness. In some ways they work: It is, indeed, hard not to look at them. But then all you want to do is look away—as soon as possible: even if it means leaving the site or scrolling down the page.

where to advertise?

When placing your ad, you should think less about what sites you want to target, and more about the users.

Ask yourself

- Who do you want to reach?

- When do you want to reach them?

Hopefully, you already have a profile of your site's audience (see profiling your users, p. 50), so you know who your ads should target and where on the web you might find them.

But also consider timing: If you reach the right people at the wrong time (when they're involved in an unrelated task) they may ignore your ad altogether. But if you hit the same user when they're thinking about your product—or even when they're in a more relaxed state of mind—they may be more likely to follow through.

choosing a site

Different types of sites offer different benefits to advertisers.

search engines offer a chance to reach the broadest swath of web users and target only those searching for specific keywords. It's an excellent way to target users with very specific needs. But its benefit is also its weakness. Nowhere are people more focused than on a search engine. If your ad doesn't relate to a user's specific need at the time, it's doubtful it will be seen at all.

portals also reach a mass audience online, and give advertisers a chance to target users. They differ from search engines because they're destinations as well as starting points. Some users go there to accomplish goals as well as find sites, making it an appropriate venue for a wider range of ads (including those that aim to draw the user's eye, without necessarily inspiring clickthrough.)

---

4 ways to pay for ads

1. By impression. With impression-based ads, you pay each time your ad is displayed to a user. This system is based on a CPM (cost per thousand impressions) model, and is typical of visual ads, like banners and pop-ups.

2. By performance. With performance-based ads, you pay each time a user clicks through on your ad. This pricing scheme is measured in CPC (cost-per-click) and is typical of text ads, including "sponsored links" and text-based search engine ads.

3. By percentage of sale. Some ads are priced based on a percentage of sales generated by the people who click on it. These ads are the least risky, in terms of investment, but they're very rare. This pricing scheme is more typical of affiliate programs than advertising.

4. By barter services. Usually called banner exchanges, services have evolved that help sites trade banners without exchanging money. Using their system, you earn credits by running ads on your site and spend these credits to place your ad elsewhere.

---

news sites offer a chance to reach a broad-based audience (sometimes with very desirable demographics) when they're in the mindset of consuming news. The advantage here is that readers will often treat an entire publication as an information source, taking in the ads along with the articles.

recreational sites offer a chance to reach users when they've slowed down from their normal break-neck browsing speed. Whether they're chatting, playing games, watching a video, or cruising the personals, users become less task-oriented and more open to suggestion on recreational sites. Visits tend to be longer and more leisurely, so users have more time to absorb ads.

what to ask before you place an ad

Before buying ads on a web site, you should learn who they are, how they do business, and what—exactly—you're signing up for.

traffic and users

How many monthly pageviews does the site have?

_____

How many monthly visitors does the site have?

_____

Who are their users?

_____

_____

_____

_____

types of ads

What types of ads does the site accept?

❏ Standard banners ❏ Skyscrapers ❏ Text-based

❏ Buttons ❏ "Rich-media" ❏ Pop-ups

❏ Sponsorships ❏ Email ❏ Video

❏ Other:

Are there technology restrictions on the ads?

_____

_____

Are there other restrictions on the ads?

_____

_____

payment and performance

How will you be charged for the ads?

❏ Based on impressions (CPM)

❏ Based on performance, or clicks (CPC)

❏ Based on the sales you make from new customers

❏ Based on barter (no money changes hands)

❏ Other:

_____

Is there a minimum amount you must spend with them?

❏ Yes ❏ No

If so, how much? _____

Do they bundle less-valuable ads with desirable ones?

❏ Yes ❏ No

What percentage of users normally click on any given ad?

_____ %

What performance guarantees—if any—can they offer?

_____

_____

How do they track the performance of an individual ad?

_____

_____

Are their results audited?

❏ Yes ❏ No

How quickly can you see the results?

_____

Will they work with you to improve your ad's performance?

❏ Yes ❏ No

targeting ads

All advertisers in all media target their ads: They choose specific venues in order to reach a particular type of audience at a particular moment. But ad targeting is more powerful online, because we have the ability to track what users are viewing and dynamically match ads to their interests, with great precision.

2 ways to target ads:

- **Content targeting** delivers ads only to pages that cover particular topics (including keyword-specific search results).

- **User targeting** delivers ads only to specific types of users.

content targeting

Content targeting takes two forms: keyword targeting, used on search engines, and channel (or topic) targeting, primarily used on portals and news sites.

keyword targeting Since 1995—beginning with a site called Infoseek—search engines have targeted ads against specific search terms. So when a user searched for "rhododendron," he was likely to see an ad for a gardening store.

This quickly became one of the most powerful and effective ways of advertising: It's a great coup, after all, for companies to reach users at the exact moment they're thinking about their products.

All search engines now sell ads based on keywords, and some (like Google and Overture) make it easy for small sites to run ads against specific words.

channel targeting Beginning in 1997 and led by Excite, most portals added subject-oriented sections, called "channels." These channels, which included topics like "Computers & the Internet" and "Cars," became prime advertising areas, because they narrow down the user's interests. A user who clicks on "Cars," for example, is the best possible candidate to see a car company's ad.

eBay Cars ad on HotBot. This ad (for eBay cars) is targeted to appear on any search for car-related words, such as this one for "Subaru." And it works: If you're looking to buy, it's bound to catch your eye.

Of course, this isn't far afield from what newspapers and magazines have always done—creating a weekly section on Autos, or running ads near related content. The model works well online and is applied widely across portals and news sites.

user targeting

Online ads can also be targeted toward specific users, based either on the profile they've created with a particular site or more generic facts about their computer.

Most user targeting is still quite primitive—focused mainly on simple facts like computer type. Because web servers can detect what platform (Windows, Macintosh, Unix) a user is on, ads can be displayed to one platform or the other. So Apple Computer could—if it wanted—show its ads only to people who already use a Mac.

Eventually, though, user targeting will become far more sophisticated, as our ability to collect and analyze data on individual users grows. And it's bound to raise a few legal and ethical eyebrows.

On a personal level, I'm deeply conflicted about these developments. On one hand, I'm concerned about the privacy issues raised and about corporate control of personal information. On the other hand, I love getting ads that are targeted to my needs. If I could live in a world where all ads catered to my personal interests in historical fiction, strong coffee, rugged winter wear, and Cynthia Rowley dresses, I'd be a very happy shopper. Except, as I said, for that whole privacy thing.

types of ads

Since October 1994—when HotWired first launched and brought advertising to the web—the basic unit of online advertising has been the banner ad, a simple strip along the top of a web page. Over time, the banner has morphed into many shapes and sizes, and bent to accommodate a range of technologies, from simple animated graphics to increasingly complex interactive programs.

But other methods—some more intrusive, some less—are nipping at the heels of the banner. Techniques like pop-ups, skyscrapers, and text-based ads have all been used with some success. And while nothing has yet toppled the supremacy of the banner, they've all become part of the online advertiser's arsenal.

Types of online ads:

- Banners
- Buttons
- Skyscrapers
- Pop-ups and leave-behinds
- "Rich media" ads
- Text-based ads
- Sponsored links
- Endorsements
- Sponsorships
- Product placement
- Video ads
- Interstitials

banners

While different sizes have been introduced and other more innovative approaches attempted, the banner, for better or worse, remains the bread-and-butter of web advertising.

The basic banner is a horizontal strip, generally placed at the top of a web page. But over the years,

alternate sizes and shapes have developed, with varying levels of success.

Because advertisers usually develop banners that appear across multiple sites, it was essential early on to regulate the size of ads. Toward this end, the Internet Advertising Bureau was founded in 1996. Among other things, the IAB produces a set of standards governing the size and shape of ad banners. (See online ad standards, p. 303.)

buttons

The distinction between banners and buttons can seem arbitrary at first. Basically, buttons are smaller and simpler. Banners may be—and invariably are—animated, while buttons are usually static or perhaps primitively animated (with, say, blinking text).

skyscrapers

Although some may argue that any banner-like ad should be called, simply, a banner (modified perhaps by the descriptive "vertical banner," "half banner," etc.) different names have evolved for different styles of banner ads,

Skyscrapers. This ad for M&M's candy, which appeared on iVillage, takes advantage of the skyscraper's dramatic dimensions to tell a story and draw the user's eye.

such as skyscrapers. As their name implies, sky-scrapers are large, vertical ads that tower over a web page, usually running down the right-hand side, adjacent to the content.

pop-ups and leave-behinds

As new online technologies develop, advertising models follow. Pop-up ads take advantage of the technology, JavaScript, introduced by Netscape in 1996. (See <u>learning to use javascript</u>, p. 165.) JavaScript allows the browser window to spawn a new (usually smaller) window, which "pops up" on the screen, along with the user's existing window.

This trick is sometimes used by sites to enhance navigation or functionality—the same way many software applications employ "floating toolbars." But more often than not, it's used for promotional messages or pop-up ads.

Leave-behinds also appear in a pop-up window, but these ads pop up as the user exits a site. A parting gift? Or the online way of saying, "And STAY out!" You make the call.

"rich-media" ads

Rich-media ads take advantage of new, Java-based technologies to embed a richer, more interactive experience into a banner ad. Rich-media ads are usually shaped like a thick rectangle and sit in the middle of a web page. They usually entice the viewer with quirky games or eye-grabbing visuals.

The advantage of rich media is that it makes possible exciting ads that engage the user more completely than a banner ad ever could. But the drawback is in the technology: It can be slooow. At times, the entire web page will hang as the ad loads—or fails to load, as the case may be. And this doesn't help anyone: The user, the advertiser, and the site all lose.

text ads

Text ads are exactly what they sound like: short, pithy lines of text, used to succinctly and simply promote a site or product. These low-key pitches are used on a wide variety of sites, but they find the most success on search engines, where they can be targeted precisely toward those users looking for a site like theirs.

Leave-behinds. Subtle, they are not. Nothing annoys users more than pop-up ads, except maybe leave-behinds, like this one, which pop up as you exit a site. They definitely get seen, but you have to decide whether the exposure is worth the ill will.

sponsored links

Sponsored links appear as a short, simple line of text on a web page, with words like "Find a car" or "Cheap airplane tickets," etc. These links, which draw the user back to an advertisers' site, often appear under the heading "Sponsored links," but they may also be integrated into a site without any particular label.

I have mixed feelings about sponsored links. On one hand, they're the least invasive ad available online. On the other hand, they can be the most insidious—because it's so difficult to distinguish them from a "normal" link.

While banner ads are generally purchased on the CPM model (meaning that payment is based on the number of times the ad is viewed), sponsored links are usually purchased on a CPC—or cost-per-click—basis. This means the advertiser only pays when a customer clicks through the link.

endorsements

Endorsements usually present themselves on a web site by a small line of text followed by a logo, which announce the web site's preference for or use of a particular product. You might see the words, "Powered by Compaq" on Yahoo's front door, or the words "HotBot prefers Visa" on your favorite search engine.

online ad standards

From their origins as standard banners (measuring 468 x 60 pixels) with simple animations, online ads have gone forth and multiplied. The Internet Advertising Bureau publishes official IAB-approved ad sizes to keep up with industry changes and suggest sanity-preserving standards. These are the latest IAB standards as of January 2003. Find updates at http://www. iab.net.

The Button

Cute, aren't they? Buttons are the miniature counterparts to the omnipresent banners. Smaller, yes. But they're also less animated. Whereas banners usually contain complex sequential animations, buttons are either static or very primitively animated, featuring simple blinking text or the like.

88 x 31 micro-bar

120 x 60

120 x 90

125 x 125

The Banner Ad

Banner ads are the bread and butter of online advertising. These horizontal strips often appear at the top of a web page, and are usually animated. Increasingly, advertisers are experimenting with the inclusion of so-called "rich media"—interactive applications embedded in the small space.

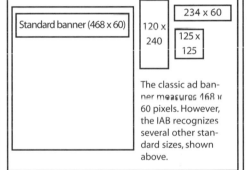

Standard banner (468 x 60)

120 x 240

234 x 60

125 x 125

The classic ad banner measures 468 x 60 pixels. However, the IAB recognizes several other standard sizes, shown above.

The Skyscraper

A variation on the banner ad, skyscrapers are just about what you'd imagine: large, vertical ads that tower over the web pages they adorn. They typically run down the right-hand side of a web page, adjacent to the content.

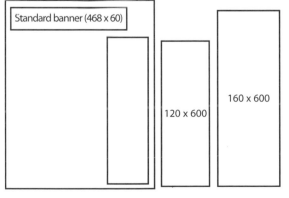

Standard banner (468 x 60)

120 x 600

160 x 600

Skyscrapers come in 2 sizes:
120 x 600 (regular)
160 x 600 (wide)

The Pop-up Ad

Pop-up ads use JavaScript to let a new, smaller window "pop up" when a user accesses the page.

Most pop-up windows conform to one of the following IAB standards:

Standard pop-up (250 x 250)

250 x 250
300 x 250
180 x 150
336 x 280
240 x 400

Endorsements can be a tricky proposition for a web site. On one hand, they can be easy money. Companies often are willing to pay a mint (tens of thousands of dollars) for this kind of placement. On the other hand, sites should be careful about handing out endorsements, lest they lose their meaning.

sponsorships

The idea for sponsorships was borrowed from other media, especially broadcast TV. In the early days of television, many programs were sponsored entirely by a single advertiser, creating a strong link between the program's content and the product or company that made it possible. Few can forget Mutual of Omaha's "Wild Kingdom," or "The Milton Berle Show," which was alternately named "Texaco Star Theater," "The Buick-Berle Show," and "Kraft Music Hall"—depending on that year's sponsor—over the course of its long run in the 1950s.

This sponsorship model is still used widely by public broadcasting stations (TV and radio) that don't accept conventional advertising. And it's used on commercial TV for spot sponsorships, in which advertisers sponsor particular segments of a program—the weather report during a news broadcast, for example, or the instant replays during a sports game.

Print media also dabble in sponsorships. Magazines may produce special issues funded by a single advertiser or run an ongoing feature linked to a single sponsor. For example, the San Francisco newspaper, *SF Weekly,* always runs a list of upcoming concerts, sponsored by Miller Beer.

On the web, both models of sponsorship—complete and partial—are used. Some sites, like HotWired's Dream Jobs (circa 1995) were entirely sponsored by a single client, whose ads appeared in all available banner spaces. Others use partial sponsorships to finance a site feature, such as "Email this to a friend."

product placement

Paid product placement has become a staple in film and TV, where actors may conspicuously display a Coke can or make an off-hand remark about using, say, pore strips to keep their skin blemish-free (seriously, these things happen). Online, these opportunities are less common. But as visual, time-based media becomes more common, product placement may take its place among the roster of online advertising options.

video ads

Although it's still quite rare, some sites with video-style content—TV stations being the best example—will incorporate short video ads before or during the video clip or animation being screened.

interstitials

As a web producer at HotWired, the mere mention of the word "interstitial" would make my face twitch. These ads, which never have been widely implemented, appear as a full-page diversion between two pages on a web site. So when a user clicks on a link, she's first taken to the ad, which runs its course and then "pushes" her to the page she really wanted.

Basically, we're looking at a TV model of fully interruptive advertisements (not that there's anything wrong with that, theoretically). The appeal to advertisers is obvious: they get the full attention of the user, and the full browser window to play with.

But the drawbacks are severe. First, web users—as opposed to TV viewers or radio listeners—are prone to rapid departures; they expect lightning-fast results and are likely to bolt if they have to wait too long for the page they requested. They're also prone to disorientation. If the interstitial page takes too long to load or too long to leave, they may well lose their train of thought and pick up something else instead. Finally, interstitials are technically difficult—which is probably why they haven't been implemented widely.

cross-media strategies

As much as you love the web and could think about it and talk about it all day long, at some point, you have to look outward. Most people spend about 20 minutes per day online, leaving 23 hours and 40 minutes for other pursuits. Subtract 8 hours for sleep (don't you wish!), and you have roughly 15 waking hours to reach your users off the web.

Problem is: It's a great big, expensive world, filled with people who may not even be Internet users. But the ranks of the wired are growing at an astonishing pace. And as the online population increases, it makes more sense to reach them through traditional venues. At last count, 88% of the U.S. population was online, and that number (220 million Americans) is growing, according to Nielsen NetRatings.

So it's actually easy to reach Internet users when they're not on the Internet. The challenge is getting them to follow through.

"One of the hardest things about marketing a web site is getting people to cross media," says Hunter Madsen. "There are a lot of opportunities to put your URL on an ad in a public place like a urinal, or on one of those postcards you can pick up at a bar—a tactic I don't recommend," Madsen says. "These are low-cost opportunities, and we tried a lot of them. But they tend to perform very poorly."

The problem, he said, is human memory. People don't often remember your site's message — or address—the next time they're online. "There's a huge fall-off in memory from the offline venue to the online venue, because you're not usually close to a web access point when you see the ad."

The trick, Madsen said, is to reach the user when they're as close as possible to an Internet access point. So you could target them on their way to work, through billboards or transit ads, or at home, with direct mailings intended for placement near the computer.

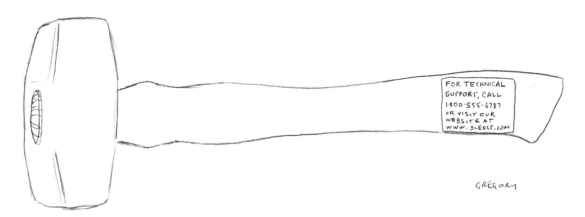

FOR TECHNICAL SUPPORT, CALL 1-800-555-6787 OR VISIT OUR WEBSITE AT WWW.SLEDGE.COM

GREGORY

Cross-media marketing tactics:

- **Press coverage** has two advantages: It's free and it's legitimizing. News stories give your site an air of importance, but they seem to have little effect on its popularity.

- **Industry awards** like the webbys, provide a badge of honor (you can call yourself an "award-winning site" if you snag one) and give you exposure to the press.

- **Newspaper and magazine ads** reach potential customers when they're already in the mindset of absorbing news, especially if you can get them to take the ad with them when they next head to their computer to go online.

- **Billboards and transit ads** can be effective at reaching users on their way to work. This is useful, because most people access the web from work, and they can follow up on the ad when they get to their desk.

- **TV ads** reach a mass audience and reinforce your brand's legitimacy as a major player and a safe place to shop or surf. Also, some sites have seen immediate results from the roughly 20 million home users who use the web while watching TV (Media Metrix).

- **Postcards, fliers, stickers** and other guerrilla tactics are low-cost ways of getting the word out and reaching some younger and hard-to-reach audiences. They're not known to be terribly effective, however.

"There's no food or medicine—just free online service.

- **In-store promotions** are useful for businesses that exist both on and off the web, because they let your existing customers know they can also find you online.

- **Direct mail** reaches home users at their primary web access point and gives them the opportunity to literally carry your message with them. If your offer is good enough, they're likely to place the mailing near their computers, to use when they next go online.

- **Promotional merchandise**—like clothing, pens, or bags with your site logo—helps strengthen your relationship with existing customers (if they're wearing a ski hat with your logo, they're likely to think about your site during the day) and also spreads the word to their friends.

how will you promote your site?

You've got what it takes. Now you have to let the world know. Your promotion plan should take advantage of everything the web has to offer: hassle-free linking from site to site; measurable advertising techniques; grass-roots energy; and ,of course, email—the best thing to happen to marketing since…well, perhaps ever.

word-of-mouth strategies

How will you let users spread the word?

From your site, will they

❏ Email their friends (an article, for instance)

❏ Poll their friends

❏ Fax their friends

❏ Instant message their friends

❏ Show their friends something

❏ Include their friends in the fun

Explain:

_____

_____

cross-media strategies

How will you promote yourself off the web?

❏ Nominations in industry awards

❏ Press coverage

❏ In-store promotions

❏ Web address written on real-world takeaways
   (receipts, etc.)

❏ Fliers, postcards

❏ TV, radio, print ads

❏ Billboards, outdoor, transit ads

linking strategies

How many sites link to yours?

Google says:

HotBot says:

Alltheweb says:

Which sites should link to yours?

Competitive/similar sites:

Complementary sites:

Get other sites to link to you

site	link requested?	link listed?
_____	❏	❏
_____	❏	❏
_____	❏	❏
_____	❏	❏
_____	❏	❏
_____	❏	❏
_____	❏	❏
_____	❏	❏
_____	❏	❏
_____	❏	❏
_____	❏	❏
_____	❏	❏
_____	❏	❏

how will you promote your site?

email strategies

To whom will you send email?

_____

_____

When will you send email?

_____

_____

Why will you send email?

_____

What kinds of email will you send?

❏ Newsletter

❏ Headlines

❏ Bite-size content:

_____

❏ Customized report:

_____

❏ Announcements for

    ❏ Events

    ❏ Sales

    ❏ Activist alerts

    ❏ Content updates

Email check-list:

task	done?
Start collecting addresses	❏
Integrate newsletter sign-up form on site	❏
Choose email software	❏
Send first round of email messages	❏
Experiment with email frequency	❏
Experiment with approaches to email	❏

(Those were trick questions.
You're never "done" experimenting.)

online advertising

Who are you trying to reach?

_____

_____

When are you trying to reach them?

_____

_____

What will go in your banner ads?

```



```

This ad is

❏ Compelling (visually)   ❏ Contextual   ❏ Functional

❏ Compelling (financially) ❏ Entertaining ❏ No-nonsense

```



```

This ad is

❏ Compelling (visually)   ❏ Contextual   ❏ Functional

❏ Compelling (financially) ❏ Entertaining ❏ No-nonsense

What will go in your text-based ads?

Google Ads _____

Title = 25 characters

Short pithy ads. Targeted to _____
keywords. Available now. _____

2 lines = 70 characters

http://www.google.com _____

URL = 35 characters

"Right now, I'm just the village idiot, but I'm thinking about going global."

improving your search rank

"Nothing succeeds like the appearance of success."
—*Christopher Lasch*

No matter what the focus of your site, search engines will likely be a significant source of traffic. If someone out there is looking for a site like yours, she'll probably turn first to a search engine to find it. And you want to make sure she finds you, not your competitor.

Search, after all, is big business. Nine out of 10 Internet users visit search engines or portals, according to Nielsen NetRatings. And they visit nearly five times each month. Users depend on them to find direction. And many sites depend on them for traffic. Whatever your business, you stand to gain a great deal if you play your search engine cards right.

first understand how it works

For starters, understand that search engines are automated—the results determined by sophisticated software, rather than human intervention. To get listed, all you have to do is submit your site's address. But to appear high on the list for any particular search, you have to anticipate what the search engine scripts are looking for.

So what *do* they look for? These all-knowing, judgment-making search engines? Well, they look at a few things—including page titles, links to your site, and the content itself—to determine what they call "relevance." For example, when a user searches on "camel trek," the search engine asks questions like: How often do the words "camel" and "trek" appear on this page? Do they appear close together? Near the top of the page? Do they also appear in the page title? Do other sites link to this one? Are the linking sites relevant to the search? Are the linking sites popular?

They weigh these different elements against each other to estimate how likely it is that the site will be relevant to the user. Then they rank it accordingly. But each search engine weighs the factors differently. This is why identical searches yield different results on different search sites.

then make a plan...

It's best to start thinking about search before you build your site, because a sensible strategy focuses on site structure and content. It's harder to make these changes once the site's launched.

To rise through the ranks

- Focus on specific keywords

- Target different words for different pages of your site (people search for pages, not sites)

- Integrate words into page titles and headlines

- Get other sites to link to you

- Make sure design issues aren't sabotaging your efforts

But don't be disappointed if you don't see immediate results. It can take a long time to improve your search engine ranking. And if there's too much competition for the keywords that matter, you may never hit the first page of search results.

"Search engines are virtually impossible to manipulate," says online marketing expert Hunter Madsen. And this is why so many services are lining up to help you, with search-optimization books, tutorials, conferences, and consulting services.

It's important, of course, to educate yourself (there are several excellent, inexpensive resources), but think twice before signing on with an expensive search consultant.

"I have watched company after company—indeed, I've *been* in company after company—that paid money to services that promised to get one's website high listings in search engines," says Madsen. "And I have yet to see any serious results."

if all else fails ...

While the best things in life may well be free, most of them can also be bought. And if you can't quite earn a place on your search engine of choice, you can always buy one. Several search engines, like Google, have excellent paid-link and advertising programs, which let you target ads toward specific keyword searches. (See paid links, p. 292.)

🛒 **Buy this book!**
Search Engine Visibility
Shari Thurow (New Riders, $35.00)

getting listed in search engines

Let's assume for the moment that your site offers advice on successfully growing asparagus. Well, every time a user types "asparagus gardening" in Google, you want him to find a link to your site. In fact, every time *any* user types "asparagus gardening" on *any* search engine, you want them to find your site. (Oh, and if your site really does offer advice on growing asparagus, my mom has some questions for you.)

Your first step is to submit your site to the search engines in question. You've gotta be in it to win it, as they say.

All search engines have simple submission forms that request your site name, URL, and perhaps a description, so they can locate and index your site.

Once submitted to a search engine, your site will be automatically added to (or "crawled into") its database whenever it's next updated. Be warned, however, that this may take months; search engines aren't always as current as they could be.

If you're in a hurry, and have cash to burn, some search engines offer an expediting service, which guarantees your site will be crawled—and its listings updated—regularly.

getting listed in directories

Directories, such as Yahoo! or About.com, also have a simple submission process. But they use a slower and more subjective system to evaluate sites. Since these directories are hand-assembled, simply submitting a site doesn't guarantee inclusion. Your site must first be deemed relevant by one of the site's category editors: an evaluation process that can take months.

Again, if you're willing to pay, there's a faster way. Most directories will evaluate your site more quickly if you pay an expediting fee.

Keep in mind that the expediting fee doesn't guarantee placement, only a timely evaluation. Comforting, it is not.

To give yourself the best possible chance carefully choose the category under which your site

getting listed

search engine dos & don'ts

- Submit your site to each search engines individually.
- Submit the URL for an index page that links to all others.
- **Don't** submit an unfinished site with an "under construction" sign.
- **Don't** submit an unreliable site. If it's "down" when the crawler visits, you could miss your opportunity.
- **Don't** submit a site without page titles and meta tags.
- **Don't** submit the same site over and over.

directory dos & don'ts

- Submit your site to each directory individually.
- Carefully choose the category to which you submit your site.
- Use important keywords in the site description.
- **Don't** use over-hyped language or slogans in your site description.
- **Don't** pretend to be something you're not.
- **Don't** submit a site that doesn't work.

belongs. Sites must be submitted directly to the category editors. Spend some time choosing the appropriate category and be specific. Don't choose "gardening," if the sub-category "container gardening" is more accurate.

On the web

Search Engine Watch
http://www.searchenginewatch.com
Searchengines.com
http://www.searchengines.com
Search optimization tutorial
http://www.webmonkey.com/01/23/index1a.html
Rankwrite
http://www.rankwrite.com
Submit-it
http://www.submit-it.com/subopt.htm

getting into Yahoo!

For many small sites, a listing in Yahoo! is like an admission ticket to the world of web legitimacy: The first step toward becoming a site of significance.

But how do you clear that bar? The first thing Yahoo! Editor-in-Chief Srinija Srinivasan wants you to know is that the editors don't pass judgment on the sites they review. "We're not trying to make fine-tuned editorial judgments on how a site stacks up against every other site or how important it is in the world."

"Given our breadth and diversity of audience, we have to work on the assumption that everything is important to someone," she says. "And it's amazing how much that turns out to be true."

> **"We work on the assumption that everything is important to someone."**
> —*Srinija Srinivasan*

So if your site works, and it's important to someone (besides you), it will get listed. That is, if anyone ever looks at it. Sheer volume is the biggest challenge Yahoo! editors face. "There are always more sites submitted than there are eyeballs to look at them," she says.

For this reason, many sites choose to use Yahoo!'s express service, which costs around $200 and guarantees an evaluation within seven business days. If you're a commerce site (listed under Business to Business or Shopping and Services), you must go this route.

Keep in mind, however, that the express service doesn't guarantee that you'll be included—only that your site will be evaluated promptly.

To improve your chances of getting in:

1. **Pay the fee to guarantee evaluation.** "This doesn't increase or decrease your likelihood of getting listed. But it guarantees that you'll be looked at."

2. **Don't pretend to be something you're not.** It's the Yahoo staff's biggest pet peeve: sites that pretend to be more than they are—claiming, for example, to have thousands of real estate listings across the country, when they only have a few for their own city.

"This is the biggest mistake that site owners make," Srinivasan says. "One of the key phrases we use nearly every day—talking to small businesses and larger clients—is that we can't list them for anything that doesn't actually exist on their site."

3. **Make sure your site works.** "These brass-tacks functionality issues are important. The site has to be up and running, and has to work in different browsers."

4. **Make sure your site makes sense.** "It shouldn't be unreadable or incomprehensible."

5. **Make sure your site is relevant** to someone, somewhere, other than yourself.

6. **Make sure your site has some shelf life.** "We avoid sites that are here today, gone tomorrow."

And take heart: "We're not capricious," Srinivasan says. "It's pretty darn likely that if you think your site should be listed—and your friends agree—then we will too."

improving your rank in search engines

Let's begin by stating the obvious: To rank well in search engines, you first need to be listed with them. So be sure to submit your site's address to all the major search engines before wondering why you don't appear on the first page of results (getting listed in search engines, p. 311).

To rise through the ranks, your best bet is to build your site with search engines in mind— making sure that your page titles are meaningful, keywords are emphasized in the right places, and other sites link to yours. Also, make sure that your site design isn't sabotaging your efforts.

But search engines are a tricky business. Each engine ranks sites differently: Some emphasize popularity; others stress keyword counts or placement. And each weighs the different factors using a slightly different formula. Don't obsess over these details! Just make sure you have your bases covered, and leave it at that.

1. focus on keywords

The first step toward search engine success is to **choose the keyword searches for which you want to rank well**. Most of your energy will be focused around these keywords or phrases, so it's important to choose well.

Target different keywords for different parts of your site. Search engines strive to match every query with the most relevant page—not the most relevant site. So you should take the time to target keywords for each sub-topic on the individual pages of your site. If you have a gardening site, for instance, you should focus not only on how your site ranks overall (on searches like "gardening" or "container gardening") but also how your interior pages rank on searches for their specific topics (like "begonia" or "petunia").

Target the right keywords. You may optimize your site flawlessly, but if you're not optimizing it for the right keywords, you're efforts will be wasted. Be sure to choose:

■ **Keywords that are relevant to your site.** This may sound obvious, but you'd be surprised by how many sites waste their time chasing a good rank on keywords that are perceived as valuable (like "sex") but have little to do with their site. Don't try to trick the engine! Just stick with keywords that apply to you.

■ **Keywords that are specific.** Competition is fierce for generic words, like "car" or "design." You'll have better luck coming up with two- or three-word phrases that describe your site's content more specifically ("fuel-efficient car" or "user-centered design"). These phrases are searched less often, but have fewer sites competing for them.

■ **Keywords that people actually type.** You may optimize your site perfectly for the words that perfectly describe your site. And you may skyrocket through the results for those searches. But if no one actually searches on those terms, you won't get much reward for your efforts.

improving your search rank (continued)

2. integrate keywords

Once you choose the keywords that are most relevant to your site—and for which you would most like your site to rank well—you need to **integrate those words into your site, focusing on the places that search engines look**. Note, however, that there's no technical trick to integrating keywords—they're simply words that appear on your site, either in headlines, the text, or the page titles. (See how a top-ranked site got there, p. 316 for a visual explanation of a site that did it well.)

■ **URL (or web address).** Although it's not always possible, it helps to have a URL that contains one or more of the important keywords. This helps both the search engine and users understand what your site is about. (See choosing a name, p. 31.)

■ **Page title.** Often ignored— because it doesn't actually appear within the web page— the page title is an important indicator for search engines. Most sites use the same title for every page on the site. But it's smarter to customize each title to reflect the content of that particular page, incorporating the most important page-specific keywords or phrases.

■ **Page text.** Page title, URL, and meta tags all matter, but the real proof is in the page text. If your targeted keywords don't actually appear on your pages, you'll have a hard time improving your rank.

Some keys to placing keywords in the page:

■ **Use keywords frequently**

■ **Place keywords close to each other**

■ **Place keywords near the top of the page**

■ **Meta tags.** Meta tags are pieces of information included with a web page that offer general (or "meta") information about the page, including the language in which it's written, the topics it covers, and a general description of its content.

A few years ago, meta tags were the most important factor affecting a site's search ranking. This is no longer true: Search engines have developed new techniques and few use meta tags to determine a site's relevance for any particular keyword. But they're still important. The information in your site's meta tags is often used to describe your site in search engine listings. And this description will determine whether or not people follow your link.

3. get links from other sites

This is the most important—and most overlooked—step in improving your search rank. **You need other sites to link to yours, because links measure popularity.** And most search engines now consider popularity the most important factor in determining a site's relevance. Popular sites—the thinking goes— are more likely to fill a visitor's needs. Otherwise, why would they be popular? So to rise through the ranks, you'll need to channel your inner Homecoming Queen and get other sites to link to you.

Get links from as many sites as possible. To measure popularity, search engines look first at how many sites link to yours. So it's important to encourage other sites to link to you, whether by earning, buying, or bartering for the link. (Many sites follow an I'll-link-to-you-if-you'll-link-to-me philosophy.)

Get links from bigger and better sites. Search engines look not only at the number of sites linking to you, but also the quality of the linking sites. Quality, here, is measured both by popularity and relevance. So a single link from a large, established site like Yahoo! may be worth a dozen links from smaller operations. And a link from a site that's relevant to your topic area (say, gardening) may be worth a dozen links from unrelated sites. But the exact weight of each factor will vary from search engine to search engine, each of which follows its own formula.

The catch-22. The increasing emphasis on popularity creates a catch-22 for site owners. In order to attract visitors, you must rank well in search engines. But in order to rank well in search engines, you must have a lot of visitors.

4. modify site design

In some cases, design issues may be standing between you and a higher ranking. Poor site design is always a problem, but **some design errors can prevent search engines from understanding your site's focus, or even from indexing your site at all.** It's important to address these issues before moving more deeply into search-engine optimization. If a search engine can't access or read your site, your efforts will be for naught.

Search-specific design problems include:

■ **Dynamic pages.** If the pages on your site are generated dynamically—like those in many data-base-backed sites (stores, directories, news sites, etc.)—search engines may not be able to index them. The problem is with the URLs, such as http://www.store.com/gift.jsp?nc=40384&BV, which contain suspicious characters, like "?" and "&." Humans can't read this gobbledy gook, and neither can most search engines. One solution is to create a set of static pages (with normal URLs) that parallels every unique page in your database. But that quickly becomes unwieldy. A better solution is to modify the way URLs appear on your site, making them both human- and search-engine readable.

■ **Flash.** Search engines can't "read" or index the text that appears in Flash files on your site. To get around this problem, consider creating a non-Flash version of your site or limiting your use of Flash.

■ **Image maps.** Search engines can't read the text that appears in images on your site. So if your site makes use of image maps— or if you use images to replace important words like headlines— you should always offer "alt" text, which translates the words in the pictures.

■ **JavaScript.** The use of JavaScript won't prevent search engines from indexing your site, but it may hurt your ranking. To determine relevance, search engines look at where keywords appear on a page: The higher, the better. But bulky JavaScript programs, inserted at the top of the page, push the page content down in the eyes of the search engine.

■ **Frames.** Most search engines can now index sites that are built in frames. But some of the smaller and older engines still have trouble, because the content stored within frames-based sites lacks individual URLs or page addresses.

5. don't try to trick the search engine

Search engines are constantly tweaking their formulas to prevent sneaky sites from fooling (or "spamming") them. It's an elaborate cat-and-mouse game that's gone on for nearly a decade now: Search engines set rules; spammers get around them; search engines change the rules. For instance, search engines used to rate sites based on the number of times a keyword appeared. So spammers laid the keywords on thick. Search engines then ousted sites with too many keywords; spoofers figured out the ideal number.

For every trick that tricksters try, search engines develop an antidote. Search engine teams are constantly developing new ways to sniff out and rebuff the sites that try to throw the rankings with deceptive methods. Unless you are very, very good at fooling software and have a lot of free time on your hands, search engine spoofing is not a game you should play. You will lose.

Instead, focus your energies on (a) finding legitimate ways to better reflect your site's content through keywords; (b) attracting more links from other sites; and (c) improving your site, so you can attract more users, grow in popularity, and rise through the ranks that way.

how a top-ranked site got there

When it comes to search engines, it often helps to follow the leader. By examining the top-ranked sites on any particular search, you can get a sense for what the site's doing right—and what you can do to follow in its footsteps.

When you investigate, be sure to notice

1. Where the keywords appear

2. How often the keywords appear

3. How many sites link to theirs

what this site does right

1. **Good site description.** The description within the search engine lets users know what they'll find on the page and encourages this user to choose the second-listed site over the first.

2. **Good page title.** The page title is short and concise, and it includes the specific phrase, "Indira Gandhi." This lets the search engine know that Indira Gandhi is the main subject of the page and not just a footnote.

3. **Headline includes the keyword phrase.** This shows that "Indira Gandhi" is central to the content on the page.

4. **Keyword phrase is near the top of page.** The keyword phrase, "Indira Gandhi" appears at the beginning of the first paragraph, which reinforces the idea that these words are important to the text.

5. **Keyword phrase reappears within text.** The repetition of the words "Indira Gandhi" throughout the text further reinforces their importance (without overdoing it).

6. **Many other sites link to it.** A search for links to this site turns up hundreds of referring sites. This shows that other sites consider it helpful.

a search for the keywords "Indira Gandhi"

A top-ranked site for "Indira Gandhi"

A search for links to this top-ranked site

how will you improve your search rank?

There's no sure-fire way to improve your search ranking: Methods that work in one search engine fall flat in another. But that's no reason not to try. These common-sense approaches—submitting your site, focusing on important keywords, improving site design, and getting links—can only help your chances. And in some case, they'll help your business as well.

get listed

Submit your sites to search engines:

search engine	submitted?	included?	rank on key search?
Alltheweb	❏	❏	____
AltaVista	❏	❏	____
AskJeeves	❏	❏	____
Google	❏	❏	____
Goto.com	❏	❏	____
HotBot	❏	❏	____
Inktomi	❏	❏	____
Lycos	❏	❏	____

Submit your sites to directories:

directory	submitted?	included?
LookSmart	❏	❏
Open Directory	❏	❏
Yahoo!	❏	❏

get links from other sites

How many sites link to yours?

Google says:

HotBot says:

Alltheweb says:

Get other sites to link to you:

site	link requested?	link listed?
_____	❏	❏
_____	❏	❏
_____	❏	❏
_____	❏	❏
_____	❏	❏
_____	❏	❏
_____	❏	❏
_____	❏	❏
_____	❏	❏
_____	❏	❏
_____	❏	❏
_____	❏	❏
_____	❏	❏

modify site design

task	done?
Provide "alt text" for headlines	❏
Provide "alt text" for all navigation	❏
Provide "alt text" for all images, Flash files	❏
Create human-readable URLs to replace gobbledygook from dynamic pages	❏

how will you improve your search rank?

focus on keywords

What keywords or phrases matter most to you?

keyword	current top-ranked sites
_____	1._____
	2._____
	3._____
	4._____
	5._____
_____	1._____
	2._____
	3._____
	4._____
	5._____
_____	1._____
	2._____
	3._____
	4._____
	5._____
_____	1._____
	2._____
	3._____
	4._____
	5._____
_____	1._____
	2._____
	3._____
	4._____
	5._____

How do you rank on searches for important keywords?

keyword	site	listed?	your rank?
_____	AOLsearch:	❑	_____
	Alltheweb:	❑	_____
	Google:	❑	_____
	HotBot:	❑	_____
	Lycos:	❑	_____
	MSNsearch:	❑	_____
_____	AOLsearch:	❑	_____
	Alltheweb:	❑	_____
	Google:	❑	_____
	HotBot:	❑	_____
	Lycos:	❑	_____
	MSNsearch:	❑	_____
_____	AOLsearch:	❑	_____
	Alltheweb:	❑	_____
	Google:	❑	_____
	HotBot:	❑	_____
	Lycos:	❑	_____
	MSNsearch:	❑	_____

integrate keywords

task	done?
Consider a new URL—one that uses keywords	❑
Target different keywords for different pages	❑
Integrate keywords into page titles	❑
Integrate keywords into headlines	❑
Integrate keywords near top of page	❑
Integrate keywords close together	❑
Create metatags that are readable & concise	❑

chapter 15

managing a web project & team

"Whoa, whoa, whoa—is that _work_? I thought we were outsourcing that."

don't miss ...

managing a web project

In some ways, this whole book is about managing a web site. But project management is a science in its own right. Strategy must be set, decisions made, a team hired, and a site built—all on schedule and budget. But there's no single correct way to accomplish this.

The best methods will vary with the size and scope of the site, and the temperament of the team. Some projects rely on tight schedules with firm deadlines, regular meetings, and structured documentation. Others leave deadlines loose and documents simple.

So the details will vary. But certain key principles apply to web projects of all shapes and sizes.

4 golden rules for web project managers:

1. Clarify what you're creating
2. Decide how decisions will be made
3. Learn how to say no
4. Create a "process"

clarify what you're creating

The first step to web success is simple: You have to describe what—exactly—it is you're creating. This may sound obvious, but it's startling just how many projects get started without a clear idea of what's being built or what it's supposed to accomplish.

"It sounds strange," says Kris Carpenter, former VP of Excite. "But we had projects get pretty far along before we realized that the team just wasn't clear on what they were building. They hadn't fully comprehended the application experience they needed to enable. They could describe features and benefits in a PowerPoint presentation— they used all the right language—but at the end of the day, they didn't have a clear understanding of what the end product needed to be or how they would enable that application."

To make sure everyone on your team is rowing in the same direction, it's important to articulate the site's mission and set concrete goals. These clear directives will save you time and energy down the road, and they may be the key to hitting a tight deadline.

"I had only six weeks to build my first major web site," says former MSN managing editor Martha Brockenbrough. "Six weeks! That's barely enough time to give birth to a rabbit!" Clarity, she says, was the key to her team's success. "Everything moves really, really quickly. So what you have to do is get everyone clear on the goals, on board with the mission."

See writing a mission statement, p. 12, and setting goals, p. 14.

decide how decisions will be made

Over the course of developing your site, you'll have to make decisions, large and small. How will these decisions be made? Who has input into the decisions, and who makes the final call? These questions—about who *answers* the questions—are important to resolve before you begin work.

"The most important thing that makes web projects go well is when the team structure and the decision-making process are clear and agreed-upon from the beginning," says Lance McDaniel, VP of Creative for SBI and Company.

"Frequently, we'll ask a new client, 'Who's running the project?' and they say 'We all are!' And I say, 'Okay. But when it comes down to whether your web site is blue or green, who decides? What if it's a 3-3 vote? Is it a blue-green site?'"

It's a simple example that speaks to a larger truth, McDaniel says: "Ultimately, you need one person who has the ability to cast the deciding vote. You can only build a site in one direction."

But the solution isn't as simple as naming a leader (although that's an important step). Web projects are usually collaborative ventures that affect an entire organization. In order to get everyone on board, you need to identify key stakeholders in the organization and involve them early— soliciting their opinions on site direction and goals. (See how to get everyone on board, p. 341.)

You also need to know whether anyone—the CEO for instance—has the ability to overturn decisions. If so (and this is usually the case!), take care to get their input early on. You may have to lobby for their attention, but better to put the effort in early than have them object later on.

Finally, do what you can to avoid design-by-committee. Many companies create a large task force—or several—to oversee their web site. And while the idea is well-intentioned (collaboration is an important goal), too many cooks—without rules in the kitchen—create a big mess.

learn how to say no

The dirty little secret of every successful web producer is that they know how to say no. They may have learned to say it in the most charming way possible ("That's a great idea! I'll put it on the feature list for version 3.0.") But say it they must. And here's why: Every web site runs the risk of "feature creep," which happens when different team members get excited about different ideas, and the site gets pulled in too many directions. If creativity is left unchecked, the To-Do list will stretch endlessly and the site will lose its identity. A strong product manager can head off such silliness with a single word: "No."

"If your product manager can't say no to people who ask for features, that's a red flag," says Peter Merholz, a partner with Adaptive Path. "Probably the single most valuable thing an organization can have is a product manager who can step back and see the whole picture. If they have a coherent vision of what the product ought to be, then they can say "No" because what's being requested doesn't match the vision for the product."

🛒 Buy these books!

Developing Effective Websites: A Project Manager's Guide
Roy Strauss and Patrick Hogan ($26.95)
Collaborative Web Development: Strategies and Best Practices for Web Teams
Jessica Burdman ($39.95)

"I actually don't know why I called this meeting. I guess it was just a reflex."

create a "process"

Who does what? And when? And how? These are the questions to answer before you begin working, not a week after your first missed deadline. Every good project manager (and every consultant, good or bad) will talk about "process."

Process covers things like:

- Schedule & budget
- Meetings
- Deliverables
- Documentation

Though these topics make non-manager eyes glaze over, a good process goes a long way toward the success of web projects. And the key to a good process is consistency: Design a system you think will work for your team, and then stick with it. As Greg Dotson, Chief Information Officer of Guru, advises: "You all have to agree that you're using this process, and you're not just going to throw it out the window when the first deadline is missed."

Schedule & budget   Time and money—or the lack of them—are facts of life on web projects. In an ideal world, the schedule and budget would be built from the ground up, based on what you need to create your ideal site. But usually, it's the other way around: You have to look at available time and resources, and figure out what you can afford to

how to save a schedule that's slipping...

Its an all too familiar situation. Your deadline is looming, and it's clear you're not going to hit it. What to do?

1. Extend the deadline. Although it causes managers deep distress, there's nothing wrong with extending a deadline. Don't just let the project float. Set a new schedule, and make it stick.

2. Do less. If you have a hard launch date that can't be changed, your only attractive option is to cut back on features. "The best thing to do at that point is chop off a piece of the project, whichever is the least important," says Pamela Statz, former production manager for HotWired and Lucasfilm. Focus your energy on the site's essential elements; others can be phased in later.

> **"You should never throw more people at a project at the last minute."**
> *—Pamela Statz*

3. Expand the team. You can also bring in more people to help finish the work. But this, Statz says, is perhaps the worst thing you could do. "You should never throw more people at a project at the last minute," she says. "It just never works. You might think, 'Oh, this project is running behind schedule, let's add 10 more people to the staff.' But you can't! It becomes a management nightmare, with all of these new people who don't know the project or the company. Then you have to spend all your time training them, and you can't get the actual work done."

make. But don't despair: These constraints actually help you place limits on a project, and a few scheduling tricks can help keep you on track. (<u>how to set a schedule that sticks</u>, p. 324.)

meetings No one likes meetings. And some people prefer to call them "working sessions." But whatever you call them, they're important. They keep the project on track and help team members remember that they're a team. To make them as painless as possible, decide ahead of time when they'll be held, how long they'll run, and what will be accomplished. And, oh yes, serve food. See <u>how to run a brainstorming session</u>, p. 326.

deliverables Over the course of the project, different team members will have to produce work— site maps, technical specs, marketing plans, etc.— so that everything else can proceed. Which of these "deliverables" must be produced at each stage? Make sure each team member knows what he's expected to deliver before his deadline looms.

documentation What sort of written documents must the team produce? Will the producer write a product plan? Will the engineer write a technical spec? Some teams go heavy on documentation, and some barely write down the site's name. It's important to write something down; how much is a question of style. See <u>writing a plan</u>, p. 21.

apply what you already know

If you're new to the web—but not to project management—don't hesitate to apply what you already know. "The web is very similar to other disciplines, other industries," Pamela Statz. "Architecture, software development, filmmaking— they all work basically on the same premise: You need to do a lot of planning, you need to keep people on schedule and on budget throughout the process. And you need to have a really big party when you're done."

how to set a schedule that sticks

Although few people would list schedule-setting as one of their favorite things, it's an indispensable skill. Nearly every successful web site has a task-master behind it. Someone—or several some-ones—has to make sure the trains run on time and the site launches when it's supposed to. Here's some expert advice on setting a schedule that sticks.

1. Define the project before setting the schedule. It's impossible to set realistic deadlines for a vague, ill-defined project. You'll need to describe the scope of a web site before you can figure out how long it will take to create.

2. Set a real schedules with real dates. It's essential to have a launch date, even if it proves wrong. Without a deadline, it's difficult to motivate a team and impossible to measure progress.

3. Ask each person, "How long will this take?" A solid schedule is built from the ground up, by asking team members how long each task will actually take. This empowers the team, builds confidence in the schedule, and allows you to hold people to their own estimates.

"The schedule needs to be agreed upon by the people who do the actual work, or at least a valid representative," says Lance McDaniel. "Of course, one of the tricks is turning managers into valid representatives of the people they manage."

4. To hit hard deadlines, make hard decisions. It's rare to be handed a blank slate on which you can draw your ideal schedule. Usually, you'll be working against an external deadline, which you don't control. Work with your staff to decide which steps must be skipped or features cut to make the date work. You may even decide to focus on key features while fudging the others.

A risky approach—but it worked for software engineer Jim Morris when launching an online store: "We had only six weeks to build the site, so we focused on the features that had to be built first," he says with a mischievous smile. "When it launched, we didn't have the billing software written. But customers didn't care. They don't care if you don't bill them."

5. Set smaller deadlines along the way. Establishing—and hitting—milestones builds confidence among team members and also makes hard deadlines easier. "You can't just say, 'We've got to be done in six weeks! Go! Go!'" says Martha Brockenbrough. "You have to break it down for people. A good manager, and a good producer, is capable of breaking everything down into easily digestible parts."

> **"The key is setting some early deadlines. When a team hits a deadline early on, it sets them up for success."**
>
> *—Greg Dotson*

"I've found that teams can be pretty resilient around hard deadlines, even if they seem unreasonable at first," says Greg Dotson. "The key to staying on schedule is setting some early deadlines. They're not only early for the sake of being early, but also for the sake of being attainable. When a team hits a deadline early on, it sets them up for success."

6. Look for red flags. Always double-check the schedule, looking for ill-defined tasks, over-loaded team members, or deadlines set too close together. These may indicate aggressive scheduling or confusion about tasks. "A good manager can quickly spot the things that just visually are red flags," says Greg Dotson. "Like tasks with long timelines or nebulous names like 'database work.'"

7. Make progress visible. Teams build momentum when they can see the progress they're making. Create daily builds of the site, print out new designs, create a chart tracking percent completion—whatever you can do to help people see the progress around them.

8. Require progress reports. If you're managing multiple teams or a large project with many facets, you may need team leaders to submit progress reports, explaining what they accomplished that week. No one likes writing them—or reading them, for that matter—but they're a necessary evil in bigger companies. They hold producers responsible for their projects and allow senior managers to identify projects that are falling behind.

9. Clear obstacles. If you can see that your team is stuck, ask them why. They may have questions, or they may be running into problems they can't solve on their own. "A lot of times, a problem is difficult for a team member, but incredibly easy for the manager to solve," says Martha Brockenbrough. "People love it when you clear an obstacle for them, and, as a manager, that's your job."

10. Pad the schedule. To be on the safe side, it's always best to build some extra time into the schedule. You'll need it! "Padding, padding, padding! It's very important! Put that in your book," says Pamela Statz, who has managed web sites for companies like HotWired, Lucasfilm, and Future Farmers. "You have to pad your schedule, because some things will take more time than you think they will. Other things take less. But if you've properly padded your schedule, you should be okay. A good rule of thumb is to always set QA to be a few weeks longer than neccessary. There you go! There's your extra time."

11. Don't agree to an unrealistic schedule. Too often, entire teams sign on to hit impossible deadlines, and no one's willing to speak up and admit it. "That's what's called 'delegated delusion,'" says Greg Dotson. "There's an unrealistic deadline, and everybody knows they're not going to hit it,

but nobody wants to admit to upper management that it's all delusional."

It's important to be realistic, and also to ask: Why the rush? "In retrospect, now that I'm out of the business, I think people kid themselves about timeframes all the time," said Cate Corcoran. "People think things are more urgent than they are."

12. If you're running behind, do less. If your project is slipping off schedule, you can either cut back on the site's scope or extend the deadline. (See how to save a schedule that's slipping, p. 323.)

13. If the schedule slips, set a new one. Web projects are complicated, and there's no great shame in falling a bit behind. But when you realize you're going to miss a deadline, it's important to set a new one—and make it stick. More than one slip causes everyone to lose confidence. "My rule is that if you're going to slip, try to slip only once and know what you're slipping to," says Greg Dotson. "Don't set another bad deadline."

14. Don't despair when things go wrong. It's important to remember that web development is complex and sometimes unpredictable; you have to expect some slippage in the sched-

> **"The schedule needs to be agreed upon by the people who do the actual work."**
>
> **—Lance McDaniel**

ule. "It's important to remember that software is hard to develop; it's hard to keep everything on track," says Greg Dotson. "If you slip only a week, you're doing a great job, especially if it's a project of any complexity."

Pamela Statz is even more emphatic. "75% of the time, things go terribly wrong, in spite of your best efforts. And you should be thrilled when something actually gets done and works well," she says with a completely straight face. "Then again, I'm something of a pessimist."

15. Throw a party when you're done! Regardless of how successful a project was, it's good for morale to celebrate its completion. Have a party—or at least eat cake!

how to run a brainstorming session

At some point, nearly every web producer will hold a brainstorming session to generate ideas for the site. Unfortunately, few will do it well. It isn't enough to get people in one room (although this alone can be a challenge), you have to know how to draw good ideas out of them, and what to do with the ideas, once drawn.

The key is participation, says Emily Simas, a trained facilitator, web veteran, and former Kindergarten teacher who knows a thing or two about group dynamics. "If you're going to run a really good brainstorming session," she says, "you have to get everyone involved."

No small task. As facilitator, you'll need to draw out the people who shy from public speaking, force the guy with the laptop to pay attention, rein in the noisy Nellies who usually dominate meetings, and keep everyone focused on the task at hand.

"Imagine a typical brainstorming session," Simas says. "You walk into a room, you sit around a table, and someone just spouts out questions and expects you to spout answers back."

Typically, only a few people—and always the same people—will participate. "These are the people who think while they're speaking," Simas says. "They're the noisier people in the room."

But they're not the only ones with ideas. "Some people need to take in all the information and absorb a lot more before they come up with ideas. And if you're going to run a good brainstorming session, you have to give them a chance to think around the question in different ways."

Circulating the questions before the meeting, breaking off into small groups, allowing "think"

> **"You have to give people a chance to think around the question in different ways."**
> —*Emily Simas*

time, and requiring everyone to write down their ideas—on Post-its, perhaps—are all ways to draw creative ideas out of everyone in the room.

And while it's worth it for the ideas alone, brainstorming sessions—ones where people actually participate and feel involved—have another benefit: They help team members feel invested in a project. And when people see that their ideas are being heard and integrated, they're likely to work harder toward the site's success.

1. Have an agenda. Like any other meeting, brainstorming sessions run best when participants know what to expect. Give an overview of the process, set a time limit, and outline your goals."

2. Explain how decisions will be made. "You've got to somehow get agreement on how the decision-making process is going to work. People should feel that they're heard at the beginning, that their ideas are part of the process, and that there is a structure for how the decision will be made."

"If people don't feel they're part of the decision—part of the process—they're not going to work as hard toward the end product."

3. Carefully craft your questions. Brainstorming usually revolves around questions that are posed to the group, with the goal of generating as many ideas as possible. "But if your questions are too narrow, you'll get run-of-the-mill answers," Simas warns.

"You have to somehow challenge people to break out of thinking within their normal limitations in the working world. You have to craft your questions in a way that will inspire creativity."

4. Create an idea board. Throughout the session, all the ideas that are discussed should be written on a board where everyone can see them. This might be a white board, or butcher paper, or just the wall. But be sure everyone can see it, and that the ideas can be permanently recorded later on.

5. Get everyone to write their own answers. Rather than shouting out suggestions for a moderator to scribe, invite participants to write their own answers down—perhaps on Post-its. Limit them to one idea per Post-it, and have each person explain their ideas before sticking them on the board.

"I'm a huge fan of the Post-it note," says Emily Simas. "It's a brilliant brainstorming tool for a number of reasons. First, if people write their idea in their own handwriting, they feel more ownership of it when it hits the board."

"It's also a phenomenal tool for organizing similar ideas. Seven people can say the same thing, and you can just stack those seven on top of each other, and they're naturally organized."

6. Give people time to think. Most people need a little time to mull things over. Always offer some "think time" between questions.

7. Break into small groups. Some people think better when they have a chance to talk through a problem in a small group. And many shy people are more likely to speak up in a small setting. So breaking into small groups and reporting back to the overall group can be very effective.

8. Draw out the "quiet ones." Many of the ideas here— breaking into groups, writing ideas down—will encourage participation from the less usual suspects in the room. But Simas encourages facilitators to take more direct action, as well. "If you see someone who continually looks like they have something to say, but just isn't talking, take a moment and say, 'June, you look like you had an idea. Was there something you wanted to share?' Call those people out."

9. Rein in the noisy ones. In any meeting, certain people are more likely to speak out than others. But if your noisy ones are particularly dominant, or prone to interrupting, you might want to use a "speaking object" to control who has the floor. Only the person holding the object (a "Koosh" ball is a good one) gets to speak at any given time.

10. Ask people to represent their departments. To help people take the process less personally, you can ask individuals to represent their departments or disciplines: "As a designer, I get excited about…." "As an engineer, I'm worried about…."

11. Appoint a timekeeper. You should set a time limit on each group activity and appoint a timekeeper to enforce it. "If you know someone who generally drifts off or does work through meetings, make them the timekeeper," Simas suggests with a smile. "It's a great way to keep them involved."

12. Serve food. Food brings double benefits to a brainstorming session. First, people are more likely to attend meetings where food will be served. Second, food can help get creative juices flowing.

13. Don't penalize people or award prizes. Some facilitators like to reward people for participating or penalize them for being late. Don't do it, Simas says. "If you want people to sit and pout in the back, charge them each $10 for being 10 minutes late," she says. "Tried and true way to kill a meeting."

Similarly, you shouldn't reward certain participants over others. "I'm just not into competitions," Simas explains. "I don't think they inspire creativity, and they definitely don't inspire teamwork. If it's the culture of your company, it might work. But personally, I'm way too Kindergarten teacher for that. I've seen some facilitators use food as a prize: 'The best idea gets a snack!' I hate that. Everyone's ideas should get a snack!"

managing a web team

Managing a web team raises many of the same issues as managing any other group. People are people, after all. And they bring the same insecurities, incompatibilities, petty jealousies, and poor communication to web projects as they do to any other.

But a web site throws certain aspects of management into high relief. You have to assemble a multi-disciplinary team, combining individuals with a wide range of technical, visual, editorial, and business skills. These team members—who speak very different languages—have to learn to communicate and collaborate with each other. And they often have to navigate a minefield of office politics, because the web site affects the entire organization and everyone (it seems) has a stake in their work.

No wonder, then, that management issues were the number-one challenge web veterans say they faced, in the course of creating successful sites. No matter whether the person was an engineer or an animator, a producer or a production specialist—people and politics were the main roadblocks to success.

"Corporate politics and corporate culture are the biggest problems I have to deal with," says Jesse James Garrett, an information architect and partner with Adaptive Path consulting. "Bigger than any information architecture problem, bigger than any design problem, bigger than any technology problem."

5 key challenges for web managers:

1. Assembling a multi-disciplinary team

2. Getting everyone on board

3. Encouraging collaboration

4. Motivating without money

5. Avoiding burn-out

assembling a multi-disciplinary team Although a small site can be built by a single person, most web sites require people from different backgrounds— technical, visual, editorial, financial—to bring their skills to the table. It's a challenge to assemble such a multi-disciplinary team: Simply finding good people is hard enough, but defining their roles and

getting them to play well together is a full-time job.

"You have to try to teach people to understand how each other's minds work, and respect that, and realize that if any part of it were missing, the site would fail," said Margaret Gould-Stewart, former VP of Media & Community Development for Tripod. "If there weren't talented sales people, you'd be out of business. If there weren't talented developers, you'd be out of business."

"We've all been a part of projects that were too strong on one side and too weak on the other," she said. "And it just never works, in the long run."

An effective web team is small, but balanced— with different disciplines given a equal voice at the table. "When one department or discipline has too much power, you have problems," agreed Luke Knowland, principal of LGK Productions. "Web development done right is so interdisciplinary. Everyone has to be responsible and accountable to each other." See <u>assembling a web team</u>, p. 332, and <u>structuring your web team</u>, p. 338.

getting everyone on board Web projects are almost always political. It takes special skills to get an entire team—not to mention an entire organization—working toward the same goals.

"You end up being quite a diplomat," Garrett says. "I sometimes feel like Colin Powell doing a tour of the Middle East. You go around to [the company's stakeholders], and you cajole and you wheedle and you make little deals, and you try to convince everybody that they're getting what they want, even when that's not the case." See <u>how to get everyone on board</u>, p. 341.

encouraging collaboration Web sites require people from different disciplines to work well together. But they usually need some help getting there. From the seating plan to the structure of teams, there's a lot you can do to encourage good work. One of the best ways to improve understanding is to show team members what the other really does. "I spent a lot of time helping people build a better understanding of what the other side was about," said Margaret Gould-Stewart. "I would send designers on sales calls so they would see what the sales people had to do—what hoops they had to

how to speak the language(s)

When you took your job, you may not have known you needed a phrasebook. Not just one, actually, but several. For collaborative web teams join people from different disciplines, who think differently, work differently, and speak utterly different languages.

It falls to the producer to translate. "It's important to understand who your audience is and communicate in a way that's meaningful to that audience," said Margaret Gould-Stewart. "You may need to get a salesperson and a designer the same information, but it needs to be delivered in a totally different way."

"All these people have their own way of thinking about the problem," explains Jesse James Garrett, an information architect whose work often makes him the middleman. "So you have to learn to say the same thing—in different ways—to an engineer and the VP of marketing. The languages required there are mutually exclusive: The terms that work for an engineer are absolutely not going to work for the VP of Marketing and vice versa."

If you're going to motivate or persuade them, he says, you have to make sure you're speaking the right language: No easy task. After all, the concepts and strategies you're discussing are often difficult to grasp on their own. "How do you explain an already ambiguous and complicated concept to people who approach the world in totally, totally, totally different ways?" asks Martha Brockenbrough.

For managers, it can feel like translating Ulysses to Chinese—when it's hard enough to explain in English.

"What it takes is an understanding of how different people understand things," Brockenbrough says. "You have to create good metaphors, good models. You have to know enough about the different disciplines so you can talk to people. You have to build a bridge between different types of minds."

As Gould-Stewart says, "It took time to gain fluency in different areas, but it was time well-spent."

jump through. There's nothing like going on a sales call to understand what sales is about."

On the flip side, she also tried to impress on the sales staff why usability mattered. "We'd bring sales people to usability tests," she said. "They'd watch users try to complete tasks with products that had been designed by committee, and—over and over again—not be able to complete them."

motivating without money In some industries, motivation is a numbers game: Pay people well, and they'll perform. Not so on the web, where managers often exert only indirect influence over the people working on the site. What motivates people besides money? "A lot of times it's just gratitude," says Kristin Windbigler, former Executive Producer of Webmonkey. "People just want to be thanked. And a little gratitude goes a long way."

> "Web development can be a lot like the movie Saving Private Ryan.
> In the end, they saved Private Ryan.
> But the team's all dead and Private Ryan is lost."
> —*Jim Morris*

Avoiding burn-out Unrealistic deadlines, outsized egos, and over-inflated expectations are hardly unique to the web, but they sure are common. In an atmosphere of high hopes, rapid development, and long hours, it's easy to push your staff too far.

"Web development can be a lot like the movie, *Saving Private Ryan*," said software engineer Jim Morris. "In the end, they saved Private Ryan. But the team's all dead and Private Ryan is lost."

Similarly, you may succeed against all odds, launching a web site that no one said could be done—only to find you've burned out your staff to launch a misguided site. To avoid a Private Ryan situation, always remember to ask yourself: Is what I'm trying to do realistic? Is it worth it?

> "The art of choosing men is not nearly so difficult as the art of enabling those one has chosen to attain their full worth."
> —*Napoleon Bonaparte Emperor of France*

lesson from the trenches

how to encourage collaboration

The challenge of web management can be summed up in one word: Collaboration. More than anything, a web producer must know how to bring together people of drastically different backgrounds and get them to work together toward a common goal. No easy task, you say? Well, we agree. But a few good ideas can go a long way toward building the bridges you need.

1. Be truly open to ideas. It's not enough to say a project is collaborative, you have to mean it. "You have to become genuinely willing in your own mind to receive other people's input," says Janice Fraser. "Often people go through the motions of collaboration, and it doesn't work because it's not genuine. If you really don't care what other people have to say, they'll figure that out. And it'll show. So you've got to change your own mind set first."

2. Include key people early in the process. True collaboration requires people of different disciplines to be involved from the beginning, when goals are being set and direction determined. Everything flows from those initial ideas, and a person brought in later will never feel a full partner in the process.

3. Clarify roles and the decision-making process. Although it's helpful to break out of narrowly defined roles, it's still essential to define who does what. "The structure needs to be laid out from the beginning," says Wendy Owen, a partner in Giant Ant Design. "The team needs to know who has input into the decisions, who makes the decisions, and who's the tie breaker: the person who makes the final call if team members can't agree."

4. Work in small groups. Although there's a definite time and place for large teams, smaller is better when it comes to collaborative work. A small team allows individuals to build personal relationships, and establish a work style that suits them. "Tight teams work best," says Wendy Owen.

"When too many people are involved, the process gets too complicated."

5. Change the seating plan. Most offices divide employees by department, rather than project. So the engineers sit in one section, design in another, and marketing in another still. "That is always a mistake," says Taylor, an interaction designer. "When people don't sit next to each other, they don't talk to each other, or go out for coffee together or collaborate well."

"I believe in collaboration that proximity is everything," agrees Margaret Gould-Stewart, former VP of Creative for Tripod." You can work really hard and do an okay job working together from a distance. But face time is a critical part of the creative process. Your relationship outside of the project totally affects your ability to communicate."

> **"I believe in collaboration that proximity is everything."**
> —*Margaret Gould-Stewart*

6. Be open to multiple directions. Collaboration is difficult when team members come to the table with rigid ideas about the end product. To build something truly collaborative, you must be receptive to new ideas. "The key to leaving yourself open to possibilities is starting with a wider pool from the beginning," says Wendy Owen." So you come up with three design directions at the beginning, and then evolve from there. You're so much more open to change than you would be if you only explored one direction."

7. Learn how to brainstorm. Brainstorming is a great way to generate ideas and enthusiasm for a project—or rather, it should be. "There are probably three people in the world who know how to run a brainstorming session," says software engineer Jim Morris. "It's so hard to be an unbiased collector of good ideas." (See how to run a brainstorming session, p. 326.)

Dig Deeper
How to work with engineers, p. 236

lesson from the trenches

8. Solicit opinions one-on-one. Group meetings are an important part of collaborative process, but they're not the only way. "The best way to get ideas out of people is to sit down one-on-one and talk to them," says Janice Fraser, a partner at Adaptive Path. "If you genuinely care about what they have to say, and you sit down, and you look them in the eye, and you listen, and you write down what they're saying, they're going to tell you a lot more."

9. Showcase good work. If one of your collaborative teams has done a great job, reward them with public praise. Mention their work at a company meeting, highlighting the role of cross-disciplinary collaboration. Better yet, ask the team to make a short presentation—as a team—to talk about what they accomplished and how.

10. Learn what other people do. Ignorance is probably the biggest organizational barrier to collaboration: It's hard to value another person's role when you don't understand it. "You should try to learn as much as you can about what your co-workers do," says Kristin Windbigler, former executive producer of Webmonkey." You should at least know what they need from you to do their job well. But always keep in mind that you aren't the expert."

11. Draw people out. One way to encourage collaboration is to draw individuals out. Sometimes a star player will hang back because she's uncertain of her role or her strengths. Take her aside, and tell her that she counts. "It's very effective to let people know that you think they're special, and that you admire them and their talent, and you're excited to learn from them," says Martha Brockenbrough.

12. Recognize your biases. Many—if not most—companies have a significant bias toward one discipline over another. As interaction designer Taylor puts it, "One group gets favored based on what the boss used to do, or what the boss sees as important." That's bad news for the web site. "A web project can go astray if the team is too beholden to any one department," says Peter Merholz. "A web site needs to reflect on the company as a whole. When one department steers it, it will reflect poorly—or at least improperly—on the other departments."

13. Hold team meetings—and serve food. No one likes meetings, but they're essential for collaboration. If teams don't meet regularly, they never learn to work as a team. "A lot of times, unfortunately, disparate groups only come together in times of crisis," says Margaret Gould-Stewart. "Something big comes up, something's wrong, and all of a sudden the engineers are meeting with the designers, or the sales people are meeting with the product manager. So instead of being proactive, you're constantly in crisis mode."

> **"The team needs to know who has input into decisions, who makes the decisions, and who's the tie-breaker."**
>
> **—Wendy Owen**

A spoonful of sugar—or a powdered doughnut—always helps the medicine of meetings go down. So serve food. People come together more easily when they're sharing a delicious meal, or even a nice snack. But beware of those doughnuts! The sugary rush is fleeting, and will leave your team deflated.

14. Know when to make changes. Sometimes, despite your best efforts, a team just won't gel. The individuals may have different work styles or may just lack the right chemistry as a group. In these cases, don't be afraid to make changes. "You can't keep investing in a team that's never going to be able to function correctly," says Greg Dotson. "Sometimes teams just don't work."

> "Everyone has the right and duty to influence decision making and to understand the results. [But] participative management is not democratic. Having a say is not the same as having a vote."
>
> —Max DePree
> Former CEO, Herman Miller

assembling a web team

Although it's the last topic covered in this book, many would argue it's the most important. The team you assemble to create a web site will determine what you can do, and how well and how fast you do it.

It's probably true in any industry, but it's certainly true on the web: You're only as good as your team. Ask Andrew Anker, a partner with August Capital, who focuses on Internet-related investments. When considering a company for their portfolio, they put people first.

"Absolutely, the number one thing we look at is the team," Anker said. "We, as a partnership, bet on people. We think you need to have someone who's passionate about the product, someone who wakes up in the middle of the night worried that it doesn't look good."

And this passion should extend not only to the management team of the company (or the lead on a project) but through every person you hire. Ideally, you want to find people who are not only talented in their own discipline, but who can think broadly about the site and its goals.

"The better people you can get on your team, the better the site will be," said Mark Hurst, founder of consulting firm Creative Good. "So it's important to build out that team the right way. Don't bring someone on the team unless they're passionate about the user experience, holistically."

And if people can make a web company, they can also break it. The wrong people—or simply the wrong chemistry between team members—can cripple a project.

"Hiring bad people is the number one mistake companies make," Anker explained. But it's also unavoidable. As a company gets started, they often have to ramp up quickly, he said, hiring 10 or 15 key people as fast as they can.

"When you make 10 or 15 hires, you're probably going to get one or two wrong," he said. "That happens. That's life. The best manager in the world is going to get one or two wrong out of 10 or 15 people—especially when you're also trying to build a business and find real estate and lawyers and everything else."

In those cases, the best thing to do is admit you made a mistake. "Realize that you've hired the wrong person, and make the change," Anker said.

building the right team

The key to building a strong team is balance. You have to assemble a team that possesses—among them—all the necessary skills to design and build your site. But the size and composition of a web team will vary considerably depending on the task at hand. If you're taking your small business online, you might just work alone—or with a single consultant—and use a web host like Big Step to handle your technical needs. But if you're launching a full-featured web site, you're going to need a full staff, including design, production, and technical roles.

There's a lot of ambiguity about roles and titles on a web team. Much of this confusion stems from the way web companies evolved. Some—like my alma mater, HotWired—evolved from media companies. Others, like the Microsoft Network, evolved from software companies. Others from ad agencies, business consultancies, retail firms, and specific industries like real estate or even photo development. Each company borrowed terms from its own industry to define the roles on the web team, and each struggled with its own unique roadblocks in mapping their old systems on to the web.

But over time, a consistent approach evolved. While companies in different sectors still use different names to describe roles, and while many roles are still shaped to fit the skills of a specific employee, there's enough consistency in the industry to create a model for building web teams.

the core team

Different projects demand different permutations of the web team. But the core needs of a site—any site—are fairly predictable.

The core roles on the web team:

- Producer

- Technical lead

- Design lead

- Production lead

producer (a.k.a. product manager, project manager, project lead) At the core of every web team is the producer or project manager, who's responsible for defining project direction. The producer must be an excellent communicator and a synthesizer of information. She has to weigh all the different factors—technical, visual, financial, creative—that will make her site succeed and collaboratively guide the team down the best path.

> **There's a lot of ambiguity about roles and titles on the web team. Each company borrowed terms from its own industry.**

To arrive at the best decisions, the producer should know when and how to put research to work for her. She should have a sense of who the audience is and how they'll use the site, and she should know how to learn more about both. She should be intimate enough with the site that she can develop theories on how to improve it but responsible enough in her methods to know how to test ideas, rather than simply follow hunches.

The producer isn't necessarily a formal manager of others on the team; often, she's the first among equals. She's usually the "tie breaker" in disputes that others on the team can't resolve. As such, she must often mediate between the needs of the end user and the financial needs of the business (considering also the needs of her staff). At Wired, I would tell producers that their job was to mediate between the twin gods of user and advertiser—angry, capricious gods at that!

To fulfill this diplomatic task, it's important that the producer learn to speak the languages of her team members. She need not be an expert in engineering or design, but she should be comfortable in technical conversations and know when to ask questions.

In addition to this conceptual and diplomatic work, the producer has to handle tactical issues, such as keeping the budget, setting and hitting deadlines, maintaining documentation, and calling team meetings. She is usually expected to bring the doughnuts.

In some cases—especially on smaller projects—the producer may double as one of the other core roles.

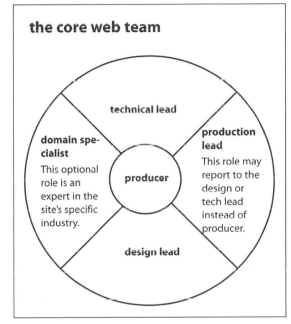

the core web team

technical lead

production lead

This role may report to the design or tech lead instead of producer.

domain specialist

This optional role is an expert in the site's specific industry.

producer

design lead

technical lead (a.k.a. lead engineer, IT lead.) The technical lead provides technological leadership for the site, which begins with the question of scope. He'll work with the core team to determine just what the site will do.

The technical lead should have a strong grasp on the state of web technologies, so he can advise the team about what's possible. He should be able to explain to the rest of the team how feasible certain ideas are and whether they should be accomplished by purchasing available tools or building applications from scratch.

The technical lead should also be able to address back-end needs: What infrastructure will be needed to support the site? Should you invest in new servers, lease more bandwidth, change databases?

Once direction's been determined, the technical lead usually designs the technical architecture of any site applications, or manages the engineer who does. He also manages the teams of software, database, and network engineers for the project, and oversees—at least in part—the QA team.

design lead (a.k.a. creative director, creative lead, designer.) The design lead is responsible for the visual presentation of the site. But the design process begins long before colors or fonts are chosen. Web design begins with site organization (which may be described as information architecture or experience design, or both, depending on the project), and the design lead should be comfortable with the task.

A well-designed web site should be both functional and visually expressive. And while most designers will lean in one direction or the other, the best designers can combine both qualities. So the design lead must have a grasp on usability issues. (Is this site functional? Can visitors accomplish their goals?) as well as the less measurable but perhaps equally important principles of visual design. (What impression does this give about our company? How does it feel to use this site?)

Depending on the size of the site and company, the design lead may do all the work himself or may oversee other specialists, including usability experts, graphic artists, photo editors, animators, and multimedia experts, such as Flash designers.

production lead (a.k.a. production manager, HTML lead) The web production manager oversees the physical creation of the site. This work begins with infrastructure: She'll map out the site's directory structure and set up the servers on which development will be done (the development server or staging server) and prepare the live site. She'll organize a templating system to ensure consistency across the site's pages.

She'll work with the design and technical leads (if they exist) to make decisions about site structure and determine how certain visual and technical features will be accomplished. In setting these standards, she must also consider such issues as site speed, accessibility, and compatibility across web browsers and platforms.

The production lead oversees the teams producing the actual pages and ensures the quality of the HTML or ASP code created, as well as all the images and multimedia elements. In some organizations, the production—or HTML—lead may be more junior than the other members of the core team, and they may report to either the design or technical lead, instead of the producer.

domain specialist Depending on the scope and type of site, other core roles may be added, bringing in key specialist skills. For instance, content-based sites will always have an editor within the core team. Commerce sites will have an expert in merchandising or marketing.

the extended team

Depending on the size and scope of a project—and the skills of the core employees—any number of specialists may be brought in to round out the team. Some specialists may join the team full-time, others may be called in for a specific task or short-term consulting. Often, a single team member may play several of these specialist roles. A single designer, for instance, may replace all the design specialists, or the technical lead may double as the software engineer.

Some of the roles on an extended web team:

- **Design roles**
  - Information architect
  - Interaction designer
  - Usability (or user experience) expert
  - Visual designer
  - Graphic artist
  - Photo editor

- **Production roles**
  - Media production specialist
  - HTML or ASP coder

- **Technical roles**
  - Software engineer (programmer)
  - Database engineer
  - QA engineer
  - System administrator
  - Data analyst

- **Editorial & community roles**

  - Copywriter
  - Copyeditor
  - Community specialist
  - Community moderator

- **Financial roles**

  - Sales manager & staff
  - Marketing manager
  - Merchandiser
  - Business development manager

information architects These designers specialize in the organizational structure of a site. They're adept at organizing and categorizing large sets of information or tasks so that users can both grasp the scope of the site and quickly find what they need. Information Architects are usually logical thinkers—able to impose a sensible hierarchy on shapeless data—and skilled wordsmiths, able to categorize and effectively label site areas.

interaction designers These designers specialize in creating a coherent user experience, especially when the site involves a multi-step process (like a stock-trading application or a shopping cart) or an

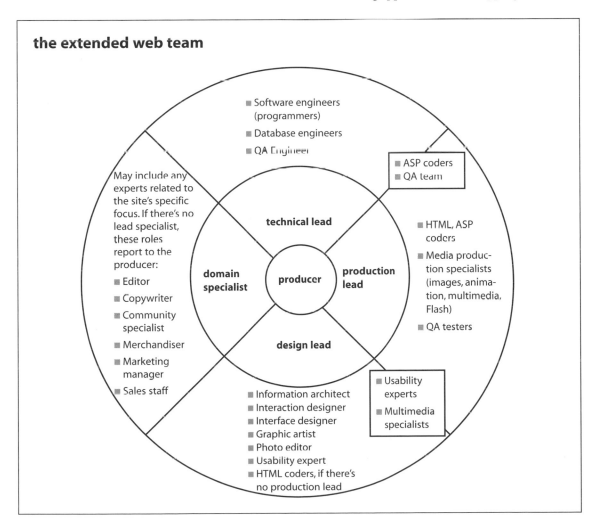

the extended web team

- Software engineers (programmers)
- Database engineers
- QA Engineer

- ASP coders
- QA team

technical lead

- HTML, ASP coders
- Media production specialists (images, animation, multimedia, Flash)
- QA testers

May include any experts related to the site's specific focus. If there's no lead specialist, these roles report to the producer:
- Editor
- Copywriter
- Community specialist
- Merchandiser
- Marketing manager
- Sales staff

domain specialist

producer

production lead

design lead

- Information architect
- Interaction designer
- Interface designer
- Graphic artist
- Photo editor
- Usability expert
- HTML coders, if there's no production lead

- Usability experts
- Multimedia specialists

open-ended sensory experience (like games or interactive exhibits). Interaction (or "experience") designers tend to think in terms of pacing and have a deeper understanding of time-based media and multi-sensory input (sound, video) than other design specialists.

usability (or user experience) experts Usability experts focus on the user's ability to interact with the site, identifying those areas that may trip users up. However, any usability expert will tell you that usability research must begin before the site is designed. Usability begins with an understanding of who the users are and what they want from your site. So many UE experts will push you (or help you) to conduct customer research and answer critical questions before the site's designed.

visual designers translate your site's underlying functionality into a visual interface. They design the navigation elements and all the related buttons and toolbars. They're skilled at expressing the essential and abstract nature of a brand through visual elements, such as colors, type, and imagery. They usually design company logos, as well as other site elements, and they can work closely with marketing specialists to both articulate and then express the brand identity.

graphic artists Artists create the illustrations, logos, cartoons, graphic headlines, and simple animations needed for your site. Many—but not all—designers are also graphic artists.

photo editors These editors locate and produce the desired images for your site by assigning photographers, searching archives, or negotiating with image banks.

media production specialists These specialists convert various media forms—images, audio, video, animation—into formats that are usable on a web page. Different specialists may focus on particular types of media (audio, say) or even specific technologies (like Flash). Within a company, this role is often played by the HTML coders.

html or asp coders Coders create the actual web pages for your site. Although the basics of HTML can be learned in a day, it takes some time to develop the expertise to implement complicated designs. ASP is a step more complicated than HTML and requires light programming skills. For this reason, ASP coders often report into the engineering department, rather than "creative" or "design."

software engineers (programmers) Programmers create or customize applications for your site. The specific skills needed depend on the application you're building: Some must be written in a particular programming language, like Java or C++. Others require specific knowledge of databases or content management systems. An experienced engineer can learn new programming languages with relative ease, but if you're hiring a consultant, you don't want to pay for their learning curve.

qa engineers (or testers) Testers specialize in testing completed software or sites for problems or errors that weren't anticipated. The QA (or quality assurance) program usually involves running many different scenarios to test the durability of the application under different conditions and uses.

system administrators These administrators manage all the computers and networks for a company, including the web servers that host the company web site and the mail servers, which schedule and send emails to members. Systems administrators usually handle a wide range of tasks, which may include setting up new computers and accounts for individuals, wiring cables and phone systems, installing and maintaining new system-level software, administering UNIX systems, and configuring printing and mail systems.

data analysts Data analysts specialize in extracting meaningful information from the morass of data that a site collects, usually pertaining to the use of the web site. This data may deal with traffic patterns, purchase patterns, or other key metrics to the business.

copywriters Writers craft the text that appears on your site. Words play a fundamental role in how a user experiences your site, and a skilled wordsmith will translate your site's identity into a verbal style. Good web writers know, however, that less is more. Web sites don't need elegant prose. They need clear labels and pithy blurbs that express meaning in as few words as possible.

copyeditors These editors do a lot more than dot i's and cross t's. In a web environment, copyeditors ensure proper spelling, usage, and style—all of which contribute to a site that appears precise and professional. Editors will usually develop a "style" for the site, which dictates how certain words or phrases should be addressed: How will dates be written? What gets capitalized? Does email have a hyphen? These issues may seem small, but they significantly affect the overall coherence of your site.

community specialists These team members understand how to foster an online community—whether it's through message boards, user reviews, mailing lists, online chat, or less direct methods, such as incorporating user feedback. Different specialists have different areas of expertise, depending on the type of communities they've worked with: real-time or delayed, visual or verbal, topic-specific or free-form.

community moderators Moderators hold leadership roles within specific online communities, keeping conversations focused and behavior acceptable. They're basically the hosts of the party, setting the tone of the environment and making sure everyone's looked after. If you have discussion areas on your site, you must have moderators—whether they're volunteers or paid employees.

merchandisers Merchandisers specialize in placing, combining and displaying products in a way that fosters increased sales. In the web environment, they may choose which products to promote on a site's front door or through targeted emails. They may also choose which products to bundle together or which to recommend when a customer views a similar item.

advertising sales managers These team members sell advertising space on the site. Depending on the type of site, sales managers may work with large-scale media buyers, who represent many corporate clients, with the corporate clients themselves, with smaller businesses making smaller-scaled buys, or with a combination of the above.

marketing managers Marketing managers specialize in promoting the site or the company. In web companies, the expertise of marketing managers will vary. Some may focus on traditional areas of marketing: advertising across media, generating press interest, planning events. others may specialize in online marketing techniques: online ads, email marketing, or the development of other programs. Still other marketing managers may focus on market research or even product development. In some companies, there may be significant overlap between the role of the producers and marketing managers.

business development managers These managers specialize in establishing new partnerships between your site or company and others. Business development is charged with drumming up new business but also with exploring new business directions.

structuring your web team

Depending on the nature of your team (employees or consultants), and the scope of your site, you may draw on one of several models for structuring your web team. Consider these prototypes as starting points for developing the best managerial structure for your team.

3 typical web teams:

1. **The web company** in which the entire organization is focused on producing a web site.

2. **The small business & the web consultant** in which a small business, whose focus is on its store or service (and not the web site) hires a consultant to build its site.

3. **The corporation & the web agency** in which a large company hires an established web agency to set their internet strategy and build or redesign their web site. The corporation may also have its own in-house web team.

the web company

Web companies are those in which the entire organization is focused on producing a web site (or sites), which they both own and operate. The web site may not be their sole business, but it's a central part of their mission and their corporate identity.

the challenge For web companies, the challenge is to develop an effective organizational hierarchy. In these companies, people from different disciplines come together in different combinations to work on different projects over time. Should the reporting structure be based on project, discipline, or a combination of the two?

> "Some single mind must be master, else there will be no agreement in anything."
>
> – *Abraham Lincoln*

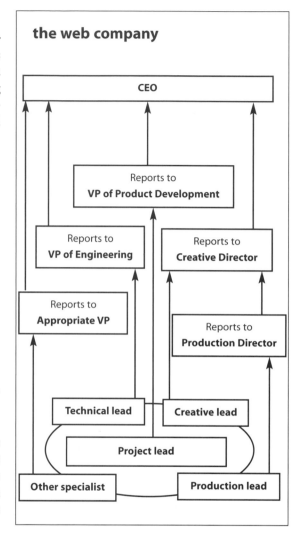

the web company

- CEO
- Reports to **VP of Product Development**
- Reports to **VP of Engineering**
- Reports to **Creative Director**
- Reports to **Appropriate VP**
- Reports to **Production Director**
- Technical lead
- Creative lead
- Project lead
- Other specialist
- Production lead

one solution Use a matrix reporting system, in which individuals report to both a project manager and a department head. Temporary teams are formed around projects, and team members are responsible to the project manager for the duration of the project. But they officially report to a department head from their own discipline. So a designer may report to a project manager on a day-to-day basis, but her salary would be set and performance reviewed by the company's creative director.

4 keys to success for a web company:

1. **Create dedicated teams** for individual projects.

2. **Give project managers authority** to manage their team—or at least their team's time—on a day-to-day basis.

3. **Offer continuity in management.** Individuals may change teams with some regularity, but they shouldn't change managers every time they change teams. If they keep a single manager, they won't get lost in the organization.

4. **Provide job-specific feedback.** Each employee should receive guidance from a senior manager within their own discipline. So a designer's work should be reviewed by the creative director, an engineer's work by the head of engineering.

the corporation & the web agency

For large corporations, the web site is only one small part of their business. While some have established in-house web teams, most rely on consulting firms to guide them on web strategy and build their web presence. Note, however, that problems can arise if you completely outsource your web site: People inside your organization must feel invested in—and responsible for—your site if it's to succeed long-term.

the challenge This scenario's challenge is to build consensus among two teams of people, each of which reports back into a larger organization with its own politics and power struggles. The challenge for the corporation is get their entire organization on board and to keep the agency focused on their core needs. The challenge for the agency is to gain broad-based support within the corporation, even though they report into a single department (typically marketing).

one solution Have a small dedicated team from the agency—headed by a single producer—work with an interdepartmental task force from the corporation, also headed by a single project manager.

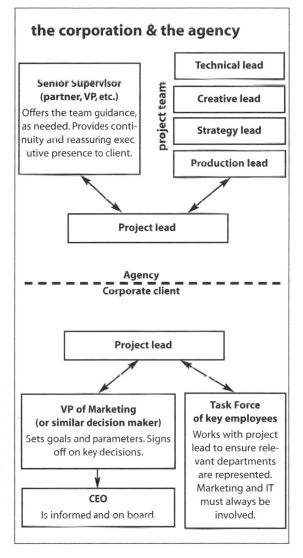

3 keys to success for a corporation:

1. **Name a single project lead for each side.** And have them stick with the project through the duration.

2. **Bring the IT group in early.** Most web sites are managed by the marketing department, but the IT group should be an equal partner. If you don't have IT on board, you're setting yourself up for technical missteps, as well as a possible mutiny: The IT group can get an agency fired faster than you can say, "Why aren't we using IBM?"

3. **Make sure the CEO is on board.** CEOs don't like surprises. Make sure the people at the top of the company—as high as you can possibly get—know about, and agree with, your plans for the web site. Otherwise, you could have the plug pulled on your project, even after the work is completed.

the small business & the consultant

A web site can provide an enormous lift to a small business—both in customer leads and actual sales. But most small businesses are, well, small, and they don't have enough employees to even think about a web site, much less build one.

the challenge   This scenario's challenge is to find time and money. All small business owners wear more hats than they can count, and a web site is just one more thing to worry about. The challenge for the consultant is getting the business owner to sit still long enough to focus on their web strategy. Also, there's the question of getting paid….

one solution   Have the business owner—or a dedicated, computer-literate, and sufficiently senior project manager—work with a single consultant or designer, who can sub-contract work to others, as needed. Keep the site basic, and consider a barter arrangement, where the web consultant is paid with products or services instead of cash.

3 keys to success for a small business:

1. **Name a single project lead on both sides.** In this case, what's true for corporations is true of small businesses: A single person must be in charge if things are to get done. Employees of small businesses often share responsibility communally. But this doesn't work well for web sites.

2. **Keep meetings simple and small.** Although the consultant may hire specialists to supplement her own skills, these specialists need not meet the business owner. Keep

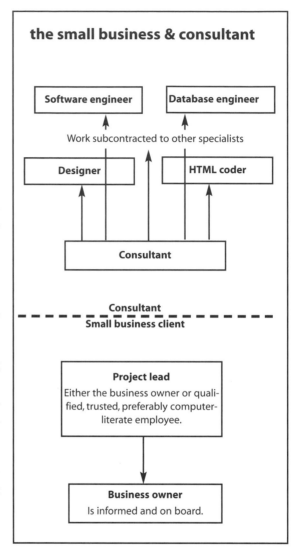

meetings between consultant and client intimate. This saves the owner time and shields them from conflicting or confusing opinions.

3. **Consider a barter arrangement.** Many web consultants will trade web services for the client's product, whether it's yoga classes, Szechwan noodle soup, or stylish shoes. Everyone wins.

how to get everyone on board

Web sites can be highly political projects. Everyone, it seems, has their own ideas on what their company's site should do and how it should look. One of the biggest challenges for web producers is how to untangle all the divergent opinions and get your entire team—indeed your entire organization—working toward a common goal. In other words, how do you get "buy-in" on a web project?

"The first thought I have is on the word 'buy-in,'" says Janice Fraser, a partner with consulting firm Adaptive Path, who's known for her well-honed diplomatic skills. "I've stopped using it because I think it masks the problem. It collapses several ideas into one word, and by collapsing them you forget to do all the steps."

> **"Buy-in only becomes a real problem when you lack clarity in the decision-making process."**
> —*Janice Fraser*

"The first part," she explains, "is awareness. People need to be aware of what's being done, because if they're taken by surprise…well, most people do not react positively to surprises."

The second step is involving those people who have a real stake in the project. Regardless of whether they're on the web team, per se, those people who have a material investment in the work you're doing should be included in the development process." But the opposite is also true. "If they do not have a material investment, then you need to keep them out."

Timing is key here. You have to include people early in the process, Fraser says. And it can't just be lip service. You have to give them a real opportunity to influence the product." You bring people in for input and you make it meaningful input. You break down their ideas and genuinely incorporate their ideas into the products. Then you tell them how you did that."

This last point can't be over-emphasized. It's not enough just to take in ideas and use them. You have to let people know how their ideas are being used. Remind them what they suggested and how it influenced the site. This let's them know you're listening, and also makes them feel more invested in the outcome.

"It's important to come back to people at the mid-point, before the product is launched," Fraser explains. "Tell them how their input has been integrated into the product. I even do periodic reviews with stakeholders, telling them, 'Here's where we are. I'd like your opinion about this…'"

The final step is in many ways the hardest, Fraser said. You have to be as explicit as possible about who makes the ultimate decisions. "Buy-in only becomes a real problem when you lack clarity in the decision-making process."

It's best when you can collaboratively arrive at decisions. But complete consensus is usually impossible and not necessarily desirable.

"Sometimes you get a lot of agreement around a point," she says. "It's more common, though, to have a lot of disagreement. Different people will always believe that their way is the right way. So you have to depersonalize the decision-making."

"Take decisions out of the 'I-think-this' realm and put them into the 'research-shows-this' realm. When you have a culture that supports user testing, you can use test results as the decision-making criteria: 'Here's what our pre-design research indicated,' or 'Here's what the last card sort indicated.' That's a rhetorical device that helps you not look like a demagogue."

"This is slightly manipulative," Fraser admits. "But I'm not afraid to be slightly manipulative. One of the things I'm always wary of is the idea of democracy. I try not to give the impression that this is a democracy. There's always someone who ultimately has authority."

> "A genuine leader is not a searcher for consensus but a molder of consensus."
> – *Martin Luther King, Jr.*

appendix

expert advice

"Look, son—I'm not a financial guru, an Internet guru, a P.R. guru, or a weight-loss guru. I'm just a guru."

Over the course of writing this book, I had the good fortune to interview around 50 experts in the web world. All of them graciously gave me at least an hour of their time—and years worth of ideas — about what was working on the web, and what had worked for them in particular.

In choosing these industry veterans, I focused less on individuals who were well-known (though some of them are) and more on the people in the trenches—the ones who are deeply involved in the day-to-day development or operations of their sites.

By way of disclosure, I must point out that my choice of subjects was skewed geographically. Most of the people I interviewed came out of the San Francisco, New York, or Seattle schools of web development (though Austin, Boston, and Chicago are all reasonably represented). By this, I mean they based their careers in one of these three cities—and I suspect that people in the same city develop similar outlooks on the web. Also, many of them passed through HotWired's doors before moving on to other companies and other sites. So similar threads run through their careers.

But the main thing these experts have in common is experience. Most of them had been working on the web for 5–8 years when I interviewed them in 2002–2003, but their experience varies widely in terms of discipline, company, and sites.

The experts range widely on

- **Discipline and company role.** Among these experts, you'll find executives, entrepreneurs, designers, engineers, producers, production managers, writers, animators, marketing specialists, business strategists, and venture capitalists, to name a few. Some are consultants, some work at web companies, and some comprise the web staff at non-web organizations.

- **Type of company.** These experts have worked at Internet start-ups, large corporations, consulting groups, small businesses, non-profits, universities, and libraries. Their organizations have ranged in size from one-person web shops to enormous multi-national corporations.

- **Type of site.** Most of these web veterans have worked on several sites over the course of their careers. Their experience runs the gamut from online stores to corporate intranets to search engines to art galleries. Plus news sites, community sites, match-making sites, software companies, music sites, company sites, film sites, and many tiny, personal labors of love.

It was striking, then, how consistent their conclusions were. Many themes were heard again and again: the primacy of the user, the need for simplicity, the importance of evolving a site, the problems with office politics. They didn't necessarily repeat each other—each brought a fresh perspective and new insight to the table—but they didn't contradict each other either.

Their insights reinforced most (though not all) of my initial inclinations, and also pushed the book in new, important directions. After completing the interviews—and reading and re-reading the transcripts—I felt I had a clear, if incomplete, picture of what we've learned so far. I hope, after reading the book, that you do, too.

Without further ado, I give you the experts.

the experts

Andrew Anker is a partner at August Capital (www.augustcap.com), a venture capital firm in Menlo Park, CA. He focuses on internet-related investments, and has funded sites like Emode, Listen.com, Ebates, and Evite. He was previously the CEO and co-founder of HotWired. Andrew has also worked as a programmer and an investment banker.

Adam Berliant is a Group Manager at Microsoft, where he oversees web development for Windows Media. He was previously the lead product planner for the MSN programming team. Before the web, he was a newspaper reporter in Tacoma, WA.

Carrie Bickner is a digital librarian with the New York Public Library. She's an active proponent of web standards, and the online style guide she produced for the NYPL is widely referenced by other sites transitioning to XHTML.

Hilary Billings is the Chairman and Chief Marketing Officer of RedEnvelope (www.redenvelope.com), a specialty gift store. She was previously Senior VP of Brand Development and Design at Starwood Hotels, where she oversaw the development of the W Hotels. Before that, she was VP of Product Design and Development at Pottery Barn, where she was in charge of directing and developing the design of all product lines for the stores and the catalog.

Doug Bowman is founder and principal of Stopdesign (www.stopdesign.com). He was previously Network Design Manager for Terra Lycos, and Design Director for HotWired. He works across media, designing for print and the web.

Rick Boyce is widely regarded as the father of the ad banner. He was a founder and Senior VP of Advertising Sales at HotWired, which introduced the ad banner to the web in 1994. He later served as the VP of Advertising for Lycos, and the president of IGN Entertainment, a network of sites targeted to gaming enthusiasts. Boyce was a founding board member of the Internet Advertising Bureau (IAB). Before the web, Rick was a vice president at the advertising agency Hal Riney & Partners in San Francisco.

Martha Brockenbrough is the former Managing Editor of MSN.com. She's now the principal of Martha Bee Productions (www.marthabee.com), a content and web consulting firm that caters to small businesses in Seattle. She writes a humor column for the online encyclopedia Encarta and another column on motherhood (The Mommy Chronicles). Before the web, she was a high school teacher and newspaper reporter in Tacoma, WA. Her first book, *It Could Happen to You: Diary of a Pregnancy and Beyond*, was published in 2002.

Sheryl Cababa is a designer for Microsoft, where she focuses on web and product design. Previously, she designed e-commerce sites for Getty Images.

Kris Carpenter is VP of Operations for Grand Central Communications, Inc. She was previously the VP of Excite Products & Services at Excite@Home, where she oversaw product development and engineering. During her five years with Excite, Inc and Excite@Home, Kris also held VP of E-Commerce Products & Services and Sr. Director of Search & Directory Products & Services positions.

Jason Cook is a former producer of Webmonkey. Previously, he was a product manager for HotBot and a production engineer for HotWired. He writes frequently about technology for Webmonkey and Wired magazine.

Cate Corcoran is the former Director of Online Communications for PeoplePC. Before that, she was the Executive Editor of HotWired. Most recently, she worked as a content specialist on the massive redesign and content overhaul of eBay's help system.

Greg Dotson is the Chief Information Officer for Guru (www.guru.com), where he oversees product development and architecture.Previously, he was CTO of Adam.com.

Esther Drill is the co-founder and Editor-in-Chief of gURL.com, the No. 1 site for teenage girls. She's written two books for gURL: *Deal With It* and *The Looks Book*.

Janice Fraser is a partner with Adaptive Path (www.adaptivepath.com), a user experience consultancy in San Francisco. She also teaches at S.F. State's Multimedia Studies Program. She started her web career at Netscape, where she pioneered consumer web applications. Before the web, she was managing editor for IDG Communications.

Jim Frew is a designer who splits his time between print and the web. He was previously Design Director at One and ThirdAge, and a designer with HotWired and Wired magazine.

Jesse James Garrett is the author of *The Elements of User Experience* (New Riders) and a partner with Adaptive Path (www.adaptivepath.com), a user experience consultancy in San Francisco. His site, jjg.net, is a popular resource for information architects, many of whom use his Visual Vocabulary, an open notation system for information architects.

Margaret Gould-Stewart is the former Senior Director of Network Design & Integration for Terra-Lycos. Prior to that role, she was General Manager and VP of Media & Community Development for Tripod.

Lara Hoyem is the senior marketing manager for BabyCenter (www.babycenter.com).

Mark Hurst is the founder and president of Creative Good (www.creativegood.com), a web consulting firm focused on improving the online user experience. His clients have included Blue Cross/Blue Shield, Gateway, Macy's, Nokia, Disney, MetLife, and Procter & Gamble. More than 30,000 people subscribe to his Good Experience newsletter.

Luke Knowland is the principal of LGK Productions (www.lgkproductions.com). He was previously Director of Web Production and Development at VolunteerMatch. Before that, he was Director of Product Development at Eyetide Media, interface director at ClearStation, and a technical designer for the @Home Network. Before that, he was a producer of Webmonkey.

Mike Kuniavsky is the author of *Observing the User Experience*, and a partner with Adaptive Path (www.adaptivepath.com), a user-experience consultancy in San Francisco. Previously, he established Wired's User Experience Laboratory, and worked on some of the web's earliest ecommerce sites.

Hunter Madsen has led the marketing efforts for several innovative web start-ups. He was VP of Marketing for Wired Digital, MoodLogic Software, and ImproveNet, before heading up product marketing at H Corporation, a provider of Internet-based data services. Madsen originally began his career at the advertising firm J. Walter Thompson, where as a Senior Partner he founded and directed JWT/Interactive, and developed pioneering online marketing programs for Sprint, Sun Microsystems, the California Board of Tourism, and others.

Matt Margolin is a web consultant living in Oakland, CA. He writes frequently about the web, and is at work on a book about web accessibility. He's also executive editor of the music site, Angry Coffee, and a former senior editor of Webmonkey.

Lance McDaniel is the VP of Creative for SBI and Company, a web consulting firm based in New York City. He was previously VP of Creative for Scient in London, Director of Client Services for iXL in San Francisco, and an account manager with Organic Online in San Francisco. During his eight years working on the web, Lance has helped build and manage sites for a variety of clients, including Disney, Harley Davidson, Levi's, Sara Lee, Starbucks, Star Wars, and Virgin Atlantic.

Noah Mercer is the Chief Technology Officer of Kalat Software. He was previously Chief Technology Officer of Nextdoor Networks, a local services start-up. Before that, he was Director of System and Software Design for The New York

Times Electronic Media Co. and Manager of Systems Development for The Washington Post/Digital Ink.

Peter Merholz is a partner with Adaptive Path (www.adaptivepath.com), a user-experience consulting firm in San Francisco. Previously, he was Creative Director at Epinions.com, and a consultant with San Francisco's Phoenix Pop. He lectures frequently on design, information architecture, and site strategy.

Jim Morris is the former Director of Software Engineering for Fogdog Sports and Global Sports, Inc (now GSI Commerce).

Steve Mulder (www.muldermedia.com) is the Manager of User Experience at Terra Lycos, where he leads a global group of information architects and usability researchers focused on increasing revenue by improving the user experience. He was previously an Experience Lead and Information Architect with the web consulting firm, Razorfish.

Peter Naylor is the VP/GM of Advertising Sales for iVillage. He was previously a VP of advertising sales at Terra-Lycos. Before the web, he sold advertising at *Vanity Fair* and *Spin* magazines.

Wendy Owen is a principal with Giant Ant Design (www.giantant.com). She was previously the Director of User Experience at Guru, and a senior producer with HotWired, who founded the site Animation Express.

Derek Powazek (www.powazek.com) is the author of *Design for Community: The Art of Connecting Real People in Virtual Spaces*. He's currently the Director of Online Projects for the Independent Media Institute, a nonprofit company in San Francisco that publishes AlterNet.org. He previously worked with Electric Minds, and has consulted for many corporate clients, including Nike, Netscape, and Sony. He also runs several independent content and community sites, including {fray} and SF Stories.

Josh Quittner is the Editor of Business 2.0. Previously, he was the managing editor of Time Digital. In 1995, he founded the Netly News, Time Inc.'s first venture into original, independent online content, and he later edited Time.com. Over the years, he has written frequently about the web in *Time* and *Wired* magazines. His influential essay, "Birth of the Way New Journalism," appeared on HotWired in 1994.

Nadav Savio is a principal at Giant Ant Design (www.giantant.com). He was previously an independent interface designer and a design engineer for HotWired.

Randi Shade is the founder of CharityGift.com, which simplifies the process of making donations in someone's name. Previously, she founded the Texas Commission on Volunteerism and Community Service (under Govs. Ann Richards and George W. Bush), where she was responsible for launching AmeriCorps. She's also worked for Procter and Gamble and Teach for America.

Emily Simas is a former Product Manager for BabyCenter, where she oversaw their multimillion mailing email program. She was previously a content manager at an online education start-up, and before that, a Kindergarten teacher. She also runs leadership programs, and facilitates workshops and brainstorming sessions for corporate and nonprofit clients.

Srinija Srinivasan is the VP and Editor in Chief of Yahoo! She joined Yahoo as employee No. 5 in 1995, and was responsible for the organization and evolution of the Yahoo! Directory. Since then, she has managed a team of editors and directed the development of Yahoo!'s original content.

Pamela Statz (pam@actionpam.com) is a freelance web developer based in San Francisco. She was previously Web Production Manager at Lucasfilm and Production Director at HotWired. Most recently she has worked on a variety of projects from writing, teaching, producing web-based software applications, and building web sites for grass-roots political organizations.

Taylor is the lead interface designer for Secret Level, and principal of Captain Cursor Creations. He was previously a partner at Red Industries, a web development shop in San Francisco, and a design engineer for HotWired.

Evany Thomas is the managing editor of Webmonkey. She's been building web sites since 1995, and her personal site was featured on many leading sites. She was previously a columnist for MSN.

Thau is the Director of Engineering at the All Species Foundation and author of *The Book of JavaScript*. He's been creating web applications since 1993, when he co-founded bianca.com, the first web-based community. He was previously Director of Engineering and senior scientist at HotWired. He teaches several courses on web technologies at San Francisco State University, and a graduate-level course on database-driven web sites at Mills College.

Michael Twidale is a professor of library and information science at the University of Illinois Urbana-Champaign. He specializes in user interface design and computer-supported cooperative work. He frequently leads workshops on web site usability design and usability testing.

Beth Vanderslice is the former General Manager of Lycos San Francisco, and former President of HotWired. Previously, she was a Vice President at H.W. Jesse & Co. a San Francisco investment banking firm. She's on the Board of Directors for Xilinx, Inc. (NASDAQ:XLNX) and the Bay Area Discovery Museum, and received her MBA from the Harvard Business School.

Jeffrey Veen is author of *The Art & Science of Web Design* (New Riders), and a partner with Adaptive Path (www.adaptivepath.com), a user experience consulting firm in San Francisco. He was previously Executive Interface Director for HotWired. He lectures frequently around the world.

Omar Wasow is the founder and CEO of BlackPlanet (www.blackplanet.com), the No. 1 site for African-Americans. He's also a TV Internet analyst for Newschannel 4 and MSNBC. In 1993, he founded the virtual community, New York Online.

Kristin Windbigler is the former Executive Producer of Webmonkey. She's currently a freelance web consultant, and based in San Francisco. She's also the founder of HITS, a non-profit offering technology education in rural Humboldt County, CA. Before moving webward, she was an award-winning newspaper reporter in northern California.

Jason Wishnow is the founder of New Venue (www.newvenue.com), the first curated showcase of movies made specifically for the Internet, and the Aggressively Boring Film Festival, the first film festival for the Palm Pilot platform. He speaks and writes frequently about digital video, and his award-winning film, *Tatooine or Bust*, was one of the first documentaries shot on mini-DV.

Indi Young is a partner with Adaptive Path, a user-experience consulting firm in San Francisco. She's been developing web applications since 1995, for clients ranged from technology start-ups to large financial institutions. Previously, she was a software engineer, focused on user interface design.

Jeffrey Zeldman (www.zeldman.com) is the principal at Happy Cog Studios, a web design consultancy, and the author of *Designing with Web Standards* (New Riders: 2003). He lectures and writes frequently about web design, and standards in particular. He also runs the popular site, A List Apart (www. alistapart.com), which offers advice "for people who make web sites."

Tim Ziegler is the founder of Family Album.com. He previously founded LostRock.com, which helped independent musicians promote themselves online. Before that, he was Executive Editor of NotHarvard.com (later Powered.com), and Senior Editor of Webmonkey.

what have you learned about the web?

1. The users call the shots. Users are in control, not you. So you have to focus on what they need, not what you want to do.

Mike Kuniavsky, author of *Observing the User Experience*, has watched company after company learn this lesson. From 1999–2000, he did user research for more than a dozen Internet start-ups.

"Every company I worked with failed," he said. "And they all failed for the same fundamental reason: They hadn't thought about the value they were giving people—and whether people wanted that value."

"So the main thing I've learned is that before you make a product, you need to know that it satisfies someone's need, and that someone will want to pay for it," he says. "This is true for just about any business, but it's especially true for web sites."

> **"People don't click if they're not sure what they're going to get. That's why it's important to have clear labels."**
> —*Martha Brockenbrough*

"You have to respect your audience," agreed Jason Wishnow, founder of the film site New Venue. "This is something I picked up as a film director, but it applies to web design as well. You don't need to pander to the lowest common denominator, but you do need to acknowledge that people will visit your site from different computers running different browsers, with different plug-ins, and with different levels of savviness when it comes to interface. You can be creative and accommodating at the same time."

2. Less is more. "I have really learned that less is more," says Janice Fraser, a partner with Adaptive Path who has developed many multi-million-dollar sites. "Doing a few things really well is far more important than having so-called full-featured web sites."

A simple, pared-down approach benefits both the organization and the user. "The first lesson I learned was that less is more—not only in staffing, but in what you put on your web site," said Josh Quittner, who founded the NetlyNews for Time, Inc. in 1995, and is now editor of *Business 2.0*.

"Initially, we had no respect for people who were on narrowband connections—and 90% of our audience was on narrowband connections. We'd give them junky pages with sound and confetti and huge images. They'd take 45 minutes to download, and we didn't care, because we could do

it! We'd have six people producing something that would cost $15,000 and would be seen by eight people. It was crazy. It was cool. It was so stupid!"

Naturally, he said, it proved hard to build an audience. "So the lesson we learned was: Simplicity. It's not about how much you can put in; it's about how much you can get rid of."

"Of course, we should have known this. I mean, that's what programming is all about. That's what information technology is all about. That, in fact, is what good writing is all about. It's what you do at Time Magazine: You just keep removing words until you've got something that's so lean, and so mean, and so smart that it's as perfect as you can get it."

"We should have applied that reasoning to what we were doing on the web…But of course, we were having too much fun."

3. Pay attention to what's working. The web gives you unprecedented opportunities to learn what's working (and what isn't) on your site—and in your business. Take advantage of it!

"Quantitative research on the Internet is so luxurious," said Adam Berllant, a Group Manager for Microsoft who oversees the WindowsMedia web sites. "I cannot pick up an issue of *Newsweek* and tell you which article was read the most. Or how much time people spent on each article. Or which headline was the most effective. On the Internet, I can tell you what 100% of the people who used this site did."

"You end up with this ever-building cumulative picture of what works and what doesn't work on a particular web site," Berliant said. "And the beauty of the web over software is I can take that learning and act on it tomorrow."

4. Your site must evolve. In just about every other industry—media, retail, software, you name it—you produce a finished product and hand it off to customers. But the web is different. Successful site owners learn quickly that the real power of the web is your ability to adapt your site to better serve users.

"It's the process, not the product," says Andrew Anker, a partner with August Capital. "In almost every other area of business—certainly in technology—the focus is on the product. But on the web, it's really the process. The easy part is getting the product out. The real challenge is figuring out what you did right and wrong, and changing quickly. The biggest mistake you can make on the web is thinking you're done."

"A lesson I've had to learn just about every day is you can't focus enough on the boring day-to-day execution," says Omar Wasow, founder of BlackPlanet. "It's important to focus on continuous improvement. The difference between success and failure is in these subtle changes."

5. Amazon gets it right. "One thing I've learned in the last seven years is that Amazon keeps doing everything that you should do, when it comes to website design," said Peter Merholz, a partner with consulting firm Adaptive Path. "You can do a lot worse than starting by copying them."

6. People are the problem. The greatest barrier to web site success isn't technology or funding or usability design. It's people. Organizational politics and inter-departmental turf wars cause companies to stumble more than anything else. "Corporate politics and corporate culture are the biggest problems I have to deal with," says Jesse James Garrett, an information architect and partner with Adaptive Path. "Bigger than any information architecture problem, bigger than any design problem, bigger than any technology problem."

7. Like begets like. Anyone who's participated in online communities—or even published a personal home page—has witnessed this phenomenon: what you put out into the world is very often what you get back. "Like begets like," says Derek Powazek, author of *Design for Community*. "If you put up a web page that says, 'All Republicans are stupid,' and then add a forum, then the responses you get are, 'No. You're stupid.' If you put up a web page that says, 'Here's this emotional rant about being a teenager and being lonely,' you will get back emotional teenage angst. Anything you put out gets amplified and comes back to you. That's the number one thing I've learned."

> "The biggest mistake you can make on the web is thinking you're done."
>
> —*Andrew Anker*

8. Pull-down menus are not for navigation. "I've learned that you should never use pull-down menus for anything other than filling in forms," says Peter Merholz, a partner with Adaptive Path. "They should not be used as navigation elements."

"Pull-downs are a highly effective way of burying information that you want your user to see."

9. Section names should be clear, not clever. "People don't click if they're not sure what they're going to get," says Martha Brockenbrough, former managing editor of MSN.com. "That's why it's important to have very clear labels."

expert advice

what's the biggest mistake you see web sites make?

Everyone in the web industry's made their fair share of mistakes, so they can easily spot where others are going astray. What are the biggest mistake that sites are still making?

1. Thinking that they are their users. "The number one misconception that clients have is that they are the target audience for the site," says Lance McDaniel. "But they are not, and their wife is not, and their kids are not. So the biggest misconception is that their opinion matters. We ask them, 'What's your user's opinion? Because we're designing the site for your users, not for you. And that's why you're paying us.'"

2. Not setting goals. "Often, a client's first question is 'How much is this going to cost?'" says Martha Brockenbrough. "But the real question is, 'What do you want this web site to do? What do you want it to do for your business?' I primarily work with very small businesses. And they usually have no idea what a web site can do. They just feel like they should have one. But that's the biggest mistake you can make! You should have very clear goals for what the web site can help you achieve."

3. Lack of focus. "Lack of focus is the major, major, major mistake I see," says Dave Thau, author of *The Book of JavaScript* and former senior scientist for Nerve and Wired. "Because the medium's flexible, you get the feeling you can do anything. But you only have so many hours in a day." And even if you finish what you set out to do, it isn't always the best thing for your business. Sites often stumble when they're "trying to do too much," says Jason Cook, former product manager for HotBot. "Often, the web site that's fastest, wins. And speed isn't just about download time, but helping people

solve things more quickly. You should think about the one or two things that customers want to do, and center your site around that."

4. Obscuring their main purpose. "As silly as it sounds, a lot of sites don't put their primary purpose on their homepage," says Mark Hurst, founder of consulting firm Creative Good. "Or it's there, but it's obscured."

"The best counter example of this is Google. It puts its primary purpose first, and doesn't distract from letting you know what it is. What's Google? It's a search site. And I don't have to tell you that, because it's kind of hard to miss."

> **"Sites aren't paying close enough attention to hierarchy. When the user arrives… they have no idea where to start."**
>
> —*Doug Bowman*

5. Skipping straight to design. "The biggest mistake that I see repeated most often is that people jump too quickly into the design process," says Indi Young, a partner with Adaptive Path. "Because design is something you can see, it's interesting to everyone. Everyone wants to jump to that first."

"Also, everybody has an opinion about it. Everybody has opinions about colors and fonts and layouts and the balance of the screen. But they skip the functionality stage and start designing backwards. They put the cart before the horse."

Continuing the analogy, she goes on to describe the cart that such a team might build: "They figure out that the cart is going to have two wheels, and those wheels need to be toward the front, because they're *prettier* up there. And one wheel is going to be bigger than the other wheel, because we want variety. And the bottom of the cart is going to be made out of a metal grid. So now, here you have this lopsided cart that's really hard to harness a horse to, and you can't hold anything in it, and everything falls out the bottom."

"Sorry," she says with a smile. "I love analogies."

6. Too much jargon. "One of the hardest transitions for people in a given business to make is from the mind of the seller to the mind of the buyer, and from the language of the seller to the language of the buyer," says online marketing expert Hunter Madsen. "So what you often see in web sites is jargon—sometimes hilariously piled upon itself."

7. Lack of a clear hierarchy. "More often than not, sites aren't paying close enough attention to hierarchy," says Doug Bowman, principal of StopDesign. "When the user arrives on a page, they have no idea where to start. Or if they do, the hierarchy's reversed compared to what it should be."

8. Prioritizing short-term over long-term goals. "A lot of companies will think in terms of the short-term, quick financial gain instead of the long-term relationship building with users," says Steve Mulder, manager of user experience for Terra-Lycos.

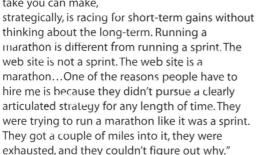

Information architect Jesse James Garrett agrees. "The worst mistake you can make, strategically, is racing for short-term gains without thinking about the long-term. Running a marathon is different from running a sprint. The web site is not a sprint. The web site is a marathon…One of the reasons people have to hire me is because they didn't pursue a clearly articulated strategy for any length of time. They were trying to run a marathon like it was a sprint. They got a couple of miles into it, they were exhausted, and they couldn't figure out why."

9. Blindly trusting web consultants. Handing off responsibility to an outside firm is always risky. "Consultants make you feel like you can trust them, and that they're going to do whatever is in your best interest," says Pamela Statz. "And in most cases they are. But sometimes they'd rather do stuff that's new and fun. I've seen this happen many times with web development companies."

"If you're going to pay someone a lot of money to build your web site, it's your responsibility to pay very close attention to the details and decisions regarding the design and technology," Statz said. "Your web consultants cannot read your mind and they cannot possibly understand the needs of your company the way you do."

10. Confusing error messages. Left to its own devices, your server will spit out confusing messages when something goes awry. But sites can customize these messages, if they bother to. "Poor error messaging" is the bee in Luke Knowland's bonnet. "You should realize that someone's going to make mistakes and allow for it. Prompt them about what to do next. This is so easy to take care of—it takes 10–15 minutes!"

> **"Using their site as a teaser area for future, unformed plans, rather than for current offerings."**
> —*Srinija Srinivasan*

11. Generic design. "We don't buy dull books or watch plotless, indifferently photographed movies. We don't go out of our way to buy generic products," says Jeffrey Zeldman. "Yet many site owners seem unaware of the importance of creating a strong visual and verbal identity. Of course, your site must be usable. But if it is indifferently written and designed, it will not engage anyone; if it lacks a memorable and appropriate identity, few will bookmark it or remember to visit again. The web is not Muzak."

12. Pretending to be something they're not. No one sees more web sites—or more mistakes—than the editorial team at Yahoo!, which evaluates every site submitted to their directory. Their biggest pet peeve? Sites that claim to offer more than they actually do. "The biggest mistake I see websites make is using their site as a teaser area for unformed future plans, rather than as a relevant, functional hub for current offerings," said Srinija Srinivasan, editor-in-chief of Yahoo!. "Beyond other media, the web is differentiated by being immediate and interactive. Great websites incorporate that rather than ignore it."

what are the red flags that a project is trouble?

After working on the web for a while (after working anywhere for a while) you start to pick up the signals that a project is going to run into problems. What red flags do industry experts look for?

1. An unrealistic schedule. "An unreasonable timeline is, to me, the biggest red flag," says Lance McDaniel. "Because if it takes eight weeks, it's going to take eight weeks. No matter what you promise, no matter what the penalty clauses are, no matter when your marketing campaign launch is. If it takes eight weeks to code 8,000 pages in HTML, that's how long it takes."

2. Unrealistic scope. A web project that's trying to do too many things at the same time, without sufficient resources, is setting itself up for trouble. "Unrealistic scope is the biggest red flag," says Carrie Bickner, a librarian and web specialist with the New York Public Library. "I just had a group of librarians come to me with a project idea. I looked at their outline, and I said to them, 'Boy, this is really great, but it's actually five different projects.' So my job is to parcel all that out, and say, 'Now, these four projects would each cost a million dollars. But this one, that might be about $60,000. Maybe there's a grant we could find to do this one small part of it.' Yes, that's usually the problem: An unrealistic sense of scope."

3. Missing early deadlines. If a team doesn't hit the first deadlines on the schedule, it's a warning sign that something's not working. "Missing a lot of early deadlines—that's a key indicator," says Greg Dotson, Chief Information Officer of Guru. "Maybe

> **"It's easier to collaborate when you're in the same time zone."**
> —*Nadav Savio*

the team doesn't have enough information. Maybe they're not functioning well together. Maybe they don't have enough resources. Or maybe they have too many people on the team, and they're not splitting up their roles properly.

4. A leader who can't say no. "If your product development person can't say no to people who ask for features, that's a red flag," said Peter Merholz. "You need someone who can say 'No,' because what's being requested doesn't match the vision of the product. When it comes to a web

product, probably the single most valuable thing an organization can have is a product manager who can step back and see the whole picture: the design, the technology, the business. A product is most likely to succeed when there's a single vision driving it."

5. A vague or poorly defined product. "The first thing I look at is the quality of the definition of the product," says Noah Mercer, former software director for *The New York Times* and *The Washington Post*. "An ill-defined product just makes me extremely nervous. An ill-defined product with no one around to define it makes me more nervous. An ill-defined product with someone around to define it who doesn't have the time or skills to do it makes me want to run away in panic."

6. A geographically dispersed team. "Distance, I should say, is a big red flag," says Jim Morris, Director of Software Engineering for Fogdog sports. "If I can do a project with me and my engineer, it has a high rate of success. if I have to work with someone back east [Morris is based in California], it's going to have a lower rate of success. If it involves a systems administrator from back east, even lower—because they're very busy and they get distracted very easily. "It's easier to collaborate when you're in the same time zone," says Nadav Savio, principal of Giant Ant Design. "There's a direct correlation between how many time zones you're off and how much harder it is."

7. Imbalanced or uncollaborative team. "When one department or discipline has too much power, you have problems," says Luke Knowland, former Director of Product Development for VolunteerMatch. "Web development done right is so interdisciplinary. Everyone has to be responsible and accountable to each other. It's important to have respect. But engineering teams and design teams almost never respect each other.

8. Dependence on a new technology. The biggest red flags for Taylor, a design engineer who's worked on many cutting-edge sites, is reliance on unproven technologies. It's a problem, he says, "if the success of the site—or the entire business—hinges on a certain deal coming through, or a certain technology being adopted. Beware new technology. Most new technologies, like most new businesses, fail."

9. Turf wars and personality conflicts. Successful web projects require collaboration. But if individuals or departments are fighting for dominance, that gets in the way. "Most of my red-flags are personality-related," says Indi Young. "One is turf wars. That happens a lot between engineering and design, engineering and marketing." Personal conflicts can also get in the way. It's a problem, when you have "key decision-makers who are battling each other," says Kristin Windbigler, former

Executive producer of Webmonkey. "If you go into a meeting and it's obvious that the marketing VP can't stand the engineering VP, it's not going to end well."

10. Unclear reporting structure. "A huge, huge red flag is when there's not a clearly organized chain of command for who gets to make decisions," says Tim Ziegler. "The lack of a clear decision-making structure and someone with the authority to mediate conflicts is just death." It's a problem in any company, he says, but it's amplified on technical projects: "There's always competition for backend resources and for development resources. And someone has to mediate that. Otherwise, you're left to fight it out in the trenches."

> **"Key decision makers who are battling each other. If the marketing VP can't stand the engineering VP, it's not going to end well."**
> —*Kristin Windbigler*

11. Unrealistic expectations. Sometimes, companies have expectations for a site that far outstrip its ability to deliver. "When clients say, 'We want to change our brand image, so build us a new site.' That's a red flag to me, because you're not going to change a brand image through the web alone," says Lance McDaniel. "If a client isn't taking into account the $350 million they're spending elsewhere, and they expect your $100,000 web site to change the world, that's usually a red flag."

12. Crazy visionaries. "I tend to stay away from companies where projects are being led by crazy visionaries," says Kristin Windbigler. "I've already seen behind the wizard's curtain."

one piece of advice for someone launching a web site?

Hindsight is always 20/20. And every web veteran would do things differently were they relaunching past sites. Here's their advice for you as you launch your web site.

1. Know your user. This is probably the biggest single piece of learning throughout the industry. Almost every successful web site starts with a strong sense of who it's for. "You have to be really truthful about who your customer is, and what your business stands for in the eyes of that customer," said Hilary Billings, chairman and chief marketing officer of RedEnvelope. "Know who your customer is, and what they need from you. And let that guide you. Don't try to outsmart your customer. Build a business for them."

> **"Get over yourself! This is not about *you*. You need to think about your user and their goals."**
> —*Cate Corcoran*

   "Know who you're building the site for, and why you're building it," says Mike Kuniavsky. "Know that very, very well. And give yourself enough time to know that before you pick up Dreamweaver and start building the site."

2. Build a site for the user, not you. "Honestly, my advice would be something like 'Get over yourself,'" said Cate Corcoran. "This is not about *you*. You need to think about your user and their goals." Similarly, you need to make sure you're building a site that someone needs. "Don't invent the gadget and then try to find a market for it," says Randi Shade, founder of CharityGift. "Find an unmet need, and develop a solution to meet that need."

3. Let your site evolve. Don't try to launch a polished, finished site. "Rather than try to build the perfect system, do something faster and fix it later," says Nadav Savio, principal of Giant Ant Design.

4. Know your business. It's less important to know the web than it is to know your own business. "Make sure that you know your business, and know your customers, and know what goals you're trying to accomplish with this web site—because the web site is a tool for your business," says Noah Mercer. "If you have that stuff nailed down—and usually you don't—the web site is the easier part of things. The harder part is really knowing what you're trying to do."

5. Always make a plan. It's important in just about any endeavor, and it's crucial for web sites. "Take the time to plan," advises Lance McDaniel. "Spend twice as much time as you think you need to figure out what you're trying to accomplish as a business. Because all the problems that you don't solve up-front will add time during the build, and make it twice as expensive."

   "Do your homework," advises Adam Berliant, a Group Manager for Microsoft. "Building a website is not like sitting down at a canvas and painting a picture of whatever comes out of your head."

   "That's why so many dot-coms failed," Berliant said. "They didn't do their homework. They weren't sure who their customers were. They weren't sure if their goals were realistic. They weren't sure how it was all going to work. But you can take care of a lot of that up front, if you do your homework."

6. Start small and keep it simple. It's easy to get swept away with big plans for a big site. But on the web, smaller is usually better. "Keep it simple," advises Omar Wasow. "Start small, learn from your mistakes, and grow incrementally. It's really easy to spend a lot of money on something that's massively useless. So try to have real clarity about what It Is you're trying to do, and do those few things well."

Keeping a sharp focus is helpful in more ways than one. "Think small," says Josh Quittner, editor of Business 2.0. "Think small in every way. Create a web site that's really as simple as you can possibly make it. Make it as obvious as you possibly can, and don't expect that because you're in a space where 100 million people *can* see you that 100 million people *will* see you.

The bigger your site is, the harder it is to get attention. But if you have a really wonderful, small, beautifully designed, simple-to-navigate, obvious site that provides real value to whoever you identify as your market, people will find it, and sooner or later it will take off."

7. Make your site easier to use. The easier you make it, the more people will participate, says Mark Hurst, founder and CEO of consulting firm Creative Good. "The web is too hard to use," he says "That's what's holding back businesses—the companies that do business on the web. The key piece [they're] missing is the user experience. A quick and easy user experience."

8. Copy your competition! You probably don't want to completely copy a competitor's site, but feel free to borrow! You definitely want to learn from what's out there, before you build your own. "Find a site doing something similar, and learn everything you can from it," says Evany Thomas, managing editor of Webmonkey. "View source. The web is all about viewing source. "

9. Collaborate. The web requires a multi-disciplinary approach. And this means not just assembling a complete team, but helping them to communicate. "Do as much as you can to have all the disciplines being represented talk to each other," says writer Matt Margolin.

10. Mind the details. A lot of things—small and large—have to come together to create a successful site. You'll need to make a lot of decisions in the course of developing a web site. "Make sure that everything the user experiences on your site is the result of a conscious decision on your part—that nothing is there by accident," advises Jesse James Garrett.

11. Test your site. No matter how many sites you've built, you can't know how a given site will be used until you see someone try. "Have your mom test it," recommends Derek Powazek. "My mom is my best beta tester. The smarter she gets about the web, the worse of a tester she is."

> **"Keep it simple. Start small, learn from your mistakes, and grow incrementally"**
> **—Omar Wasow**

12. Make sure you have authority. Web projects are notorious for their convoluted reporting structures and unclear chains of command. When you take on a site, make sure things are clear. "For the project manager, make sure you have enough authority over the project," says Pamela Statz. "Before you get involved, make sure you're introduced to the team and to others in management as the person who's in charge."

13. Register variations on your domain name. When you're choosing your domain name, remember that people won't always type or spell things correctly. "Register all the misspellings of your domain name," advises Cate Corcoran. "And the dot-org, dot-com, and dot-net addresses too."

A site that does it right? Crate & Barrel. "Crate & Barrel knows that no one knows how to spell the word 'barrel,'" Corcoran said with a smile. "How many R's and how many L's? So you can type in anything that's somewhat close to Crate & Barrel and still get to crateandbarrel.com."

index

b

C

d

e

f

g

j

k

l

m

q

r

S

t

V

VOICES THAT MATTER

HOW TO CONTACT US

VISIT OUR WEB SITE

WWW.NEWRIDERS.COM

On our web site, you'll find information about our other books, authors, tables of contents, and book errata. You will also find information about book registration and how to purchase our books, both domestically and internationally.

EMAIL US

Contact us at: **nrfeedback@newriders.com**

- If you have comments or questions about this book
- To report errors that you have found in this book
- If you have a book proposal to submit or are interested in writing for New Riders
- If you are an expert in a computer topic or technology and are interested in being a technical editor who reviews manuscripts for technical accuracy

Contact us at: **nreducation@newriders.com**

- If you are an instructor from an educational institution who wants to preview New Riders books for classroom use. Email should include your name, title, school, department, address, phone number, office days/hours, text in use, and enrollment, along with your request for desk/examination copies and/or additional information.

Contact us at: **nrmedia@newriders.com**

- If you are a member of the media who is interested in reviewing copies of New Riders books. Send your name, mailing address, and email address, along with the name of the publication or web site you work for.

BULK PURCHASES/CORPORATE SALES

The publisher offers discounts on this book when ordered in quantity for bulk purchases and special sales. For sales within the U.S., please contact: Corporate and Government Sales (800) 382-3419 or **corpsales@pearsontechgroup.com**. Outside of the U.S., please contact: International Sales (317) 581-3793 or **international@pearsontechgroup.com**.

WRITE TO US

New Riders Publishing
1249 Eighth Street
Berkeley, California 94710

CALL US

Toll-free (800) 571-5840
If outside U.S. (317) 581-3500
Ask for New Riders

WWW.NEWRIDERS.COM